ADVENTURES OF PERCEPTION

The publisher gratefully acknowledges the generous support of the Humanities Endowment Fund of the University of California Press Foundation.

Adventures of Perception

Cinema as Exploration: Essays/Interviews

SCOTT MacDONALD

UNIVERSITY OF CALIFORNIA PRESS

Berkeley Los Angeles London

University of California Press, one of the most distinguished university presses in the United States, enriches lives around the world by advancing scholarship in the humanities, social sciences, and natural sciences. Its activities are supported by the UC Press Foundation and by philanthropic contributions from individuals and institutions. For more information, visit www.ucpress.edu.

University of California Press
Berkeley and Los Angeles, California

University of California Press, Ltd.
London, England

For acknowledgments of previous publication, please see page vii.

Library of Congress Cataloging-in-Publication Data

MacDonald, Scott, 1942–.
Adventures of perception : cinema as exploration : essays/interviews / Scott MacDonald.
p. cm.
Earlier versions of several of the essays and interviews, or portions of them, have been previously published.
Includes bibliographical references and index.
ISBN 978-0-520-25854-9 (cloth : alk. paper)
ISBN 978-0-520-25856-3 (pbk. : alk. paper)
1. Motion pictures. 2. Independent filmmakers—Interviews. I. Title.

PN1994.M3135 2009
791.43'611—dc22 2009003367

Manufactured in the United States of America

18 17 16 15 14 13 12 11 10 09
10 9 8 7 6 5 4 3 2 1

This book is printed on Cascades Enviro 100, a 100% post consumer waste, recycled, de-inked fiber. FSC recycled certified and processed chlorine free. It is acid free, Ecologo certified, and manufactured by BioGas energy.

Contents

Acknowledgments

Earlier versions of several of the essays and interviews in this book, or portions of them, have been published previously. Thanks to Anthology Film Archives for permission to reprint "The Attractions of Nature in Early Cinema," which originally appeared in *Unseen Cinema: Early American Avant-Garde Film, 1893–1941*, a catalogue that accompanied the release of the DVD collection of that title (New York: Anthology Film Archives and Black Thistle Press, 2001), 56–63; to *Afterimage* for permission to reprint "Program Notes: An Interview with Karen Cooper," which appeared in vol. 11, no. 4 (Summer 1983): 4–6, and a revised, shortened version of "Putting All Your Eggs in One Basket: A Survey of Single-Shot Film," which appeared as a special supplement in vol. 16, no. 8 (March 1989): 10–16; to *Artforum* for permission to reprint "Testing Your Patience: An Interview with James Benning," which appeared in vol. 56, no. 1 (September 2007): 428–37, 494, © Artforum; to *Esopus* for permission to reprint a portion of my interview with Peter Hutton, which appeared in no. 10 (Spring 2008): 25–28; to *Film Quarterly* for permission to reprint "Confessions of a Feminist Porn Watcher," which appeared in vol. 36, no. 3 (Spring 1983): 10–17, "Up Close and Personal: Three Short Ruminations on Ideology in the Nature Film," which appeared in vol. 59, no. 3 (Spring 2006): 4–21, and a condensed version of "Gentle Iconoclast: An Interview with David Gatten," which appeared in vol. 61, no. 2 (Winter 2007–8): 36–44; to the *Independent* for permission to reprint "Storm Chaser: An Interview with George Kuchar about the Weather Diaries," which appeared in vol. 20, no. 6 (July 1997): 38–42; to *Mohawk Valley History* (Oneida County Historical Society, Utica, New York) for permission to reprint "The Mohawk Valley Journey to *The Journey* with Film Director Peter Watkins," which appeared in vol. 2, no. 2 (Winter 2005–6): 83–109; to NAMAC (National Alliance for Media Arts and Culture) for permission to reprint "Film History and 'Film History,'" which appeared in *A Closer Look: Hidden Histories* (2005): 32–41; and to *Poetics Today* for permission to reprint "Poetry and Avant-Garde Film: Three Recent Contributions," which appeared in vol. 28, no. 1 (Spring 2007): 1–41.

Acknowledgments

Introduction

Imagine an eye unruled by man-made laws of perspective, an eye unprejudiced by compositional logic, an eye which does not respond to the name of everything but which must know each object encountered in life through an adventure of perception. How many colors are there in a field of grass to the crawling baby unaware of "Green"? How many rainbows can light create for the untutored eye? How aware of variations in heat waves can that eye be? Imagine a world alive with incomprehensible objects and shimmering with an endless variety of movement and inumerable gradations of color. Imagine a world before the "beginning was the word."

Stan Brakhage[1]

For me, cinema has always been primarily an arena for direct exploration, for various forms of sensuous learning and interchange, rather than a pretext (a "pre-text") for the production of a literature that articulates a discourse *about* cinema. While I am indebted to many learned and brilliant essays and books about media by my colleagues in the world of film studies, the focus of my learning about cinema has always been and continues to be the experience of individual works that in one way or another function as interventions into my complacency as a spectator, as a chronicler of film history, and as a person. The final essay in this collection, "Film History and 'Film History,'" details what seem to me some of the pivotal cinematic adventures in my experience, though in truth the instances described in that essay are little more than memorable (and pedagogically useful) moments in what has been a lifetime of such experiences.

The films that have forced me to redefine my sense of cinema and of myself as a cineaste and as a person have nearly always come to my attention during moments when I am exploring cinema, sometimes when I have decided to take a chance on a film someone else has recommended to me, sometimes when I am trying to develop a clearer sense of still another tendency

1. Stan Brakhage, opening lines of "Metaphors on Vision," originally published as a special issue of *Film Culture,* no. 30 (Fall 1963).

in this now-immense history. The discoveries made possible by some of these explorations may be immediately pleasant or infuriating, but I know an intervention has occurred when I feel an energy that, at first, keeps me thinking about the particular work, and in the end, motivates me to work with this film or video on a long-term basis in the classroom and/or as a subject for further research.

While this book is the product of my own personal and professional explorations into particular films and filmmakers and particular cinematic issues over a period of twenty-five years, it also reveals a good many other kinds of exploration. Almost always, the films that interrupt my complacency are either avant-garde films or experimental documentaries: that is, nearly all of them offer alternatives to the cinematic status quo and function as cine-interventions for the audiences that discover them. In addition, however, the filmmakers discussed in the eight essays included here, and the filmmakers interviewed in the eight interviews, have generally used media-making to explore their own lives and what they see as the crucial social and cultural issues of the moment. In most cases, they have investigated the elements and boundaries of the particular media they have chosen to work with. In other words, this is a book of one scholar-teacher's explorations of the explorations of a good many filmmakers and videomakers.

For some years, my frustration with the way in which the current divisions between academic fields tend to inhibit explorations across the conceptual boundaries that come to separate them, and especially the ways in which these divisions impact the history of independent cinema, led to attempts to demonstrate the relevance and value of particular avant-garde films for the fields of American studies, literature and comparative literature, and art history. The resulting essays were collected in *The Garden in the Machine: A Field Guide to Independent Films about Place* (University of California Press, 2001). Several of the essays in this new collection developed from the same frustration; others, from my disappointment about the ways in which certain accomplished and pedagogically useful films and videos tend to be ignored, even by those who could make the most productive use of them.

"Desegregating Film History: Avant-Garde Film and Race at the Robert Flaherty Seminar, and Beyond," the longest and newest essay in the book, was instigated by a comment from a frustrated Flaherty seminarian, curious about why the filmmakers generally identified as "avant-garde" and the audience that supports their work seem "white." I have come to believe that this comment was a reflection of our ways of categorizing film history, and that these habits of categorization have tended to create a sense of difference and a practice of exclusion where they are counterproductive. My discussion attempts to demonstrate the theoretical and pedagogical value of the considerable, if usually ignored, overlaps between American avant-garde cinema and African American cinema. Films and videos by Oscar Micheaux, Spencer Williams, Jack Smith, Spike Lee, William Greaves, J. J. Murphy, Anthony McCall, Robert Nelson, Yvonne Rainer, Peter Watkins, Melvin Van Peebles, John Waters, George Kuchar, Raphael Montañez Ortiz, Martin Arnold, Su Friedrich, Marlon Riggs, James Benning, Tony Cokes, and others are discussed as instances of a single, expansive response to the commercial media industry.

"Poetry and Film: Avant-Garde Cinema as Publication" is an attempt to combine my interest in avant-garde cinema with a lifelong interest in poetry, as a means of luring academics who teach literature into an exploration of the long history of films and videos that incorporate poetry, or in some cases are themselves forms of poetry. "Poetry and Film" focuses on a particular group of films—*Waterworx (A Clear Day and No Memories)* (1982) by the Canadian Rick Hancox; *nebel* (2000) by the German Matthias Müller; and *Trains of Winnipeg—14 Film Poems* (2004) by the Canadian Clive Holden. Each of these films re-presents a previously published poem or body of poems in a new cinematic "edition": specifically, Wallace Stevens's "A Clear Day and No Memories" (1955); Ernst Jandl's *gedichte an die kindheit* ("Poems to Childhood," 1980), and Holden's own *Trains of Winnipeg* (2002). These films are as interesting and useful as part of an ongoing engagement with poetry as they are within the history of independent cinema.

"Up Close and Political: Three Short Ruminations on Nature Film" was an attempt to bring nature film (or "wildlife film") into the larger film-historical conversation. Like the following essay, "The Attractions of Nature in Early Cinema," this piece grew out of my interest in issues of the environment and place but was, in particular, a response to the recent spate of successful feature-length nature films, most of them from Europe: Claude Nuridsany and Marie Pérennou's *Microcosmos: Le peuple de l'herbe* (1996; "The People of the Grass") and *Genesis* (2004); *Winged Migration* (2001, directed by Jacques Perrin); *Deep Blue* (2003, directed by Andy Byatt and Alastair Fothergill); and *March of the Penguins* (2005, directed by Luc Jacquet). These films and the tradition they have revived had received relatively little attention from film scholars, and I wanted to question what I saw as an implicit resistance to a remarkable and remarkably committed body of work—and, more important, to model new forms of engagement with these films. As it turns out, a number of scholars were being drawn to this field at the same time that I was, but nature cinema is such a prolific genre that, as yet, there has been little overlap in our work.

"The Attractions of Nature in Early Cinema" recounts a foray into the Library of Congress's paper print collection, specifically to consider whether American landscape painting during the nineteenth century—the Hudson River School, the Rocky Mountain School, Luminism, and Tonalism—created enough interest in landscape to produce effective cinematic imitations. While landscape film *was* a mini-genre during the era of the cinema of attractions, the first attempts to represent American nature had less to do with reenergizing the landscape art of the previous century than with singing the excitement of new technologies: the modern railroad and cinema. It remained for a later generation of filmmakers to create films that evoke the work of Thomas Cole and the many painters who, in one way or another, expanded on Cole's work.

"Putting All Your Eggs in One Basket: The Single-Shot Film" focuses on six remarkable single-shot films (the original version of this piece, published in *Afterimage* [March 1989], includes a "glossary" of several dozen such films). As film stock and processing became increasingly expensive after the mid-1960s, a central challenge faced by independent filmmakers was how to produce interesting work on a limited budget. Within this moment, a return to the Lumière Brothers' approach, to the discipline of trying to make an interesting, memorable film experience using only a single, uninterrupted running of the camera, seemed promising; a new mini-genre was the result. Of course, in recent years the development of new, inexpensive digital ways of making moving-image media, combined with the option of making far longer continuous shots, seems to have rendered the single-shot film archaic. But just as the arrival of modernist poetry has not rendered the haiku obsolete (quite the reverse, in fact), the new video equipment has not diminished the accomplishments of earlier single-shot filmmaking.

The essays in *Cinema as Exploration* range from the scholarly to the frankly personal. "The Mohawk Valley Journey to *The Journey*" is a detailed report on my involvement in the process of producing a portion of what became the Peter Watkins megafilm, *The Journey* (1987). By 1984 I had become something of a devotee of Watkins's filmmaking, partly as a result of seeing *The War Game* (1965) when it toured the American art theater circuit in the mid-1960s. When the BBC, the producer of *The War Game,* refused to broadcast the film, Watkins created a public furor, and in the end the BBC compromised by releasing the forty-seven-minute film as a feature documentary. *The Journey* was an attempt to expand the media critique of *The War Game* and to model new ways of using media to engage political and social issues, or, to locate it within the parameters of this book, a new, progressive way of using media to explore the world and interact with it. I have analyzed *The Journey* elsewhere (see, for example, the final chapter of my *Avant-Garde Film / Motion Studies* [New York: Cambridge University Press, 1993]), but this more recent essay details the unusual five-year experience that resulted from my agreeing to instigate and oversee the participation of my community in Watkins's project. Since many of Watkins's films are meant to be indices of the processes he initiates to produce them, as well as finished works of film art, an in-depth look at one major dimension of the process that produced *The Journey* may be of value in appreciating this controversial film and Watkins's unusual career.

"Confessions of a Feminist Porn Watcher (Then and Now)" is my most embarrassingly intimate piece; the original version was written in 1981 during a moment of considerable personal stress brought on by the illness of a loved one, as a means of distracting myself—though I had been trying to find the nerve to write it for years. "Confessions" was instigated during the 1970s and early 1980s by the questions of feminist women who were engaging the issue of why men use pornography, and by my own questioning of why *I* was drawn to precisely what I *was* drawn to and what I seemed to be looking at on those occasions when I used porn. The addendum provides some perspective on the original essay from twenty-five years later.

The final essay in *Adventures of Perception*, "Film History and 'Film History,'" is a self-indulgent autobiographical review of my development as a cineaste. "Film History and 'Film History'" was written in 2005 as an explanation of why, after having retired from full-time teaching for several years, I found I could no longer be satisfied simply doing research and writing (and teaching the occasional class), and needed to return to programming film events both in the classroom and for the public.

Once particular films or moving-image works in other media have interrupted my habits of thought about cinema, I have regularly made interviewing the makers of these works a crucial part of my research. Indeed, it has been my great good fortune that the University of California Press has supported my interviewing by publishing what is now a five-volume series of interviews called *A Critical Cinema* ("critical" cinema, because the films and videos that are the subjects of these discussions can be understood as critiques of commercial media and its audience, and because I believe that experiencing these films and videos is of critical importance for anyone interested in the full range of accomplishment in cinema). Obviously, filmmakers' ideas about their own work are merely one input into our thinking, but they can be revealing and a particularly helpful catalyst for further exploration.

My interest in diarist and feature director Gina Kim was a result of a screening of her *Invisible Light* (2003), an elegant and inventive experimental narrative, at the New York Video Festival in 2004. Seeing her other work, I came to understand her career as emblematic of the many overlaps between ethnic cinemas and avant-garde work (Kim is a Korean national who studied media-making at the California Institute of the Arts; she lives in Los Angeles), and evidence of how a particular sensibility can express itself with considerable style and impact in both avant-garde work and commercial filmmaking. Kim's early videos were made as personal diaries focusing on her struggles to accept her own physicality; she used diary-videomaking as a form of companionship and therapy, with, she says, no expectation that what she recorded would be seen by anyone else. Her most recent film, on the other hand, is a feature melodrama during which her protagonist, a young European American woman (Vera Farmiga), is caught between loyalty to her husband (David Lee McInnis) and his desire to have a child, and a lover (Jung-Woo Ha), who helps her come to terms with her body.

My interview with Clive Holden focuses on his film suite *Trains of Winnipeg—14 Film Poems,* the culminating work in his "Trains of Winnipeg" project, which began as a website but subsequently yielded a book of poetry, a CD of poetry readings by Holden, a 35mm film, and, finally, a DVD of the film. The "Trains of Winnipeg" project and *Trains of Winnipeg—14 Film Poems* in particular reveal Holden's fascination with exploring the overlaps of and the spaces between various moving-image technologies and various art forms. The film poems in *Trains of Winnipeg—14 Film Poems* combine poetic narrative, new and recycled imagery, and music in a variety of ways that reflect Holden's development as a man and as an artist.

In 2007, I began an e-mail interview with Claude Nuridsany and Marie Pérennou because I wanted to find out how they saw their nature photography and filmmaking in relation to the larger history of cinema. Further, I had come to feel that their implicit environmental politics and the level of commitment required by the kinds of films they make—each takes years to shoot and requires considerable technical skill— represent a new kind of film avant-garde, one that, as I suggested earlier, deserves a good bit more attention and respect from those who teach and historicize cinema than has been evident until very recently. At their best, the great nature films are aesthetically remarkable and deeply interesting and powerful for a very wide range of spectators; they offer a vision of nonhuman nature that, one hopes, might help to instigate a more activist, progressive engagement with issues of species protection and environmental conservation.

In recent years, Peter Hutton and James Benning have taken the lead in the production of interesting place-oriented cinema. Hutton's films reveal many parallels with Benning's; both filmmakers engage viewers with often gorgeous and visually subtle, tripod-mounted extended compositions of landscape and cityscape that create experiences closer to contemplation or meditation than to what seems normal in local multiplexes. Benning's and Hutton's work can be read as a form of perceptual retraining that attempts to move us away from the hysterical consumption that characterizes commercial society and commercial media and toward a more serene, engaged, more deeply respectful sense of the physical world. Both filmmakers have developed a considerable following outside of the United States, particularly in Germany, Austria, and Holland (the first book on Benning was published by the Austrian Film Museum in 2007 on the occasion of a major retrospective);[2] and in recent years the work of both filmmakers seems to have become increasingly engaging for audiences looking for a different relationship to cinema.

David Gatten's *Secret History of the Dividing Line: A True Account in Nine Parts,* a projected sequence of nine films, is emblematic of the idea of cinema as exploration. The ostensible subject of the set of films is the life and surround of William Byrd II of colonial Virginia, who founded the city of Richmond, led the surveying expedition that drew the original boundary (the "dividing line") between Virginia and North Carolina, wrote one of the first detailed descriptions of American nature, *History of the Dividing Line* (written soon after the surveying expedition, but not published until 1841), and assembled one of the two largest libraries in colonial North America. Byrd's daughter, Evelyn, who is said to have died of a broken heart, is among the most famous ghosts of Virginia. Gatten uses the Byrds' lives as a focal point for exploring a wide range of conceptual, formal, and cultural issues—all of them relating to the evolution of the ways in which information has been encoded and communicated in writing and in imagery since the publication of the Gutenberg Bible, and the ways in which this evolution relates to the digital revolution we are in the midst of.

The series of Weather Diaries George Kuchar made with an inexpensive video camera in the 1980s and early 1990s in the heart of "tornado alley" during tornado season must be included in any listing of this prolific filmmaker's most interesting and controversial work. The first video in this series, *Weather Diary 1* (1986), is a kind of trash version of Thoreau's *Walden.*

2. *James Benning,* ed. Barbara Pichler and Claudia Slanar (Vienna: Österreichisches Filmmuseum; SYNEMA—Gesellschaft für Film und Medien, 2007).

Alternately beautiful and humorously shocking (because of its directness in dealing with bodily functions), it caused considerable controversy at the 1993 Robert Flaherty Seminar. Kuchar channeled his Flaherty experience into *Vermin of the Vortex* (1996). Kuchar and I discuss the *Weather Diary* series and Kuchar's experience in the Flaherty "vortex."

The final interview, with Karen Cooper, director of New York City's Film Forum, draws attention to the heroic efforts of one woman who for thirty-five years has made inventive documentary, experimental animation, and avant-garde shorts and features available to New York audiences. Cooper transformed an alternative screening space with fifty folding chairs on the Upper West Side into a three-screen theater on Houston Street in lower Manhattan that is open 365 days a year and draws more than 250,000 admissions annually. An exhibitor with Cooper's talent and accomplishments may be rarer than a great filmmaker. Indeed, without courageous exhibitors, much of the greatest film art would languish in obscurity. The Cooper interview is in two parts: the first was recorded in 1982; the second, in 2007.

The interviews in *Adventures of Perception* are organized so as to function in relation to the essays, sometimes as confirmations or extensions of ideas evident in the essays, sometimes as counterpoints. Often, the connections are obvious (this is true of the juxtaposition of "Desegregating Film History" and the interview with Gina Kim, for example, and of "Poetry and Film" and the Clive Holden interview). In other instances, the relationships are more subtle and complex. Of course, few readers ever read a collection like this from front to back, even though those of us who prepare such books often structure them as metanarratives. My hope, then, has to be that the different sectors of the book will engage readers in different ways at different times, and that those who do explore the entire volume will enjoy both the individual contributions to it and the implications of their particular combination.

The majority of this book consists of new material. In those instances where I am reprinting essays published some time ago, I have revised them so as to speak more fully to our present moment and to a more general audience. Only one of the interviews reprinted here (the interview with George Kuchar) was published in its present form; others (those with Hutton, Benning, and Gatten) were published in much shorter versions. Within the essays, documentation is presented as footnotes; in the interviews, what little documentation is necessary is included within the text.

I have, of course, had the help of a number of people and organizations in finishing this collection. My attendance at several Flaherty Film Seminars has been important to the project; the fiftieth-anniversary Flaherty instigated the longest essay in the collection, and other seminars resulted in my interviewing Clive Holden and George Kuchar. Teaching at Hamilton College and Harvard University has provided a variety of support for my interviewing and writing. Ian P. MacDonald, Frank Bergmann, Roy Grundmann, Haden Guest, Martine Guyot-Bender, Tom Gunning, Richard Herskowitz, Robb Moss, Patricia R. O'Connor, Patricia O'Neill, Bruce Posner, Jacqueline Stewart, Linda Williams, and Patricia R. Zimmermann provided various kinds of instigation and assistance. At Hamilton, my colleagues Marianita Amodio and Krista Siniscargo helped me deal with the imagery used in this volume; Sharon M. Britten (then at Burke Library) assisted with permissions; and Terri Viglietta helped me get the manuscript ready for submission. Thank you.

Desegregating Film History

Avant-Garde Film and Race at the Robert Flaherty Seminar, and Beyond

When national and ethnic [I would add aesthetic] identities are represented and projected as pure, exposure to difference threatens them with dilution and compromises their prized purities with the ever-present possibility of contamination.

Paul Gilroy[1]

At the final Friday evening discussion session of the fiftieth annual Robert Flaherty Seminar,[2] held at Vassar College in June 2004, there was a remarkable moment. We were in a large classroom lecture hall; the evening's filmmakers—Morgan Fisher, who had shown his *Standard Gauge* (1984), and Louise Bourque, who had shown four short films—were sitting at a table in front. It was the end of a week of screenings and discussions and late-night conversations about the mixture of documentary and avant-garde films that had been programmed by Susan Oxtoby in conjunction

1. Paul Gilroy, *Against Race: Imagining Political Culture beyond the Color Line* (Cambridge, MA: Harvard University Press, 2000), 105.

2. The Robert Flaherty Seminar was begun by Frances Flaherty, the director's widow, as a testament to her husband's commitment to independent filmmaking, in 1955. What began as a small gathering of filmmakers to discuss work in progress became in time an annual seminar attracting filmmakers, programmers, teachers, librarians, and independent media aficionados. The primary focus of the Flaherty has been documentary, though a strong secondary focus has been avant-garde cinema—reflecting two rather different ways of understanding Flaherty himself: he is generally recognized as the first great documentarian (though he himself did not think of himself as a documentary filmmaker in our current sense of the term) *and* as an experimental narrative filmmaker.

In recent years, attendees at the annual weeklong gathering have numbered approximately 150. Programmers are hired to curate shows of generally recent films and videos several times a day for a week. Each program is discussed by the assembled attendees. The mood of the annual Flaherty Seminar has depended on the programmers, the topic, and the era when a program is offered. While particularly volatile discussions have become the stuff of Flaherty legend, most seminars are generally affable gatherings.

with several Flaherty stalwarts; the end-of-the-seminar party would begin in an hour or so.[3] A hand was raised, and ethnographic documentarian Sarah Elder broached an issue that had been hovering around the seminar all week. "Why is it," Elder asked, "that all the avant-garde filmmakers, and their films, seem so *white?*"[4]

The potential volatility of this question could be heard in the silence that followed. All faces turned slowly from Elder to Fisher, who had been brilliant and witty during discussions throughout the week. Fisher paused for a moment, then said tersely, "I think we all *know* why." It was a clever and amusing evasion that allowed members of the seminar to feel that perhaps they *did* know, or ought to know, without actually knowing precisely what it was that they knew. And it was pure Morgan Fisher, whose films resonate with subtle, dense conceptual moments. Fisher's response led into a brief discussion of the issue of race and avant-garde film that cannot have satisfied anyone present.[5]

This Flaherty moment was far from my first confrontation of the issue of race and avant-garde cinema at the seminar. Indeed, it has been a perennial issue, especially during those seminars that have made avant-garde film a substantial part of the programming. Since many documentaries are explicit polemics for progressive political and social change, and most avant-garde films are not, it is easy to suspect that the avant-garde filmmakers are comfortable with the political status quo, including the status quo of race relations. This suspicion is exacerbated by the fact that the Flaherty Seminar itself has long had difficulties in attracting people of

3. In honor of the Flaherty's fiftieth anniversary, a group of Flaherty stalwarts—Ruth Bradley, Richard Herskowitz, Louis Massiah, William Sloan, and Patricia R. Zimmermann—programmed a retrospective of films of particular importance in the history of the seminar; their selections were interwoven with Oxtoby's programming.

4. I am working from memory vis-à-vis Elder's question; her exact words might have been other than what I have quoted her as saying, but I am confident that this catches her meaning, and it represents my memory of this moment as precisely as I can render it.

5. I do not mean to suggest here that Fisher, as a filmmaker, avoids the issue of race. In fact, race is one of the issues engaged by *Standard Gauge*. In that film, Fisher presents us with a series of filmstrips of 35mm film ("standard gauge") that he has collected over the years while working in various businesses that service the industry. The filmstrips are presented in one continuous 16mm shot, as Fisher tells us the context for each filmstrip and the reasons he finds it of interest; often this has to do with the words and other symbols on the filmstrip, signals of one kind or another to lab technicians, projectionists, and others who, while outside the spotlight, help to get films made and keep theaters working. After Fisher discusses I.B. Technicolor, he focuses on several versions of the "China Girl," usually the frame (or frames) of a colorfully dressed European American woman included on film leader that allows film labs to correctly adjust the color of prints, using as a guide the correct tonality of "flesh" (that is, the color of white skin).

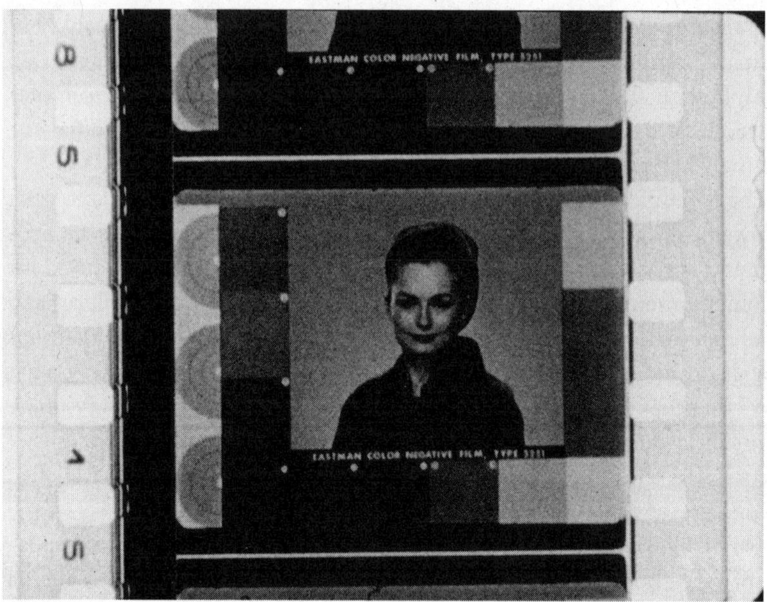

Frames of a China Girl in Morgan Fisher's *Standard Gauge* (1984). Fisher's discussion of the China Girl foregrounds the issue of skin color (for more information, see note 5). Courtesy Morgan Fisher.

color, except as guest filmmakers or curators.[6] To some considerable extent, this seems to have been an economic issue, but it also seems clear that African Americans are not particularly drawn to the seminar, despite the apparent desire for diversity on the part of most of those who attend the annual seminar and those who have served on the board of International Film Seminars, which sponsors the annual gathering.

The legendarily volatile 1989 seminar, programmed by Pearl Bowser and Grant Munro, was probably the most fully integrated Flaherty (guests included Ignacio Aguero, John Akomfrah, Orlando Bagwell, Ayoka Chenzira, Julie Dash, Mouse Diakite, William Greaves, Henry Hampton, Phillip Mallory Jones, Gaston Kabore, Olley Maruma, Louis Massiah, Susana Muños, Kwate Nee-Owo, Horace Ove, Pratibha Parmar, Lourdes Portillo, Jacqueline Shearer, Cheick Omar Sissoko, Valery Solomin, Osamu Tezuka, Trinh T.

6. Interestingly, "whiteness" is also an oft-noted reality at gatherings of avant-garde film aficionados. For example, the annual shows at Views from the Avant-Garde, curated by Mark McElhatten and Gavin Smith as a sidebar to the New York Film Festival, are rarely attended by anything like a significant percentage of people of color—much to the consternation of many who do attend.

Minh-ha, and Csaba Varga), but even this seminar was read in some quarters as not exactly racially progressive. For Toni Cade Bambara, it was

> a predictably mad proceeding in which colonialist anthro-ethno types collided with "subject people" who've already reclaimed their image, history, and culture for culturally specific documentaries, animations, features, experimental videos, and critical theory (the program of lectures and screenings of works primarily drawn from the African diaspora was curated by Pearl Bowser; an unprecedented commandeering of the guest curator's program time was used to screen post-glasnost works from Eastern Europe, and the highlight of the usurping agenda was a screening of the spare-no-expense-to-restore Flaherty/Korda colonist work *Elephant Boy*).[7]

I did not attend the 1989 seminar, but I am sure that some white seminarians would have been shocked to be considered "colonialist." At the 1987 seminar, which was my first, seminarians made clear their hostility to anything that smacked of colonialism, and the same attitude has been pervasive at every seminar I have attended since. Flaherty seminarians certainly think of themselves, and hopefully are, progressive about issues of race and culture.

The fact that Flaherty attendees and programmers have long been concerned about the seminar being, or being seen as, elitist and racially unfriendly has been particularly obvious at moments when filmmakers have seemed to straddle the categories of "black filmmaker" and "avant-garde filmmaker." At the 1991 seminar, programmed by Coco Fusco and Stephen Gallagher, William Greaves presented his *Symbiopsychotaxiplasm: Take One* (shot in 1968, first version finished in 1972), a brilliant exploration of the filmmaking process. The excitement generated was a function of the film's sophistication and ingenuity, and the fact that the seminar was playing a role in the rediscovery and long-overdue appreciation of a remarkable

7. Toni Cade Bambara, "Reading the Signs, Empowering the Eye: *Daughters of the Dust* and the Black Independent Cinema Movement," in *Black American Cinema*, ed. Manthia Diawara (New York: Routledge, 1993), 143.

Bambara's complaint that the screening of the Flaherty film and Grant Munro's programming represented an "unprecedented commandeering of the guest curator's time" seems to me a mistaken assumption. Since its inception, the Flaherty has always shown at least one Flaherty film at the annual seminar. In some instances, programmers meld the Flaherty screening into their curating; in others, it takes the form of a ritual observance, an interruption in the programming, a gesture of respect to Flaherty himself and to Frances Flaherty, who instigated the seminar to promote the study of Flaherty's films and related work. Further, it has not been uncommon for the seminar to use multiple programmers for individual seminars. A listing of those who have programmed Flaherty seminars up through 1995 is included in Erik Barnouw and Patricia R. Zimmermann, eds., *The Flaherty: Four Decades in the Cause of Independent Cinema*, special issue of *Wide Angle* (17, nos. 1–4 [1995]): 415–16.

work (completely misunderstood when it was first shown, *Symbiopsychotaxiplasm: Take One* had disappeared for nearly twenty years).[8] But many at the 1991 seminar (and I include myself) seemed particularly excited because here was an undeniably important African American contribution to avant-garde cinema. Much the same response was evident at the 1992 Flaherty, which included a considerable presence of avant-garde film, to Cauleen Smith's *Chronicles of a Lying Spirit (by Kelly Gabron)* (1992), a short film by and about an African American woman that was clearly within the avant-garde traditions of collage filmmaking and personal diaristic work. Seminarians were so excited about it that many demanded, and received, a repeat screening of the film—the only time I remember this happening during the dozen or so seminars I have attended.

However, when Elder asked her question about avant-garde filmmaking and race at the fiftieth seminar, it was the first time—or at least the first time that I am aware of—that this particular issue has been put in front of the assembled seminar in such a straightforward manner, and Elder's question stayed with me after the seminar was over. During the brief discussion that followed Fisher's response to Elder, I commented that I thought that while many of us who follow, write about, and teach avant-garde film *are* embarrassed by the degree to which our field seems "white," the issue is more one of terminology than of the racism of avant-garde filmmakers or programmers. And while, at that moment, I was not entirely convinced that this was correct, I have come to think that the issue *is* largely one of terminology or, more precisely, of categorization and segregation.

During the past generation, as film studies has become ensconced within American academe, various threads in the weave of film history have been delineated, in part as a way of defining and focusing college courses. Specific films have tended to become identified with individual threads. There are exceptions, of course: the "city symphonies" of the 1920s—Walther Ruttmann's *Berlin: Symphony of a Big City* (1927), Cavalcanti's *Rien que les heures* (1926), Vertov's *The Man with a Movie Camera* (1929), and the proto–city symphony *Manhatta* (1921) by Charles Sheeler and

8. Greaves had hoped the film would get into the Cannes Film Festival, but the "problem was that Louis Macorelles, the influential critic, went to a pre-screening of the film and the projectionist got the reels all fouled up. *Take One* is already chaotic. It's so fragile that if you mix it up even a little, you lose the film. Macorelles and I had dinner after the screening, and he said, 'I couldn't understand what the film was about!' I was surprised at his reaction, and then later, too late, I discovered that his projectionist had screened the reels out of order. I like to think of that incident as divine intervention: it has kept this film buried for almost twenty-five years." Greaves in Scott MacDonald, *A Critical Cinema 3* (Berkeley: University of California Press, 1998), 49–50.

Paul Strand—have traditionally been considered important contributions to both documentary history and avant-garde history (the city symphony is one of the earliest cinematic forms to privilege experimental composition and editing over storytelling).[9] But for the most part, until very recently the histories of documentary and avant-garde film have been seen as quite separate.[10]

Much the same has been true of African American cinema and avant-garde film. The few clear instances of crossover have been European American directors working with African American performers. The unusual career of Dudley Murphy is a useful example. Murphy began as an avant-garde filmmaker, most notably as a collaborator on one of the quintessential films of the 1920s European avant-garde: *Ballet mécanique* (1926; Fernand Léger and Man Ray were the other collaborators; George Antheil composed his *Ballet mécanique* as an accompaniment to the film). When Murphy returned to the United States from Paris, he became the director and scriptwriter of two of the best early jazz films—*St. Louis Blues* (1929) with Bessie Smith, and *Black and Tan* (1929) with Duke Ellington and Fredi Washington—and in 1933 he directed the screen adaptation of *The Emperor Jones*, starring Paul Robeson.[11] For the most part, however, at least as these fields have generally been understood, there have been relatively few significant intersections of avant-garde film and African American film.

Historians of American avant-garde film have traced the trajectory of the field from the 1920s European avant-garde, focused primarily on dada and surreal work, to the emergence of Visual Music in the 1930s and 1940s (Oskar Fischinger, Len Lye, Norman McLaren) and the "psychodramas" or "trance films" of Maya Deren, Kenneth Anger, Sidney Peterson, Curtis Har-

9. The city symphonies document aspects of the industrial societies that have developed and supported filmmaking; in several senses, they are the polar opposites of the exploratory films of Robert Flaherty—*Nanook of the North* (1921), *Moana* (1926—and Miriam C. Cooper and Ernest P. Schoedsack's *Grass* (1925), which function as early cinematic forms of salvage ethnography, capturing images of preindustrial cultures whose disappearance, or transformation, is implicit in the fact that they are being filmed.

10. That a change is occurring became evident at the end of the 1990s, in such books as Barry Keith Grant and Jeannette Sloniowski's collection *Documenting the Documentary* (Detroit, MI: Wayne State University Press, 1998), which includes essays on Flaherty, Basil Wright, Joris Ivens, *and* Stan Brakhage and Bill Viola; Catherine Russell's *Experimental Ethnography* (Durham, NC: Duke University Press, 1999), which discusses an ingenious combination of men and women identified either with ethnographic documentary or with the avant-garde; and Patricia R. Zimmermann's *States of Emergency* (Minneapolis: University of Minnesota Press, 1998), which explores political dimensions of documentary and avant-garde film and video.

11. Susan Delson's biography of Murphy, *Dudley Murphy: Hollywood Wild Card* (Minneapolis: University of Minnesota Press, 2006), carefully reviews Murphy's involvement in all these projects.

rington; to the diverse accomplishments of Anger, Stan Brakhage, Andy Warhol, and Jonas Mekas; to "found-footage film" or "recycled cinema" (Joseph Cornell, Bruce Conner, Ken Jacobs, Raphael Montañez Ortiz); to "structural film" (Tony Conrad, Michael Snow, Ernie Gehr, J. J. Murphy); to the feminist critiques of cinema of the 1970s, 1980s, and 1990s (Yvonne Rainer, Su Friedrich, Peggy Ahwesh); and to "trash" or "punk" film (Jack Smith, the Kuchar Brothers, early John Waters).[12] More recent years have seen remarkable accomplishments in films on place (James Benning, Peter Hutton, J. Leighton Pierce, Sharon Lockhart), in a widening sense of recycled cinema (Alan Berliner, Phil Solomon, Robert A. Nakamura), in various forms of hand-processed work (David Gatten, Jennifer Todd Reeves, Lawrence Brose), and in "polyvalent montage" (Warren Sonbert, Nathaniel Dorsky). The field is complex and has developed a complex cinematic discourse, as well as its own history of distribution and exhibition.

The academic field of African American cinema began to develop in the 1970s, when scholars—most important, perhaps, Donald Bogle, in his *Toms, Coons, Mulattoes, Mammies, and Bucks,* and Thomas Cripps, in *Slow Fade to Black: The Negro in American Film, 1900–1942*—mined Hollywood film history for instances where blacks had been negatively stereotyped and in some instances had found ways of triumphing over stereotyping and limited opportunity.[13] But the late 1960s and the 1970s also saw the development of filmmaking projects that were rebelling against Hollywood and its

12. Crucial historical texts include Sitney's *Visionary Film: The American Avant-Garde* (New York: Oxford University Press, 1974), and the revised edition, *Visionary Film: The American Avant-Garde, 1943–2000* (New York: Oxford University Press, 2002); Paul Arthur's *A Line of Sight: American Avant-Garde Film since 1965* (Minneapolis: University of Minnesota Press, 2005); and Jan-Christopher Horak, ed., *The First American Film Avant-Garde, 1919–1945* (Madison: University of Wisconsin Press, 1995). David James's *Allegories of Cinema: American Film in the Sixties* (Princeton, NJ: Princeton University Press, 1989) and *The Most Typical Avant-Garde: History and Geography of Minor Cinemas in Los Angeles* (Berkeley: University of California Press, 2005); William C. Wees, *Light Moving in Time: Studies in the Visual Aesthetics of Avant-Garde Film* (Berkeley: University of California Press, 1992); Ed Small, *Direct Theory: Experimental Film/Video as Major Genre* (Carbondale: Southern Illinois University Press, 1994); James Peterson, *Dreams of Chaos, Visions of Order: Understanding the American Avant-Garde Cinema* (Detroit, MI: Wayne State University Press, 1994); and Jeffrey Skoller, *Shadows, Specters, Shards: Making History in Avant-Garde Film* (Minneapolis: University of Minnesota Press, 2005) are also important contributions toward the chronicling of this history, as I hope are my five volumes of *A Critical Cinema: Interviews with Independent Filmmakers* (Berkeley: University of California Press, 1988, 1992, 1998, 2005, 2006).

13. Donald Bogle, *Toms, Coons, Mulattoes, Mammies, and Bucks* (New York: Continuum, 1973) and Thomas Cripps, *Slow Fade to Black: The Negro in American Film, 1900–1942* (New York: Oxford University Press, 1977), respectively; the fourth edition of Bogle's book appeared in 2006. Other important contributions to chronicling the history of African American cinema include Daniel J. Leab, *From Sambo to Superspade: The Black Experience in*

depictions of African America, by such directors as Melvin Van Peebles, William Greaves, Bill Gunn, Charles Burnett, Kathleen Collins, Billy Woodberry, Haile Gerima, Julie Dash, and Charles Lane. These filmmakers, and the rediscovery of the underground "race films" of the 1920s, 1930s, and 1940s—particularly those by Oscar Micheaux—allowed the history of films made by, and for, African Americans to seem a coherent project with a particular ongoing purpose: to critique and revise the assumptions about African America communicated in the mass media and, by doing so, to assist in righting some of the wrongs with which African America has struggled.

Related developments have occurred in other ethnic cinemas as well. In his programming for the 1993 Flaherty seminar, Chon Noriega demonstrated that "Chicano cinema" has a similar history: the recognition and exposure of stereotyping and the rebellion against bigotry have produced a variety of Chicano alternatives to commercial Hollywood. The same is true, of course, for the history of Asian American filmmaking/videomaking, though Asians and Asian Americans have been making important contributions to avant-garde cinema, as well as to Asian American cinema, for decades: Teiji Ito composed the sound track for Maya Deren's *Meshes of the Afternoon* (1959); Taka Iimura has been a fixture on the independent film and video scene since the 1960s; and Nam June Paik and Yoko Ono made major contributions to video art and avant-garde film in the 1960s and 1970s.

The fact that some African American, Chicano, and Asian American filmmakers have made work that is closely related to films produced by filmmakers identified with the avant-garde seems generally to have been less interesting and important to many filmmakers and scholars than dealing with issues of ethnicity. Of course, this "interest" and "importance" is both a theoretical/critical matter and a practical one. In both academic contexts and governmentally funded arts contexts, African American cinema, Chicano cinema, and Asian American cinema sell more effectively than avant-

---

Motion Pictures (Boston: Houghton Mifflin, 1975); Thomas Cripps, *Making Movies Black: The Hollywood Message Movie from World War II to the Civil Rights Era* (New York: Oxford University Press, 1993); the collection *Black American Cinema*, ed. Manthia Diawara (New York: Routledge, 1993); Jane M. Gaines, *Fire and Desire: Mixed-Race Movies in the Silent Era* (Chicago: University of Chicago Press, 2001), which includes a detailed overview of scholarship relating to race films; Jacqueline Stewart, *Migrating to the Movies: Cinema and Black Urban Modernity* (Berkeley: University of California Press, 2005); and two books focusing on Oscar Micheaux: Pearl Bowser and Louise Spence, *Writing Himself into History: Oscar Micheaux, His Silent Films, and His Audiences* (New Brunswick, NJ: Rutgers University Press, 2000), and Pearl Bowser, Jane Gaines, and Charles Musser, *Oscar Micheaux and His Circle: African-American Filmmaking and Race Cinema of the Silent Era* (Bloomington: Indiana University Press, 2001).

garde cinema does. This has been especially true in recent years, since most colleges and universities have been at pains to diversify (or at least to seem to diversify) their faculty and their student bodies, and since most governmental arts organizations feel pressure to spread whatever resources they have at their disposal across as many geographic and ethnic constituencies as possible.

As practical as the decision to align oneself with one's ethnic comrades in a collaborative effort at social change can seem, and as understandable as a rejection of avant-garde film on the grounds that it is apolitical may be for some, the maintenance of these different histories as separate and unrelated cultural projects obscures important aesthetic, historical, and practical realities and creates divisions where they need not be. Most obviously, both avant-garde filmmakers and the makers identified with the various ethnic cinemas see the commercial media as at best a mixed blessing that has regularly distorted and obscured social reality in the name of the status quo, has generally reduced human beings to consumers, and has often stifled many forms of resistance and creativity. Both cultural projects evolved as countercinemas to these tendencies, and both have explored a range of alternatives to the mass media with generally limited means.

Often, the makers within these two traditions have worked in ignorance of each other. As a result, filmmakers uninformed about avant-garde film history can see dimensions of their work or the work of their comrades as aesthetic breakthroughs, even as instances of a specifically black aesthetic when, in fact, these aspects of their work are echoes of avant-garde projects of earlier decades; and those in the avant-garde who are not aware of Oscar Micheaux or of Spencer Williams's *Blood of Jesus* (1941) may assume that certain approaches to independent filmmaking were new in the 1960s, when in fact aspects of these approaches were part of African American cinema a generation earlier.

For much of American film history, filmgoing was a segregated activity; and even once theaters were finally integrated legally, African American and European American audiences seem to have remained largely distinct in terms of both their preferences and their modes of reception. The eight discussions that follow do not deny this troubled history, but I do attempt to suggest some specific areas where avant-garde film and African American cinema can be usefully integrated in our thinking and, for those of us who are film educators, in our teaching and our programming. With a single exception, I am focusing on African American film and video history, rather than the other ethnic cinemas, because the gap between this ethnic cinema and avant-garde film seems especially troubled and because their intersections are of considerable interest. Obviously, none of these brief discussions is exhaustive; hopefully, each suggests ways of thinking beyond conventional cine-historic categories.

EARLY CROSSOVERS

One of the earliest attempts to build a bridge between the histories of avant-garde film and African American film involved the rediscovery of Oscar Micheaux by film aficionados during the late 1970s and the 1980s. In his "Bad Cinema," published originally in *Film Comment* in 1980, J. Hoberman (a critic long identified with American avant-garde film) argued that what had usually been considered Micheaux's ineptitude as a director and/or the result of his having to work without adequate financial resources—the many strange narrative constructions, the awkward editing, the cheesy sets, the unconvincing acting—can be understood as the formal expression of Micheaux's anger and rebellion against American society and the Hollywood cinema produced for it: "Micheaux's films are so devastatingly bad that he can only be considered alongside Georges Méliès, D. W. Griffith, Dziga Vertov, Stan Brakhage, and Jean-Luc Godard as one of the medium's major formal innovators. . . . And if Oscar Micheaux was a fully conscious artist, he was the greatest genius the cinema ever produced."[14] What Hoberman calls Micheaux's "badness" as a filmmaker (referring not only to his supposed ineptitude as a director, by Hollywood standards, but to his rebelliousness toward those blacks who were more committed to protesting African American disenfranchisement than to taking advantage of the entrepreneurial opportunities available in the United States), J. Ronald Green argues "might be understood better as a retention of early film traits, from before the advent of glossy illusionism, than as a failed imitation of White movies"; and sometimes, Green suggests, Micheaux's "bad" production values "can be read as part of a representation of desire for financial means."[15]

If one approaches Micheaux in this way, it is easy to see him as closer to certain avant-garde filmmakers than to some of his race film colleagues. *Ten*

14. J. Hoberman, *Vulgar Modernism: Writing on Movies and Other Media* (Philadelphia: Temple University Press, 1991), 22. Hoberman was educated in the Cinema Department at what is now Binghamton University (then the State University of New York at Binghamton), the now-legendary department established by Larry Gottheim that nurtured a considerable number of the leading filmmakers, programmers, and writers of the American avant-garde.

15. J. Ronald Green, "'Twoness' in the Style of Oscar Micheaux," in *Black American Cinema*, ed. Manthia Diawara (New York: Routledge, 1993), 40, 44.

Minutes to Live (1932), for example, has a good bit in common with Luis Buñuel and Salvador Dali's *Un chien andalou* ("An Andalusian Dog," 1929). The Buñuel-Dali film has become the best-known avant-garde surrealist film and is, of course, a virtual compendium of anti-Hollywood gestures. Seemingly unrelated actions are combined within a structure that provides constant surprise to anyone expecting a normal narrative, starting with Buñuel's slicing the eye of the central female protagonist in the film's opening sequence, which relocates the "climax" of the film to the beginning. From then on, virtually every conventional cinematic trope is defied. When a young woman is hit by an automobile, the action is presented with a "mistake" in continuity: we see three shots of the woman (actually it is difficult to be confident about the gender of characters in *Un chien andalou*); in the first, she is holding a striped box, then her hands are in the air and no box is sight; then, she is holding the box again. This refusal of conventional continuity is so obvious that we cannot imagine it was not a conscious choice on the part of the filmmakers. Once the woman has been hit by the car, the focus moves to a young man and woman who have been looking down at the events from a second-story apartment; the man is suddenly sexually aroused and begins to molest the woman, to the accompaniment of tango music. Surprises to our conventional expectations, affronts to the "rules" of commercial narrative filmmaking, continue throughout the film.

As Arthur Jafa has suggested, "Some of the most interesting aspects of Micheaux's films are their refusals, what they don't do . . . how they resist certain Hollywood tropes and ways of organizing things."[16] Many moments in *Ten Minutes to Live,* for example, seem to draw attention to themselves as mistakes. In one instance, we see, in succession, what were apparently two versions of the same shot, recorded from slightly different distances, and I believe we hear "cut" at the end of the first. In another instance we see exactly the same sequence, during which the character Letha Watkins (Willor Lee Guilford) reads a note telling her she has ten minutes to live and discusses the situation with her boyfriend, twice in succession. The repetition is obvious and seems as obviously conscious as Buñuel's inclusion of the same sequence twice at the beginning of his *The Exterminating Angel* (1962). The location of much of the action in *Ten Minutes to Live* within a nightclub, the Lybia, is a device familiar from many early sound films, including a number of race films, but Micheaux's nightclub scenes simultaneously provide moments of conventional entertainment (singing and

16. See "The Notion of Treatment: Black Aesthetics and Film," an interview with Arthur Jafa by Peter Hessli, in *Oscar Micheaux and His Circle,* 14.

dancing, a comedy routine) *and* resist the usual conventions for presenting such action: as Jafa says, "The way Micheaux uses those music and dance sequences is both entertaining and formally radical. They're totally jagged and they completely disrupt the narrative flow."[17] Further, just as *Un chien andalou* presents one primary location, the apartment, to which we return almost at random, in *Ten Minutes to Live* the Lybia serves as the location for two separate, unrelated stories (adapted, according to the opening credits, from two stories of "Negro night life in Harlem") during both of which some of the same characters participate and some of the same moments occur: it is almost as if we are seeing two options of events that might happen in this nightclub milieu.

There are, of course, a good many differences between *Un chien andalou* and *Ten Minutes to Live.* The Micheaux film seems to mean, however jaggedly, to reveal the climaxes of two stories that do have some continuity, whereas *Un chien andalou* avoids story altogether. And the Buñuel-Dali film is full of subconscious images culled from the dreams and hallucinations of several people, whereas it would be a stretch to call Micheaux's film "surrealist" in this sense. Nevertheless, both films assume an audience that can enjoy discontinuity and absurdity within a film experience that simultaneously alludes to Hollywood commercial cinema in a variety of ways, while refusing to abide by conventional moviegoing expectations. They are two instances of conscious rebellion, made at the opening of the sound era by independent filmmakers working with limited resources and using formal abrasions as a means of expressing their distance from the industry.

In recent years, Spencer Williams—and especially the first feature he directed, *Blood of Jesus*—has been of particular interest both to those chronicling African American filmmaking and to those who keep abreast of avant-garde cinema. Unfortunately, at this point we know relatively little about Williams or about the context and production of *Blood of Jesus;* indeed, we may never know as much as we would like because, as is true of so many early African American directors, whatever paper trails were created by the production of their films seem to have disappeared, or at least have not yet resurfaced.[18] While *Blood of Jesus* exemplifies the low-budget quality of so many race films, it is, for many viewers, charming and revealing, precisely because of its limitations. Compared with King Vidor's *Hallelujah* (1929),

17. "The Notion of Treatment," 13.

18. Jacqueline Stewart is currently doing research for a book on Williams—a challenging, frustrating (and exciting) project, as she has suggested to me, because of the lack of good information about Spencer and his directing.

another film that focuses on some of the same aspects of African American religion, *Blood of Jesus* seems almost intimate, as if it were made by a group of Christian friends from inside an African American religious community. Indeed, at times the film seems like a church pageant, where the dramatization is less about creating a believable illusion than about the community's providing a wholesome and intimate entertainment for the congregation. The fact that Williams and his collaborators were willing and able to complete the film, despite what must have been their recognition that the result could not compete with conventional commercial movies, at least in terms of its production values, is evidence of their commitment as filmmakers, and apparently as Christians, to the story the film tells and the belief it seems to express. That is, the "spirit" of the filmmakers seems to transcend their material limitations, a perfect reflection of the rural southern African American Christianity the film depicts and the particular vision of Christ at its center.[19]

Blood of Jesus could not, at first glance, seem more different from such early "trash films" (see the discussion of trash cinema in section 4 of this essay) as Jack Smith's *Flaming Creatures* (1963) or George and Mike Kuchar's *A Town Called Tempest* (1963) in terms of the kinds of people it depicts and the story it tells. However, the commitment of Smith, the Kuchars, and their colleagues to make films despite limited financing and questionable talent suggests a comparable faith in the spirit of a disenfranchised community to transcend its own limitations—in films that will probably be of interest only to like-minded souls. And in all three instances, this community spirit seems embedded within the stories enacted, in related ways: all three films evoke the idea of divine retribution. In *Flaming Creatures* and *A Town Called Tempest*, an earthquake and a tornado, respectively, are presented as divine responses to communities immersed in sin, just as in *Blood of Jesus* the near accidental death of Sister Martha at the hands of her husband, Rastus, forces him to reconsider his resistance to being part of her religious community. Of course, *Blood of Jesus* was presumably made by true believers in Christianity, while the Kuchar and Smith films seem made by men in rebellion against what are usually considered Christian values—but the use of filmmaking as a dramatization of a level of spiritual life deeper and more committed than what is seen in the commercial cinema

19. I say "seems to" because there may have been commercial motives to *Blood of Jesus* that might have made its producers decide to use what had become one of the conventions of race movies: that is, the struggles of believers to resist the temptations of urbanity, symbolized by the nightclub.

unites the three projects. Indeed, one can see *Blood of Jesus, Flaming Creatures,* and the Kuchar Brothers' early films as cinematic forms of folk art that relate in a number of ways to the work of self-taught painters like Mose T (Tolliver) and Howard Finster, and to the New York City graffiti artists of the 1980s who did what Martha Cooper and Henry Chalfant called "Subway Art"—to the whole history of self-taught artists whose impassioned work has been created entirely outside of recognized institutional channels of financial and critical support.[20]

DO THE RIGHT THING: ETHNIC CITY SYMPHONY

One of the dangers of using our usual categories, and especially with distinguishing African American cinema from other strands in the weave of film history, is that even obvious connections between these different strands can be missed. Earlier, I mentioned that the city symphony has traditionally been claimed by both documentary and avant-garde film. American filmmakers have made a number of memorable city symphonies: Pat O'Neill's *Water and Power* (1989), Weegee's *Weegee's New York* (c. 1952, co-made with Amos Vogel); the several New York city symphonies made by Rudy Burckhardt; and the remarkable *Forest of Bliss* (1986), a city symphony of Benares, India, by American Robert Gardner. But this country's most remarkable city symphony is usually considered neither a documentary nor an avant-garde film. Like Ruttmann's *Berlin: Symphony of a Big City,* which established the city symphony form, Spike Lee's *Do the Right Thing* (1989) begins in the early morning as the city is waking up, moves through an entire day, in this case a hot summer Saturday (most city symphonies have focused on workdays), and continues into the night.

Do the Right Thing not only conforms to the overall temporal structure of the city symphony but also incorporates crucial dimensions of the classic 1920s European city symphonies that are usually considered the most characteristic instances of the form (I have detailed this idea in chapter 6 of *The Garden in the Machine*), while at the same time broadening our definition of the form and using it to redefine what a city *is.* The overall organizational similarity between *Berlin* and *Do the Right Thing* is obvious, but while Ruttmann's film ends with literal fireworks, Lee's film focuses on so-

20. I am referring to Martha Cooper and Henry Chalfant's *Subway Art* (New York: Holt, Rinehart and Winston, 1984). I mention Howard Finster and Mose T in particular here because the work of both painters is featured in *North on Evers* (1991) by James Benning, who is discussed in section 7 of this essay.

cial "fireworks": the late evening conflict that ends in the death of Radio Raheem and the fire that destroys Sal's Famous pizza parlor.[21]

Like Dziga Vertov in *The Man with a Movie Camera,* Lee is at pains to draw attention to the fact that his film is a constructed artifact. Vertov means to define cinema as the quintessential art form for a society in the throes of industrial modernization, and he depicts the filmmaker as a worker, like other workers, committed to the new, industrialized communist society. During the film, Vertov draws continual attention to the three processes cinema requires: a central motif within his film is an actual cameraman (Mikhail Kaufman, Vertov's brother) shooting imagery; the process of editing (conducted by Vertov's wife, Elizaveta Svilova) is also demonstrated; and *The Man with a Movie Camera* begins and ends in a theater, where we watch an audience arrive for a screening and the projectionist and the theater orchestra prepare and present the screening.

Lee draws attention to his filmmaking by giving free rein to the expressionist tendency that is evident at some point in most of his films. Beginning with the opening credits, during which Rosie Perez dances to Public Enemy's "Fight the Power" in continually changing outfits in front of what is obviously a projected image of a portion of a city neighborhood, Lee is continually at pains to punctuate the flow of his narrative with aspects of image and sound that draw attention to themselves as cinematic devices, as directorial flourishes, including, most obviously, several instances where characters address Lee's camera directly, in one instance to perform a now-famous set of racist diatribes; in another, to reveal Radio Raheem's philosophical side (while simultaneously alluding to a cinematic progenitor of Lee's film: Charles Laughton's *Night of the Hunter* [1955]). Of course, the fact that most people who see *Do the Right Thing* know that Lee not only is the film's director but also plays Mookie, one of the film's central protagonists, helps maintain our awareness of Lee-as-director, as does the casting of Joie Lee, Lee's sister, as Jade, Mookie's sister.

While Vertov's goal in drawing attention to the various processes that make cinema possible is to demonstrate his excitement about modern, socialist Russia, Lee's goal in drawing attention to himself as director is to demonstrate an alternative to Mookie's inability to find a way to move beyond maintaining his personal status quo. Although Mookie, to use an early description of the character from Lee's journal for *Do the Right Thing,* "has

21. Other city symphonies—*Weegee's New York,* for instance, and several of the Burckhardt city symphonies of the 1940s, as well as Francis Thompson's *N.Y., N.Y.* (1957)—substitute the lights of theater marquees and advertisements for Ruttmann's literal fireworks.

no vision. . . . The future might be too scary for kids like Mookie, so they don't think about it. They live for the present moment, because there is nothing they feel they can do about the future,"[22] Lee himself *is* a person of vision who *does* think he can affect the future. Indeed, in the case of *Do the Right Thing,* he is at pains to demonstrate that an African American man can do more than maintain his own economic status quo; he can produce a film that offers immediate (if admittedly limited) benefits to a disenfranchised New York neighborhood, and he can model a creative alternative to the feeling of powerlessness. To put it succinctly, *Do the Right Thing dramatizes* the unfortunate consequences of a neighborhood's inability to work through its ethnic differences, while *demonstrating* the potential for New Yorkers (the director, his crew, the cast, the residents of the neighborhood) to overcome their differences during the production of a work of cinematic art.

Lee's decision to ask St. Clair Bourne to document the making of *Do the Right Thing* (in what became *Making "Do the Right Thing" with Spike Lee* [1989]) reveals that, even before the production got under way, Lee recognized that the process of producing this new film was something his audience needed to be aware of. Bourne's documentary helps to make clear the degree to which Lee saw his project as a contribution to the history of African American cinema: during the documentary, Lee is filmed talking about Oscar Micheaux, and Melvin Van Peebles visits the set and is introduced to the neighborhood and to the filmmakers as one of Lee's cinematic forefathers.

Do the Right Thing makes a significant contribution to the genre of the city symphony in several ways. First, it expands the fictional component of the form.[23] From early on, the city symphony sometimes included fictional elements. This was particularly the case with the now least known of the major European city symphonies of the 1920s: Cavalcanti's *Rien que les heures,* which develops several characters whose lives intersect during a day in the life of Paris. Lee's film is full of characters; indeed, it is clear that for Lee, New York *is* the immense cluster of personalities who inhabit the city and whose interactions are its life. Indeed, it is evident throughout *Do the Right Thing* that it is the particular multiethnicity of New York that makes it distinctive and quintessentially American. The directors who invented the city symphony form emphasized industrialization, transportation, and the commercial energy of the modern city. For Lee what energizes the modern

22. From Spike Lee's book companion to the film: *Do the Right Thing,* ed. Spike Lee and Liza Jones (New York: Simon and Schuster, 1989), 63.

23. Federico Fellini used this structure before Lee did, in *Fellini's Roma* (1972), which Lee saw "as a good model for this film" (Lee and Jones, *Do the Right Thing,* 28).

Vito (Richard Edson) and Mookie (Spike Lee) argue sports in *Do the Right Thing* (1989). Courtesy Museum of Modern Art.

city is not industrial or commercial labor, though, of course, many of his characters presumably have jobs, and much of the action in *Do the Right Thing* occurs in and around the three commercial establishments on the single block of the Bedford-Stuyvesant neighborhood to which the action of the film is confined. Lee's focus is evident in his setting *Do the Right Thing* on a summer Saturday, when most of the neighborhood is not away at work and when the neighborhood children and young people are not in school. The modern city in *Do the Right Thing* is not simply a place where people work; it is where concentrations of individuals of a variety of ethnic heritages make their homes.

Lee sees the fundamental energy of his city as the interaction of the many ethnic groups that have been drawn to New York as a result of several centuries of immigration from all over the United States and the world. This is obvious within the narrative of *Do the Right Thing,* during which various ethnic individuals and groups interact—sometimes with pleasure, sometimes causing friction, sometimes both—and it was evident within the production process. Lee saw John Turturro as "ideal" to play Pino, Sal's openly racist son, because Turturro grew up "in a Black neighborhood in Queens."[24] One of the most interesting moments in Bourne's documentary

24. Lee and Jones, *Do the Right Thing,* 109.

is a conversation between Danny Aiello (who plays Sal) and Giancarlo Esposito (who plays the most volatile anti-Italian African American character, Buggin' Out). Aiello explains that he feels no particular connection to Italy and thinks of himself not as an Italian American, but as an American Italian. Esposito, who is (Lee explains in his journal) "half Black and half Italian," responds that he *does* feel a connection to his Italian roots and considers himself an Italian American. That is, not only are Lee's cast and crew ethnically mixed, but the actors themselves play across ethnic lines.

Lee's commitment to the idea of the modern city as distinctive in its ethnic diversity and in the interchange among ethnic groups that inevitably occurs in such an environment is expressed not only by the unusual ethnic range of the characters he includes in *Do the Right Thing* but also through his expressionist use of color throughout the film. This immensely "colorful" city block functions as a synecdoche not only for modern American urban life—every American city is increasingly a "colorful" mixture of ethnicities that is a major determinant of the nature of life in that environment—but also for urbanization throughout the world. The city symphonies of the 1920s include, or at least emphasize, very little diversity, less than might have been emphasized had their directors been less swept away by modern industrial processes (and perhaps less prejudiced against certain groups). The evolution of modern transportation so important in *Berlin: Symphony of a Big City* and *The Man with a Movie Camera,* even in *Manhatta,* had already helped to transform many of the world's urban areas into increasingly complex ethnic mixtures; and the past seventy-five years have seen an expansion of this development that previous centuries could hardly have imagined. Lee's film is the first city symphony (or at least the first I am aware of) to fully recognize this development and to simultaneously mourn its frustrations and failures, and not only celebrate, but *demonstrate,* its potential.[25]

"STRUCTURAL FILM" AND *SYMBIOPSYCHOTAXIPLASM: TAKE ONE*

From 1965 to 1975, the most important cinematic development, at least in American avant-garde film (or, perhaps more precisely, in the minds of those who functioned as critics and chroniclers of American avant-garde cinema)

25. Many of Rudy Burckhardt's New York City films emphasize and celebrate the city's diversity: *The Climate of New York* (1948), *Doldrums* (1972), and *Zipper* (1987) are excellent examples. Much the same can be said of Weegee's *Weegee's New York.*

was what came to be called "structural film." P. Adams Sitney gets credit for the term, which was defined in his breakthrough book *Visionary Film:* "There is a cinema of structure in which the shape of the whole film is predetermined and simplified, and it is the shape which is the primal impression of the film"; "Four characteristics of the structural film are its fixed camera position . . . the flicker effect, loop printing, and rephotography off the screen."[26] Sitney was trying to account for what was clearly a new kind of cinema, though in the long run his attempt to characterize a set of films by what he saw as their unusual formal elements was not particularly successful, or at least, not nearly as successful as the term "structural film" itself. Indeed, what the diverse films designated by Sitney's term have in common is not so much a set of formal elements but a particular goal: to transform explorations of fundamental elements of the cinematic apparatus into aesthetic experiences. Thus, and here, of course, I am oversimplifying, Andy Warhol (whom Sitney saw as the forefather of structural film) can be said to explore duration; Tony Conrad explores flicker in *The Flicker* (1966); Michael Snow and Ernie Gehr explore the zoom lens in *Wavelength* (1967) and *Serene Velocity* (1970); Snow, the panning camera in *Back and Forth* (1969); Taka Iimura, duration, in *1 to 60 Seconds* (1973); Gehr and J. J. Murphy, different aspects of the filmstrip in *Eureka* (1974) and *Print Generation* (1974), and so forth.

Understood this way, structural film can be seen as part of the larger social and political context of that period, during which the fundamental structures of a good many traditional elements of American culture and society were being reexamined. One crucial subject for cinematic exploration during this moment—one not reflected in Sitney's discussion of structural filmmakers—is cinema's status as a collaborative medium, both during its production and during its reception. Certainly, all the films I list here were confrontations of the traditional audience expectations for both mainstream and avant-garde cinema, and, in many cases can be said to have demanded, and to some extent to have created, new forms of film audience. Further, some films identified as structural films made an examination of the social nature of film reception a subject; Anthony McCall's *Line Describing a Cone* (1973), for example, literally reconstitutes the film-viewing audience: spectators move around a smoky, nontheatrical space (often an art gallery) that allows for mobility within the darkness, as a cone of light gradually forms between the projector, which is placed within the darkened space, and the

26. Sitney, *Visionary Film,* 407, 408.

Line Describing a Cone (1973), during a projection of the film at Artists Space in New York City in 1974. Photograph by Peter Moore. Courtesy Anthony McCall.

opposite wall (no screen is used). For McCall, *Line Describing a Cone* was a way of exploring a particular dimension of cinema—projected light—and using it as a metaphor for a reconsideration of the assumptions that underlie the "normal" screening situation, where audience members sit in regular rows of seats, all looking in the same direction, and are led by a set of visual and auditory cues through a generic narrative that is broadcast from the projection booth, a space separated from the theater and accessible only to a class of experts.

During the half hour of *Line Describing a Cone,* most viewers become physically active in examining the developing cone of light and in keeping it visible (originally, smoking was considered intrinsic to the experience of the film; that smoking is no longer allowed in public spaces has changed the experience, and to some extent the meaning, of the film), and as the growing arc on the far wall becomes a circle, they form a new kind of social circle. McCall's film creates a democratic screening situation and places the "means of production"—of the look of the cone, at least—"in the hands of the people." Further, McCall reduces the social class gap between producer and consumer, since the various pleasures of *Line Describing a Cone* (its loveliness as a light sculpture, its political insights) were produced with virtually no expenditure: the film was produced by animating the drawing of a circle with a simple protractor on a three-by-five-inch card.

William Greaves's *Symbiopsychotaxiplasm: Take One* can be understood as a contribution to structural film, specifically, as an exploration of the social dimensions of the cinematic apparatus of independent film *production*. While it is widely assumed that many avant-garde films, including most of those Sitney describes as structural films, were made by individuals working alone, in fact filmmaking is virtually always a social activity. To take a particularly extreme example, even when Ernie Gehr shot *Serene Velocity* in a hallway at Binghamton University (then the State University of New York at Binghamton), absolutely alone during an exhausting single summer night in 1970, he had already bought film stock from someone (and he would subsequently take the resulting footage to someone to have it developed and good prints struck); also, he needed to work within the social reality of the university to be sure he would be alone and uninterrupted as he shot; and of course, he would not have considered the process complete until he had shown the finished film to an audience. All film production, including avant-garde film production, has social dimensions, and at least as inventively as any other American independent film, *Symbiopsychotaxiplasm: Take One* explores aspects of this fundamental dimension of the filmmaking process.

Greaves's particular approach to investigating the social aspects of film production evokes another structural film. When J. J. Murphy made *Print Generation* (1974), he designed an unusual procedure for generating imagery—he made a one-minute diary film, then asked a film laboratory to make a set of contact prints: a contact print of the original, then a contact print of that contact print, then a contact print of *that* contact print, and so on, until no significant change was visible from one contact print to the next (this was true after the fiftieth print). In other words, he allowed this process to generate his imagery, which was subsequently organized so that during the first half of the film, we travel up through twenty-five layers of emulsion on the filmstrip to the original contact print, then, during the second half, down through another twenty-five layers to the final contact print included in the finished film.[27] The stratification of color emulsion is usually hidden territory; Murphy allows us to explore it.

For *Symbiopsychotaxiplasm: Take One,* Greaves designed a (social) process that would produce imagery of pairs of actors performing a screen test using a scripted argument between a man and a woman.[28] Greaves decided at the outset that this set of screen tests would take place within the "symbiotaxiplasm" (Arthur Bentley's term for any social organism and all that is contingent to it) that included the actors, the group of men and women working as Greaves's crew, and the social space of Central Park, where the film was shot. Greaves added "psycho" to emphasize his interest in the psychology of collaborative creative activity. Having provided the script and generally organized the shooting so that the camera and sound people would simultaneously record the actors, *and* the shooting *and* the surround, depending on where most of the psychic energy seemed to be at any given moment, Greaves stepped away from the usual film director's role to allow his process to generate its own experiences and its own imagery. Greaves's assumption that his refusal to direct in the conventional sense would, sooner or later, create rebellion among both cast and crew and his expectation that the visibility of the filmmaking process in Central Park would create interest among those moving through the park were correct: many of the crew began to meet secretly to discuss what for them was a most unusual and frustrating filmmaking experience, and at various times, individuals and groups of New Yorkers did become involved in the shooting.

Originally, Greaves had hoped to produce a series of *Symbiopsychotaxiplasm* films, but only *Take One* was completed, and that not for several years (in 2005 Greaves would revisit the project in *Symbiopsychotaxiplasm: Take 2½*).[29] After an introductory passage and the opening credits (visually, the credit sequence evokes Edward Steichen's photo sequence *The Family of*

27. Contact printing this way creates one set of prints organized left to right (A wind), another right to left (B wind); in order to see all the images in the same right-to-left configuration, alternating prints need to be flipped. This results in one set of prints with the imagery slightly nearer the projector lens than the imagery on the other set of prints. Murphy wanted all the prints seen in the same configuration and decided to divide them so that viewers see all the A-wind prints, then, after an adjustment in projector focus, all the B-wind prints.

28. To the extent that Greaves's film focuses on the repetition of the argument between Alice and Freddy, it resembles another remarkable avant-garde film of the same era, Hollis Frampton's *Critical Mass* (1971), which also focuses on an argument between lovers that is repeated over and over during the film. *Critical Mass* and *Symbiopsychotaxiplasm: Take One* might make a fascinating double bill.

29. So far as I have been able to determine, the version of *Symbiopsychotaxiplasm: Take One* finished in 1972 was the one shown at the Brooklyn Museum retrospective and at the 1991 Flaherty Seminar. In 1994, presumably because of the interest the film had created, Greaves added four minutes. At the beginning of the new version, we briefly see several of

William Greaves (left) and Victor, a homeless man who walks into the production of *Symbiopsychotaxiplasm: Take One* (1972), near the end of the film. Courtesy William Greaves.

Man [1955]; the sound track combines Miles Davis's "In a Silent Way" and the sound of a rising sine wave that reminds anyone familiar with Michael Snow's *Wavelength* of that film's sound track), Greaves intercuts between one pair of actors (Don Fellows and Patricia Ree Gilbert) repeatedly trying to play Freddy and Alice within the group of technicians recording the dramatic scene and the Central Park surround, and several meetings of cast and crew, including those that were originally filmed without Greaves knowing, during which Greaves's goals and direction—or his apparent lack of direction—are discussed. The focus of the finished film is the complex nature of the layered social enterprise of producing a film, including the interchange between the fictional characters, between director and actors and director and crew, between the crew and the actors, between the actors themselves, between various crew members, and between members of the production unit and others in Central Park.

In *Line Describing a Cone,* McCall uses his exploration of the cone of light between projector and wall as a means to consider the social implications of film spectatorship; in *Symbiopsychotaxiplasm: Take One,* Greaves sees his exploration of the production process as more than an end in itself, however fascinating that might be. Greaves models an attitude toward production that, to that point, seems virtually unprecedented in American cinema in general and in avant-garde cinema. Greaves's cast and crew, and even the people enjoying Central Park who find their way into the shoot, are unusually multiethnic for a film—though at no point in the film does Greaves make a point of this multiethnicity; it is never overtly mentioned.[30] In part, this is because Greaves saw his collaborators as people who had moved beyond the issue of race ("The people who worked on *Symbiopsychotaxiplasm*

the other pairs of actors playing Alice and Freddy; and one pair—Susan Anspach playing Alice—later does the scene as a musical, or tries to do the scene (they cannot stifle their own laughter). I must say that I prefer the original version—though it is interesting to see what other "takes" Greaves had in mind.

30. It is clear at least in one instance that Patricia Ree Gilbert is conscious of the issue of race: when Greaves makes a joke about George Wallace, Gilbert's laughter suggests that she is at pains to prove she is not racist.

were Age-of-Aquarius-type people, who were in many respects shorn of the encumbrances that many white Americans are burdened with. If you investigated the psychology of these people, you wouldn't discover racism or prejudice").[31] During an informal meeting with cast and crew, Greaves goes so far as to refer to himself as "the establishment" against which his collaborators should feel free to rebel—and neither Greaves nor any actor or crew member seems to find his inversion of the "normal" racial power structure worthy of comment. They may not understand why Greaves is ignoring, or seeming to ignore, the usual prerogatives of directorial power, but their puzzlement and resistance never seem to involve the issue of race.

Greaves is certainly not unaware of the history of American racism, and its then current realities—one of the primary sites where Alice and Freddy argue is the small knoll that includes a monument erected in honor of fifty-eight men of the New York National Guard's Seventh Regiment who were lost during the Civil War, and at one point Greaves lists racial strife as one of the contexts for his film—but *as a filmmaker* he is at pains to create a collaborative community that can model ways of constructively building on and moving beyond this history. From the beginning of his career as a documentarian, Greaves "wasn't interested in just making movies. I was interested in social issues and corrective social action,"[32] and over the years, this interest has taken a wide variety of forms, including a series of formally conventional but widely admired documentaries about important but under-recognized contributors to African American history, as well as a good number of films that have experimental elements.[33] The angel financing that made the *Symbiopsychotaxiplasm* project possible, however, allowed Greaves to demonstrate that working interethnically should not be considered strange or unusual, that, in a sensible world, it *shouldn't* even inspire comment.

In 2005 Greaves returned to the *Symbiopsychotaxiplasm* project in a major way (over the years, he had made minor changes to the 1972 version of *Take One,* in order to make clearer the nature of the original project). In *Symbiopsychotaxiplasm: Take 2½* Greaves focuses on the interracial couple introduced during the final credits of *Take One* (they are played by Au-

31. Greaves in MacDonald, *A Critical Cinema 3,* 57

32. MacDonald, *A Critical Cinema 3,* 47.

33. Greaves has made documentaries on Booker T. Washington, Frederick Douglass, Ida B. Wells, and Ralph Bunche. Among his more experimental works are *In the Company of Men* (1969), a cinema verité film that focuses on frustrated white foremen in a factory and the frustrated blacks who work under them (psychodramatic techniques are used to break through racial barriers); and *From These Roots* (1974), a brief history of the Harlem Renaissance, using only photographs, music, and narration. Greaves's career is in need of serious exploration.

Audrey Henningham and Shannon Baker as Alice and Freddy in 1968 during the shooting of *Symbiopsychotaxiplasm: Take One* (1972). Thirty-seven years later, they would be reunited to play Alice and Freddy, thirty-seven years older, in *Symbiopsychotaxiplasm: Take 2½* (2005).

drey Henningham and Shannon Baker) as the focus of the upcoming *Take Two,* which was never completed as planned.[34] *Symbiopsychotaxiplasm: Take 2½* confirms the interethnicity of the original production while focusing on Freddy and Alice, decades later, as Freddy convinces Alice to become involved in nurturing a talented young African American woman who reminds him of Alice—she is the daughter of a lover who has recently died of AIDS (in *Take 2½* Freddy is infected with HIV).

"TRASH": *PINK FLAMINGOS* AND *SWEET SWEETBACK'S BAADASSSSS SONG*

While structural filmmaking was, for many who were following the evolution of American avant-garde cinema, the crucial development of the late

34. What was for a time called *Symbiopsychotaxiplasm: Take Two* was the slightly modified version of *Take One* discussed in note 29 of this chapter, in which Greaves includes bits of Freddy and Alice's argument as played by several pairs of actors, so that viewers can understand the original serial conception of the project. *Symbiopsychotaxiplasm: Take Two* was made during the aftermath of the rediscovery of Greaves's project; it is now the version of *Symbiopsychotaxiplasm: Take One* in distribution through Criterion DVD.

1960s and early 1970s, it was, of course, not the only game in town. Indeed, for some the structuralist project of exploring various dimensions of the cinematic apparatus was little more than an intellectual and aesthetic exercise that had no impact on social reality; for others, it was an utter bore that was destroying the audience that had been developing "underground" for non-Hollywood filmmakers unafraid of sexuality and politics. Not surprisingly, a range of filmmakers demonstrated their rebellion against both Hollywood convention *and* what they saw as avant-garde effeteness in what became known as "trash film" and, later on, "punk" or "no wave" cinema. Crucial figures in the early development of trash film include Jack Smith, George and Mike Kuchar, John Waters, Paul Morrissey, and Melvin Van Peebles, whose *Sweet Sweetback's Baadasssss Song* (1971) is usually considered a pivotal film in the history of African American cinema.

Like structural films, trash films are aggressive in their confrontation of conventional filmgoing expectations, but unlike structural films, trash films do not ignore commercial film history; rather, they often "liberate" its methods and storytelling approaches and use them for overtly anti-industry, sometimes revolutionary goals. Both *Pink Flamingos* (1972) and *Sweet Sweetback's Baadasssss Song*, for example, employ the good-guys-against-bad-guys paradigm so intrinsic to the Western and other mainstream genres, but they invert its normal assumptions. The "good guys" in *Pink Flamingos* are "the filthiest people alive," characters (and actors) willing to do *anything* in order to defy "good taste." The heroine of the film, Divine, is played by the late Harris Glen Milstead, a fat man who dresses in drag outfits that flaunt his/her deviation from Hollywood standards of beauty and fashion. In *Sweet Sweetback's Baadasssss Song*, the hero is a sex-show performer, a black man who has sex with black and white women, then becomes a cop killer who shows no remorse for his defiance of authority and, in the end, escapes to Mexico. Just as Divine and her/his director Waters were heroes to those who were sick of the repressions of bourgeois American culture and the cinema produced for it, Sweetback and Van Peebles became heroes to those who were sick of a nation, and a film industry, that repressed the realities of African American life in order to maintain the bourgeois canons of good taste. "Good taste" for Waters and Van Peebles, and for trash filmmakers in general, is an index of a soulless society; in cinema it represents the repression of all dimensions of society that might reveal the failures of commercial capitalist culture.

As Mario Van Peebles makes clear in *Baadasssss* (2003), his entertaining paean to his father's struggle in getting *Sweet Sweetback's Baadasssss Song* produced and released, financing was the elder Van Peebles's biggest hurdle. *Sweet Sweetback's Baadasssss Song* was shot in nineteen days on a budget of half a million dollars, using nonunion personnel (feasible only because Van Peebles pretended he was making porn). While this can still seem a small budget by Hollywood standards—and by Van Peebles's standards at the time, since *Watermelon Man* (1970) had made him a bankable African American director—this was a considerable budget for a trash film. John Waters was establishing his reputation as an independent filmmaker with *Multiple Maniacs* (1970) and *Pink Flamingos* (1972) at exactly the same moment Van Peebles was making and distributing *Sweet Sweetback's Baadasssss Song;* according to Waters, *Multiple Maniacs* cost $5,000, and *Pink Flamingos,* $10,000. And Waters's predecessors, Jack Smith and George and Mike Kuchar, made films for far less than this: J. Hoberman explains that Smith shot *Flaming Creatures* (1963) on film stock he stole from the outdated film bin at Camera Barn: "According to [Tony] Conrad [who produced the sound track for *Flaming Creatures*], Smith made particular use of Perutz Tropical film—a German stock designed for shooting at high temperatures—because, thanks to its counter location, it was the easiest to shoplift."[35]

The fundamental aesthetic of trash filmmakers is to demonstrate their defiance of financial limitations and their outsider status by producing films that are in one way or another *more* powerful than big-budget commercial films. Van Peebles may not have stolen the film stock he used in *Sweet Sweetback's Baadasssss Song,* but his choice of film gauge was driven by related considerations:

> At the beginning, I swore that I wasn't going to use 16mm, that I was going to make a big film, that I was going to shoot entirely in 35mm. I over-used the rule of thumb about 35mm being Big, Professional, etc., and 16mm equaling amateursville, low-budget. Both production value and professional quality are determined more by what's going on in front of the lens and how it is recorded than by what film stock is in the camera magazine. We decided to use 16mm in the streets for four reasons: its two usual advantages, economy of the stock and the mobility of 16mm equipment; third, security reasons: 16mm is less noticeable, minimizing police hassles[,] and 16mm is taken less seriously by Hollywood types, minimizing Union hassles. My last reason for using 16mm was for its texture—a paradox, because texture is exactly what is considered the big drawback of 16 over 35. 16mm is more grainy, less slick than 35mm, i.e.,

35. J. Hoberman, *On Jack Smith's Flaming Creatures (and Other Secret-Flix of Cinemaroc)* (New York: Granary Books, 2001), 27.

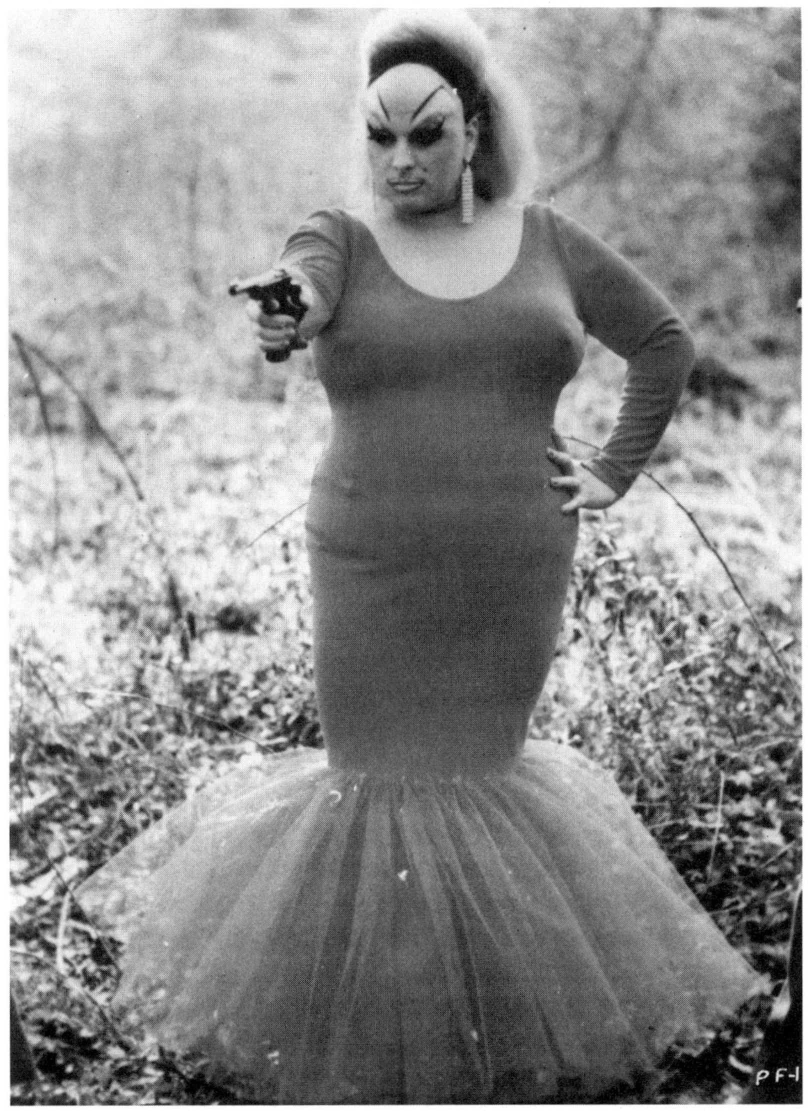

Divine (Harris Glen Milstead) dressed to kill in *Pink Flamingos* (1972). Courtesy John Waters.

> more newsreely, more documentary. The more I thought about it, the more I felt 16 would even add to the flavor of realism I wanted in the street.[36]

Coming to *Sweet Sweetback's Baadasssss Song* from working in the industry, Van Peebles had come to the same conclusion that the previous generation of American avant-garde filmmakers had reached: not only can interesting and important cinema be made using small-gauge film, but the supposed limitations of smaller gauge can be transformed into its strengths by committed, imaginative filmmakers interested in alternatives to the status quo. Of course, for Van Peebles, 35mm was the gauge of choice because his goal was not simply to make a film that undercut the assumptions of conventional, commercial depictions of African America and African Americans, but to make a film that might challenge the mainstream in its own theaters.

The idea that what are normally conceived of as limitations can be a film's strengths is also evident in other dimensions of trash film production. In avant-garde film circles, Jack Smith is famous for arguing that what is considered bad acting is better than good acting. In defense of his favorite movie star, Maria Montez, who in her time was considered by some "the World's Worst Actress," Smith argues that acting may be "lousy," but if "something genuine got on film why carp about acting—which HAS to be phoney anyway—I'd RATHER HAVE atrocious acting." Speaking of Montez, Smith explains, "Her real concerns (her conviction of beauty/her beauty) were the main concern—her acting had to be secondary. An applying of one's convictions to one's activity obtains a higher excellence in that activity than that attained by those in that activity who apply the rules established by previous successes by others."[37] In other words, what often shines through a poor acting performance is a kind of personal integrity, a glimpse of a real person (who does not have the ability or does not feel the motivation to create an illusion) *through* the role, rather than a person successfully creating a character invented by a screenwriter.

Trash films frequently have what would conventionally be considered terrible acting, but often, the very attempt and failure to create a believable illusion through acting reveals a level of personal commitment quite rele-

36. Melvin Van Peebles, in *Sweet Sweetback's Baadasssss Song*, Voices of Conscience Edition (Ann Arbor, MI: NEO Press, 1994), 64–65.

37. Jack Smith, in "The Perfect Filmic Appositeness of Maria Montez," collected in *Wait for Me at the Bottom of the Pool: The Writings of Jack Smith*, ed. J. Hoberman (New York: High Risk Books, 1997), 25, 34.

vant to the goals of the filmmakers. One famous instance occurs in the final sequence of *Pink Flamingos.* In order to create a buzz for his low-budget feature, Waters was determined to end the film with something "no one would ever be able to forget."[38] In a single continuous shot, he has Divine reconfirm her status as "the Filthiest Person Alive" by literalizing a common slang phrase: the actor, dressed in spectacular drag, follows a miniature poodle, catches some poodle shit as it comes out of the dog, and eats it. A "good performance" of this action, given the premise of the film, would have involved Divine enjoying "eating shit." But the subsequent close-up of Divine's face reveals him attempting to stay in role, while gagging and struggling not to reveal his obvious disgust. What comes through is Divine's commitment to the film and his poignant willingness to do whatever is necessary to make a place for himself and for his director in the wide world of cinema.

Sweet Sweetback's Baadasssss Song is full of bad acting that often functions in similar ways. While Divine's shit-eating is the grand finale of *Pink Flamingos,* the most controversial sequence in Van Peebles's film occurs early on, when the young Sweetback, a foundling taken off the streets by the prostitutes in a brothel, has sex with a prostitute who discovers the talent that leads to Sweetback's subsequent occupation and, during her orgasm, provides the young boy with his moniker.[39] The young Sweetback is played, awkwardly, by Mario Van Peebles, at age fourteen; and as is true of the shit-eating sequence in *Pink Flamingos,* the scene is less effective as illusion (we certainly do not believe actual sex is occurring, though the nude child is clearly lying between the up-drawn legs of a nude woman) than as evidence of the elder Van Peebles's commitment to put himself and his family on the line for a film that would defy not only white society but those elements of African America that in Van Peebles's view had found ways of working within white society's strictures (the sex scene with the child and the prostitute is pictured as a baptism and is accompanied by a chorus singing religious music). The use of a child in this sex scene was widely criticized by reviewers and others who saw the film; indeed, I would conjecture that one of Mario Van Peebles's reasons for deciding to make *Baadasssss* was to demonstrate that Melvin was in fact a good father who "became the ulti-

38. Waters, in MacDonald, *A Critical Cinema,* 236.

39. There are other instances where *Sweet Sweetback* works at shocking viewers, including an interracial sex scene with an audience, and, near the end as Sweetback nears the Mexican border, his eating a lizard raw (this is less effective than it might be, since the lizard seems to be rubber!) and his urinating and using the urine to sterilize an open wound on his leg.

mate role model for my career choice and continues to be a strong influence on my life."[40]

More fully than some of the better-known trash films, *Sweet Sweetback's Baadasssss Song* makes use of techniques of shooting and editing familiar from avant-garde film of the 1950s and 1960s.[41] Indeed, at pivotal moments in the film, these techniques are crucial. After the sex performance that follows the credits, which is witnessed by several policemen who enjoy the performance so long as it does not become interracial, the police strong-arm Beatle, who runs the brothel and its sex shows, demanding that he loan them Sweetback for a day so they can pretend they have apprehended a criminal. On the way to the police station, the cops are directed to a political demonstration, where they apprehend a young man, Moo Moo, apparently the demonstration's ringleader. They handcuff Moo Moo to Sweetback and decide to take the troublemaker somewhere where they can work him over without being seen, which turns out to be an oilfield. The cops uncuff the men and begin beating Moo Moo up. For a while, Sweetback allows this to go on (as the larger society always has), but then he makes a decision to become involved and attacks the cops, using the handcuffs still attached to his wrist as his weapon. After Sweetback beats the cops unconscious and bloody, he escapes, along with Moo Moo. From this point on, *Sweet Sweetback's Baadasssss Song* is about Sweetback's avoidance of capture.[42]

For this transformative moment in Sweetback's life—his direct involvement in a rebellion against racist oppression and brutality, and his subsequent decision to escape from the authorities—Van Peebles employs a technique used only during this one sequence: the multiple imposition of color solarizations of the oil derricks and of Sweetback running from the scene of the "crime." This particular set of effects was added during postproduction at a small company run by avant-garde filmmaker Pat O'Neill

40. Mario Van Peebles, introduction to Melvin Van Peebles, *Sweet Sweetback's Baadasssss Song*, Voices of Conscience Edition, iv.

41. Of course, Van Peebles was no stranger to cinematic experiment. His experimental narrative film *Three Pick-up Men for Herrick* (1959) was shown at Cinema 16, a leading American exhibitor of experimental cinema during the 1950s, and it was part of the Cinema 16 rental collection; his first feature, *Story of a 3-Day Pass* (1967), is full of experimental touches. However, the experimentation in these films is of a different order from what happens in *Sweet Sweetback*.

42. In some senses, John Waters's *Female Trouble* (1974) is more fully related to *Sweet Sweetback* than *Pink Flamingos*. In *Female Trouble*, the protagonist, Dawn Davenport (played by Divine), becomes a criminal (she kills her own daughter for becoming a Hare Krishna and during a nightclub performance shoots into the audience) who leads police on a chase, though unlike Sweetback, she is caught and sentenced to the electric chair, where she defies law enforcement and convention by delighting in her execution.

(a master of the optical printer, whose *Water and Power* was mentioned earlier), Marty Muller (Neon Park), Burt Gershfield, and Cisco Curtis.[43] That Van Peebles had decided to use a special effect for this particular sequence reflects his assumption that the sequence is pivotal within the larger narrative of *Sweet Sweetback's Baadasssss Song*. And it encapsulates the multileveled formal rebellion that had characterized 1960s avant-garde film: that is, as Sweetback violently breaks with authority, the look of Van Peebles's film breaks from the "authority" of traditional Hollywood imaging of violent scenes by using a process that literally reveals action in a new light and transforms the image from a single, clear representation into a multilayered, colorful, alternative expression.[44] In other words, the use of this effect to interrupt the look of Van Peebles's narrative per-

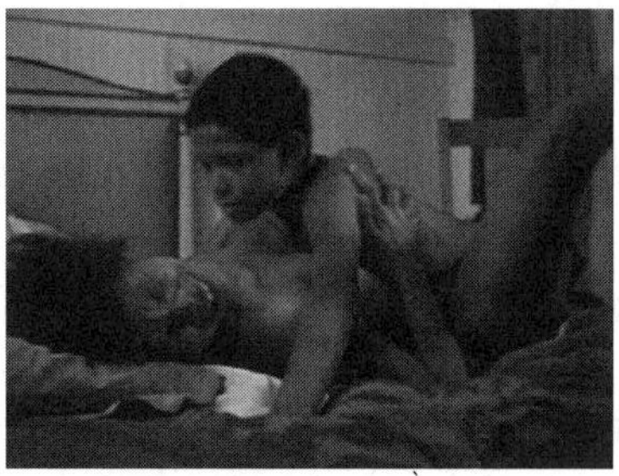

The young Sweetback (Mario Van Peebles) having sex with the prostitute who provides his moniker in *Sweet Sweetback's Baadasssss Song* (1991). Courtesy Melvin Van Peebles.

43. O'Neill, in an e-mail to the author, July 15, 2007: "Not much to relate about Mel Van Peebles—I met him in about June 1970 when he brought some work in for opticals. Marty Muller (Neon Park), Burt Gershfield, Cisco Curtis, and I had a little production company in a rented house on De Longpre Street in Hollywood. I was in the process of leaving that relationship at the time, as I was about to start a new job at CalArts. I sat in on the meeting, which took place in the driveway, as it was too hot inside. Mel was clever and fast talking, and wanted to try a lot of things, but as I recall had almost no budget to work with, as was so often the case with projects we were offered. The lease on our optical printer was overdue, one of our clients was actually living in the kitchen, and I was looking forward to a new start. Mel showed us his tattoo—a dotted line all the way around his neck just below the collar line. Discussion got down to just what we could do with what was there. I remember some shots of an oilfield, a man running past oil derricks. I'm sure there were others. We were to convert the picture to a high-contrast black and white, and then print it back to color through a range of bright colors. Cisco ran the job, it got done in a week or so, and Mel paid in cash. I have never seen the film."

I assume Van Peebles is referring to O'Neill in his book *Sweet Sweetback's Baadasssss Song* when he says, "I had to use two sets of optical people to get the results I wanted, one brilliant but spaced out [O'Neill?], the other expert but numb" (85).

44. Of course, by the late 1960s and early 1970s, the commercial cinema was peppering its products with comparable formal extravagances, some of them "borrowed from" or done by avant-garde filmmakers. This practice has a history, of course, which includes Hitchcock's use of James Whitney's animations in *Vertigo* and his use of Dali dream sequences in *Spellbound* (1945). One can imagine that Van Peebles was signaling that increasingly common tendency, in a hope that echoed the industry hope that such formal freedom might help attract the young moviegoing population. But his use of an avant-garde tactic in *Sweet Sweetback* seems quite sensitive to the social meanings of formal experiment.

fectly reflects Sweetback's decision to enact a violent break with the conventional way of dealing with the LA police.

Throughout the remainder of *Sweet Sweetback's Baadasssss Song* Van Peebles's style is characteristic of sixties avant-garde film's rebellion against Hollywood stylistics. Much of his imagery is handheld, and in a gestural manner as reminiscent of the avant-garde tradition instigated by Marie Menken in the 1940s and elaborated by Stan Brakhage, Jonas Mekas, and others in the 1950s and 1960s as it is of cinema verité documentary. There is also frequent use of superimposition, including much superimposition of gestural imagery—again a characteristic of much personally expressive avant-garde cinema.[45] At times Van Peebles uses looped images and sound, a tactic employed by any number of structuralist filmmakers. Finally, during the concluding section of *Sweet Sweetback's Baadasssss Song,* once Sweetback escapes into the desert, Van Peebles controls duration in a manner highly unusual for a Hollywood film, then or now.

One of the most frequent tactics of structural cinema is defiance of normal expectations of duration. Even once one can see that the continuous zooming employed by Michael Snow in *Wavelength* will ultimately deliver viewers to the far wall where several images are pinned up, one must endure Snow's relentlessly gradual pace—precisely the opposite experience from most Hollywood films, where climactic action usually involves acceleration. Sweetback's journey through the desert in the direction of the Mexican border seems to take forever, and its duration is emphasized by a vocal chorus that repeatedly addresses Sweetback, commenting on his progress toward freedom using variations on the lines "They bled your Mama; they bled your Papa, but they won't bleed me!" By testing viewers' patience in this way, Van Peebles provides an ongoing emphasis of the persistence and stamina needed by blacks in their struggle toward freedom and embeds the chorus's poem in the consciousness. Indeed, when I have screened *Sweet Sweetback's Baadasssss Song* for classes, students have difficulty refraining from singing this poem in the hours and days following the screening.

In one of the classics of early trash film, *Hold Me While I'm Naked* (1966), George Kuchar plays a young filmmaker struggling to make a romantic melodrama with as much nudity and sexuality as he can get away with. His protagonist is clearly a version of himself—though it appears that Kuchar, as director, has had more success than his protagonist in getting actresses to take off their clothes for their romantic scenes (looked at another way,

45. In several instances, Van Peebles includes multiple images by embedding frames within the frame, a tactic used also by Greaves in *Symbiopsychotaxiplasm: Take One.*

the finished film can be understood as the final product of the protagonist's efforts). In a sense, *Hold Me While I'm Naked* is a confession; it is clear that Kuchar's protagonist's commitment to filmmaking includes his recognition that being a filmmaker gives him the power to ask people (women especially) to do things that he otherwise would not have the nerve to ask them to do. Of course, the director does not always receive what he asks for: the central plot of *Hold Me* involves a woman refusing to work with the voyeuristic director any longer and leaving the production with her boyfriend and costar, and the director's failed attempt to find another couple to play the role of lovers. In *Hold Me While I'm Naked,* Kuchar functions in many capacities: he is his own lead, he is the director, the cameraperson, the editor; he even dubs the voices of all the actors himself (*Hold Me While I'm Naked* was not shot in sync).

Like Kuchar in *Hold Me,* Van Peebles plays the protagonist in *Sweet Sweetback's Baadasssss Song,* and he functioned in a variety of capacities as director (the film's final credit line: "Written, Composed, Produced, Directed and Edited by Melvin Van Peebles"). It cannot have been lost on the film's original audiences that while, on one level, Sweetback is a mythic black hero who does the right thing for African America and gets away with it, on another, Sweetback is a metaphor for the film's director, who breaks the "rules," escapes the authority of Hollywood and its censors (Van Peebles refused to submit the film to the ratings board), and gets away with making this outrageous film, despite the odds. Indeed, if the first major result of *Sweet Sweetback* was to instigate blaxploitation (commercial films with black heroes as sexual, as rebellious, and as unstoppable as Sweetback), the longer-lived result has been the recognition and honoring of Van Peebles for *his* efforts in getting his film made, and thereby demonstrating that blacks in America could in fact produce films for black Americans, films that confronted, in no uncertain terms, conventional white society and the cinema produced for it.

FILM PRODUCTION AS ETHNIC UTOPIA

When William Greaves returned to the *Symbiopsychotaxiplasm* project to make what would become *Take 2½,* he confirmed the attitude about race and ethnicity implicit in *Take One.* Despite the fact that this time Alice and Freddy are an interracial couple (Audrey Henningham is black; Shannon Baker, white), once again the issue of race is never referred to by the characters or the actors who play them, or by anyone involved in the production. In *Symbiopsychotaxiplasm: Take 2½,* as in the original film, Greaves

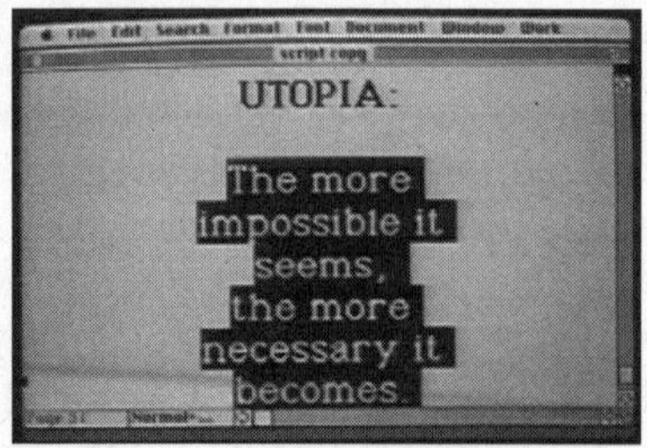

The final computer-screen text in Yvonne Rainer's *Privilege* (1990). Courtesy Yvonne Rainer.

and his collaborators seem to assume that whatever is going on in the American culture that surrounds them, the essential function of filmmaking is to model a productive, creative social utopia. Indeed, as is clear in *Take 2½*, this utopia has achieved longevity: not only are two of the original actors who performed in *Take One* involved in a related production more than thirty-five years later, but many of the original crew members returned to work with Greaves on *Take 2½*.

The lack of comment about race becomes particularly obvious during the early portion of the new film, which focuses on Alice and Freddy in 1968: as the couple argue, their ethnic difference is never mentioned, despite their anger and frustration with each other. And during a moment when some members of the 1968 crew are filmed off-duty during the original shoot, we see that a romantic relationship has developed between Henningham and Jonathan Gordon, who is white (Gordon is a central character in both films, and worked as sound recordist for both productions): he and Henningham exchange a passionate kiss. A final confirmation of Greaves's refusal to mention race involves the fact that, in the conversation that Greaves wrote to function as the central focus of the contemporary story within *Take 2½*, Freddy, whose health is now deteriorating, asks Alice to become responsible for Jamilla (Ndeye Ade Sokhna), the daughter of a woman with whom Freddy had a relationship. Before the woman died, Freddy promised to look after the daughter, a talented young African American singer who is recovering from a drug problem. At first, Alice refuses this responsibility, but Freddy is able to overcome this resistance: we see Alice meeting Jamilla at the end of the film.

Greaves's decision to work creatively with a remarkably diverse group of people in a way that celebrates their ability to rise above ethnic distinction and racism places both *Symbiopsychotaxiplasm* films within a mini-tradition in independent cinema where the filmmaking process is imaged as a form of ethnic utopia: films that are particularly noteworthy in this context include Robert Nelson's *Oh Dem Watermelons* (1965), Peter Watkins's *Punishment Park* (1971) and *The Journey* (1987), and Yvonne Rainer's *Privilege* (1990).

Of course, any number of films can be seen as premonitions of this tendency, including Jack Smith's *Flaming Creatures* and Kenneth Anger's *Inauguration of the Pleasure Dome* (1954), even if these earlier films do not obviously suggest an *ethnic* utopia, the way *Symbiopsychotaxiplasm: Take One* and the Nelson, Watkins, and Rainer films do. And this tendency is evident in two commercial films that have already been mentioned. I have suggested that the production process of *Do the Right Thing* is the implicit answer to the problem dramatized in the film; and in *Baadasssss,* Mario Van Peebles reveals that during the making of *Sweet Sweetback's Baadasssss Song,* actors and crew members of various backgrounds collaborated across ethnic and class lines in ways virtually unheard of in Hollywood.

Oh Dem Watermelons was commissioned by the San Francisco Mime Troupe, perhaps the best-known guerrilla theater group of the decade, as an entr'acte for *A Minstrel Show, or Civil Rights in a Cracker Barrel,* a frontal attack on American racism using the minstrel show format. *A Minstrel Show* was written (or at least instigated) by Ron Davis, Saul Landau, and Nina Serrano and performed during a nationwide tour in 1966.[46] Once Nelson had decided to focus on the watermelon as an emblem of negative stereotyping and had a general idea of the approach he would use, he met with Landau and Davis, who suggested further ideas, and then shot the film over a two-week period mostly on the streets of San Francisco, with members of the mixed-race Mime Troupe.

The twelve-minute film begins with a nearly two-minute continuous opening shot of a watermelon positioned like a football ready for kickoff.[47] Then, a voice-off instructs the audience, "Follow the bouncing watermelon!" The watermelon bounces wildly, completely out of sync with the words of the song, mocking the idea of singing along with these lyrics (in the film they are presented all in capitals): "Down in de corn-field / Hear dat

46. Alternately subtitled "Jim Crow a Go-Go," *A Minstrel Show* "consisted of a series of skits performed by a racially integrated cast, all but the white, straight-man 'interlocutor' in blackface. The self-designated 'darkies' were costumed in blue and ivory satin suits, white cotton gloves, and topped off with short-haired wigs like jet-black scouring pads. Audiences found it perplexingly difficult to discern the true racial identity of the six masqued *[sic]* performers, a predicament which rendered the actors' raucous banter all the more unsettling." Michael William Doyle, "Staging the Revolution: Guerilla Theater as a Countercultural Practice, 1965–1968," available online at the Digger Archives, www.diggers.org/guerilla_theater.htm.

47. Actually, this is more than one shot, though it has the impact of a single shot. At one point, end-of-roll perforations interrupt the audience's contemplation and subtly suggest (as do the opening, narrated credits that precede the watermelon-as-football shot) that this frustrating beginning will not be the entirety of the film.

mourn-ful sound / All de darkies am a weep-in / Mas-sa's in de cold, cold ground / Mas-sa make de dark-ies love him / Cause he was so kind / Now they sadly weep a-bove him / Mourn-in cause he leave dem be-hind." A chorus follows: "Den oh, dat wat-er-mel-on / Lamb ob good-ness you must die / Gwine to join the con-tra-band child-dren / Gwine to get home bye and bye." The lyrics come partly from Stephen Foster's "Massa's in de Cold Ground" (1852): specifically, from the chorus and from the first half of the third verse. The chorus of the song in *Oh Dem Watermelons* is not part of "Massa's in the Cold Ground"; I assume it is a Nelson–Mime Troupe invention.[48] We see the lyrics and bouncing watermelon once; then when other imagery replaces the text and watermelon, the phrase "oh dem watermelons" is repeated several times, after which "watermelon" is chanted, until we return to the chorus at the finale.

After the "singalong" portion of *Oh Dem Watermelons* is over, Nelson and his cast insert paper watermelons into outrageous animated and live-action contexts (little watermelons are inserted into a newspaper photo of black delegates to the United Nations, for example) as a way of reminding viewers of the pervasiveness of this stereotype and the racism it represents; and they attack and destroy actual watermelons in every conceivable way. Nelson and the Mime Troupe members are able to foreground the stupidity of the watermelon stereotype, which has played a role in film history since *A Watermelon Feast* (American Mutoscope and Biograph, 1896), *Watermelon Eating Contest* (Edison, 1896), and Edwin S. Porter's frightening "comedy," *The Watermelon Patch* (1905), and of stereotyping in general, by taking control of the watermelon image in the context of race, in much the way Ice-T takes control of the word "nigger" in his "Straight Up Nigga" from the *O.G. Original Gangsta* album (1991).[49]

For Nelson, making films during the 1960s and 1970s was usually a collaborative experience, and the collaboration needed to be a pleasure if

48. Of course, Nelson is satirizing not only Stephen Foster but also the experience of going to a commercial theater and being faced with singalong cartoons that encoded various kinds of racism.

49. For a discussion of early films that made the blacks-and-watermelons stereotype part of film history, see Stewart, *Migrating to the Movies*, 55, 75–78.

Of course, the stereotype of African Americans loving watermelon has also played an important role in African American filmmaking. Melvin Van Peebles's *The Watermelon Man* has already been mentioned. In *Chronicles of a Lying Spirit (by Kelly Gabron)* (see above), Cauleen Smith uses the image of the watermelon to represent stereotyping of blacks. Of course, the titles of Cheryl Dunye's *The Watermelon Woman* (1996) and *How to Eat Your Watermelon in White Company (And Enjoy It)* (2005), the documentary about (and with) Melvin Van Peebles by Joe Angio, suggest how pervasive this stereotype (or, more precisely, at least within academe these days, an awareness of this stereotype as a stereotype) still is.

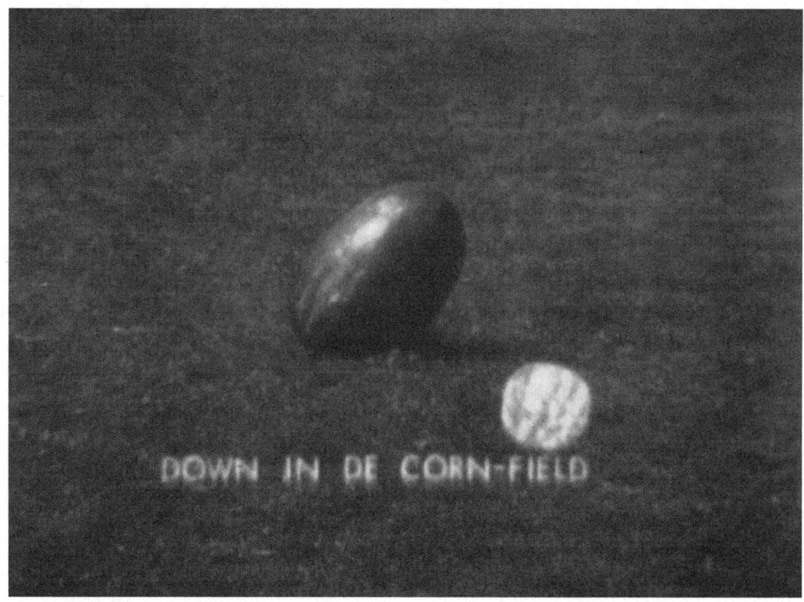

The bouncing watermelon in Robert Nelson's *Oh Dem Watermelons* (1965). Courtesy Robert Nelson.

the resulting film was to be worth watching: "The artists I knew at that time felt pretty genuinely that if the process got too heavy or ponderous or worried, if you weren't having a good time at least part of the time, something was wrong. We were bent on having a good time."[50] It is obvious in *Oh Dem Watermelons* that Nelson and his Mime Troupe colleagues are having a blast working together to confront the fundamental imbecility of racism and the absurd forms it has taken during several centuries of American history. *Oh Dem Watermelons* was made quickly and for almost nothing, but it remains one of American cinema's most telling attacks on racist stereotyping. The film does not expand on the interrelationships among those who participated in the production; we can only deduce from the evidence of the finished film that a brief, ethnically utopian collaboration produced what we see.

Peter Watkins's *Punishment Park* was one of this inventive director's most remarkable experiments. Usually identified as a documentarian—largely because of *The War Game* (1965), which won an Academy Award

50. Nelson, in Scott MacDonald, *A Critical Cinema* (Berkeley: University of California Press, 1988), 263.

for Best Documentary Feature—Watkins has made films that have generally defied easy categorization, and this is certainly true of his fifth feature. Made in California at the height of resistance to the Vietnam War, *Punishment Park* is a social psychodrama that asks viewers to imagine a near future during which China has become involved in the Vietnam conflict, simultaneously instigating further American resistance to the war and more elaborate attempts on the part of law enforcement authorities to deal with this resistance. The film intercuts between the trial of seven ethnically diverse war resisters (closely based on the Chicago Seven) and a previous group of ethnically diverse resisters, all of whom were found guilty in a previous tribunal, as they attempt to navigate an expanse of California desert called "Punishment Park": they are told that if they can reach the American flag some fifty miles across the desert before law enforcement officials can apprehend them (they are given a head start), they will earn their freedom.

Instead of scripting the dialogue, Watkins created a basic scenario and then cast the roles according to type: that is, the resisters, law enforcement people, and tribunal members are generally played by people who closely identified with these roles,[51] and Watkins allowed cast members to generate their own dialogue on the basis of what they really felt and believed. The result is a level of candidness that expresses that volatile moment of American history to a degree that few other films do. One can certainly not claim that this production process created anything like a harmonious group, but it was utopian in the sense most important to Watkins: a politically and ethnically wide range of individuals came together to express themselves to each other about real issues and to collaborate in imagining the horror of a future that might still be avoided. The film "creates a framework within which the very participants in the film release their pent-up emotions and frustrations and fears; these that are common to us all, and which are created by the pressures of contemporary society."[52]

Watkins's *The Journey*, shot during 1984–85 and completed in 1987, was the epic (14½ hours) result of an attempt to use the making of a film to create a grassroots global utopian community of like-minded souls (the film was shot in several American locations and in Mexico, Canada, Australia, Japan, the Soviet Union, Norway, Germany, France, Scotland, Mozambique,

51. In a few cases, cast members played roles that did not represent their own opinions, apparently in an attempt to imagine how people committed to very different attitudes thought. The most extensive discussion of *Punishment Park* can be found in Joseph A. Gomez, *Peter Watkins* (Boston: Twayne, 1979), 99–122.

52. Peter Watkins, "Open Letter to the Press," Oslo, Norway, January 1972 (unpublished, author's files).

and on the island of Tahiti). Watkins seems to have imagined that once the various support groups that produced the film learned to work together despite national, linguistic, and ethnic differences, they would become a transnational community that could continue to work together for the global common good once the film was completed—and might use the film as part of their ongoing work. That the community Watkins imagined did not last beyond the production and release of the film, except in relatively minimal ways, represents a failure of imagination on the part of those of us who were involved in the project: except for Watkins, few of the many participants in *The Journey* were able to conceive of a film production as a catalyst for a new form of mediated, politically active, global community.[53]

Yvonne Rainer's *Privilege*, a feature that focuses on issues of gender, aging (menopause, in particular), and ethnicity, was made in the wake of a controversy that erupted over a series of screenings and panels presented at the Collective for Living Cinema in 1988, curated by Rainer and Bérénice Reynaud: the general title was "Sexism, Colonialism, Misrepresentation."[54] Media artist Coco Fusco attacked the events on the grounds that while the organizers proposed to deal with the ways in which gender, age, and race problematized cinematic representation, they were unable to see beyond their own whiteness: as Rainer would explain later, "By not examining our own 'otherness'—in the panel discussions—we 're-centered' our whiteness."[55] Rainer revisits these issues in *Privilege*, within which both Yvonne Rainer and an alter ego, "Yvonne Washington" (played by African American Novella Nelson), are working on a documentary on menopause—the implication being that the trials of aging are fundamental to all ethnicities. At one point, Yvonne Washington vehemently argues against the psychoanalytic explanation for racial difference advanced by the film's other pro-

53. See "The Mohawk Valley Journey to *The Journey*" in this collection for further information on the production of *The Journey*. For a detailed description and analysis of the finished film, see Scott MacDonald, "The Filmmaker as Global Circumnavigator: Peter Watkins's *The Journey*," *Quarterly Review of Film and Video* 14, no. 4 (August 1993): 31–54.

54. The program and the papers were published in the Summer/Autumn 1990 issue of *Motion Picture*.

55. Rainer in Scott MacDonald, *A Critical Cinema 2* (Berkeley: University of California Press, 1992), 349. Fusco's critique of "Sexism Colonialism, Misrepresentation" appeared as "Fantasies of Oppositionality," in *Screen* 29, no. 4 (Fall 1988): 80–93, and in *Afterimage* 16, no. 5 (December 1988): 6–9. Fusco's argument was that while "the majority of panelists were people of color, the organizing principles of the discussions were drawn from (largely French) feminist psychoanalysis. Throughout the conference there operated a Eurocentric presumption that sexual difference could be separated from other forms of difference and that the theoretical models that privilege gender-based sexual difference could be used to understand other differences" (9).

Jenny (Alice Spivak) and Robert (Dan Berkey) in the front seat enjoying their newfound passion and oblivious to the issues of ethnicity and class that surround them in the form of Digna (Gabriella Farrar), dressed as Carmen Miranda in the backseat (our foreground), and the laborers on the truck in front of them, in Rainer's *Privilege* (1990). Courtesy Yvonne Rainer.

tagonist, Jenny (Alice Spivak), an aging dancer loosely based on Rainer herself. The central dramatic narrative in *Privilege* focuses on Jenny's struggles with ethnicity—or, really, her failure to recognize the implications of ethnicity and class—during her early years in New York.

Throughout the long, concluding sequence of *Privilege,* Rainer intercuts between her extensive end credits and scenes from what is clearly the wrap party for the shooting. During the body of *Privilege,* much of which takes place within Jenny's memories, the various actors play roles that dramatize various dimensions of the ongoing struggles of African Americans and Hispanics within a New York City dominated by white wealth and power. But in the scenes of the wrap party, we see a different reality and realize that this dramatization was the result of considerable interethnic collaboration by the diverse actors and crew members who have gathered to celebrate the experience of producing this film. Periodically during *Privilege,* Rainer uses a computer screen to interject quotations that in one way or another comment on the developing action and the issues it raises. Once the final credits begin, one further computer statement is included:

UTOPIA:

The more
impossible it
seems,
the more
necessary it
becomes.[56]

Like Greaves, Rainer has always seen the collaborative creative process of filmmaking as a way of coming to a more complete understanding of social issues. By including the wrap party as the long final sequence of *Privilege,* Rainer brings this attitude toward film production into the foreground.

RECYCLED CINEMA: RAPHAEL MONTAÑEZ ORTIZ AND MARTIN ARNOLD

African Americans and European Americans often seem to have different senses of film history and different expectations of cinema. For many African Americans, the historical tendency of the commercial film industry to exclude nonwhites—both nonwhite characters who ring true to the realities of African American life as well as nonwhite directors—has posed the most important cinematic challenge. And given the power of Hollywood and its utter domination of film production and exhibition, the mere fact that some African American directors have been able to get films produced and exhibited has certainly been a cause for celebration. One, and perhaps the primary, goal of filmmaking by groups excluded from full participation in film history and its potential for affecting American society is increased inclusion, influence, and financial reward. In this context, independent filmmaking is seen as primarily a means to an end: a filmmaker may need to make films independently in order to be able to make films at all, but working independently of Hollywood is valuable primarily to the extent that this experience helps to train filmmakers for later entry into a largely segregated industry.

For the avant-garde film audience and for a good many avant-garde filmmakers, independence in filmmaking means something quite different. While they recognize the power of commercial cinema, and believe that this power is a problem, they do not believe that struggling to be part of the in-

56. According to Rainer, these lines are "a variation on a quote from an essay by Alexander Kluge. Utopia: the more we desire it the farther away it gets. Or something like that. I think mine is more optimistic." E-mail to the author, August 3, 2007.

dustry provides the best response to this problem: since the bottom line for Hollywood film production *is* the bottom line, whoever works within that system becomes part of it, at the cost of other forms of independence. Most avant-garde filmmakers, at least during recent decades, have decided to direct their filmmaking energies elsewhere. The goal of the avant-garde filmmaker is to demonstrate that great cinema can be made, if not without money, with a level of financing almost unimaginable for a Hollywood director. That is, for avant-garde filmmakers and those who admire their work, the function of independence is to offer a distinctive and accomplished alternative to Hollywood.

Not surprisingly, for many African Americans, avant-garde cinema has seemed relatively pointless, since it cannot alter the still-exclusionary status quo of the industry, while for many aficionados of avant-garde film, the African American focus on breaking into the industry is equally pointless, since inclusion, even when it does occur, functions for the most part as simply a confirmation of the cinema-as-commerce status quo. Of course, there have been instances where individual filmmakers have defied one or the other of these positions. Spike Lee's use of the city symphony form, often identified with the avant-garde, was fundamental to the considerable impact of *Do the Right Thing*. And whatever reservations one might have about some of Lee's commercial melodramas, his continuing success can hardly be said to have made him a conventional industry filmmaker. Indeed, it has allowed him not only to create a variety of works that are sometimes unusually experimental for commercial filmmaking but also to make important contributions to independent cinema, including the documentaries *4 Little Girls* (1997) and *When the Levees Broke* (2006).

While many avant-garde filmmakers try to avoid Hollywood altogether, a considerable number have made avant-garde films or videos that engage the industry by providing rereadings of Hollywood films and Hollywood gestures. The audience for this work is certainly smaller than that for commercial cinema, but it can be substantial and can have long-term impact. Two interesting instances are Raphael Montañez Ortiz, a native New Yorker with a mixed Puerto Rican, Native American, and European American ethnicity; and Austrian avant-garde filmmaker Martin Arnold.

My decision to become seriously engaged with Ortiz's work came at the end of a two-year process that, while personally embarrassing for me, is certainly relevant to the issue of ethnicity and avant-garde film. For a brief period, I was a member of the board of directors of International Film Seminars. It was during my tenure as board member that a seminar focused on "fourth world" filmmaking—filmmaking by indigenous, original peoples—

was proposed for the summer of 1992, with Faye Ginsburg as primary programmer. At a point well into the process, soon after Ginsburg had asked Jay Ruby to assist her with preparations for the seminar, several board members became increasingly uncomfortable with the idea that two "white" Americans were now programming a set of events focusing on indigenous makers. So far as I remember, no one doubted Ginsburg's (and Ruby's) expertise, but after considerable discussion, the board decided to ask Ginsburg to add a third programmer to her process, ideally a person of indigenous heritage who had had experience in programming media events.

Programming a Flaherty seminar is a considerable challenge in the best of circumstances; programming an indigenous Flaherty faced Ginsburg and the board with unusual challenges: the necessity, for example, to supply translators for the indigenous makers. For Ginsburg, the brouhaha over her ethnic right to program such events, coming in the midst of her preparations, added a complicating and distracting factor. In the end, she refused the board's request and (along with Ruby) withdrew from the process entirely—and the "indigenous Flaherty" idea was dropped.

With the 1992 seminar only a few months away, several board members—I was one of them—agreed to share the programming responsibilities.[57] I had been very excited about meeting indigenous makers and was angry with what seemed to me the misplaced political correctness that had caused the demise of the "indigenous Flaherty." I volunteered, knowing that in my programming I would, at some point, take revenge on PC, which I did by inviting Ken Jacobs to the seminar to present his *XCXHXEXRXRXIXEXSX* ("Cherries"—the *X*s are a humorous reference to X-rated films—in various versions since 1980), a "Nervous System" performance in which Jacobs explores a passage from a French pornographic film.[58] I expected that Jacobs's use of pornographic imagery, especially in a long work that involves considerable strobe effects, would be an affront to many seminar attendees, even perhaps to some members of the Flaherty board—and I was correct (I have described the reception and aftermath of this Flaherty moment elsewhere).[59]

57. I programmed the first two and a half days of the 1992 seminar. The other programmers of that seminar were Austin Allen, Ruth Bradley, William Sloan, Jackie Tshaka, and Lise Yasui.

58. The "Nervous System" is a projection apparatus invented by Jacobs that allows him to achieve a variety of effects, including moments of 3-D, by moving two superimposed prints of a filmstrip, one frame at a time, through two projectors, so that the individual frames are slightly out of sync.

59. See my *A Critical Cinema 3* (Berkeley: University of California Press, 1998), 158–65. Other writings on this event include Jesse Lerner, "Flaherty in Motion," *Afterimage* 20, no. 5 (December 1992): 3–4; and Laura U. Marks, review of the Flaherty, *The Independent* 16, no. 2 (March 1993): 26–31.

For me, however, the most important result of my programming at the 1992 Flaherty (in addition to Jacobs, I invited John Porter, Godfrey Reggio, Holly Fisher, and Chris Welsby—all filmmakers related to my focus on cinema as motion study) occurred after the screening of Martin Arnold's *pièce touchée* (1989), which I used to introduce my programming. Film scholar Chon Noriega, who had agreed to program the 1993 Flaherty, approached me to say that seeing the Arnold film had made him confident that I would be interested in the "digital/laser/videos" of Raphael Montañez Ortiz, whom he planned to feature at the next seminar.

When I saw Ortiz's videos at the 1993 seminar, I was astonished at their similarity to Arnold's work. Indeed, on first viewing, Ortiz's *The Kiss* (1985) seemed to me nearly identical to Arnold's *pièce touchée.* I had been aware of Arnold's work since *pièce touchée* had toured as part of the Black Maria Film Festival in 1990 and had been in contact with Arnold himself beginning in 1991. My first reaction to *The Kiss* was a vestige of the frustration with ethnic PC that had fueled my programming in 1992; I remember thinking to myself, "Because of his ethnicity and because the folks interested in ethnic cinemas don't realize what has been going on in avant-garde film, this guy's work may seem original, but in fact it's a rip-off of an avant-garde filmmaker." When I realized that, in fact, *The Kiss,* along with a considerable body of related work, had *preceded pièce touchée,* and further, that Arnold had seen a show of Ortiz's videos in Vienna before he made *pièce touchée,* I was forced to recognize my own obvious prejudice: it was clear that, if in fact any "ripping off" had occurred, it had been the European ripping off the Puerto Rican American.

In the years that followed, I explored Ortiz's work in detail and learned, among other things, that Ortiz had begun working with recycled cinema around the time Bruce Conner was making his breakthrough recycled work, *A Movie* (1958). In 1958, Ortiz chopped up a print of Anthony Mann's *Winchester '73* (1950) with a tomahawk as part of a ritual performance. Then he put the chopped-up bits of film into a medicine bag, which he used as a rattle to accompany some ritual chanting. Finally, he randomly reedited the shards into *Cowboy and "Indian" Film* (1958). Whereas Conner's film provides an amusing and somewhat cynical meditation on the surrealism of a violent century, *Cowboy and "Indian" Film* foregrounds and confronts the implicit racism of one of the most popular commercial film genres. Conner's focus is general; Ortiz's, quite specific.

When I interviewed Ortiz about his early work and the digital/laser/videos, I came to understand that while *pièce touchée* and *The Kiss* do have a great deal in common, the combination of their similarities *and differences* is as fascinating and instructive as the similarities and differences between *A Movie* and *Cowboy and "Indian" Film.* In *The Kiss,* Ortiz recycles a passage from an American film noir—Robert Rossen's *Body and Soul* (1947)—using a homemade apparatus: his laser disc player and an Apple computer combined with a Deltalab Effectron II sound effects generator. Ortiz unpacks a conventional Hollywood moment, the first kiss of potential lovers. *Pièce touchée* also recycles a passage from an American film noir—*The Human Jungle* (1954), directed by Joseph M. Newman—exploring the passage frame by frame, wittily foregrounding the gender politics within a conventional Hollywood moment (a husband returns home to his waiting wife) and, using a homemade optical printer, transforms a narrative cliché into an astonishing visual tour de force.

At some moments the Ortiz video and the Arnold film look nearly identical: in both there is a focus on a kiss, and in both much of the action takes place in the doorway to a living room; both use a fast-paced alternation of forward and reverse to humorous and humorously erotic effect. Both implicitly comment on the way in which, during the years when the Hays Office rigorously applied the Production Code, Hollywood filmmakers were forced to repress eroticism. Using forward and reverse, Arnold gives many passages in *pièce touchée* an erotic dimension; and Ortiz transforms an "innocent" kiss into faux sexual intercourse.

Other elements of the film and the video reveal considerable differences. In a sense, Arnold is a classicist: his patient, painstaking craftsmanship is dependent on a time-tested cinematic apparatus (the optical printer); and the almost obsessive precision of both *pièce touchée* and Arnold's more recent films, *passage à l'acte* (1993) and *Alone: Life Wastes Andy Hardy* (1996), reflects the intelligence and craftsmanship one traditionally expects of classic works of art. Arnold is much indebted to his compatriot and mentor Peter Kubelka, whose carefully wrought films have long been legendary for their brevity, their density, and their considerable insight (Kubelka's *Unsere Afrikareise* ["Our Trip to Africa" (1966)] remains one of cinema's most penetrating exposés of colonialism and one of film history's most impressive montages).[60] Like Kubelka, Arnold works very slowly; a fifteen-minute film can take him several years.

In his digital/laser/videos, Ortiz's approach is closer to cultural contributions identified primarily with African America: specifically, jazz improv-

60. Arnold is also indebted to the now considerable avant-garde tradition of "recycled cinema," whose best-known forefathers are Joseph Cornell and Bruce Conner. In fact, making new films out of earlier films has become a common, perhaps the most common, avant-garde approach.

isation and rap sampling. For *The Kiss* and the other digital/laser/videos made during the 1980s and early 1990s, Ortiz would study a laser disk of a classic film, often looking for a moment that he felt encapsulated social injustice or some other dimension of experience that was repressed in the film, and then, during a single, continuous moment, he would rework the chosen passage in an attempt to reveal its implications, improvising as he went, and recording the results. Ortiz's method allowed for the production of many works (he no longer makes digital/laser/videos) in a relatively short period of time: forty-six between 1985 and 1995.[61]

In other words, what at first appear to be (and in some ways *are*) two nearly identical works can be understood, simultaneously, as emblems of quite different ethnic, cultural, and technological backgrounds. The bottom line here, however, is that it is to the advantage of both *The Kiss* and *pièce touchée* that they are seen and worked with together. While each has been understood as an impressive contribution to a different dimension of media history—*pièce touchée,* as an instance of recycled cinema,[62] of Austrian avant-garde cinema; *The Kiss,* as an instance of video art, of Chicano media—each is more interesting within the context of the other.

Much the same is true of Ortiz's *My Father's Dead* (1991) and Arnold's *passage à l'acte* (1993); in fact, this pairing is useful in distinguishing a fundamental difference between the two artists' approaches to Hollywood filmmaking. *Passage à l'acte* recycles a brief sequence from Robert Mulligan's *To Kill a Mockingbird* (1963)—the breakfast-table scene during which Atticus Finch tells Jem to wait until his sister is finished eating before leaving for the first day of school; the presence of a female neighbor causes the group to look like a nuclear family. This sequence is presented in much the same way as *pièce touchée:* Arnold uses his optical printer to retard the progress of the filmed movement, so that many bits of the original movement (and, in this instance, sound) are seen (and heard) in forward and reverse, over and over, as Arnold teases out dimensions of the original sequence not ev-

61. For a complete listing of Ortiz's digital/laser/videos, see Scott MacDonald, "Media Destructionism: The Digital/Laser/Videos of Raphael Montañez," in *The Ethnic Eye: Latino Media Arts,* ed. Ana M. López and Chon A. Noriega (Minneapolis: University of Minnesota Press, 1996), 183–207.

62. "Recycled cinema," or "found-footage film," has a long history. The Russian Esfir Shub may have invented the form in *The Fall of the Romanov Dynasty* (1927), but its becoming one of the primary approaches in modern American avant-garde film owes more to Joseph Cornell and especially to Bruce Conner, whose ingenuity with recycling older films, especially in *A Movie* (1958) and *Cosmic Ray* (1962), inspired a generation of filmmakers, including Arnold.

Raphael Montañez Ortiz is also an early contributor to this genre of avant-garde filmmaking: his *Cowboy and "Indian" Film* (1958) and *Newsreel* (1958) are among the earliest such works—though so far as I am aware they were not widely shown.

ident at normal speed and transforms the action into a strange, exhilarating, and very funny mechanical ballet.

Arnold's decision to work with this particular moment in *To Kill a Mockingbird* was a function of the various formal options this particular family sequence offered him: at the breakfast table, "the family, home, and gender theme could pair best with my formal ambition to work with repetitions of sounds. There would be a lot of clatter and scraping at the table, the shrill voices of the kids, and the lower voices of the grown-ups who 'educate,' that is, repeat certain orders to furnish the kids with a decent behavioral repertoire."[63] In a sense, Arnold's formal intervention reflects the action in the scene: Atticus is forcing his son Jem to slow down and wait for his sister; and Arnold is forcing the viewer to slow down and examine the sequence in detail. Jem is frustrated; and we viewers would be too, except that Arnold's careful reworking of the action is very funny both in a visceral sense and because of its witty allusiveness (for example, under Arnold's control, Scout beats well-known rhythms on the kitchen table with a spoon). Arnold has made these characters, and the actors who play them, his own; they become his puppets.

Though *To Kill a Mockingbird* is a film about race, Arnold consciously avoided this theme by using a scene "that is not vital for the narrative structure of the original movie and which does not have anything to do with the central theme of racism. . . . I would have been afraid to use a scene where, for example, the black man is on trial. I wouldn't want to play around with that material."[64] The irony here is that, by avoiding the issue of race in a film where it is important, Arnold implicitly reconfirms a basic weakness of Mulligan's film.[65] The African Americans in *To Kill a Mockingbird* are for the most part passive victims, generally distanced from the viewer; the focus is on the nobility of Atticus Finch (Gregory Peck) in defending Tom Robinson (Brock Peters) against the charge of raping a white girl. For all practical purposes, Mulligan segregates his black and white characters from each other as fully as southern society segregates them. Virtually the only African American character who is visible in this southern town, outside the courtroom and outside brief trips to Tom Robinson's home, is the capable, dignified Finch

63. Arnold, in MacDonald, *A Critical Cinema 3*, 357.

64. Ibid.

65. Harper Lee's *To Kill a Mockingbird* is a thoroughly pleasant, readable novel; but for those familiar with Faulkner, and with *Intruder in the Dust* (1948) in particular, it is clear that *To Kill a Mockingbird* is Faulkner lite. Lee's novel eliminates all the moral, ethnic, and historical complexity so fundamental to *Intruder in the Dust*. The adaptations of both novels are disappointing—though at least Clarence Brown (with the help of a fine performance by Juano Hernandez) was able to portray Lucas Beauchamp, the strong, defiant African American character at the heart of the Faulkner novel, without embarrassing himself or viewers.

maid and cook, Calpurnia.[66] In the breakfast table sequence, Calpurnia is as fully in the foreground of our attention as she is in any other sequence in the film. Arnold's reanimation of the sequence eliminates her, except for the torso and arm in the background of the shot of Jem telling Scout to "Hurry up!" While this movement is visible longer in *passage à l'acte* than it is in *To Kill a Mockingbird* (she is visible for about a second in the original shot), Arnold keeps it in the background of his and our attention. Arnold's fear of dealing with the issue of race causes him to pretend, and to ask us to pretend, that we do not see race, even when it is literally in front of us.

In *My Father's Dead*, Ortiz combines material from three separate films—*High Plains Drifter* (1973; an explosion in a building), *Quest for Fire* (1981; two shots of a cave man and woman having sex), and *Excalibur* (1981; the child, Morgana, saying, "My father's dead!")—into a jagged montage that intercuts between the three excerpts forty-one times in less than four minutes. If one reads the three images as a kind of mini-metanarrative, the sequence suggests, perhaps, the precariousness of childhood and family life in general: the child seems poised between powerful social, psychological, and physiological forces. Ortiz's method of working with these materials, however, suggests a further meaning. By taking the three excerpts out of context and combining them, Ortiz "liberates" them, allowing them to be read in a manner that has little to do with their original functions, that is, in whatever way the audience pleases. If we imagine the commercial film industry as the "father" here, Ortiz's appropriation and invasion of the excerpts suggests his rebellion against the smooth continuities and simplistic meanings characteristic of commercial media-making; for Ortiz, the arrival of electronic technologies and their capacity for responding to commercial cinema are a premonition of the death of film: the media "father" that for several generations has taught Ortiz and his audience "what this culture means, what it is about, and where it should be going."[67] While the new technologies offer the possibility of an ethnic revenge on conventional Hollywood, the chance to expose the full context of the constrictions within which Hollywood representation usually works ("I found other meanings submerged in that cement that allowed me to relocate the more conventional meanings into the context of the infinite—the infinity of possible meanings"),[68] the digital/laser/videos are ultimately a means for transforming the explicit and implicit

66. Another maid is visible on the porch of a nearby home, apparently tending to an elderly woman, though she has no lines.

67. Ortiz, in MacDonald, *A Critical Cinema 3*, 339.

68. Ibid.

messages within commercial media into a kind of ritual, something like an exorcism, that might help to free Ortiz and his audience from their power.

Fathers as authority figures are central to both *passage à l'acte* and *My Father's Dead.* And both makers are responding to cinematic emblems of the corporate film industry, one of the more patriarchal institutions of modern culture. But Arnold's and Ortiz's attitudes toward these fathers are subtly different. At the end of *passage à l'acte,* Jem and Scout finish eating and run out of the kitchen through the screen door (all this in Arnold's witty retardant style); but Scout hesitates, then returns to give her father a kiss, and yells "Bye!" as she runs out the door, and we immediately see Arnold's name (as though he is also saying "Bye!" to Atticus and to us). In *My Father's Dead* there is no interaction between this daughter and the father (if indeed within Ortiz's pasticcio the man having sex can be read as the child's father): she can only cry out her loss, over and over. I read this difference in the two works as a reflection of Arnold's and Ortiz's positions with regard to Father Cinema: for all his wry detachment from the patriarchal familial scene he works with and from the commercial cinema that envisions the nuclear family as the core of modern civilization, the concluding kiss in *passage à l'acte* betrays Arnold's romance with the father and what he represents. His is an affectionate rebellion.

Ortiz, on the other hand, is pleased to kill the cinematic father, since he has been responsible for creating, or at least confirming, much of the prejudice Ortiz has become an artist to confront and move beyond. As a member of American minorities largely excluded from commercial film history and as a slum kid on New York's Lower East Side during the 1930s and 1940s, Ortiz confronted the various forms of prejudice intrinsic to the Hollywood cinema that surrounded him as he grew up. At a certain point during a viewing of a Western, he remembers wondering, "What am *I* doing cheering *the cavalry*?!"[69] His realization that by doing so, he had been unwittingly participating in his own disenfranchisement led him to the more aggressive aesthetic evident in *My Father's Dead.*

COMING OUT: MARLON RIGGS / SU FRIEDRICH

One of the crucial currents in avant-garde filmmaking at least since the 1940s has been the representation of alternative sexualities; indeed, the success of the American film society movement and of "underground film" in the 1960s seems to have had much to do with the fact that film audiences were

69. Ibid., 330.

fascinated with cinematic considerations of sexuality, including homosexuality and lesbianism. Two of the films that were of particular importance at Cinema 16, the widely influential New York film society directed by Amos Vogel from 1946 until 1963, were Willard Maas's *Geography of the Body* (1943) and Kenneth Anger's *Fireworks* (1947). *Geography of the Body* provides a visual tour of the human body in extreme close-up, accompanied by a voice-off narration by poet George Barker that takes the form of a discovery narrative by a naturalist-explorer. Maas's argument that the entire human body is mysterious sensual territory is expressed, first, by his refusal to distinguish between the male and female body in his close-ups and by the film's witty use of one body part to represent another: a close-up of a bit of tongue between lips, for example, at first appears to be a woman's labia. Maas's decision to intermix the two sexes and his refusal to see one female or male body part as more sensual/sexual than another is a premonition of what would come to be called "Queer Cinema": that is, cinema that questions those heteronormative understandings of gender and sexuality that have informed nearly all popular film and television.

Fireworks may be the first openly gay film produced in this country and presented to audiences; like *Geography of the Body,* Anger's psychodrama was shown more than once at Cinema 16 and was controversial each time.[70] *Fireworks* takes the form of a dream during which a young man (Anger himself) goes to a bar where he becomes the victim of sadomasochistic violence by a group of sailors. The violence is a dream transformation of sexuality; milk poured on the dreamer's body is clearly a dream version of semen. He awakes in bed next to a young man. *Fireworks* is full of a whistling-in-the-dark humor, simultaneously reflecting Anger's excitement about his own gay desire and his recognition that this society, which pretends to honor freedom; punishes the honest expression of any but heterosexual desire: one of the "climactic" images in the film is a man (we don't see his face) with a firecracker hard-on; when lit, it explodes into an ejaculation of sparks.

During the early 1960s, after the heyday of the American film societies, avant-garde films dealing with homosexuality often ran into legal hassles. Two of the most controversial of these films were Jean Genet's *Un chant*

70. In American avant-garde cinema, a "psychodrama" is a dramatization of a disturbed state of mind. The most famous instances include Maya Deren's *Meshes of the Afternoon* (1943, co-made with Alexander Hammid), Sidney Peterson's *The Lead Shoes* (1949), and Anger's film. In some instances the nature of the psychic disturbance is ambiguous—as it is in *The Lead Shoes*—while in others it is obvious, as in *Fireworks,* where it is clear that Anger is excited by his desire for men, even as he understands how dangerous the expression of this desire can be in a repressed society.

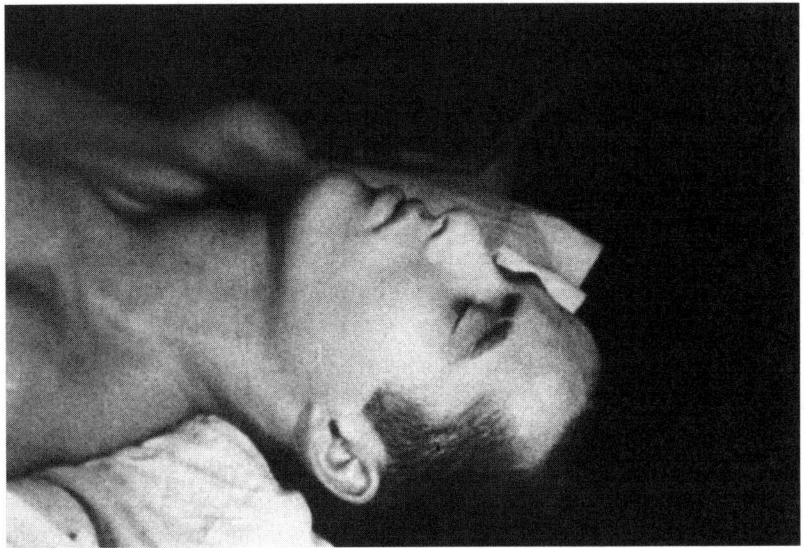

Kenneth Anger, dreaming, in *Fireworks* (1947). Courtesy David James.

d'amour (1952) and Jack Smith's *Flaming Creatures* (1963). Genet's film, which focuses on homosexual desire within an ethnically integrated prison environment, dramatizes the irony that it is only within prison that homosexual desire is "normal," that, in other words, incarceration frees men to express a form of desire that the society outside of prison obsessively imprisons. The seizing of the Genet film by the San Francisco police in 1964 resulted in an eloquent defense, "An Essay on Censorship: On Arresting Movies (Not People) in San Francisco," by Saul Landau, member of the board of directors of the San Francisco Mime Troupe—the first important longer essay published in the *Canyon Cinemanews*.[71] The arrest of Ken and Flo Jacobs and Jonas Mekas in 1964 for showing *Flaming Creatures* in New York City resulted in a court case that, in the end, found its way into the halls of Congress (Mekas was later arrested again for showing *Un chant d'amour* as a benefit for the *Flaming Creatures* defense fund).[72] The trans-

71. This essay, which appeared in the October–November 1964 issue, helped to transform the *Cinemanews* into an important source of thinking about alternative cinema during the 1960s and 1970s; it is available in Scott MacDonald, *Canyon Cinema: The Life and Times of an Independent Film Distributor* (Berkeley: University of California Press, 2007), 46–52.

72. For a review of the controversy surrounding *Flaming Creatures* and the film's legal battles, see J. Hoberman, *On Jack Smith's Flaming Creatures and Other Secret-Flix of Cinemaroc*, 36–51.

vestites in Smith's film create an orgy of self-expression that is sometimes funny, sometimes frightening (it is a struggle to excuse the "gang rape" of the woman, however obvious its unreality). Like *Un chant d'amour, Flaming Creatures* exposes both men's and women's bodies in a manner far more open than conventional films of that era (or our era, for that matter). "Normal" assumptions about gender roles are turned upside down, and America's overseriousness about sex is burlesqued. Indeed, *Flaming Creatures* is less about sex than about playing dress-up; limp male genitals are jiggled from time to time, and a large woman's breast is diddled with a finger, but generally we are looking at men—grown-up children, really—playing women playing their favorite film roles.

During the decades since *Un chant d'amour* and *Flaming Creatures,* American avant-garde cinema has continued to produce films that have argued for the honest expression and acceptance of gay desire. Two of the most pivotal are *Damned If You Don't* (1987) by the New Yorker Su Friedrich and *Tongues Untied* (1989) by the late San Franciscan Marlon Riggs (Riggs died of AIDS in April 1994). Appearing during the same cultural moment, both films use a comparable combination of approaches to provide defiant responses to the relentless commercialization of desire and to the repression of gay desire and of its depiction in cinema. Each film has also been understood as a formal breakthrough in the genre with which it has usually been identified: *Damned If You Don't,* in avant-garde film; *Tongues Untied,* in documentary.

The film that established Friedrich's reputation was *Gently Down the Stream* (1981), in which poetic texts, adapted from a dream diary and scratched directly onto the filmstrip, express the filmmaker's angst-ridden attempt to reconcile her Roman Catholic upbringing with her lesbian desire.[73] At the time Friedrich arrived on the scene, feminist filmmaking, which had been an important component of avant-garde filmmaking and videomaking in the 1970s, had found itself in a cul-de-sac. The rebellion on the part of many feminists against the conventional exploitation of women's bodies had moved feminist filmmakers toward what Laura Mulvey called "scorched-earth" cinema: an approach to moving-image making that avoided all forms of conventional pleasure—both sensual imagery (including all female nudity) and, at its most extreme, the careful crafting of beautiful images of any kind.[74]

73. For a thorough reading of *Gently Down the Stream,* see P. Adams Sitney, *Eyes Upside Down: Visionary Filmmakers and the Heritage of Emerson* (New York: Oxford University Press, 2008), 298–304.

74. See Mulvey's comments in MacDonald, *A Critical Cinema 2,* 334.

During the 1980s, Friedrich, who identified both as a feminist filmmaker and as an avant-garde filmmaker, began to rebel against the scorched-earth approach, which she had used in her earliest films, believing that to abjure sensuality and the production of beautiful imagery merely reconfirmed the conventional phallocentric idea that men had something that women lacked. By the time Friedrich made *Damned If You Don't*, this rebellion was in full swing.

Damned If You Don't combines a variety of elements into a composite of documentary and poetic narrative. Friedrich focuses on Roman Catholic nuns, a formative influence on her early life, as a metaphor for the kinds of feminist filmmaking that *Damned If You Don't* was rebelling against. Early in the film, one of her two protagonists is seen watching the Michael Powell–Emeric Pressburger film *Black Narcissus* (1947) on a black-and-white television; we see a visual synopsis of the film, as Martina Siebert offers an often ironic voice-over, describing the action in *Black Narcissus* in a manner that suggests the ways in which the film represses the complex sexual implications of the situations in the film into a love triangle between the film's protagonist, the church, and Mr. Dean, who flaunts his anti-Catholicism and sees the nuns as sensual/sexual women-in-hiding. Later, Cathy Quinlan reads passages from Judith C. Brown's *Immodest Acts: The Life of a Lesbian Nun in Renaissance Italy.*[75] Another form of information is supplied by an interview with (African American) Makea McDonald, who remembers early school experiences during which some nuns attempted to repress all sexual thoughts, while others subtly modeled the possibility of lesbian relationship. These three sources of information are supplemented with filmed images of nuns in public, here and abroad.

The documentary elements of *Damned If You Don't* provide a context for a silent, fictional, poetic narrative in which a sensuous woman (Ela Troyano), the one seen watching *Black Narcissus,* romantically pursues a nun (Peggy Healey), following her at times, planting a flower where the nun will find it, making a needlepoint of Christ—until, at the film's conclusion, the nun comes to the woman's apartment, where the two make love. Frequently, during the body of the film, the woman's pursuit of the nun is evoked by Friedrich's lovely, sensuous imagery of swans and albino whales and other creatures filmed at the New York City Aquarium (where the nun goes on her day off). This animal imagery implicitly argues that the desire felt by both pursuer and pursued is quite natural (and socially constricted). The lovemaking sequence, at the beginning of which the Troyano charac-

75. Judith C. Brown, *Immodest Acts: The Life of a Lesbian Nun in Renaissance Italy* (New York: Oxford University Press, 1986).

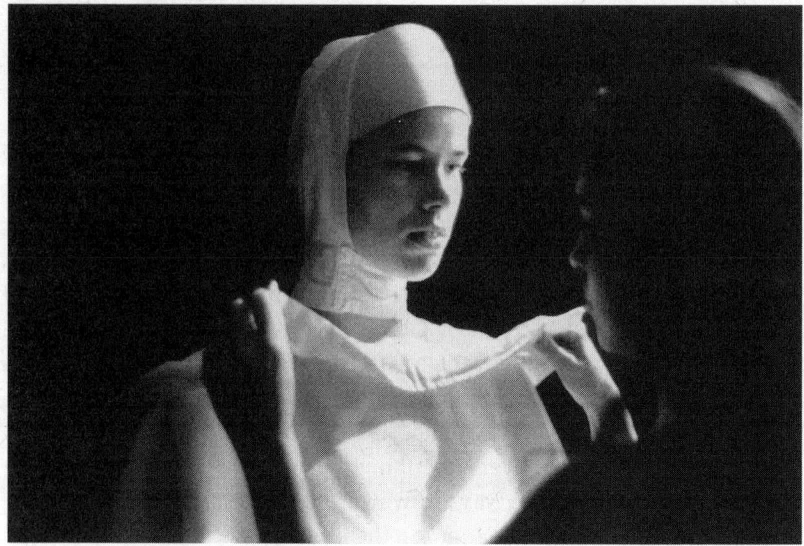

The nun (Peggy Healey) is undressed by her lover (Ela Troyano) in Su Friedrich's *Damned If You Don't* (1987). Courtesy Su Friedrich.

ter carefully undresses the nun, removing item after item of her habit until she is nude, defies not only the Catholic Church and Friedrich's upbringing but the feminist repressions of sensuality in scorched-earth filmmaking. From Friedrich's point of view, since a lesbian is damned by the church simply for recognizing her natural desires, she might as well express her true nature. Similarly, since scorched-earth filmmaking avoids all sensual pleasure, this approach can only damn the resulting films to invisibility (except perhaps for those interested in a form of sisterhood analogous to life in a convent). In other words, to quote a song Mr. Dean (David Farrar) sings in *Black Narcissus* (and that Friedrich herself sings during the film), Friedrich "can*not* be a nun" for she is "too fond of pleasure"—the pleasures of love, the pleasures of cinema.

Overall, within the evolution of Friedrich's work, *Damned If You Don't* is not particularly surprising. It seems a logical extension of *Gently Down the Stream:* the frightening conflict embodied in the dreams in the earlier film is resolved in *Damned If You Don't.* However, I cannot imagine that anyone familiar with *Ethnic Notions,* the hour-long documentary Marlon Riggs finished in 1988, would not have been surprised by his *Tongues Untied. Ethnic Notions* is formally a thoroughly conventional documentary about the stereotyping of African Americans in nineteenth- and twentieth-century pop culture. It relies on a set of talking heads (all of them college professors) to explain the development and implications of particular stereotypes (the mammy, the sambo, the coon, the savage, the uncle), illustrated by photographs, drawings, clips from film and television, and items from Jan Faulkner's collection of racist memorabilia (according to the end credits, this collection was the inspiration for the film). While *Ethnic Notions* is informative, but conventional *as a film,* Riggs's combination of a no-nonsense sexually political aggressiveness with formal experiment in *Tongues Untied* seems to me nearly unprecedented, not only within the history of Riggs's work, but within the history of cinema in general and within the histories of avant-garde cinema and African American cinema, in particular. And nearly twenty years later, it remains as surprising—and, for some viewers, as jarring—as it was on its release.

Like *Damned If You Don't, Tongues Untied* combines elements of documentary and fiction, in this case to offer a sense of the individual and collective struggles of black gay men coming of age during the era of Stonewall and the AIDS epidemic. Riggs uses a variety of sources, including, most important, readings of poems by several poets, including Essex Hemphill, whose physical presence is a central motif in the film.[76] The importance of poetry in *Tongues Untied* is suggested in the film's title, which implies not only a general rebellion of people who have been repressed but the practice of poetry as a way of freeing the spirit. Indeed, the centrality of poetry in *Tongues Untied* and the ingenuity with which poetry is presented make Riggs's film a landmark within the long and complex tradition in avant-garde cinema of incorporating poetry (see "Poetry and Film: Avant-Garde Cinema as Publication" in this collection). *Tongues Untied* also includes several group performances designed for the film (a choreographed demonstration by several "Snap Divas" of the techniques and meanings of finger-snapping; a similar demonstration of voguing by New York City gays; a black, gay doo-wop quartet, the Lavender Lovelights, singing music written for the film by Riggs and Alex Langford), and several gay pride marches and demonstrations in support of gay issues.

While Friedrich uses a dramatized narrative as the central thread of *Damned If You Don't,* the narrative thrust of *Tongues Untied* is achieved

76. Hemphill's poems "Without Comment," "Homocide," "In the Life," "Conditions," "Black Beans," and "Now We Think" are included in the film, along with poems by Reginald Jackson ("Initiation"); Craig Harris ("Classified," "The Least of My Brothers"); Steve Langley ("Confection," "Borrow Things from the Universe"); Alan Miller ("at the club"); and Donald Woods ("What Do I Do about You?"). Riggs himself supplied four "monologues": "Black Chat," "Three Pieces of I.D.," "Snap Rap," and "The Wages of Silence."

Marlon Riggs (left) and Essex Hemphill. Courtesy Richard Herskowitz.

through the ordering of a series of individual poems so that they seem to tell a roughly chronological story of a gay man growing up and coming to terms with himself. The film is organized so as to create a sense not simply of Riggs's life but of the lives of a generation of homosexuals. Riggs reads only the first poem, the one dealing with childhood and adolescence (this text is available as "Tongues Untied" in Essex Hemphill's anthology *Brother to Brother: New Writings by Black Gay Men*).[77] Riggs's reading of "Tongues Untied" suggests the perils (and fleeting pleasures) of a childhood as a black gay man in the Deep South, where he must fight not only the hatred of whites who consider him a "mutha fuckin' coon" but also the hatred of blacks, who see him as a "punk," a "homo," a "freak." The young man is momentarily saved by a white boy who helps him trust passion again ("What a joy! / That it should come from a whiteboy / with gray green eyes, / what a curse!"); then he finds his way to San Francisco and the Castro, where he becomes "immersed in vanilla" and refuses even to notice black

77. Essex Hemphill, ed., *Brother to Brother: New Writings by Black Gay Men* (Boston: Alyson, 1991), 200–204; this anthology includes Riggs's shorter monologue, presented later in the film, on discovering he had AIDS.

gay men. Finally, the young man faces the fact that by immersing himself in a white gay world, he has become an invisible man (whites see him as an exotic, not as an individual); finally, he learns to love, and to accept the love of, black men.

Of course, in an era of AIDS, even this love, once found, provides continual challenges: of remaining a passionate and sexual person under the threat of the disease; of dealing with the loss of lovers, friends, and personal heroes; of standing up to the black church's homophobia; of dealing with one's own mortality. However, it is precisely the HIV virus and AIDS—and the refusal of heterosexual American culture, white and black, to see the epidemic as more than the just punishment of homosexuals—that energizes Riggs and his colleagues to concentrate their energies to produce *Tongues Untied* and, in the end, to argue that the struggle for gay liberation is part of the struggle for civil rights (a montage near the end of the film combines images of Frederick Douglass, Martin Luther King, and civil rights marches with imagery of gay liberation activities) and to conclude that "black men loving black men is *the* revolutionary act."

Tongues Untied is not simply a message film, however. Like Friedrich in *Damned If You Don't*, Riggs expresses his understanding of gay life and culture through the film's formal means: the film's composite structure, the variety of its forms of address, the obviously collaborative qualities of its production are all implicit arguments for a pluralistic society, for an embracing of ethnic and sexual difference, and for a recognition that, in many ways, personal identity is a process, not a product. One of the strategies of a number of landmark Queer films—Kenneth Anger's *Inauguration of the Pleasure Dome* (1954), for example, and Ron Rice's *Chumlum* (1964), Lawrence Brose's *De Profundis* (1997)—is to visualize the complexity of personal and social identity by superimposing multiple layers of imagery, as if to literalize the idea that any individual or group contains a far wider range of selves than conventional media representations allow. In these films the complex, layered expressions of self are quite gorgeous in their extravagance, arguing for the beauty of a more complex sense of identity. The mixture of forms in *Tongues Untied* is closely related to this strategy of layering, though Riggs's film differs from the others I have mentioned because of the circumstances under which it was made.

Riggs's experience of the devastation of his community by AIDS and his subsequent personal battle with the disease did not allow for the kind of euphoria implicitly expressed in so many landmark Queer films, including Friedrich's *Damned If You Don't*. As was true of Anger's *Fireworks*, in *Tongues Untied* the release and acceptance of gay desire are shadowed by fear and danger. In the end, Anger fled to Europe, where he found a world more congenial to sexual variety—and where he expressed his excitement about this release from American repression in a companion piece to *Fireworks:* the gorgeous *Eaux d'artifice* (1954; Anger's title is a play on the French term for fireworks, *feux d'artifice*). Riggs refused to flee America and, indeed, could not have fled his disease. He came to see filmmaking as a way to celebrate the creative energies released by the pressures of mortality. Like *Damned If You Don't, Tongues Untied* is resonant with craft, full of sensual compositions and moments of tour de force editing; it can be thought of as a cinematic version of James Weldon Johnson's breakthrough anthology, *The Book of American Negro Poetry,*[78] which introduced African American poetry to a much expanded readership during the Harlem Renaissance. Riggs means to introduce an accomplished new group of (gay) black poets to an expanded audience—within a new form of poetic cinema.

Tongues Untied created a firestorm upon its release. Riggs had received a small Western States Regional Media Arts Fellowship from the National Endowment for the Arts (the grant request was sponsored by the Rocky Mountain Film Center in Denver), and while a substantial number of public television stations refused to show the film, it was part of the 1991 "P.O.V." series, which itself had received federal support. This government involvement with *Tongues Untied* was met with outrage by Senator Jesse Helms and others, who claimed that the NEA's support of Riggs's film was tantamount to taxpayer support of pornography. The reaction against the film was widespread enough, as was support for the film by those who understood its cinematic accomplishments, that Riggs could say, "The general desire to suppress any realistic acknowledgment or exploration of homosexuality in America has spawned the ultimate postmodern [political] coalition!"[79] *Tongues Untied* and *Damned If You Don't* can be understood as landmark contributions to the evolution of several film histories: *Damned If You Don't,* to avant-garde cinema, women's cinema, and Queer Cinema; *Tongues Untied,* to documentary, Queer Cinema, and to both avant-garde and African American cinema.[80]

78. James Weldon Johnson, ed., *The Book of American Negro Poetry* (New York: Harcourt, 1922).

79. From Marlon Riggs's "Tongues Re-tied?" reprinted from *Current,* August 12, 1991, and available on the *Current* website: www.current.org/prog/prog114g.html.

For details on the *Tongues Untied* controversy, see Jack C. Ellis and Betsy A. McLane, *A New History of Documentary Film* (New York: Continuum, 2005), 285–87.

80. Friedrich's *Hide and Seek* (1996) also caused consternation by suggesting (as does *Tongues Untied*) that young people are often aware of being gay earlier in their lives than much of conventional society is usually willing to admit.

TEXT AND IMAGE; JAMES BENNING / TONY COKES

As alternative cinemas have evolved, their histories have come to resemble the history of commercial cinema in certain ways. Most obviously, perhaps, within any particular countercinema, specific approaches develop and, as they are used over and over, sometimes become genres. During the 1970s and 1980s, UCLA became a nexus for the development of an independent black filmmaking movement, which often expressed the everyday lives of African Americans in a distinctive form of neorealism: fictional melodramatic family dramas focusing on disenfranchised blacks in Los Angeles are enacted within real locations and often with the involvement of local nonactors, in such landmark independent films as Haile Gerima's *Bush Mama* (1974), Charles Burnett's *Killer of Sheep* (1977), and Billy Woodberry's *Bless Their Little Hearts* (1984). During the same period, many filmmakers identified with avant-garde structural filmmaking created what might be called the text/image film: that is, films in which the uses of visual text were expanded and explored. Hollis Frampton's *Zorns Lemma* (1970) and *Poetic Justice* (1972), much of Yvonne Rainer's work, Patrick Clancy in *Peliculas* (1979), Su Friedrich's *Gently Down the Stream* (1982) and *The Ties That Bind* (1984), Michael Snow's *So Is This* (1983), Peter Rose's *Secondary Currents* (1983) and *SpiritMatters* (1984), Morgan Fisher's *Standard Gauge* (1984), and James Benning's *American Dreams (lost and found)* reveal ways of foregrounding the use of visual text as a means of providing a new kind of viewer engagement with film and new forms of cinematic engagement with a wide range of issues. Of filmmakers involved with the American avant-garde, James Benning has been most engaged with the issue of race, and his *American Dreams* can serve as a particularly useful instance. Further, Benning's work with image and text in *American Dreams* is interesting to consider along with the videos Tony Cokes has made during the past ten years.

American Dreams is a fifty-eight-minute film with a highly formal organization that tracks several narrative developments. One of these is Hank Aaron's pursuit of Babe Ruth's home run record, from his entry into the white major leagues in 1954 through his capturing the home run record in 1976. Benning, a Milwaukee native who grew up idolizing Aaron, details Aaron's career by using items from his collection of Aaron memorabilia—baseball cards, bottle caps, and the like—one item per year, shown from the front and from the back. A second narrative element is added through a handwritten text that scrolls across the bottom of the frame from right to left: at first, viewers may assume they are reading excerpts from Benning's own diary, but when we see that the diary writer is focused on assassinating a presidential candidate (Richard Nixon at first, Alabama governor George Wallace, later on), we realize that the diarist is not Benning but Arthur Bremer (another Milwaukee native), who shot Wallace in Laurel, Maryland, on May 15, 1972. A final major source of information in *American Dreams* is the sound track: Benning presents a series of excerpts from significant public speeches of the period (everything from an Elvis Presley news conference to a Nixon-Kennedy debate to an Angela Davis lecture) and from popular songs—a single excerpt of each kind for each year (in the film, a new year is signaled by a number representing the cumulative total of home runs Aaron had hit by the end of that year).

These several sources of information combine to create a cinematic collage that reflects a wide array of American dreams and provides a challenge to the viewer's perceptual and conceptual capacities. Most obviously, the attempt to focus on the Aaron memorabilia and to read their texts in some detail is continually interrupted by our desire to read the rolling Bremer text: Bremer's visit to a massage parlor early in the film seduces viewers away from the Aaron memorabilia, as does the evolving mystery of who the diarist is and what he means to do. The regular changing of items of memorabilia and Benning's periodic indications that one or another item is special in some way (small flashing texts signal these instances) lure us back to the image and away from the rolling text. By the end of the film, the juxtaposition of the two forms of American dreaming represented by the film's visuals, and emphasized by its structure, has become increasingly suggestive, particularly within the plethora of dreams represented by the many speeches and popular songs. In many instances we recognize interconnections between the various strands of information.

Obviously, in one sense Aaron's pursuit of Ruth's record is a quintessentially positive American Dream, while Bremer's is the epitome of a negative dream. But this distinction is more complex than it may seem. After all, the attack on Wallace, while negative in the obvious sense, is "positive" in a different sense. During this era, Wallace was the nation's primary spokesperson for segregation, easily identifiable as the kind of person responsible for impeding the many African American dreams represented on the sound track. That Bremer would attack the southern governor (though, ironically, his attack seems to have had nothing to do with Wallace's racial attitudes) is not entirely inconsistent with Aaron's final success in hitting his record-changing home runs for the Atlanta Braves (an accomplishment made all the more special by the fact that Aaron's life had been threatened). That is, the import of both Aaron's accomplishment and Bremer's success

From James Benning's *American Dreams* (1984): imagery of Hank Aaron memorabilia and handwritten excerpts from Arthur Bremer's diary. Courtesy James Benning.

in attacking a presidential candidate, at least for Benning, has mostly to do with the issue of race.

A further implication of the Aaron-Bremer juxtaposition becomes clearer once one takes Benning's approach to filmmaking in *American Dreams* into consideration. The structure of *American Dreams* was, even for Benning, unusually rigorous and minimal. Once under way, the film unfolds in an absolutely regular fashion, for fifty-eight minutes, until the final "shot" (Bremer's shot at Wallace, Aaron's shot to left field, and Benning's final image). The only movement in the film is the scrolling text. The relentlessness of Benning's minimalist organization of the film can be read as analogous to Aaron's increasingly relentless pursuit of Ruth's home run record and to Bremer's dogged pursuit of a victim. And all three of these "relentless pursuits" can be seen as emblematic of a particular male way of functioning in the world (years ago, when I suggested to Benning that the issue of gender informs all three levels of the film, he responded, "That's exactly what I was trying to suggest!")—though this implication may have been more obvious in 1984, during the heyday of feminist art production, than it is now.[81] In the 1970s, some feminists theorized that structural film was male, not simply in the sense that few women used the structural approach but because the focus on the cinematic apparatus was characteristic of a phallocentric engagement with tools and with power and control.[82]

For Benning the information overload in *American Dreams* is simply a reference to one of the realities of contemporary experience, where we often feel overwhelmed by a continual barrage of information. For videomaker Tony Cokes, however, media overload was a crucial dimension of the aesthetic of his *Fade to Black* (1991) and continues to be important in the postmodern videos he has made during recent years. Unlike most of the African American media-makers discussed in this essay, Cokes was familiar with American avant-garde filmmaking by the time he began making the videos that established his reputation. He studied with Yvonne Rainer, "whose work I admire greatly," in the Whitney Museum Independent Study Pro-

81. Benning in MacDonald, *A Critical Cinema*, 243.

82. There were, of course, instances where women did employ a structural approach, including the landmark *Riddles of the Sphinx* (1977), co-made by Laura Mulvey and Peter Wollen; and Su Friedrich's *Sink or Swim* (1992), which was Friedrich's response to her real father and to a cinematic father, Hollis Frampton: Friedrich's use of the alphabet as a structuring device recalls Frampton's *Zorns Lemma*, while simultaneously revising that earlier film's vision. While Frampton's film is an epistemological work that does not take gender into account, *Sink or Swim* argues that gender is a crucial element of what and how we learn.

gram; by the time he made *Fade to Black,* he had seen Michael Snow's *So Is This,* which he calls "a landmark" in regard to its use of visual text, and knew about the films I listed earlier.[83] Visual text was also explored during the early history of video art (for years, understood by both makers and critics as a different history from avant-garde film), and Cokes was influenced by this history as well: "There are two direct influences I can think of that aren't filmic: Richard Serra's *Television Delivers People* (1973) which is a textbook case informing my work, and Dan Graham's use of text in *Rock My Religion* (1984)."[84]

Fade to Black is framed by the trailer for the 1950 film adaptation of Richard Wright's *Native Son* (1940), directed by Pierre Chenal, with Wright playing Bigger Thomas. The trailer, a montage of Bigger Thomas being chased by the police, uses the novel's tripartite division—"Fear," "Flight," "Fate"—as a visual text. During the prologue that follows the trailer, Cokes uses a series of visual texts presented on the bottom third of the screen to consider his seduction, as a film viewer, by *Vertigo* (1958), the opening credits of which are seen, cropped, in the middle third of the screen (on the sound track we hear Jesse Jackson talking about rap music, which transforms "mess into a message," and then a reading of a Louis Althusser quotation discussing "interpellation": the way in which the implicit ideology of a society calls individuals into complicity with it). As we listen to the Althusser text and read the commentary on the experience of viewing *Vertigo,* we cannot help but notice the animated special effects in the *Vertigo* credits, which function as a series of hypnotic images, suggesting the way in which commercial film and its implicit ideology transfix us, drawing us into its way of understanding the world (these animated hypnotic images were created by avant-garde animator John Whitney).

After the opening credits, *Fade to Black* divides the screen into horizontal thirds. The middle third presents imagery, mostly opening credit sequences, from a series of commercial films that, in one sense or another, relate to the history of the cinematic depiction (and/or exclusion) of African Americans: *Intruder in the Dust* (1949), *Manhattan* (1979), *Taxi Driver* (1976), *Jailhouse Rock* (1957), *Mississippi Burning* (1988), *2001: A Space Odyssey* (1968), *Gone with the Wind* (1939), *Chariots of Fire* (1981), *Cry*

83. In his July 24, 2007, e-mail to me, Cokes mentions that my article "Text as Image (in Some Recent North American Avant-Garde Films)," *Afterimage* 13, no. 8 (March 1986): 9–20, "was quite valuable to my thinking during the late 1980s." In that article I discuss films by the text/image filmmakers I mentioned earlier in this section, including James Benning's *American Dreams.*

84. E-mail to the author, July 24, 2007.

Freedom (1987), *The Emperor Jones* (1933), *Desperately Seeking Susan* (1985), *Do the Right Thing* (1989), *To Sir, with Love* (1967), and *Babes on Broadway* (1941). In the upper third of the screen, Cokes presents titles and dates of films historically significant for the depiction of African Americans in cinema, beginning with *Uncle Tom's Children* (1903) and continuing chronologically until the Douglas Sirk version of *Imitation of Life* (1959). This listing is based on Donald Bogle's *Toms, Coons, Mulattoes, Mammies, and Bucks;* it ends with Douglas Sirk's *Imitation of Life* (1959) because it was "among the first films dealing with African-Americans that Donald and I both remember seeing."[85] In the bottom third of the frame, we read a series of texts that comment on the films recycled in the middle third of the screen and on the stories presented on the sound track.

The sound track is as complex as the visuals. During the body of *Fade to Black,* we hear montaged clips from rap songs (and other music) intercut with a series of stories narrated by Cokes and Donald Trammel (both of them, African Americans), describing incidents that keep African Americans aware of how racism continues to function in day-to-day American life. The voice-off narration of these stories is ironic and curt, even abrasive (for some white viewers, at least). The focus is on white racism toward blacks, but in at least one instance, Cokes suggests how a black man's perception of a white woman's fear of him—he is a moviegoer enjoying the aftermath of a pleasurable film in a theater lobby when he realizes she is glaring at him out of fear—triggers racism in him: he thinks to himself, "That stupid bitch—I could cut her fucking heart out! That could have been 'stupid White bitch,' or 'stupid rich White bitch' but I have trained myself not to think that way," as we read a blue text: "THERE IS NO RACISM HERE"—a phrase that is repeated periodically during the video, always in an ironic context that reflects the consistent resistance of whites to admit the presence of racism in themselves or in the here and now generally.

The primary visual and auditory motifs in *Fade to Black* are supplemented by several additional visual texts that are presented, in various colors, in the center of the frame, normally when no other imagery is visible. The texts in blue are poetically organized statements: for example,

85. E-mail to the author, August 19, 2007. Cokes goes on to say, "It was a Saturday matinee staple on WTVR, the local Richmond, VA, CBS affiliate I watched when I was a kid. I also like the idea that it was a remake, but I didn't know that until reading Bogle's book. . . . I was particularly intrigued by the idea that there was a history of cinema as an institution (and a repertoire of racial stereotypes) before we were born that preceded and informed our experience of cinema, perhaps without our knowledge, which was one of the points of Bogle's book for me as a reader. And then there's the Sirk-Fassbinder connection to melodrama as potential subversive form, which I came to appreciate after a few years of university film study."

CHAINED? FRAMED?
YOU KNOW WHAT I MEAN?

One implication here is that the way African Americans are framed, and "framed," by the history of cinema is a remnant of slavery, a modern media version of keeping blacks confined to "their place." Many of the blue texts seem to continue the set of textual statements and questions about *Vertigo* during the prologue; others refer to the stories told on the sound track (e.g., "WAITING FOR THE / LIGHT TO CHANGE," which refers to a story of how a white driver locks the doors of her car when African American men are near but pretends her action has nothing to do with race). Green texts, presented the same way, often refer to financial issues. The three sections of Cokes's frame, the two sound track elements, and these other textual bits are presented as a set of interwoven motifs revealing parallel histories that frequently intersect—much as the various elements in *American Dreams* do.

As Cokes's thirty-three-minute video draws to a close, we see "THIS MOVIE IS OVER" in blue several times (for aficionados of American avant-garde film, this is reminiscent of Bruce Conner's repetition of "The End" near the end of *A Movie*). The repetition of this statement, followed by the continuation of the film, suggests that just as the movie does not stop, the racism that is its subject continues as well, and requires a continuing struggle.[86] Finally, after the repeat of the *Native Son* trailer, a textual epilogue uses the upper and lower thirds of the frame to dedicate the video to the memory of Eleanor Bumpers, Michael Griffith, Yusef Hawkins, Phillip Pennell, Edmund Perry, Juan Rodriguez, and Michael Stewart (all of whom died as a result of racism, and several of whom are mentioned in Spike Lee's dedication at the end of *Do the Right Thing*), to the accompaniment of an excerpt from *Carmen Jones* (1954) of Joe Adams singing "Stand Up and Fight" ("The Toreador Song"). *Fade to Black* concludes with a text from Malcolm X, presented in alternating lines of green and red against a black background, evoking black nationalism and warning readers of the trickiness of whites in their dealings with blacks. Ending with this text is in part a response on Cokes's part to the final texts from Martin Luther King and Malcolm X in *Do the Right Thing:* "I

86. In her *Chronicles of a Lying Spirit (by Kelly Gabron)*, Cauleen Smith uses a similar tactic. The film works with two voice-off narrators: an apparently white man, probably an academic, and an African American woman (Smith herself). At the beginning of the film, the male voice dominates, and Smith's comments provide a counterpoint, but by the end of the film, this has changed: "The male narrator may seem to have the last word, 'Sound out,' but even if *he* thinks the movie is over, it continues regardless of what he says" (Smith, in MacDonald, *A Critical Cinema 3*, 303). In fact, nearly the entire film is repeated a second time, along with the man's once again ignored "Sound out."

thought the juxtaposition of the MLK and Malcolm X quotes Lee deploys at the end of DTRT was muddle-headed politically."[87]

While *American Dreams* and *Fade to Black* have much in common formally, there are significant differences, which can be read, at least in part, as a reflection of the racial positions of their makers (and their likely audiences) within American society. Benning's film is more elegant, more rigorously composed. Its means are simple and clear, its pace relentless and patient (and, for some, patience-testing). *American Dreams* does communicate Benning's recognition of his phallocentric approach to filmmaking, but he does not seem to see himself as complicit in racist behavior. In fact, the emphasis of *American Dreams* is on the similarity of his filmmaking to Aaron's quest and even to Bremer's desire to kill Nixon and Wallace (by handwriting the excerpts from Bremer's diary himself, Benning creates a sense, especially early in the film, that this is *his* diary; and even once we recognize that these are Bremer's words, the implication is that Benning too—like so many of us during that era—did fantasize about killing Nixon and/or Wallace).[88] Benning clearly sees himself as a racially progressive member of a certain generation with a particular history that is now, to some substantial degree, the past.

Cokes, on the other hand, at least insofar as we imagine him from *Fade to Black,* is not simply a member of a certain generation but an *African American* member of his generation, coming to terms with a racist cinematic history that has played an important role in determining his self-image and his experience. While *American Dreams* is a contemplative film, made by a loner, Cokes's more collaborative video (his primary collaborator is Trammel, who supplied text, provided voice-over narration, and did graphics for the film) reflects his frustration and anger with how the past has fed,

87. E-mail to the author, August 19, 2007. Cokes explains that he felt the quotations were muddle-headed "in the same way that the 'riot' (led by his Mookie character of all people) that preceded it seemed absurd as an expression of/response to the things happening to people of color all over the NYC metro area during the period. The film's narrative also struck me as producing an uncannily heavy identification with Sal and sons pizza shop as 'victims' of 'irrational black violence' for many critics and white viewers. (When the actual problem to be framed was state and white violence against people of color.) For these viewers Radio Raheem was expendable, or got what he deserved from the police. I thought Lee's construction functioned as a disservice to and misrepresentation of situations like the Michael Stewart case that the film allegedly sought to reference or illuminate."

88. Those who grew up during and immediately after World War II were often asked to consider (asked by the culture in one way or another) whether it wasn't prudent to kill a potentially dangerous tyrant *before* he could develop enough organization and power to, say, exterminate whole ethnic groups. In hindsight, a person who assassinated Hitler would have been a hero.

and continues to feed, into the African American present. And this unresolved frustration and anger are evident in the form of *Fade to Black*, which is less rigorous than *American Dreams*, the product, at least in part, of its maker's refusal of elegance and the detachment elegance might suggest. *Fade to Black* is fundamentally not only a rumination on the past but an attack on the racist present.

In the years since he finished *Fade to Black*, Cokes has become known for series of short video pieces, including most recently what he calls the "*Evil* Series," several of which are, formally at least, even more like *American Dreams* than *Fade to Black*—except in terms of their duration: all the *Evil* videos are brief. One particularly interesting instance is *Evil.8. A Bigger Picture (Unseen)* (2004, 8 minutes). As is true in the Benning film, in *Evil.8* all the visual elements are recycled: they include three texts, presented in two different ways, framed by two quotations: one from George W. Bush ("We don't torture people in / America and people who say / we do simply know nothing / about our country") and another from a U.S. State Department official ("It's like the song by The Who, 'Meet the new boss, / same as the old boss' [actually, "Won't Get Fooled Again"]. That's the widespread perception we have to deal with"). As in *American Dreams*, these various elements are organized in a minimal, and quite elegant, way (this is true, in fact, of all the *Evil* videos).

Two of the three primary texts—a May 5, 2004, editorial from the *New York Times* on the Abu Ghraib torture pictures; and an e-mail sent by Tony Cokes, also about Abu Ghraib, on May 7, 2004—are presented in the middle of the screen, one word at a time, against a vivid color background that changes from red to blue, or blue to red, in a right-to-left wipe, as each individual word is presented. The texts themselves are white, causing the color scheme to be, on one hand, an ironic comment on the conventional American patriotism that was invoked to enlist the American public in the war; and a way of saying that speaking out, questioning the war, *is* the real American patriotism. The third text, "A Tyrant 40 Years in the Making," a *New York Times* story written on the brink of the Iraq war by Roger Morris and published on March 14, 2003, scrolls across the screen, from right to left (white against a black background), above the red, white, and blue texts. Morris details the covert involvement of the Eisenhower and Kennedy administrations in Middle Eastern political events during the 1950s and 1960s, and specifically in the assassination of then Iraqi leader Abdel Karim Kassem, who had gained power by confronting Western interests but was seen as a useful counter to Egypt's Nasser, until he began to build an arsenal comparable to Israel's, to reenergize Iraq's long feud with Kuwait, to threaten Western oil interests, and to work to supplant American power in the region. In the end, the United States (through the CIA), along with coconspirators from Iran and elsewhere, was able to stage a coup, which ended in the execution of Kassem, the establishment of the until-then outlawed Baathists (including Saddam Hussein) as the ruling party, and a bloodbath at the hands of the Baathists of Iraqis who had benefited from Kassem's rule. On the sound track Alias provides electronic music with a repeated lyric that confirms the sad recognition, implicit in the juxtaposition of the main texts, that Bush's Iraq adventure, as horrific as it is, is nothing new.[89]

In *Evil.8,* as in *American Dreams,* the simultaneous presentation of two different texts in two different ways confronts viewers with more information than they can take in.[90] Here, however, the overload takes on a specific implication: that the entire process of this new American involvement in Iraq happened so quickly that most American citizens did not have the time, or the willingness, to consider what was going on or how it related to the past history of our engagement in the region—or, for that matter, how our racist attitude toward Arabs and Muslims might play into activities like those that occurred at Abu Ghraib. The theme of racism in *Evil.8,* however, is expressed rather differently from the way racism is dealt with in *Fade to Black.* In the earlier video, Cokes, as an African American, was in a position of blamelessness; he did not need to consider himself complicit in those aspects of American culture that were/are challenges for African Americans (or, perhaps more accurately, he was in rebellion against the idea that he or his ancestors were complicit in their own victimization). In *Fade to Black,* this blamelessness sometimes becomes a self-righteous anger that "justifies" the slight irregularities (they read as a kind of clutter) in the video's presentation—the inelegance I referred to earlier. The racism implicit in the events at Abu Ghraib is not American white-on-black racism, and as a result, in *Evil.8,* Cokes is able to detach from the issue just enough to be able to take the same sort of total control over his form as Benning does in *American Dreams.* The result is a formal elegance that gives a particular power to this video and to the others in this series.

89. The lyrics of Alias's "Unseen Sights" are "Lights, squares, a detail fakes the whole / catch the abstract all in all / a shift so small / but remembered after all / unseen sights / you're hanging on / catch the abstract all in all / a shift so small / but remembered after all / after all."

90. Another film that uses a related strategy is Paul Sharits's *Word Movie/Fluxfilm* (1967), in which a series of fifty words are shown, one word per frame, in a graphic arrangement that causes the words to "optically-conceptually fuse into one 3¾-minute long word" (Sharits's description in *Film Culture,* nos. 65–66 [1975]: 115), while, on the sound track two speakers alternate one-word-at-a-time readings of two distinct texts.

and George H. W. Bush would aid Saddam Husse

Bush

of challenging the dominance of America in the M

criminal

From Tony Cokes's *Evil.8. A Bigger Picture (Unseen)* (2004). Courtesy Tony Cokes.

• • •

For several decades, those of us involved in film education have agreed that two of the film histories we can talk about and exhibit are African American film history and avant-garde film history, and we have agreed, at least implicitly, that somewhat different kinds of people are interested in these two histories (we have not divided *entirely* along racial lines, but . . .). Of course, our division of the field in this way continues to have its uses. If one explores African American film history (or Chicano video history, or Asian American film history), one has a basic structure within which to pursue an interest, even develop a career. The same is true of avant-garde film: if I want to write an article on Michael Snow or Ernie Gehr or Su Friedrich, I know which journals might consider a piece on an avant-garde filmmaker.

The problem is that our conceptualizing of these particular histories has a tendency to blind us to important dimensions of both: to the formal variety of ethnic cinema and to the ethnic variety of avant-garde cinema, to important cinematic qualities that any number of accomplished works in both histories share, and to fascinating distinctions between works exploring similar issues. In general, our categories have caused us to emphasize the differences in these two histories by suppressing their similarities and complicities. This was evident when Sarah Elder asked her question at the fiftieth Flaherty; *Tongues Untied* had been shown two days earlier, but my guess is that Elder had categorized it as a documentary or an African American film; that it might also be seen as an avant-garde film probably did not occur to her, since she was thinking of avant-garde film as "white."

I am arguing neither for an abandonment of ethnic media histories and of avant-garde film history nor for a mindless combining of them; these historical divisions have been productive of insight and may continue to be useful. What I am arguing for is additional steps, a moving beyond these (and other) historical categories or, better yet, a synergic interchange between them that might allow us to recognize and explore the many issues, approaches, and accomplishments filmmakers share, and in the long run, to help us see each other with more empathy and ourselves more clearly.

Interview with Gina Kim

Gina Kim began as a video diarist, recording her experience as it happened, using a home-video camera. In the earliest of her works to be exhibited publicly, *Empty House* (1999; 24 minutes), Kim began to engage the issue that, more than any other, has informed her video and film work: the obsession of women with their bodies and their desire to come to terms with this obsession. Kim's first major work, the personal epic *Gina Kim's Video Diary* (2002; 157 minutes), is a subtle, often troubling, generally exquisite, surprisingly intimate, sometimes wildly narcissistic coming-of-age story. Focusing on what would normally be seen as minor domestic details, and confined to Kim's small apartment and the seemingly insignificant actions that take place there, *Gina Kim's Video Diary* tracks Kim from her arrival in Los Angeles, with few resources, no friends other than her video camera, and virtually no English, through struggles with loneliness and anorexia, to her acceptance of her physicality and her potential as a visual artist. She also rediscovers the familial heritage she hoped to escape by emigrating to the United States. *Gina Kim's Video Diary* is a major contribution to the history of personal documentary, as remarkable in its way as Su Friedrich's *Sink or Swim* (1992), Ross McElwee's *Time Indefinite* (1993), Alan Berliner's *Nobody's Business* (1996), and Jonathan Caouette's *Tarnation* (2004).

In 2003 Kim completed her first fiction feature, *Invisible Light,* which focuses on two young women living in LA who are indirectly connected through a man. Gah-in (Yoon Sun Choi) is a lover of the man (whom we never see); she is conflicted about the relationship and suffering from bulimia. Do-hee (Sun Jin Lee), the man's wife, is pregnant, though not by her husband; she flies to Korea to create some space for herself in order to decide whether to abort the pregnancy or see it to term. The first half of *Invisible Light* is Gah-in's story, the second half, Do-hee's—though it is clear from the details of the film that both stories are happening simultaneously.

In a sense, both women are running from the physical involvements their desires have led them into: after listening to Do-hee leave a message on her answering machine, Gah-in unhooks the phone, hides in her apartment,

Gina Kim in *Gina Kim's Video Diary* (2002). Courtesy Gina Kim.

binges and vomits, goes swimming, then plugs the phone back in. After Do-hee makes the call to Gah-in, she leaves for Korea; it is her first visit in eight years. She is suffering from morning sickness and cannot keep food down. She meets a bartender (Chan Jeong), who reluctantly agrees to go with her to see her grandmother (she wants her grandmother to see her as married), who raised her after her mother divorced, remarried, and emigrated to the United States. When they get to the grandmother's village, the old woman does not know Do-hee (or she is angry with her and refuses to recognize her; we cannot be sure). Do-hee and the bartender leave and talk about Do-hee's situation; and Do-hee returns a gift she had bought for the grandmother. At the end of her story, Do-hee finds a ring in a playground and sings a lullaby that suggests that she may have accepted the pregnancy—though it is unclear where this acceptance will lead her.

Invisible Light was shot on video but released as a 35mm film. It is consistently stunning. The images are rigorously composed and the editing elegant. The acting is impressive, and the narrative is convincing in its evocation of two lives in transition—and unusual, even courageous, in its refusal of an easy, conventional resolution. Indeed, for those who know *Gina Kim's Video Diary* (as impressive as that piece is in its way), Kim's adeptness at creating a believable, engaging fiction on her first try is impressive.

Kim's most recent film, *Never Forever* (2007) represents a further move toward commercial cinema, though, again, her work remains consistent in terms of theme and quality. The protagonist is Sophie Lee (Vera Farmiga), the Caucasian wife of Andrew (David Lee McInnis), a Korean businessman living in New York. They want a baby, but Andrew is sterile and so deeply humiliated about it that he attempts suicide. Wanting to please Andrew and his family (David's mother seems to disapprove of her), Sophie first asks a nurse at a fertility clinic to impregnate her with another man's sperm; when her request is refused, she follows a young Korean man, Jihah (Jung-Woo Ha), whose application to become a sperm donor at the clinic has been refused because he is an illegal immigrant. Sophie arranges to pay him to have sex with her and offers a substantial bonus if she gets pregnant. By the time Sophie does get pregnant, Sophie's and Jihah's feelings for each other have developed (in time, releasing Sophie into pleasurable sexuality). When Andrew learns about their relationship, he arranges to have Jihah deported and agrees to continue the marriage so long as Sophie aborts. Realizing that she wants the child, Sophie leaves Andrew, and a jump cut delivers us to a scene on a beach, where a little boy is running around, to the entertainment of Sophie, who is pregnant again. We assume that Sophie and Jihah are now a couple, but there is no specific evidence of this; we are not even sure where she and the child are. What seems clear is that Sophie is happy and fulfilled.

Like *Invisible Light, Never Forever* is well acted and convincing, a pleasure to watch and hear (Michael Nyman provided the score); it shows not only that Kim can work capably with established actors but that her vision of what she intends her cinema to do, both thematically and stylistically, is translatable from one level of production and kind of film to another (when she visited Hamilton College in the spring of 2007, she hinted that her next project will be a horror film). In *Never Forever*, Kim's fascination with the struggle of women to accept their physicality and their physical desires continues, as does her fascination with Korean diaspora. And as is true in her earlier feature, the resolution of this struggle is not the heterosexual couple, as it would be in a Hollywood romance, but the sensually fulfilled, emotionally self-sustaining woman.

This conversation was recorded in April 2007 and was refined online.

MacDonald: At the beginning of *Gina Kim's Video Diary*, your grandmother says, "Be a professor in Korea." That suggests to me either that you were already a college teacher or that you were aiming to become one. But your persona in the video seems to be much younger.

Kim: My family has a very strong academic background. My father is a professor. When my grandmother said that to me, I had just graduated from college; she, everybody in my family actually, wanted me to pursue my academic career and get a Ph.D., then settle down in Korea and become a professor like my father. Also, I think my granny believes that my dad did a lot for my mother (her daughter); what she really wanted to say to me was, "Please stay in Korea and take care of your mother, just like your father did."

MacDonald: Since you were leaving to go to CalArts, you must have already been making work.

Kim: I went to art school, which was a big scandal in my family. Everybody expected me to become an academic, and *I* always thought I would do that too. But when I searched my heart, I realized that what I wanted to do most was to draw, to paint, to touch things. I had thought that creating art was not something I could do for a living, but when I became a senior, I started to think, "Why not! This is what I *want* to do; it's not a crime."

MacDonald: Are there artists in your family?

Kim: My father teaches public administration and government, but when he was in high school, he wanted to become a painter. Somebody actually recognized his talent and wanted to support him, but back then, this was *completely* out of the question, so he gave up, didn't even try. Because he did well in school, and was the eldest in the family, he felt forced to be more "practical."

My mother was a semiprofessional singer and dancer when she was in high school, but in those days that was considered a vulgar occupation for a girl, and she was from a very conservative doctor's family. Even going to medical school was supposed to be vulgar for a proper girl, and that's why she was sent to a girl's school to major in pharmacy.

I knew these stories and I knew that there was this pent-up sorrow in both my parents because they never achieved what they really wanted to achieve in their lives; they sacrificed their real desires and dreams for the sake of others. I realized that I didn't want to do that, and once I knew I wanted to be an artist, I was really adamant. I remember telling my mother, "If you're not going to support me financially to go to this after-school program where students study art, I'll do some prostitution to support myself"—something like that. My mother passed out and was hospitalized. They felt they had no choice but to support me from then on. It was kind of crazy, but I'm glad I did what I did, because that's how I was able to get started.

MacDonald: How did you get into videomaking?

Kim: Pretty much all of my student works in Korea were mixed-media, installation, performance art, and I was involved in a theater group. Seoul

National University is a very conservative school, and it was very slow in terms of keeping up with new media and new trends in art, but when I was a senior, a video art class was offered. That was the first time I ever touched a video camera, and I still remember the feeling—it was thrilling. I was so excited by this new medium and its incredible potential: to make my artwork, which is very personal, become more public, to be able to distribute it, to be able to communicate with millions of people—in painting you can never do that. You can see reproductions in a book, but it's never the same.

And I was fed up with the elitism of the Korean art community; I was always looking for some new medium that was not completely conquered by the Genius, Modernist, Male Artist. Back then, there was something incredibly fresh about video, and I was especially intoxicated by the narcissistic feature of the medium: the instant feedback. I would hook up the video camera with the monitor and observe myself. It was like an I-watch-myself-film-myself kind of looking. When I think about it now, it sounds silly, vain, but that was a period when I really needed to find my own identity and to define myself as a female artist. I really didn't have any role models, any mentors.

MacDonald: Had you seen any video art from North America?

Kim: That video class was my only opportunity. The teacher, who had studied at UCLA, had these personal connections to friends who made work. I did see Bill Viola's stuff and some other North American video art, but it was pretty random. And we didn't speak English, so we'd watch the films and videos not subtitled, and the teacher would try to explain what was going on. It was like blind people trying to understand the shape of an elephant or something. It was a hard way to learn, but now I'm glad I was introduced to video art without any sort of conceptual discourse. I was a baby on a beach, finding my way to the water!

MacDonald: From watching *Gina Kim's Video Diary,* I would guess that for a period of time you accumulated a lot of work and then, later on, went back and looked at material involved with issues of the body and issues having to do with your mother.

Kim: Yes, exactly.

MacDonald: How much were you recording during those early months?

Kim: I started documenting myself in the fall of 1995, and then when I moved to the United States, I was recording every day, sometimes for five or six hours. That was pretty much all I ever did back then, because I didn't have any family around, I didn't have any friends, I didn't speak English—I didn't even have *furniture.* I was so scared to go out. The video camera became my only friend, my family, my pet, everything. Sometimes I was so lonely that I would turn the camera on just to feel that I was not alone, and to see someone, myself, moving in the monitor. This was not performative taping at all; the video camera was just there, breathing, flickering, like a small animal.

MacDonald: This was during the time when you were also going to classes?

Kim: Yes, yes. That's a bit odd, when I think about it. I was living two separate lives.

In 1998, I got *really* depressed. This was during the Asian financial crisis. My family was never rich to begin with, and after the collapse, they couldn't afford to keep sending me to CalArts. I was forced to take a semester off.

MacDonald: What did you work at?

Kim: I got tutoring jobs. I taught students art, drawing. I was still meeting with my teachers at CalArts. I got more and more depressed, and my eating disorder got worse. I was anorexic back then . . .

MacDonald: Anorexic or bulimic? There's a character in *Invisible Light* who is bulimic.

Kim: Anorexic—I was never bulimic, thankfully. I knew that once I started to throw up, there'd be no stopping things; I'd be moving into another world. I started to have the symptoms of anorexia when I was a senior in art school in Korea, I think because I didn't know what to do next with my life.

At some point during this depressed period, I compiled some very crazy footage from this home taping and showed it to my teachers: Thom Anderson, James Benning, and Bérénice Reynaud. They were shocked. They could see stylistic continuity between this new material and the works I had made for classes, but they *didn't* know that I was that crazy and suffering so much—at school I was very demure, but still I functioned well; they just never imagined what my home life was like. James was especially heartbroken, I think.

Back then, I didn't even know what anorexia meant. After a while, I realized that it wasn't just me suffering, that this was some sort of social disease and that maybe there was a way out of it. And I realized that maybe I should keep documenting myself for myself, but at the same time for other girls too. I started to have a sense of responsibility, at least subconsciously. It didn't make me self-conscious in terms of recording myself, but I began to think that maybe I could make a real documentary out of my video material.

At first, making the tapes was therapeutic, something just for myself, like going to a priest and making a confession. I wasn't even saving the recordings. Now, I began to realize that I should keep the tapes safe. I did compile some footage that I tried to edit while I was still going to CalArts, but watching that footage at that point was too painful; it seemed too weird and too raw. And there was so much of it, something like two hundred hours of footage. *Empty House* was my first successful try at a work made out of the diary material. It wasn't until two years after graduation that I managed to edit *Gina Kim's Video Diary.*

Even before I finished *Gina Kim's Video Diary,* my boyfriend back then—now he's my husband [Kyung Hyun Kim]—submitted *Empty House* to Oberhausen, one of the most prestigious short film festivals in the world. He did it just on a whim, without my knowing. I get this phone call from the festival director, saying he really likes the film and wants it to be part of the festival. Back then, I didn't even know what a film festival meant; but going to Oberhausen turned out to be an eye-opening experience for me: to be able to talk about my work with an audience and to find people who could really interpret my films was so encouraging; it helped me to continue editing *Gina Kim's Video Diary,* which I had given up on so many times. After Oberhausen, I got a letter from this French woman saying, "I went through the same thing and your film is invigorating," and a dancer e-mailed me to say, "Your film reminds me of this experimental dancer in Germany; it was really beautiful"—my film seemed to *mean* something to some people!

So when I finished *Gina Kim's Video Diary,* I had enough confidence to send it to one of the programmers at the Berlin Film Festival. She loved it. So that was another prestigious experience—but for me the film festival experience was not about glamour; it was where I learned that my films can speak to people.

MacDonald: That opening section, where you're "hiding" as the movers pack up your things for the trip, suggests that you're a fetus. *Gina Kim's Video Diary* is about rebirth.

Kim: Yes, but when I was recording that, I had no idea at all that I would do something with the material later, that it might end up *meaning* something.

MacDonald: Your mother seems very embarrassed about your grandmother's visit.

Kim: My grandmother (my mother's mother) and my mother never got along. My mother still blames her mother, even after her death, for her own unhappiness. My granny was not supposed to visit our apartment because she embarrassed my mother so much.

MacDonald: What did your mother find embarrassing?

Kim: The way she talks, the way she dresses (her flowery dress was very old-fashioned). She was just a silly old grandma, maybe a little bit senile, but my mother was overly sensitive about her.

I think I inherited some of my arts and crafts skills from my grandmother; she would make me these cute little dolls and stuffed animals when I was young. She was very creative and loved fabric; she would make a tiny pouch sort of thing to keep her money in, and wear it with her underwear; *that* would embarrass the hell out of my mother—but everything about my grandmother embarrassed my mother.

I don't know how my granny found out I was leaving that day. I was taping the movers, and the movers hated it, so I had to hide the camera underneath the piles of old clothes, which happened to be my grandmother's; my mother and I were throwing things away. All of a sudden, my grandmother is in the frame, and my mother is yelling at her. Granny telling me to stay and become a professor in Korea and take care of my mother really infuriated my mother. Early in their marriage, my father and mother flew to the United States together. My father was doing his Ph.D. at the University of Pittsburgh; he got this enormous grant from the Korean government. Because my father's family was pretty poor, the promise was that my mother would support my father, but she hoped that after he got *his* degree, she would resume *her* career as an artist. She hated being a pharmacist. But she got pregnant, and also my grandmother wanted her to come back to Korea *so* badly that my mother felt she had to. What my granny was saying to me probably reminded my mother of her own past. The last thing that my mother told me when I was leaving for the United States was, "Don't be like me. Don't come back."

In the airplane flying to LA I was thinking about how even personal history repeats itself, and it made me sad. Of course I didn't know what to do with that moving-day tape, but I kept it safe because I knew it would be something precious.

MacDonald: How was your English when you arrived?

Kim: How are you? Good Morning! I'm sorry. Excuse me. My *French* was as good as my English—meaning my English was as bad as my French [laughter]. I learned some English in high school, but that was it.

MacDonald: You mentioned earlier that you weren't performing things for the camera, but at a certain point you seem so at home with the camera that what you record seems like a dance you're doing with the camera, within carefully controlled texture and light.

Kim: Definitely. But this is the irony of my video diary: I wouldn't have

Chiaroscuro in *Gina Kim's Video Diary* (2002). Courtesy Gina Kim.

been so performative had I thought that I could possibly show what I was recording to other people. I did what I did because I was so sure that I was *completely* alone and that this was *entirely* for myself. That's the reason I could be so playful. I had a tremendous amount of fun with my camera and monitor, and looking at myself was a strangely soothing experience for me. On one level, it was like a surveillance camera that could spy on my body and see how *fat* I was and where the cellulite was: oh, my legs are like *this,* they should be like *that.* But at the same time, it was extremely pleasurable and soothing and comforting and reassuring because, of course, the person who shows up in the monitor *was* me, but at the same time was *not* me. There was a certain distance between me and my image and that helped me to face my problems with my physicality in a more objective way. Making video always had this calming effect, just as for some bulimic people, throwing up has a calming impact, for a while. I would turn on the camera and perform for myself, and by the time I would turn off the camera, I was just normal Gina again and felt as if, well, everything was okay, that I was what I was. Gina with all her problems was *in that tape.* The nontaped me was all right.

Some psychotherapists tape their patients to help analyze them; I was doing that for myself.

MacDonald: Many of us are painfully conscious of our bodies at some point in every day. When you get to my age, you regularly see mortality looking around the corner, but you're still engaged with how you look physically. The irony is that through the very personal "dance" you did with your video camera, you were externalizing a fundamental aspect of our lives that most of us repress from each other, and that is almost entirely repressed from cinema.

Kim: Thank you. That's exactly what I was hoping. My video diary is a coming-of-age story about how to survive in this world where we don't really admit our physicality.

MacDonald: On two different levels. One is your consciousness of your physical *body,* and the other is your consciousness of your *perceptions,* especially of light and of other very simple perceptual realities. This second aspect places *Gina Kim's Video Diary* within a tradition that includes Benning's recent films and Stan Brakhage's work, and the work of many other avant-garde filmmakers. At CalArts, I assume you were seeing American avant-garde film.

Kim: Definitely. James Benning was one of biggest inspirations for me, and Stan Brakhage also—I love his films. The things that I produced for my classes at CalArts were pretty much imitations of their works but on a smaller scale, since I was working in video. My student work was often very mathematical, very elegant, very photographic, in ways that related to Benning's work and other films I was seeing.

MacDonald: At one point in *Gina Kim's Video Diary* you say, "I choose narcissism; it's the only option when you don't want self-pity"; is that your line or is it a quotation?

Kim: Definitely my line—nobody else would say that [laughter]; it's a *strange* thing to say. I think my mother chose self-pity and I hated that; she always complained, "Oh, I made a sacrifice for you, and that's what made my life miserable."

MacDonald: Inadvertently, my parents did something like that too.

Kim: Even before I could talk or think, I had this fear of losing my mother, because I felt that I was the one who caused all this misery for her; it was like an original sin kind of feeling, and I think that was why I always drove myself mad to be at the top of the class. I hoped that would make my mother feel as if she had done the right thing, had sacrificed for the right reason. I don't resent her *at all* now, but when I was in my video diary period, I *did.* Now, I truly believe that she did her best, and I feel sorry for her; I feel like *I'm* the mother to *her* these days.

MacDonald: Has she seen your work?

Kim: She saw *Invisible Light.* I'm reluctant to show her *Gina Kim's Video Diary.* She would probably flip out. She cried during *Invisible Light.* I said, "Please, Mommy, it's not autobiographical!"

MacDonald: One of the turning points in *Gina Kim's Video Diary* is when you tell the story about the child, and there are the white sheets with the blood, accompanied by the song "Danny Boy." That's a remarkable and mysterious sequence.

Kim: Thank you. That's my mother singing, by the way.

I have a certain number of recurring fantasies, and that sequence is one of them. The event that I think instigated it happened when I was very young, around eight. My parents used to fight a lot then; my father had recently become a professor while my mother had to struggle with his two kids. I now think that the little girl with the nosebleed is my mother; later in *Gina Kim's Video Diary* I talk about that one very traumatic moment of my life when my mother was bleeding and telling me to call the hospital. I still don't know exactly what happened; that's the traumatic part of it.

MacDonald: Your father is never mentioned in *Gina Kim's Video Diary.* Did your parents split up at some point?

Kim: My parents never split up. They're still together, just an old Korean couple. They still fight. Actually, my father has always been more like a mother to me, the nurturing, tender one.

MacDonald: In *Empty House* you use imagery and poetic texts; by the time of *Gina Kim's Video Diary,* text is less important. Even if viewers are repelled by your narcissism, they're allured by the look of the piece, which is clearly made by somebody who knows a good image when she sees one. That's less clear in *Empty House.*

Kim: I agree. I think in *Empty House* I was trying to hide behind those texts. *Gina Kim's Video Diary is* painfully narcissistic, but that was a good starting point for me in coming to terms with myself: to grow up and *live,* you have to understand that you *exist.* The only thing I could do was to look at myself and be reassured that I exist, that I'm really here, that I don't just exist in the gaze of others, that I'm flesh and blood.

MacDonald: The end of *Gina Kim's Video Diary* transitions right into *Invisible Light;* you leave the apartment and go out into the world to film.

Kim: I think that the tagline of my life is that passage from the Russian Jewish poet Marina Tsvetayeva: "I didn't want this, not / this (but listen, quietly, / to want is what bodies do / and now we are ghosts only)." Unless you admit your physical presence, your body, you don't know how to want things, let alone how to pursue them. A woman who desires has been the most important theme in all of my works, including my new film, *Never*

Forever, which is about a woman who doesn't know what she wants until the end, when she finally accepts her desire, despite what it will cost her. Even the horror film script I'm working on is about a woman who doesn't know what she wants out of life because she hasn't come to terms with her physicality, then realizes she does know and actually pursues it. For me genre doesn't matter; it's the ideas that are important.

MacDonald: All the shots in *Gina Kim's Video Diary* have a mask around them . . .

Kim: That's from the wide-angle adapter I used. Almost all of the shots in my video diary were made indoors, in my house, which got really claustrophobic (the place was really small), so because a wide-angle lens was too expensive and I couldn't find anything compatible with my camera, I bought a wide-angle adapter. When you attach that adapter to the camera and zoom out completely, you get that vignette look.

MacDonald: It works.

Kim: You think so? [laughter] It's real amateurish, but I did it anyway; I thought it was interesting-looking.

MacDonald: Another question about a detail: Does the hat you use in *Empty House* and again in *Gina Kim's Video Diary* have significance beyond the fact that you just like it as a hat?

Kim: It's not a nod to René Magritte, if that's what you're thinking. Actually, there were two different hats. The one that shows up in *Gina Kim's Video Diary* is more like a cowboy hat; I got it at this very strange mall in Maryland when I was traveling with my father in 1992, visiting galleries and museums. I kept it as a souvenir and then, strangely enough, brought it to the United States. The hat that shows up in *Empty House* looks like a René Magritte hat, but more than anything else, I think in both cases I just wanted to hide my face. It's not until very late in *Gina Kim's Video Diary* that you finally get to see my face.

MacDonald: When you smile at the end, it's almost shocking. There's one moment early in the film where you laugh with your mother, but that's the last upbeat moment until nearly the end—except for that dance you do with the hat.

Kim: Yes, to "Everything's All Right" from *Jesus Christ Superstar.*

MacDonald: In both *Empty House* and *Gina Kim's Video Diary* there's a shot where you see your arm reaching for what looks to be a gas valve. Is that a contemplating-suicide image?

Kim: It looks like it could be, but no, that wasn't its purpose. *Gina Kim's Video Diary* uses a fuller version of that sequence, which starts with me examining my face. It's hardly audible, but when you listen carefully, you hear me say that I'm so scared I cannot feel my face. I also had this fear of getting really fat, obese; this was not really an obsession with *image,* but a reflection of my feeling that I was taking up too much space in the world. I felt as if I was a prisoner in this house and was terrified by the place. I started to touch my body in my video diary, not really thinking about what I was doing, but when I look back, I think I subconsciously thought that if I really *knew* my body, I wouldn't be so scared, and I extended this idea to my house.

MacDonald: On one level, *Gina Kim's Video Diary* and *Invisible Light* have a lot in common. I can see why you say on your DVD, "Fiction is fiction," reminding the audience that the fiction feature isn't simply a continuation of the diary. At the same time, one could imagine that the two stories in *Invisible Light* are pretty close to your own experiences, at least judging from *Gina Kim's Video Diary.* What was involved in the transition from diary to fiction feature?

Kim: As I was finishing the editing of *Gina Kim's Video Diary,* I was writing a script for what became *Invisible Light*—though it was not really a script at the beginning; it was more like notes on random images occurring to me out of the blue: a woman sitting alone cannot eat this really warm and nice-looking meal; or a woman standing on top of a bridge, looking down, as if she's considering suicide. Images just kept occurring, and I didn't know what to do with them other than to write them down, but then later, when I tried to consolidate them, I realized there were two characters living in my notebook: one person was always on the road (so I called her Do-hee, which means the woman on the road in Korean) and the one who stays at home: Gah-in in Korean.

When I came to structure the film, I had a mathematical inspiration (à la James Benning). Do you remember the $y = 1/x$ equation? The graph of that equation results in two very neat curves: one lives in a plus world and the other lives in a minus world; they seem to echo each other, but they never cross. I thought the two characters corresponded to these two curves. Exactly halfway between the curves is zero, which I imagined as the man: Do-hee's husband and Gah-in's lover. The two women never meet, but their lives are connected through this man. The women in the film have different issues; they are very different people, but they also have many things in common, so many, in fact, that they can be seen as two sides of the same personality. The point here is that both are reaching for the same goal: to come to terms with themselves and to find and admit their own physicality and their own physical desires.

These parallels are built into the structure of the film. In both stories the

Gah-in (Yoon Sun Choi) bingeing and Do-hee (Sun Jin Lee) unable to eat because of morning sickness in Gina Kim's *Invisible Light* (2003). Courtesy Gina Kim.

climax—Gah-in's bingeing and Do-hee's masturbation—come at exactly the same spot. I thought it made sense to give Do-hee the plus numbers and Gah-in the minus numbers—both having to do with pregnancy. Actually Gah-in is supposed to be suffering from PMS; I ended up deleting direct references to this, but the numbers involved her counting down to her period, which will mean she's not pregnant. The plus numbers refer to the number of days Do-hee has been pregnant. The clock is ticking for her, and she really has to make a decision about whether to keep the baby or not.

MacDonald: We don't actually see Do-hee take the pill. My sense is that the film ends before she is sure what she's going to do.

Kim: My interpretation is that she does not take the pill. I probably should have put English subtitles at the end when she hums the Schubert lullaby. She's singing the song to her baby.

MacDonald: By humming a lullaby, she might be fantasizing about what might have been.

Kim: It is a bit of an open ending, but I wanted it to be clearer.

MacDonald: You had never worked with actors before; the production process must have felt quite new.

Kim: Oh, definitely. Even after I finished the script for *Invisible Light*, I wasn't completely committed to making a narrative feature. I traveled with *Gina Kim's Video Diary* with this script in my pocket, mostly thinking of making an experimental documentary or a work of video art that would use a lot of intertitles and voice-overs. But then as I was interacting with perceptive young women, young artists and critics in the audiences seeing *Gina Kim's Video Diary*, I started to think that maybe I should make a fiction film out of it, something that could speak to a broader audience.

I was fascinated by this idea because while both characters in the script were fictional, both had certainly come from my heart; I considered them *my* babies. Having actors realize these characters was an experiment for me: I knew that it would be really challenging because I had never directed a fictional piece. At the same time, I was hoping that my documentary approach to the script and the other, fictional elements might create a really interesting tension, a dialectic, and reveal some new meanings.

As it turned out, I got really great actors and I loved working with them. And it was a lot of fun to work with a DP [director of photography].

MacDonald: Do you see *Gina Kim's Video Diary* and *Invisible Light* as feminist? How have women who consider themselves feminists responded to your work?

Kim: There are feminists who hate my work. Wow, they say, *Gina Kim's Video Diary* is really narcissistic; all you care about is yourself. And *Invisible Light*—so self-indulgent. But other feminists, who are more like me (I consider myself a hard-core feminist), the kind of people who think that the personal is the political, *they* get a broader meaning out of this work.

Things have been changing rapidly since *Empty House* premiered at the Seoul Women's Festival in 1999. At that hard-core feminist festival, that piece was quite controversial; so when I screened *Gina Kim's Video Diary* in 2001 at Jeonju International Film Festival, another big film festival in Korea, I was a little concerned. If *Empty House* is narcissistic and self-indulgent, then *Gina Kim's Video Diary* is the epic version [laughter]! But the reception was very different; things had already changed.

MacDonald: Am I right in assuming that you feel that dislocation from the motherland, dislocation of women from their bodies, and from each other, are all part of the same fundamental issue?

Kim: Yes. I strongly believe that. My work is not really about eating disorders, and it's not really about pregnancy; it's not about the body exactly, but about the feeling of isolation and loneliness experienced by all women. I see all women as nomads. If I may say so, the world is still very male-centered—especially where I come from. I didn't have any role models of female artists, which was very frustrating for me. I think that was one of the reasons why I was suffering from anorexia when I was younger. It was not about the desire to look beautiful or anything like that; I was just stressed out about the fact that in this big world, there seemed to be no place for me at all, nowhere that I could feel comfortable, nowhere that I fit in. Girls who suffer from anorexia want to disappear; they want to become thinner and thinner and thinner, so that they take up less and less space.

We women are perpetually in a nomadic state no matter where we go, since we feel we're living in someone else's world. After I was able to accept this as my fate, I became more comfortable with myself, with my physicality, and with the world in general. When I was obsessed with the idea of finding my motherland, so to speak, I was repressed as a creator. But when I finally gave up on that idea and accepted that I am a nomad, I became prolific.

In *Invisible Light,* Gah-in and Do-hee represent the feeling of woman as nomad. Gah-in is a Korean girl living in the United States, and Do-hee is a Korean girl who returns to Korea; they are nomads quite literally, but at the same time, it really doesn't matter where they come from or where they are. It's just their constant state of being—inside this burdensome female body that creates all kinds of problems and issues—that they cannot feel comfortable with, no matter where they are. If and when they do come to accept their own physicality, when they accept their own desires, then they can feel comfortable in this world. Hopefully, that's the message that I give at the end of the film when Doo-he finally sings the lullaby. That moment is not about *motherhood,* it's about Doo-he's accepting her own body and her own desires.

I wanted to break up the traditional binary definition of whore and Madonna; the sexual woman as whore; the mother as holy, pure Madonna figure. Do-hee is both, and yet neither.

MacDonald: Could you talk about the production of *Invisible Light?*

Kim: The crew size was about twelve people, and the total budget was under $150,000. Of that, more than $80,000 was for the tape-to-film transfer—we shot on video, then transferred it to 35mm film—so the actual budget for film and the actors and everything else was about $70,000, which is nothing when you're flying back and forth from Korea. Everybody, including myself, pretty much worked for free. I did all the production design and the costume design, almost everything. The film takes place in confined spaces and is really controlled; that had to happen, because I didn't want the film to look cheap.

MacDonald: There's little dialogue in the film, but sound is really important.

Kim: Because of the very low budget, there were very few things I could do to deliver what I wanted to say. One of them was sound design, which is all done postproduction; if you know Pro Tools, you can do many things with your laptop. From the very beginning of the production my goal was to use the diagetic sound as much as possible; I wanted every single sound that you hear in this film to come from the scene itself: no music, no added sound effects. Once I achieved that to the exact degree I wanted, I did put in another layer to intensify the dramatic tension. I wanted to emphasize the feeling of diaspora experienced by these two women, and for me trains and airplanes are the sounds that always trigger the idea of diaspora—though train sounds are a little too nostalgic and too beautiful. A gigantic airplane passing by is something very violent. I used a lot of airplane sounds.

Another thing that I was very careful with was the refrigerator, because that is the villain for the first part of the film. When we actually filmed the scenes, we turned the refrigerator off, since its noise drowned out all the other little sounds on set. The refrigerator sound had to be recorded later on and then planted in the sound track. Whenever Gah-in exits the kitchen, you hear the refrigerator, so that subconsciously it feels as if there is something going on inside it. The sound of Gah-in eating was very important, obviously, but surprisingly enough, that *is* all diagetic; it's just what came naturally. While I was listening to Gah-in eating as we were shooting, I was really surprised because it sounded so violent, and I was struck by the different sounds of different foods being eaten. I wanted the eating sounds to seem as if they were coming from the *inside* of her mouth. My sound guy understood what I wanted, and we ended up getting wonderful sound from a single take.

The masturbation sound was a bit of a struggle because my DP, who was fantastic, had an allergy to the dust in the room where we were shooting. For the masturbation scene I was absolutely committed to diagetic sound, because the idea of dubbing that sound, like in a Japanese porn animation, horrified me. I made it clear to my sound people what I wanted, but when we shot, the camera and the microphone were really close to Sun Jin Lee's face, and we ended up getting two voices: hers and my DP sniffling. We had managed to get something truthful in that scene so I resisted the temptation to reshoot: it took us a week to erase the sniffling from the sound track.

MacDonald: Was the interracial theme part of your original conception for *Never Forever*? While it's not really the subject of the film, it's an important element.

Kim: The race element was definitely one of the jumping-off points. The story developed when I started teaching at Harvard University. I had never lived on the East Coast before and was quite struck by Boston's lack of ethnic diversity. I became more conscious of my own race than ever before (having been born and raised in Korea, I had very little awareness of race), and I became intrigued by how Asian people are perceived in mainstream culture in the United States. I was always aware of how Asian women are sexualized in American pop culture, but had very little knowledge about how Asian men are perceived. Well, most of them are completely desexualized. Asian men are very rarely portrayed as subjects of desire in the U.S. Of course, there are exceptions, usually good-looking, successful professionals (lawyers, doctors, et cetera). Asian working-class men are often completely desexualized, unlike Latino laborers. I wanted to subvert this stereotype. Jihah is a poor immigrant, but I wanted to portray him as a sexually charged man. Andrew is a sexy upper-class Asian man, but his sperm is weak and, therefore, he is desexualized on the most basic level.

MacDonald: Were there particular models in the world of melodramatic film that were useful to you as this project evolved?

Kim: Douglas Sirk films greatly influenced me, as did some European films: *Belle de jour* [1967, directed by Luis Buñuel], for example. But the most inspiring films were Korean films from the 1960s. I was teaching a Korean cinema class at Harvard when I first started to conceptualize *Never Forever,* and I was fortunate enough to get some 35mm prints of classic Korean cinema for class screenings. Of course, I had seen the films a long time ago, but when I watched them again, I was impressed with how subversive they were—both aesthetically and thematically. The depiction of women in such films as *Madame Freedom* [1956, directed by Han Hyeong-mo], *The Housemaid* [1960, directed by Kim Ki-young], and *The Houseguest and My Mother* [1961, directed by Shin Sang-ok] moved me deeply. The women in these films are driven by their struggle to fulfill their desires. The endings are often less than satisfying, but the films inspired me nevertheless. I started to wonder what would happen if I put the same kind of woman character in a contemporary film but did not sacrifice her integrity at the end. The result is a melodrama that is strictly focused on the psychology of a woman character rather than on the happy resolution of a love affair.

MacDonald: How do you understand the somewhat ambiguous ending? I say "somewhat" because the phone call suggests that they reconnect, and, also, the young boy's orange shirt suggests that he *is* Jihah's son, even if we don't see him—Jihah wears orange a number of times during the film.

Kim: I think it is quite clear that the baby in Sophie's belly is Jihah's, but I didn't want to show Jihah because it would distract from the real question, which, for me, is "Is *she* happy? Did *she* achieve what she wanted?"—which differentiates this film from the typical melodrama, where the *couple* is the focus. In *Never Forever,* who she ends up with is really not the point.

I see *Never Forever* as a coming-of-age story of a woman (a bildungsroman) more than a melodrama, which is also true, in different ways, of *Gina Kim's Video Diary* and *Invisible Light.* For the ending, I wanted to make clear that Sophie achieves what she longed for. The best way to imply that is to make her pregnant again, since pregnancy carries a different meaning for Sophie than it does for typical female characters in melodrama. For Sophie, the fetus is what makes her realize what she really wants out of her life. It represents her desire, her dream, and ultimately, *her* life. So, when Sophie says, "This baby is mine," during the climactic confrontation scene with Andrew, she is not talking about motherhood but is explicitly expressing the desire to live her own life. The irony is that what starts as a sacrifice for her husband ends up becoming her self-fulfillment. In a way, Sophie became a whore in order to become a mother and ultimately, like Do-hee in *Invisible Light,* she blurs (and hopefully *negates*) the Madonna/whore stereotype.

MacDonald: While *Never Forever* is hardly a blockbuster, it is clearly a more expensive production than *Invisible Light.* Could you talk about how the production developed, and in particular how Vera Farmiga ended up playing the lead, and how Michael Nyman came to do your score?

Kim: Never Forever is not a dialogue-heavy film, so I was desperately looking for someone who could not only "play" the role, but who could *become* the role. I first saw Vera in *Down to the Bone* [2004, directed by Debra Granik] and was blown away by her performance. I sent her my script and we met at a small café in SoHo. The minute she walked into the café, I was convinced that Vera was the Sophie that I'd been looking for. Vera is both transparent and mysterious. Her body always creates a cinematic tension within a frame. Her face is like a map with which we can explore a character's heart.

Sophie (Vera Farmiga) and Jihah (Jung-Woo Ha) in Gina Kim's *Never Forever* (2007). Courtesy Gina Kim.

Thanks to her tremendous cinematic presence, I had a relatively easy time creating the Sophie character without having to explain much with dialogue. The chemistry between Jung-Woo and Vera as fellow artists was beyond belief. They didn't want to meet each other before the shoot, so that they could retain the mystery until the first day of shooting, and I decided to shoot the sex scenes in a sequential order so that I could exploit their real-life awkwardness and tension. Of course, that was risky, but it ended up working beautifully. I could feel the intimacy growing between the two actors from one scene to another!

MacDonald: Why did you have Jihah live in Chinatown?

Kim: It was to portray him as a total outsider. He, of course, suffers from extreme isolation in the U.S., since he is an illegal immigrant. But he refuses to be part of the Korean (or Korean American) community as well. Things could have been easier for him if he had chosen to compromise. But he stubbornly goes his own way in pursuit of his "American Dream." I wanted Jihah to be a man of strong will who is not afraid of loneliness and not willing to compromise his integrity by pretending to be someone other than himself.

MacDonald: I understand *Never Forever* had a warm reception at Sundance; what was the reception in Korea?

Kim: The film was very warmly received in Korea as well. We opened the film on ninety-three screens nationwide (for comparison, *Spiderman* opened on eight hundred screens in Korea) and attracted about a hundred thousand people. We hoped to do better, but since *Transformers* and *Harry Potter* opened the following weekend, we lost momentum almost immediately.

But I am very happy with the many wonderful comments from critics. *Never Forever* was featured on the cover of most of the major film magazines and made Vera and Jung-Woo stars. Some hard-core fans of the film launched fan sites. I'm extremely grateful for them.

I think originally we were able to attract interest from the Korean audience due to the interracial relationship that the film depicts, but so far as I can tell, when people watched the film, they found the racial element very minor compared to the emotional landscape that the characters create. Apparently, it's a story that celebrates the possibility of liberation through desire and love after all!

Poetry and Film

Avant-Garde Cinema as Publication

BACKGROUND: POETRY AND THE POETIC IN AVANT-GARDE FILM

In general, cinema has evolved by incorporating earlier art forms, or aspects of earlier forms. It developed first as an extension of the still photograph and, soon after, as an extension of the magic show; and it was not until D. W. Griffith and others recognized that theater and prose fiction, and especially the novel, offered a model for extending cinematic narrative that the feature film became a possibility.[1] Most screenplays are based on short stories, novels, or parts of novels, and the screenplay itself is, as the word suggests, a derivation of the theatrical drama. But the tendency of cinema to incorporate other art forms is not confined to the commercial feature. Even those forms of the motion picture that are generally understood as "critical"—that is, as offering critiques of the commercial feature and the audience that has developed for it—have tended to incorporate the other arts, though the particular art forms incorporated tend to be different from those usually used as sources for commercial narrative features.[2]

The most obviously critical of cinema's various histories is what is usually called "avant-garde" or "experimental" film.[3] From the outset, this history has been particularly dependent on painting and collage, on music, and to a somewhat lesser extent on the literary arts, particularly poetry.

1. For a review of the evolution of early cinema, see "Part One: Early Cinema," in David Bordwell and Kristin Thompson, *Film History: An Introduction* (Boston: McGraw Hill, 2003).

2. A number of books have explored the ways in which early avant-garde cinema incorporates the visual arts and music. They include David Curtis, *Experimental Cinema: A Fifty-Year Evolution* (New York: Delta, 1971); Malcolm Le Grice, *Abstract Film and Beyond* (Cambridge, MA: MIT Press, 1977); and, more recently, A. L. Rees, *A History of Experimental Film and Video* (London: BFI, 1999).

3. Terminology for this major strand in the weave of film history has always been confusing. "Avant-garde" and "experimental" are the most common terms, though each is problematic. Some filmmakers and critics do not like the military implications of "avant-garde." In

While much early cinema, including commercially oriented cinema, was experimental in the sense that filmmakers were often attempting things that had not been accomplished in film before, it was not until the 1920s that something like an avant-garde film movement developed.[4] What is usually considered the first film avant-garde—crucial figures include Hans Richter, Man Ray, Henri Chomette, Germaine Dulac, Viking Eggeling, Oskar Fischinger, Salvador Dali and Luis Buñuel, Fernand Léger, Dudley Murphy, Marcel Duchamp, and René Clair—was a result primarily of visual artists exploring cinema as a new artistic tool for creating dadaist, abstract, and surrealist works. Richter, Ray, Léger, and others used the capacity of cinema to combine disparate imagery in a manner that confronted traditional assumptions about narrative and pictorial logic; Oskar Fischinger found ways of animating abstract shapes into what is often called "visual music" and by 1930 was combining animated abstractions with music; and in *Un Chien andalou* (1929), Luis Buñuel and Salvador Dali used a series of shocking dream images and nonsensical intertitles to attack all forms of film that are meant to provide conventional coherence and narrative resolution.[5]

While the visual arts tended to dominate the first film avant-garde, poetry was also an important influence. For *Manhatta* (1921), sometimes considered the first American avant-garde film, the two filmmakers, both of whom were established visual artists—photographer-painter Charles Sheeler and photographer Paul Strand—intercut between modernist cinematography of Manhattan and intertitles made up of excerpts from Walt Whitman's poems "A Broadway Pageant" (1860), "From Noon to Starry Night: Mannahatta" (1860), and "Crossing Brooklyn Ferry" (1856).[6] Jan-Christopher

---

any case, "avant-garde" film cannot be said to *be* the avant-garde of cinema, since even the technology usually used to make it, 16mm cameras and film stock, would not exist if it were not for the commercial industry. Some filmmakers do think of themselves as experimental artists, but others bridle at the implication that their films are "experiments" rather than finished works of art. "Alternative cinema" is often useful too, as is "critical cinema," since nearly all the films in this general category provide alternatives, *critical* alternatives, to industrial cinema. I tend to use all these terms, depending on the particular context.

4. For a brief history of 1920s European avant-garde cinema, see Bordwell and Thompson, *Film History*, 173–84.

5. For information about Oskar Fischinger's career, see William Moritz, *Optical Poetry: The Life and Work of Oskar Fischinger* (Bloomington: Indiana University Press, 2004). For commentary on some of the various dada and surrealist strategies used by artists working in film during the 1920s, see Rudolf E. Kuenzli, ed., *Dada and Surrealist Film* (New York: Willis Locker and Owens, 1987).

"Intertitles" are the visual texts that are interspersed with other forms of visual imagery in silent film, usually providing a kind of narration, along with other forms of information.

6. Ken Kobland's stunning *Buildings and Grounds: The Angst Archive* (2003) begins with an homage to *Manhatta*, using excerpts from Whitman's "Crossing Brooklyn Ferry."

Horak has argued that this particular combination of text and image makes *Manhatta* a historically pivotal film that looks simultaneously forward into a modernist future and backward toward the romantic past represented by Whitman.[7]

In Europe and the United Kingdom during the 1920s and 1930s, an audience formed for critical forms of cinema as a result of the ciné-club movement that spread from nation to nation (a ciné-club was an informal organization dedicated to exhibiting the many forms of film that commercial exhibitors were not interested in showing).[8] For this audience and for the filmmakers who produced the films shown in ciné-clubs, visual text, and poetic texts in particular, were important as source and inspiration.[9] Some avant-garde films, widely seen on the ciné-club circuit, followed *Manhatta*'s lead in combining imagery with visual text. For example, *L'étoile de mer* ("Starfish," 1928), a collaboration of Man Ray and the surrealist poet Robert Desnos (who wrote film criticism during the 1920s), uses phrases from Desnos's poetry as visual texts. And Marcel Duchamp's *Anemic Cinema* (1926) intercuts between spiral designs and spirally arranged sentences full of puns and wordplay.[10] The arrival of sound in the late 1920s made possible the auditory inclusion of poetry, and during the 1930s, several landmark contributions to the history of documentary included recitations of poetic texts: *Night Mail* (1936) by John Grierson and Basil Wright ends with a poem by W.H. Auden, read by John Grierson and Stuart Legg; and Pare Lorenz's *The River* (1937) is narrated by Thomas Chalmers, reading a

7. Jan-Christopher Horak, "Paul Strand and Charles Sheeler's *Manhatta*," in *Lovers of Cinema: The First American Film Avant-Garde*, ed. Horak (Madison: University of Wisconsin Press, 1995), 267–86.

8. For an overview of the history of the ciné-club movement in Europe, see Richard Abel, *French Cinema: The First Wave, 1915–1929* (Princeton, NJ: Princeton University Press, 1984), chap. 3.

9. Depending on how one defines "poetry," it could be argued that the incorporation of poetry into film is one instance of a somewhat larger field: the use of visual text as imagery in the history of cinema. A good many avant-garde films have used visual texts that would not normally be considered poetry, unless poetry is understood as any text that is arranged spatially. Michael Dorland and William C. Wees, in their anthology *Words and Moving Images* (Montreal: Mediatext, 1984), explore this larger field, focusing in particular on Canadian avant-garde films, including several that are clearly combinations of poetry and cinema. My anthology *Screen Writings: Scripts and Texts by Independent Filmmakers* (Berkeley: University of California Press, 1995) includes the texts of a number of particularly remarkable films that make extensive use of visual text.

10. The verbal puns in *Anemic Cinema* are translated and discussed by Katrina Martin, "Marcel Duchamp's *Anemic Cinema*," *Studio International*, no. 189 (1975): 53–60. P. Adams Sitney discusses the use of visual texts in *Anemic Cinema* and *L'étoile de mer* in "Image and Text in Avant-Garde Cinema," *October*, no. 11 (1979): 97–112.

Pulitzer Prize–nominated poetic text written by Pare Lorenz, but clearly inspired by Walt Whitman.[11]

Soon after the end of World War II, ciné-clubs, now called film societies, proliferated in the United States as a result of the pioneering exhibition work of Frank Stauffacher at the Art in Cinema film society in San Francisco and of Amos and Marcia Vogel at the Cinema 16 film society in New York City. Both Art in Cinema and Cinema 16 specialized in reviving significant films that had been important in the European ciné-clubs and in introducing audiences to new avant-garde and documentary work.[12] In 1946, when Art in Cinema announced its first film series, the ninth show was entitled "Poetry in Cinema," with Jean Cocteau's *Le sang d'un poète* ("Blood of a Poet," 1930) planned as the feature presentation.[13] During subsequent years, *Le sang d'un poète* was widely seen and influential, in part because it represented to some what poet-filmmaker James Broughton would later describe as an "unforgettable example: a poet making a poetic film!"[14]

The meaning of "poetic" as used by Art in Cinema in its description of *Le sang d'un poète* (and of "poet" in the Cocteau title, for that matter), as well as in its descriptions of a good many other films, is quite general, and typical of the 1940s and 1950s. It refers neither to the act of writing poetry nor to particular poetic texts but to a human sensibility that can take a wide variety of forms. The men and women involved in presenting avant-garde cinema and the audiences that came to see the films seem to have shared a sense that filmmakers could create "poetic" film experiences. The actual

11. In documentary history, there is also the "poetic documentary." Bill Nichols defines the "poetic mode" of documentary as emphasizing "visual associations, tonal or rhythmic qualities, descriptive passages, and formal organization. Examples: *The Bridge* (1928), *Song of Ceylon* (1934), *Listen to Britain* (1941), *Night and Fog* (1955), *Koyaanisqatsi* (1983). This mode bears close proximity to experimental, personal, or avant-garde filmmaking." See Nichols, *Introduction to Documentary* (Bloomington: Indiana University Press, 2001), 33.

But "poetic documentary" is a slippery term that is often used more broadly to refer to other kinds of film: for example, to Robert Flaherty's evocative depictions of exotic peoples. In his study of the making of Robert Flaherty's *Man of Aran* (1934), *How the Myth Was Made* (1978), George Stoney concludes that Flaherty was America's first (and still best) "film poet."

12. For an overview of the histories of Art in Cinema and Cinema 16, see the introductions to Scott MacDonald, *Cinema 16: Documents toward a History of the Film Society* (Philadelphia: Temple University Press, 2002), and Scott MacDonald, *Art in Cinema: Documents toward a History of the Film Society* (Philadelphia: Temple University Press, 2006).

13. The program notes for the first Art in Cinema series were published by the San Francisco Museum of Art in 1947, as *Art in Cinema*, edited by Richard Foster and Frank Stauffacher. The book is now out of print, though a facsimile is available in MacDonald, *Art in Cinema*. The Art in Cinema papers are housed at the Pacific Film Archive in Berkeley.

14. James Broughton, "Frank Stauffacher: The Making of *Mother's Day*," *SPIRAL* 1 (1984): 29. In this instance, Broughton was speaking specifically of Cocteau's *Beauty and the Beast* (1946).

"Poetry in Cinema" program presented by Art in Cinema (as opposed to the program announcement) included four films: *Le sang d'un poète, Jammin' the Blues* (1944) by Gjon Mili, *Lot in Sodom* (1933) by John S. Watson and Melville Webber, and *Vormittagspuk* ("Ghosts before Breakfast," 1928) by Hans Richter. Judging from the program notes, what constitutes the "poetic" in *Jammin' the Blues* is the film's graphic qualities, particularly its use of close-ups and evocative chiaroscuro; in *Lot in Sodom* and *Vormittagspuk* it is the handling of symbolic details within a mythic tale and within a fantasy, respectively. And in *Le Sang d'un poète* it is a combination of several of these factors. Basically, what these and the many other films that were labeled "poetic" had in common, at least in the minds of those who wrote the program notes, is suggested by Luis Buñuel in "Cinema as an Instrument of Poetry," a talk delivered in Mexico in 1958: "It was agreed that the theme [of this event] would be 'cinema as artistic expression,' or more concretely, cinema as an instrument of poetry, with all that this latter word holds of a sense of liberation, subversion of reality, a passage into the marvelous world of the subconscious, and nonconformity to the restrictive society that surrounds us."[15]

During the 1940s and 1950s there was a particular strategic value to the use of "poetic" in conjunction with avant-garde film. That filmmakers can be considered creative artists may seem obvious to us, and it was certainly clear to many avant-garde filmmakers, but for most moviegoers during the first five decades of film history, films were mindless distractions, engaging and skillfully made, perhaps, but certainly not "artistic" in any serious sense. Indeed, in the United States, film was not even considered a medium of communication protected by the First Amendment until 1952.[16] By emphasizing the relationship of unusual cinematic forms to poetry (and also to painting, collage, and music), Art in Cinema, Cinema 16, and the network of film societies that imitated them were implicitly arguing for the kinds of attention and patience normally accorded to serious works of art.

While "poetic" remained relatively amorphous when used in connection with cinema, by the 1940s there were avant-garde films that revealed a more particular connection with poetry. Sometimes these films combined the earlier, more general sense of the filmmaker as a maker of "poetic" images with

15. Luis Buñuel, "Cinema as an Instrument of Poetry," in *An Unspeakable Betrayal: Selected Writings of Luis Buñuel* (Berkeley: University of California Press, 2000), 136.

16. The U.S. Supreme Court decided in *Burstyn v. Wilson,* 343 U.S. 495, that "expression by means of motion pictures is included within the free speech and free press guaranty of the First and Fourteenth Amendments." See Dawn P. Sova, *Forbidden Films* (New York: Checkmark, 2001), x–xiii for a brief review of the history of American film censorship.

sound tracks that included readings of particular poems. Willard Maas's *Geography of the Body* (1943), for example, is accompanied by the reading of a poem by the British poet George Barker, and Ian Hugo's *Bells of Atlantis* (1953) was based on *The House of Incest*, a prose poem by Anaïs Nin, who reads passages of it on the sound track. This combination of poetic texts and imagery has continued to be an option for filmmakers. James Broughton was both a prolific poet and an accomplished filmmaker. From *Mother's Day* (1949) on, his films reflect a poetic sensibility, and by the 1970s regularly included poetic voice-overs, often of previously published Broughton poems read by Broughton himself.[17] Examples include *This Is It* (1972), *High Kukus* (1973), *The Water Circle* (1975), and *Erogeny* (1975). *High Kukus* and *The Water Circle* are particularly effective; both use rather minimal visuals—a small pond reflecting sky and trees and birds; the surface of moving water, respectively—as an accompaniment to lovely, childlike, rather Blakeian verses read by Broughton. Each film evokes haiku (indeed, "High Kukus" is a play on the word) in its attempt to create meaning from deceptively simple, unpretentious combinations of visual observation and poetic statement.[18]

By the 1950s the idea that poetry and avant-garde film were closely related had become so commonplace that Cinema 16, then the most successful film society in North America, felt the need to offer a symposium titled "Poetry and the Film" for its membership.[19] On October 28, 1953, Amos

17. The early Broughton films were recognized as film poetry by other poets and filmmakers. In the catalogue description for *Four in the Afternoon* (1951), Broughton includes comments by both Willard Maas ("The best film poetry ever made") and Dylan Thomas ("Lovely and delicious, true cinematic poetry"). See *Canyon Cinema Film/Video Catalogue* 2000 (San Francisco: Canyon Cinema, 2000), 89.

Broughton's poetry, including the poems recited in *This Is It* and *The Water Circle*, is available in Broughton, *Packing Up for Paradise: Selected Poems, 1946–1996* (Santa Rosa, CA: Black Sparrow, 1977), 229, 187; "High Kukus" is available in Broughton, *A Long Undressing: Collected Poems, 1949–1969* (New York: Jargon Society, 1971), 176.

18. Probably no poetic form has had more resonance for independent filmmakers than the haiku. The mini-tradition of single-shot films that develops in the 1960s and 1970s (see "Putting All Your Eggs in One Basket: The Single-Shot Film" in this volume) owes a good deal to an awareness of the haiku form. Chick Strand's haiku-like *Kristallnacht* (1979) begins with a haiku by Yosa Buson.

19. The text of the first half of the "Poetry and the Film" symposium is reprinted in MacDonald, *Cinema 16*, 202–12. Deren's distinction there between "horizontal" and "vertical" meanings (see note 21, this chapter) made particular sense for avant-garde film during the 1940s and 1950s, and especially for her own work. Her most famous film, *Meshes of the Afternoon* (1943; a collaboration with her husband, Alexander Hammid), creates a dreamlike narrative in which the protagonist, played by Deren herself, functions within a world of seemingly symbolic objects that beg for interpretation. That is, the protagonist's record player, phone, kitchen knives, mirror are, on one level, realistic details *and* on another level, clues to the psychic disturbance that is expressed in the film's dream narrative. Without an interpretation of these details, the narrative itself seems indecipherable.

Vogel was host to Dylan Thomas, Arthur Miller, Maya Deren, Willard Maas, and the critic Parker Tyler, who discussed the relationship between poetry and film. That those coming to the discussion from the world of avant-garde film saw a clear relationship between film and poetry is obvious in Parker Tyler's opening directive to the participants: "On the one hand, there's the *theory* of poetry, its possibilities as such in the film medium, and on the other hand the *practice* of poetry, as concentrated in the avant-garde film."[20] Tyler, Maas, Deren, and Vogel seem to have been sure that there was such a thing as a "poetic film" or a "film poem." However, throughout the symposium discussions, Thomas and Miller—dignitaries from the literary world who were not familiar with avant-garde film—seem unclear as to how these two art forms are related, despite Deren's useful distinction between "horizontal" and "vertical" meaning in literature and in film: horizontal, being the forms of meaning made clear through the developing narrative of a work; and vertical, the multiple *layers* of meaning that accrue in forms of expression normally considered poetic.[21]

Poetry not only was pervasive in the thinking of the generation of avant-garde filmmakers who came to maturity in the 1940s and 1950s and of those programmers who cultivated audiences for alternative work but also was central for those chronicling this history. When P. Adams Sitney came to write his breakthrough *Visionary Film* (1974), he read the work of the particular filmmakers who were his focus—Maya Deren, Sidney Peterson, Kenneth Anger, Gregory Markopoulos, Stan Brakhage, and others—as a modern extension of British Romantic poetry, by virtue of their creation of expansive, imaginative visions of the place of poetry and the poet, in this case the filmmaker-poet, within modern society:

> The earliest American films discussed here were called "film poems" or "experimental films" when they were first seen. Both names, like all the subsequent ones, are inaccurate and limiting. Of the two, the term "film poem" has the advantage of underlining a useful analogy: the relationship of the type of film discussed in this book to the commercial narrative cinema is in many ways like that of poetry to fiction in our times.

20. MacDonald, *Cinema 16*, 202.

21. Deren's distinction between horizontal and vertical meaning: "what I called a 'horizontal' development is more or less of a narrative development, such as occurs in drama from action to action, and . . . a 'vertical' development such as occurs in poetry, is a part of plunging down or a construction that is based on the intent of the moment" (MacDonald, *Cinema 16*, 211); "in what is called a 'horizontal' development, the logic is a logic of actions. In a 'vertical' development, it is a logic of a central emotion or idea that attracts to itself even disparate images which contain that central core, which they have in common. This, to me, is the structure of poetry" (ibid., 208, 211).

> The film-makers in question, like poets, produce their work without financial reward, often making great personal sacrifices to do so. The films themselves will always have a more limited audience than commercial features because they are so much more demanding. The analogy is also useful in that it does not put a value on the films in question. Poetry is not by essence better than prose. . . .
>
> Just as the chief works of French film theory must be seen in the light of Cubist and Surrealist thought, and Soviet theory in the context of formalism and constructivism, the preoccupations of the American avant-garde film-makers coincide with those of our post-Romantic poets and Abstract Expressionist painters. Behind them lies a potent tradition of Romantic poetics.[22]

By the late 1960s and the early 1970s, filmmakers were less likely to think of themselves as film poets and their work as film poems even though Broughton and some others—Jonas Mekas is a particularly noteworthy instance—continued to incorporate their poetry into their films. There are a number of reasons for this. One of the more obvious is that once "foreign film" (especially the feature-length commercial films arriving from Italy, France, Sweden, Japan) and, to a lesser extent, avant-garde film had demonstrated to a substantial portion of the educated filmgoing audience that film *was* an art form rather than just a set of entertaining distractions, the designations "filmmaker" or "film artist" developed enough cultural cachet that most filmmakers, and most apologists for avant-garde film, no longer felt the need to argue cinema's artistic importance by referencing more established and more respected cultural forms.

In any case, regardless of whether they thought of themselves as "film poets," a good many filmmakers continued to see poetry as closely related to their work. Jonas Mekas was an established poet in Lithuanian before he left Lithuania, and he continued to write poetry in exile, first in a German displaced persons camp and then in the United States.[23] However, from the

22. P. Adams Sitney, *Visionary Film: The American Avant-Garde* (New York: Oxford University Press, 1974), vii–viii, ix. In 2002, Sitney published a revised, expanded version of *Visionary Film,* which provides a more extensive survey of the field, though with less emphasis on Romantic poetics.

Sitney's newest book, *Eyes Upside Down: Visionary Filmmakers and the Heritage of Emerson* (New York: Oxford University Press, 2008), uses Ralph Waldo Emerson's poetics as the basis for his approach to a panoply of American avant-garde filmmakers, including Robert Beavers, Stan Brakhage, Abigail Child, Hollis Frampton, Su Friedrich, Ernie Gehr, Ian Hugo, Jonas Mekas, Marie Menken, Andrew Noren, and Warren Sonbert.

23. Mekas's *There Is No Ithaca* (New York: Black Thistle Press, 1996) makes available-Mekas's *Idylls of Semeniskiai* (*Semeniškiy idilės*), written in Germany in 1947–48 before Mekas

moment he immigrated to the United States, Mekas was both literary poet and a film poet. At the beginning of *Lost Lost Lost* (1976), he explains in an intertitle that a week after arriving in New York, he and his brother Adolfas borrowed money and bought "their first Bolex"—as though a new continent required a new poetic medium. Within a few years, the Mekas brothers were making important contributions to independent cinema. Jonas Mekas has remained a prolific filmmaker, and throughout his career he has included poetry in his films, in the form of intertitles and spoken in voice-over (and it is not unusual to see a Mekas poem or poetic reminiscence in a film or art journal).

In the final reels of *Lost Lost Lost*, Mekas includes two suites of haiku, "Rabbit Shit Haikus" and "Fool's Haikus." "Rabbit Shit Haikus" includes fifty-six brief filmic moments, some of them silent single images, some of them combinations of imagery (often of Mekas himself in the Vermont countryside in winter) and brief, spoken poetic phrases or words. Later in the final reel of the film, there are thirteen "Fool's Haikus" filmed in Manhattan. These two sets of filmic haiku are lovely and inventive in their own right, and are fitting additions to a film that is "poetic" in all the senses mentioned earlier. They are also emblematic of Mekas's rebirth into the new, creative life that, in the final third of the film, replaces the longing for Lithuania he experiences in the first two reels of *Lost Lost Lost* (the Soviet Union made Lithuania off limits for Americans and for those who had left the country during World War II soon after the surrender) and concludes the dark night of the soul he experiences as he works to find a place for himself in New York.

Stan Brakhage yearned to be a poet and became the most prolific and influential of American avant-garde filmmakers, never ceasing to see his work in relation to modern poetry or to be aesthetically fed by his reading of poetry and by its formative influence on him: "I had thought I was a poet, and I had continued to think so into my early twenties when I was living with Robert Duncan in the middle of the San Francisco Beat poetry movement. I met Michael McClure and Kenneth Patchen and Jack Spicer and Robin Blaser, Kenneth Rexroth and Louis Zukofsky and began having a sense of what a poet really is. All this powerfully confirmed my poetic aspirations."[24]

---

came to the United States, and *Reminiscences* (*Reminiscensijos*), written in 1951–52 as Mekas was coming to terms with living in Brooklyn. Both collections are published both in the original Lithuanian and in a translation by Vyt Bakaitis.

24. Brakhage, in Scott MacDonald, *A Critical Cinema 4: Interviews with Independent Filmmakers* (Berkeley: University of California Press, 2005), 46. The most efficient access to writing about Brakhage's prolific career, both his own writing and that of critics and historians,

Hollis Frampton gave up his aspirations to be a poet, first to become a still photographer and subsequently a filmmaker, but continued to see Ezra Pound (whom he visited during the poet's hospitalization in Baltimore) as a major influence on his life and work. Two of Frampton's films—*Poetic Justice* (1972) and *Gloria!* (1979)—use visual text in ways closely related to poetry. *Poetic Justice* is a film of a 240-page screenplay, divided into four tableaux, filmed one page at a time for a few seconds per page; the third tableau and Frampton's propositions about his maternal grandmother in *Gloria!* take a form closely related to catalogue poems like Whitman's *Song of Myself*, no. 6 ("What is the grass?") and Wallace Stevens's "Thirteen Ways of Looking at a Blackbird."

During the 1970s both Abigail Child and Henry Hills became fascinated with L=A=N=G=U=A=G=E P=O=E=T=R=Y and the L=A=N=G=U=A=G=E P=O=E=T=S—a diverse group of poets and language artists who worked at radically defamiliarizing conventional reading habits. Child's and Hills's films often revealed close relationships with language poetry: see, for example, Child's *Ornamentals* (1979) and *Mutiny* (1983) and Hills's *Kino Da!* (1981) and *Money* (1985). As editors of Canyon Cinema's publication, the *Cinemanews*, during its final years, Hills and Child championed a variety of language experiments, including their own.

The idea that the "film poem" constitutes a particular field continued to have adherents long after most avant-garde filmmakers no longer saw themselves as film poets. Herman Berlandt organized the first Poetry-Film Festival in Bolinas, California, in 1975, for reasons he makes clear in a letter published in the January–February 1977 issue of the *Cinemanews:*

> I've been peculiarly obsessed with the concept of the poetry-film for a long time. I feel that its magic has hardly been made use of technically, aesthetically or conceptually. For more than twenty years I responded to my environment and inner troubles by reaching for a pencil to transform my vision into words. For a lazy, inept, borderline schizophrenic like myself, written poetry was the next best thing to dreaming. But, when I started attending readings and began listening to my colleagues, I became aware

---

is the website of Fred Camper: www.fredcamper.com/Brakhage. Brakhage often talked about poetry and its relation to his filmmaking. See, e.g., "Poetry and Film," an edited transcription of a lecture recorded at the University of North Carolina, Chapel Hill, on March 22, 1977, reprinted in Bruce R. McPherson, ed., *Essential Brakhage: Selected Writings on Filmmaking by Stan Brakhage* (Kingston, NY: Documentext, 2001), 174–91.

In "A Crucible of Document: The Sequence Films of Stan Brakhage, 1968–1984" (Ph.D. diss., New York University, 1999), Marie Nesthus explores the ways in which Brakhage's series films make use of his understanding of the history of modern and modernist poetry.

> of the incredible isolation that printed and narrated poetry had suffered. Too many poets mumbled and bungled a good poem through a poor reading. Those who remained active poets tended to become self-centered, morose and bitter, not simply in reaction to the karma of human existence, but because of their failure to communicate their feelings and thoughts to their fellow mortals. Those who were published were often infected with delusions of self-importance through incestuous bonds with other "recognized" poets and a small snobbish public. It occurred to me that it was too easy to abide with and re-enforce the sick and very romantic tradition of the poor struggling and troubled poet. The popular image of the poet had become far more masochist than that of the composer, the painter or the filmmaker.
>
> I made a very personal decision to change that state of affairs. The medium itself must become better "show business," more interesting "theatrically." New forms of presentation must be found for talented poets. Why not publish in film form rather than in esoteric quarterlies?[25]

The Poetry-Film Festival was a fixture in the Bay Area for seventeen years.

Poetry continues to be a significant influence on avant-garde film. Quite recently I learned during interviews with Nathaniel Dorsky, Abigail Child, and Phil Solomon that all three see the work of John Ashbery as inspira-

25. Berlandt's essay is reprinted in Scott MacDonald, *Canyon Cinema: The Life and Times of an Independent Film Distributor* (Berkeley: University of California Press, 2008), 231. I never attended the Poetry-Film Festival, but Berlandt is certainly a subject for further research. His commitment to using film as a means of "publishing" poetry and of developing a more public community around poetry now seems, on one hand, a means of carrying on the oral tradition of poetry (a late manifestation of the Beats, perhaps) and, on the other hand, prescient of such recent developments as rap and poetry raves.

In a flyer designed for the Poetry-Film Festival Workshop, held in conjunction with the twelfth Poetry-Film Festival in December 1987, Berlandt lists the "Three Basic Elements in Poetry-Films": "I. POETRY: lettered or spoken"; "II: IMAGES: stills, moving or animated, abstract or recognizable"; and "III: SOUNDS: music, environmental sounds (nature, street, machinery), deliberate beats for special emphasis or rhythms." This listing would seem to accommodate nearly all of what is called avant-garde film.

In "Words and Images in the Poetry-Film," included in Dorland and Wees, eds., *Words and Moving Images*, William C. Wees quotes another Berlandt statement about the poetry-film: a poetry-film must incorporate "a verbal poetic statement in narrated or captioned form," and defines four types of poetry-film: the first is "the poem 'as seen by' the filmmaker. In other words, the poem already exists, and in addition to providing the words for the film's soundtrack, was the originating idea for the film, a kind of 'first treatment,' that may also become the film's scenario and even its 'shooting script.'" The second type "reverses that relationship: the film comes first—in conception and perhaps even in execution—and then the filmmaker finds a poem that suits the film's images." Wees considers *Waterworx (A Clear Day and No Memories)* an instance of this second type. The third type "is one in which the film—either completed or in preparation—leads to the writing of a poem which is then incorporated into the film" (Wees uses Hancox's *Beach Events* as an instance, along with *The River, Le sang d'un poète,* and *Geography of the Body*). See Wees, "Words and Images in the Poetry-Film," 11.

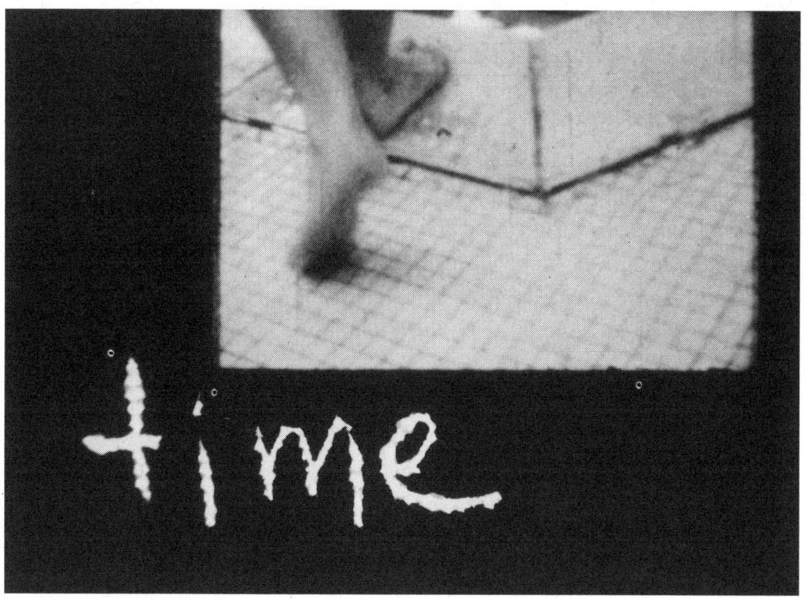

Word scratched into the emulsion in Su Friedrich's *Gently Down the Stream* (1981). Courtesy Su Friedrich.

tional and some of their own films as closely related to his poetry.[26] Each of these filmmakers seems to take somewhat different things from Ashbery, though all share an approach to editing that often results in sequences during which successive shots are not related by any apparent narrative logic but accumulate impact through subtle, mysterious, surprising changes in subject and tone, a quality common in Ashbery's work. And there continue to be instances where filmmakers use their own poetic texts or the poetic texts of others as central dimensions of films. Noteworthy examples are *Gently Down the Stream* (1981) by Su Friedrich, *Tongues Untied* (1989) by Marlon Riggs, and David Gatten in his *Secret History of the Dividing Line* project.

26. See Scott MacDonald, *A Critical Cinema 5*, 94–95, 210–11. Child remarked on her admiration for Ashbery in conversation with me. Child has been a practicing poet for years and uses analogous strategies for organizing her poems and her films. And she thinks of poets as a primary audience for her work: "Poets—people who are used to speed, density, complication, ambiguity— *they've* always been an enthusiastic and comprehending audience." See my interview with Child in Scott MacDonald, *A Critical Cinema 4*, 221. Child's poetry collections include *A Motive for Mayhem* (Hartford, CT: Potes and Poets, 1989), *Mob* (Oakland, CA: O Press, 1994), and *Scatter Matrix* (New York: Roof Books, 1996). See also Child, *This Is Called Moving: A Critical Poetics of Film* (Tuscaloosa: University of Alabama Press, 2005).

For *Gently Down the Stream,* the film that, as P. Adams Sitney has said, marked "her maturity as a filmmaker," Friedrich scratched a series of texts—edited versions of dreams recorded in a dream diary—word by word into the film emulsion so that the texts themselves become the visual foreground and the photographed imagery the background of a psychodrama that expresses the filmmaker's internal struggle with the conflict between her Roman Catholic background and her lesbianism.[27] I say Friedrich's words are the "foreground," since words have particular power in film, especially words represented visually. If a particular shot in a film includes both photographic imagery and visual text, the tendency is to read the text first; as Hollis Frampton once said, "Once we can read, and a word is put before us, we cannot not read it."[28] Friedrich's texts are arranged within *Gently Down the Stream* with considerable attention to their visual spacing and temporal rhythm; it is difficult not to see the texts as a poem.[29] The experience of watching *Gently Down the Stream* has something of the impact of a public reading, though in this instance, we do the "listening" *and* the reading.

In *Tongues Untied,* Marlon Riggs was determined to reveal "all the poetry that was coming out by black gay men"[30] as a crucial component of his aggressive response to the history of the repression and suppression of African American homosexuality within American society. Riggs's controversial film gives voice to a range of openly gay black men in a performance-oriented, confrontational form that is full of visual and auditory performances of poetic texts (see section 6 of "Desegregating Film History: Avant-Garde Film and Race at the Robert Flaherty Seminar, and Beyond" in this collection, for a more substantial discussion of Riggs's film).[31]

Finally, David Gatten takes the final section of the poet Susan Howe's *Frame Structures* (1996), "Secret History of the Dividing Line" (1978), as a structural model for a cycle of films focusing on the life, writings, and personal life of William Byrd II of colonial Virginia. Byrd's *History of the Dividing Line* (1841), which chronicles his experiences drawing the boundary line between Virginia and North Carolina, is considered one of the forma-

27. Sitney provides a thorough reading of *Gently Down the Stream* in *Eyes Upside Down,* 298–304.

See note 70 in "Desegregating Film History" in this collection for a definition of psychodrama.

28. Frampton, in Scott MacDonald, *A Critical Cinema,* 49.

29. A small, hand-made book called *Gently Down the Stream* that presents the texts, arranged as poetry and illustrated with stills from the film, was self-published by Friedrich in 1982.

30. Chuck Kleinhans and Julia Lesage, "Interview with Marlon Riggs: Listening to the Heartbeat," *Jump Cut* 36 (1991): 119.

31. When *Tongues Untied* was broadcast on television in 1991, it created considerable controversy. See p. 68 for details.

tive American nature writings. (For details about Gatten's project, see the interview with Gatten in this collection.)

While the intersection of poetry and cinema could (and should!) sustain a book-length exploration, the particular focus of this essay is three underappreciated, relatively recent films, which are distinct from most all the combinations of poetry and film I have described (except for several of the Broughton films). Each makes available to an audience a previously published poem or set of poems in a new, cinematic form; and each makes the presentation of the poems, which are included in their entirety, the foreground of the film experience: that is, these films do not *adapt* the poems (revise them for use in a new context), they deliver the original words in their original senses, as precisely as possible, to new audiences through a different medium. They are, in other words, closer to new *editions* than to adaptations.[32] *Waterworx (A Clear Day and No Memories)* (1982) by the Canadian Rick Hancox and *nebel* (2000) by the German Matthias Müller make available to viewers poems by recognized poets: specifically, Wallace Stevens's "A Clear Day and No Memories" and Ernst Jandl's *gedichte an die kindheit* ("Poems to Childhood"). Canadian Clive Holden's *Trains of Winnipeg—14 Film Poems* recycles Holden's own poems. The "Trains of Winnipeg" project began as a website, then produced a CD of Holden reading his poetry, followed by a book of thirty-eight poems, *Trains of Winnipeg*;[33] by the 35mm feature film *Trains of Winnipeg—14 Film Poems*; and, finally, by a DVD of the film.

The idea of using cinema as a means of providing poetry with a new form of public life still seems unusual enough, and these recent films engaging enough, to deserve more detailed discussion. My goal here is not to provide anything like an exhaustive exploration of the films discussed, or to deal with the many theoretical issues raised by the translation of a work of literature into a work of cinema.[34] Rather, I hope to alert readers to three particularly accomplished contributions to the recent history of avant-garde film, in the

32. I do not mean to split hairs here. Cinema has a long history of adapting literary texts to its own uses and, by doing so, creating endless debate about whether this or that film was true to the original story or novel adapted by the filmmaker. Certainly, the three films I discuss provide new contexts for the poems they "republish," and these new contexts may create somewhat different readings of the poems for readers/viewers—any change in context tends to do this. But there seems a firm commitment on the part of all three filmmakers to the original poetic texts, which are used not as raw material but as finished works, each with its own integrity. In this sense, I see the films as closer to new editions of the poems than as adaptations of them.

33. Clive Holden, *Trains of Winnipeg* (Montreal: DC Books, 2002).

34. For a discussion of the history of attempts to understand the practice of adapting literature to the screen and for a remarkable new approach to the issue of adaptation, see Kamilla Elliott, *Rethinking the Novel/Film Debate* (Cambridge: Cambridge University Press, 2003).

hope that at least some readers will be drawn toward the three films I discuss and to the remarkable history of which they are a part. Not only are these films interesting and unusual, and quite relevant to the study of poetry, but my experience tells me that they can be of considerable use in college courses where the relationship of poetry and the other arts is a topic.

FILM AS EDITION: *WATERWORX (A CLEAR DAY AND NO MEMORIES)* AND *NEBEL*

Between 1969 and 1994, Rick Hancox made several films that explore the cinematic possibilities of poetry and other forms of visual text.[35] Of these, the most interesting is *Waterworx (A Clear Day and No Memories)*. Its straightforward presentation of a brief but powerful poem by a well-known poet within a context that is quite personal to the filmmaker continues to seem, after a quarter century, both novel and powerful. Like so many accomplished but unconventional films, *Waterworx* has not received much attention, either from programmers or from critics. This lack of attention belies not only the film's quality but its value for those who teach poetry in general and the work of Wallace Stevens in particular.

"A Clear Day and No Memories" is not particularly well known and is brief enough to reprint here:

No soldiers in the scenery,
No thoughts of people now dead,
As they were fifty years ago,
Young and living in a live air,
Young and walking in the sunshine,
Bending in blue dresses to touch something,
Today the mind is not part of the weather.

Today the air is clear of everything.
It has no knowledge except of nothingness
And it flows over us without meanings,

35. In the *Canyon Cinema Film/Video Catalogue 2000*, Hancox explains that he sees *Waterworx, Landfall* (1983), and *Beach Events* (1984) as a trilogy "of landscape/poetry films" (214), each of which has an autobiographical dimension: *Waterworx (A Clear Day and No Memories)* was shot near his grandmother's home, and the other two films, at his family home on Prince Edward Island. *Landfall* combines the poetry of D. G. Jones, which we hear read and see phrases of on-screen (the on-screen words and phrases move in and out of the frame and around the screen like animated characters), superimposed over images of landscape. *Beach Events* combines a poem by Hancox himself with imagery recorded on a beach—feet making footprints, a crab, mussel beds—in a more formal way: poetic lines are presented, in a cursive typeface, at the bottom center of the frame. While *Waterworx (A Clear Day and No Memories)* is the most interesting of the three films, the other two are capably filmed and

As if none of us had ever been here before
And are not now: in this shallow spectacle,
This invisible activity, this sense.[36]

Stevens's poem is rich with subtle paradox. The speaker's list of the memories he is *not* having—soldiers in the scenery; people, now dead, as they were fifty years ago; and young women in blue dresses bending to touch something—*is,* of course, a list of memories: he cannot name these people and moments without remembering them, and without in fact creating in us a memory of them. And yet, there is another sense in which his statement may be true, for even if he *is* having thoughts about these past moments, he seems not to be in pain about them, or at least not in a depth and immediacy of pain that we might assume has been an inevitable part of these (seemingly wartime) memories, at least until this "clear day." Whatever the speaker has lost and has felt the loss of, "Today the mind is not part of the weather": that is, he seems to be able to be conscious of the weather, of being alive in a particular moment, without the mind's projection of painful memories into this moment.

"Today the air is clear of everything. It has no knowledge except of nothingness" adds a further dimension to our sense of the speaker's experience. Stevens's use of "nothingness" recalls the pun on "nothing" in Hemingway's "A Clean, Well-Lighted Place": in the atmosphere "today" there is, at least at first glance, *nothing* of the speaker's projected awareness of the past, or of the speaker's previous pain; but the air *does* seem full of an existential nothingness, a feeling that nothing any longer makes sense, or at least that nothing makes the kind of sense it may have seemed to make in the past. It is as if the very idea of recovering from the losses implicit in the speaker's memories, his no longer openly feeling the pain of these losses, renders life meaningless and this clear day, a "shallow spectacle." The particular "invisible activity" of thinking about what is no longer—or what is,

edited and, with *Waterworx,* do chart a range of the possibilities of visual text, particularly poetic text, within the film image. The particular success of *Waterworx,* in my view, is Hancox's decision to use his filmmaking to deliver the Stevens poem to us as directly as possible, rather than to use film as a way of interacting with the text of the poem, as he does in the other two instances.

36. "A Clear Day and No Memories" was originally published with three other poems in "Four Poems," *Sewanee Review* 63, no. 1 (Winter 1955): 72–74; subsequently, it was included in Wallace Stevens, *Opus Posthumous,* ed. Samuel French Marse (New York: Knopf, 1957); in Wallace Stevens, *Poems by Wallace Stevens* (New York: Vintage, 1959); and in Wallace Stevens, *The Palm at the End of the Mind,* ed. Holly Stevens (New York: Knopf, 1971). This item is reproduced by permission of the Huntington Library, San Marino, California (WAS 4122).

for this *unusual* moment (unusual enough to be the subject of the speaker's reverie), no longer causing pain—is a "sense" of things that is on one hand *sensible* (it is usually sensible to move past the pain of loss) and, at the same time, *senseless,* since forgetting what one has lost, and the concomitant surrender to meaninglessness and nothingness, seems to create a psychic state where nothing is as it seems and everything is empty.

Stevens's use of "us" suggests further complexities. The air "today" flows over "us" without meanings, "as if none of *us* had ever been here before," revealing that the speaker is not "here" alone (wherever he is). But whoever else we assume is with him, the use of "us" includes the reader: even if we have not been wherever the speaker is, we *are* here now, "today," *here* reading Stevens's poem (and this speaker's psyche) once again, and over and over as we attempt to come to a clear sense of "A Clear Day and No Memories," remembering how we understood it before and gaining fresh insights, or at least forming additional conjectures, *now.*[37]

Obviously, Wallace Stevens does not need Rick Hancox to re-present his poem: "A Clear Day and No Memories" is engaging, complex (I have only begun to unpack the poem), complete, and powerful in its own right. And yet, Hancox's presentation of the Stevens poem not only brings a relatively obscure poem to a new audience but also visualizes it in a manner that simultaneously confirms its complex implications and includes it within a cinematic work that has its own integrity and power.[38] *Waterworx (A Clear Day and No Memories)* begins with the poem's title, in computer-generated text (throughout the film, the text is all in capitals), which fades out.[39] Unless one already knows the Stevens poem, there is no way to know that this first text is a title, especially since it is not until the second half of the film that the poem itself is presented. This opening text is followed by eighteen shots of a large waterworks near a body of water, accompanied by what seems to be the sound of machinery operating behind the waterworks walls. The first shot of the waterworks reveals the corner of a building with well-kept

37. "A Clear Day and No Memories" has not attracted criticism. Harold Bloom does mention the poem, though Bloom's reading of the line "Today the mind is not part of the weather" suggests that he does not see it as ironic: "In the beautiful poem of the year before, *A Clear Day and No Memories,* he finally had said, 'Today the mind is not part of the weather.' But until then, he mixed mind and weather, not wanting to know how much of the weather came from the light of his own mind, the breath of his own spirit." Bloom, *Wallace Stevens: The Poems of Our Climate* (Ithaca, NY: Cornell University Press, 1977), 156.

38. *Waterworx (A Clear Day and No Memories)* won first prize at the eighth Poetry-Film Festival, held on December 3–4, 1983.

39. Hancox generated the text on a VAX 11/780 and filmed directly off the terminal that appears at the end of the film. See Hancox, "Engaging Poetry with Film: A Personal Statement," in Dorland and Wees, eds., *Words and Moving Images,* 100.

The waterworks in Rick Hancox's *Waterworx (A Clear Day and No Memories)* (1982). Courtesy Rick Hancox.

grounds visible to the right of the building. It is a twenty-one-second still shot, the only still shot of the eighteen shots in the waterworks sequence; the other seventeen are filmed with a camera moving horizontally or forward in stable tracking shots, presenting various views of the waterworks installation.[40] The pacing of the sequence is quite serene, matching the lack of apparent activity at the waterworks. Until the final shot, no person is visible, and nothing is moving except apparently the wind.

The sequence of the waterworks is accompanied by what seems to be the persistent hum of machinery behind the walls and the sound of wind. We also hear, first, with the opening image of the waterworks, some children playing in the distance and then, during the remainder of the waterworks shots, a radio playing in the distance; through static, we can make out bits of a romantic song sung by a woman, a nostalgic song the words of which are for the most part inaudible, though we can make out the phrases "it's only the moon again" and "I'll never forget." In fact, we are hearing Vera Lynn, "England's Sweetheart" during World War II, singing "White Cliffs of Dover";

40. Hancox shot his dolly shots in slight slow motion, thirty-two frames per second, from an automobile (he had let twenty pounds of air out of each tire to ensure smoothness). Phone conversation with author, September 2, 2004.

Lynn was the host of the BBC radio program *Sincerely Yours,* immensely popular with British overseas servicemen. The song becomes audible as the camera begins to move and remains audible until the final shot, when the camera moves toward a railing by a walk overlooking Lake Ontario and then stops.

Immediately after the conclusion of the two-minute ten-second waterworks sequence, it is repeated: we see the exact same sequence of shots, accompanied by the hum of machinery and the radio static and song, heard exactly as before (we do not hear the sound of the children playing during the first shot, or the wind). This time, the poem is presented, one line at a time, in a computer text that, after the first line of the Stevens poem, scrolls across the screen from left to right. Each line disappears as it fades out.[41] The visual arrangement of the lines of Stevens's poem is altered—lines 6, 7, 9, 10, 11, and 12 are presented as two lines each—though the overall timing of Hancox's presentation approximates the experience of reading the poem. At the conclusion of the repetition of the waterworks sequence, there is a dissolve (just after we read "THIS INVISIBLE ACTIVITY") to a computer terminal. There is a momentary refocusing of the camera, and we can see, in this final, still shot, the reflection of the camera and the filmmaker in the monitor, along with, superimposed, "THIS SENSE."

In fact, Hancox's project began not with Stevens's poem but with the images of the water filtration plant we see in the film, which were shot and edited before Hancox decided to use "A Clear Day and No Memories."[42] The Harris Water Filtration Plant on Queen Street East in Toronto overlooking Lake Ontario was a landmark in the neighborhood where Hancox was born and where he continued to visit his grandmother once the family moved west. He recalls: "As a child, I was always told, 'Don't go down there by yourself!' My mother had wheeled me around there in the pram when I was a baby; she was a war bride who had emigrated from England, and I guess she looked out over this vast lake and imagined she was looking back home. She was very lonely. So it's a place that goes back to my infancy."[43] Hancox had been moved by Stevens's essay "The Noble Rider and the Sound of Words," which argues that the poetic imagination protects the idea of nobility from the pressure of reality, and he decided to use "A

41. I can find no clear rule as to when Hancox uses the fade-out versus the simple disappearance of the text. I assume the choices had to do with his sense of how Stevens's poem should be read.

42. See Hancox, "Engaging Poetry with Film," 99–100.

43. Hancox, in phone conversation with author, September 2, 2004.

Clear Day and No Memories" within his film, "since it conceptualized a particular relation between time and memory I had been wrestling with in the film."[44]

Hancox has described the structure of *Waterworx (A Clear Day and No Memories)* as "modeled on human memory processing, with the first half, which has no text, permitting the viewer to record a strong, eidetic-like image directly, via the senses; the second half is actually a repeat of the first, emulating recollection, with the soundtrack attenuated and the image cluttered now by the superimposed poetic text, forcing its way through the intellect."[45] On the most obvious level, this organization evokes dimensions of Stevens's poem. As we read "A Clear Day and No Memories" in the film, line by line, we are, as Hancox suggests, not only making sense of Stevens's words and the speaker's sense of things but also reseeing, *remembering,* the images of the waterworks and the song. Of course, once again, there is nothing in this scenery—certainly no soldiers—and, as in the poem, the day is clear. The "spectacle" of the film is "shallow"—nothing happens, and seeing the waterworks sequence the second time adds nothing except our awareness that we are remembering, and remembering nothing much, certainly nothing that causes us pain—though the combination of the unpopulated spaces and distant sounds does evoke a feeling of emptiness, a feeling of distance from human interaction, and, in conjunction with the music on the sound track, a sense of nostalgia. The intersection of the experiences of poem and film is particularly emphatic at the line "As if none of us had ever been here before," since the viewer can hardly fail to realize that "we" *have* been *here*—at the railing of the walk overlooking Lake Ontario—before, regardless of who the "us" in Stevens's poem refers to.

The dissolve to the computer screen and the reflection of filmmaker and camera doubles the implications of *this* shallow spectacle, *this* invisible activity, *this* sense—since "this" now refers simultaneously to the speaker's remembering/nonremembering, the poet's representation of it, the filmmaker's activity in communicating his sense of the Stevens poem to us, and our understanding of the finished film. It is also significant that we are looking at a computer screen (and, throughout the second half of the film, at a computer-generated text that is typed presumably, and actually, on the com-

44. See Hancox, "Engaging Poetry with Film," 100–101. Stevens's essay was published in *The Necessary Angel: Essays on Reality and the Imagination* (New York: Vintage, 1951), 1–36.

45. See Hancox, "Engaging Poetry with Film," 101.

Computer screen with filmmaker visible in reflection, and final text, from Rick Hancox's *Waterworx (A Clear Day and No Memories)* (1982). Courtesy Rick Hancox.

puter we see), which in 1982 was not yet a conventional film image. According to Hancox, "The idea of using the artificial memory of a computer to generate poetry about the absence of memory, is consistent with the kind of complex imagery central to Wallace Stevens' poem."[46] The film's concluding "This sense" seems at first to refer specifically to the new computer technology as confirming the distance between the present and the past. Of course, the "sense" of the computer screen is no more an answer to the complexity of passion and of loss, of pain, of memory than is the speaker's reverie or the poet's representation of it.

Hancox has said that his inclusion of Stevens's "A Clear Day and No Memories" in *Waterworx* was in part a formal decision: "The film was stalled. The nostalgic imagery was simply available too readily to the senses; the viewer was lured into consuming the image, lured into an illusionary sense of possession. . . . Something was needed to block penetration into the image—something flat across the screen, to draw attention instead to a kind of transparent partition, made apparent through the use of superimposed text, preferably contrary in style to the background image."[47] Nevertheless, once he had decided to use a poetic text, and "A Clear Day and No Memories" in particular, Hancox's care in presenting Stevens's work in such a way that the poem can be read, understood, and enjoyed for itself, even within a context that has powerful personal implications for Hancox, allows *Waterworx* to achieve something that seems quite unusual. By delivering Stevens's original text to a new set of readers within a new, cinematic context, Hancox has done the work of a creative editor: essentially, *Waterworx* provides the opportunity for a new kind of public "reading" of Stevens's poem, within the experience of a personal film. Even the fact that the title *Waterworx* is not present at the beginning of the film (or, for that matter, at the end), and that the film privileges *Stevens's* title as its opening text, confirms Hancox's respect for the poem he delivers to us and suggests that

46. Ibid., 100.
47. Ibid., 99–100.

the way in which what we read often comes to be as "personal" for us as our memories of our firsthand experiences.[48]

Matthias Müller's *nebel* was, in some ways, a quite different project from *Waterworx (A Clear Day and No Memories)*. The film came about when Müller agreed to contribute to what was planned as a cinematic homage, "an episodic film about Ernst Jandl's work, containing different filmmakers' contributions."[49] While the larger homage to the widely known Austrian experimental poet fell through, Müller finished *his* homage, which premiered at the Vienna Film Festival in 2000 shortly after Jandl's death.[50] Originally Jandl, who was widely known as a performer of poetry and for his innovations in the "sound poem," was to read his *gedichte an die kindheit* in *nebel*, but in the finished film, the reading is by Ernst-August Schepmann. According to Müller, although Jandl is a recognized figure in Europe, the cycle of poems called *gedichte an die kindheit* was not widely known, despite the accomplishment of the work. "As I read these poems, my own images were immediately released," Müller remembers; as a result, he decided to work with this particular set of poems.[51] Further, until *nebel, ge-*

48. Hancox had originally planned to use the Stevens title as the title of his film but thought better of it and in the end decided on "Waterworx." He explained his unusual spelling of "waterworks" this way: "In my own mind, while the film is in fact shot at a waterworks, the reason for the 'X' is to signify how its original purpose seems crossed out by its stronger metaphoric presence." Phone conversation with author, September 2, 2004.

49. Müller, in Scott MacDonald, *A Critical Cinema 5*, 301.

50. Ernst Jandl (1925–2000) is well known for a wide range of experimental poetic forms. According to Sharon K. Hall, "Although he is little known to the public, Austrian poet and dramatist Ernst Jandl is regarded by critics as one of the most prominent and influential figures in German avant-garde literature. His career, which has spanned over thirty years [Jandl died in 2000], is marked by tireless linguistic invention and experimentation. Jandl has been linked to the school of 'concrete poetry,' which emphasizes the acoustic and visual properties of words rather than their representational qualities. He has explored a variety of styles but is best known for his *Lautgedichte*, or sound poems, which he has performed in public, preserved on recordings, and published in numerous collections." See Hall, *Contemporary Literary Criticism Yearbook 1984* (Detroit, MI: Gale, 1984), 194.

51. Müller, in MacDonald, *A Critical Cinema 5*, 301. In *The Oxford Companion to German Literature*, 3rd ed. (Oxford: Oxford University Press, 1997), the editors, Mary and Henry Garland, mention *gedichte an die kindheit* as an example of what in the collection *der gelbe hund* (1980) was an experiment with "'infantile language' (verkindlichte sprache)": "The volume [*der gelbe hund*] expresses oppressive resignation, a preoccupation with ageing and death; writing has become a 'duty' ('was ein gedichte ist'), a means of survival in an existential crisis in which the lyrical 'I' thinly disguises personal despair ('von sinnen')" (423). Sharon K. Hall (in *Contemporary Literary Criticism Yearbook 1984*, 194) confirms this estimate: "The poems in *Die Bearbeitung der Mütze* (1978) and *Der gelbe Hund* (1980) are dark and self-analytical, revealing Jandl's profound depression and mounting fear of old age and creative decline. There are fewer of his characteristic sound and visual experiments, and a striking

dichte an die kindheit had not been translated into English; Peter Waugh provided Müller with the translation he used in his subtitles.

Like Rick Hancox, Matthias Müller is considered an avant-garde filmmaker, though his means are usually quite different from Hancox's. Müller's early films, shot on Super-8mm, are sensuous, diaristic evocations of complex, sometimes disturbed psychic states. More recently Müller has made a name for himself as one of the cinema's premier "recyclers"—that is, many of his films are made by imaginatively recycling material from earlier works (his own films, films recorded off of television, old home movies, etc.).[52] In one sense, the *nebel* project was unusual for Müller. Though many of his films have evocative voice-overs and sometimes include bits of text photographed from books, he had never made a film dedicated to presenting a poet's work. But, in another sense, *nebel* is a typical Müller film. Not only does *nebel* "recycle" the entirety of Jandl's *gedichte an die kindheit,* but the visual imagery Müller uses to accompany the Jandl poems is, in many cases, borrowed from diverse filmic sources: *nebel* includes at least two shots from *The Wizard of Oz* (1939), for example, and a number of passages from home movies made by Müller's father when Müller was a child.

The Jandl poems, at least in translation (I do not read German), are deceptively simple, easy to read but full of subtle humor, irony, and mystery. The title poem for the series, or really, the second of two poems in the collection called "der nebel," gives a clear sense of Jandl's method:

nebel (mist) is leben (life),	der nebel ist das leben,
if you start from the end.	wenn man es von hinten beginnt
everyone wants to do that at times,	das möchte manchmal jeder,
to become a child again,	zu werden noch ein kind
I'd like to, more and more,	ich möchte es immer mehr,
the older I get,	je älter ich werde,
and the closer and closer I get	und komme doch immer näher
to my mother the earth,	meiner mutter der erde
which might also mean:	was auch heißen kann;
my mother under the earth.	meiner mutter in der erde.[53]

new stylistic device is his use of a reduced language similar to that spoken by children or foreign workers."

52. For the most extensive discussions of Müller's work, see Karen Becker, ed., *Matthias Müller/Album: Film, Video, Photography* (Berlin: Neuer Berliner Kunstverein, 2004); and Stefanie Schulte Strathaus, ed., *The Memo Book: Filme, Videos und Installationen von Matthias Müller = Films, Videos, and Installations by Matthias Müller* (Berlin: Vorwerk 8, 2005).

53. *gedichte an die kindheit* is included in Ernst Jandl, *Gesammelte Werke,* vol. 2, edited by Klaus Siblewski (Darmstadt: Luchterhand, 1985), 346–50.

What begins as a straightforward statement of our desire, from time to time, to move against the flow of time, to become children again (this reverse movement is subtly dramatized by the fact that "nebel" is "leben" in reverse), takes on a somewhat macabre tone, even a humorously macabre tone, from the final lines. While the adult might dream of returning to childhood and the security and protection of the mother, the reality is that we *are* relentlessly moving forward to our future in Mother Earth, and into the same earth as the mother we long for is buried in. We *will* be reunited, but not in the sense we dream about—though there is a kind of security in this reunification too. The reality of what happens after death—whether, as Jandl dearly hopes in "the soul shepherd," the first poem in *gedichte an die kindheit,* "we return at death to somewhere else / to this one great soul body, to this immortal joy"—is lost in the mist. We *will* be reunited *under* the earth with our mothers, but whether any further form of reunification will occur, we cannot know. Indeed, the closer to the end we come, and the hungrier we may grow for some transcendent reunification, the more "in the mist" we can feel: as Jandl suggests in the first "der nebel," "over the distant things . . . [mist] lays itself down thickly. / I can't see them / and often don't know/if they're really there at all."

Müller's approach to presenting the poems in Jandl's *gedichte an die kindheit* is reasonably consistent throughout *nebel* and, since there is no space for a thorough exploration of his film, I'll use his version of the second "der nebel" to suggest the nature of this approach. Of course, since my experience of *nebel* is with the English version of the film, which translates the narrator's reading into visual text (there is also a version without the visual text for German-speaking audiences), the translated lines of Jandl's poem tend to function as the visual foreground of the film, and the photographed images, the background—the cinematic *interpretation* of what is read. Of course, even in the German version, the audience's attention would primarily be devoted to hearing the reading of the poems, and the visual imagery would be seen in relation to that reading. The narrator's tone *is* consistently a part of our understanding of what we read: Schepmann's reading is full of humor and wit—in a sense, the opposite of Hancox's presentation of the Stevens poem by means of the neutral, deadpan computer text. And the imagery Müller uses to accompany the Jandl poems is far more diverse and expressionistic than the imagery used in *Waterworx:* there are many shots, and the camera is generally handheld in an informal manner. The result is a very different film experience of a "republished" poetic text. Nevertheless, Müller's method is as fully appropriate for *gedichte an die kindheit* as Hancox's imagery is for the Stevens poem.

Ball in Matthias Müller's *nebel* (2000). Courtesy Matthias Müller.

The first visuals we see during "der nebel" are shots from an old regular-8mm color home movie of a young boy and his mother playing ball at a beach. This home-movie material is followed by an image of a ball flying through the air, across the film frame, back and forth; after a moment, we realize that while we are seeing the ball fly forward, from left to right, when it flies from right to left, we are actually seeing the original shot in reverse. That we are seeing alternating forward and reverse motion is confirmed by the sound track: the tape of the music, composed for *nebel* by Claus van Bebber, is played forward and in reverse in time to the movement of the ball. When we get to the end of the poem, and to the line "which might also mean: my mother under the earth," the image darkens and we see a brown-tinted image of a ball lying on the muddy ground among puddles, then a fade to black. The music fades out just before the final line of the poem.

The visual images used for "der nebel" function on several levels. Most obviously, within the context of Jandl's short poem, the use of home movies of a child and his mother visualizes our periodic yearning "to become a child again," and the increasingly frequent desire to reverse the flow of time is imaged in the forward and reverse of the ball and the sound. That is, Müller provides a clearly appropriate visual accompaniment to the Jandl poem and a metaphor for the essential hunger it expresses. More subtly, the fact that we are seeing what are clearly *old* home movies—the color has faded and there are scratches in the emulsion; the surface of the old movies has decayed—of *early childhood* is a way of combining the new and the old or, more precisely, of creating a cinematic emblem of the hopeless irony of our desire to return to a past that is itself in a state of decay.

A third level of suggestion—one not self-evident within Müller's version of "der nebel" from the words, imagery, and sound—is available to those who know Müller's other films, in the same way that Jandl's rumination on childhood must be more fully evocative for anyone who is familiar with the evolution of his career. The home movies we see in "der nebel," and throughout *nebel,* were made by Müller's father, who died when Müller was a child. In fact, Müller did not know that his father had made home movies, or at least did not remember, until the 1980s, long after his father had passed on.[54] And then, he began to use them in his own work, to render the old new and embed, within the new, intimations of what had already passed. The imagery of the filmmaker and his mother, filmed (from outside the frame) by Müller's father, can be read as a prescient metaphor for the mother's and son's subsequent lives together without the presence of the father. This relationship of mother and son is the subject of what may be Müller's best-known, and most accomplished, film: *Alpsee* (1994)—the title refers to another home movie made in 1964 by his father, also called "Alpsee" (after a lake in the Alps the family was visiting). Müller's *Alpsee,* which ends with imagery of his mother wading in the lake—dramatizes moments in the life of mother and son in a manner that, in its visual design, evokes (consciously, says Müller)[55] Douglas Sirk's American films. The theme of *Alpsee* is the evolution of the boy's creative sensibility within the repression and boredom of a middle-class life. For those of us familiar with Müller's oeuvre, *nebel* evokes the evolution of the filmmaker from child to the person who can make the film we are seeing, and who, like Jandl, can now feel the poignancy of the lost past, and is becoming fearful about what is to come.

But most of all, Müller—like Jandl—has learned not only to find but to *create* consolation within his work. In the tenth (untitled) poem in *gedichte an die kindheit,* Jandl remembers how "dazzling and marvelous" Christmas

54. See Müller's comments on home movies in MacDonald, *A Critical Cinema 5,* 284, 292.
55. Ibid., 295.

was when he was a child, and how, "for more than forty years," he no longer "believed in any of that." But now, he explains, "things are beginning to change":

> everything can suddenly
> dazzle me
> namely each commonplace
> thing.
> I hold
> nothing in my hands
> after such a long time.
> but it's no longer
> as far to get there
> as it used to be.
> it becomes the whole
> room
> in which I'm imprisoned,
> big and white and
> dazzlingly marvelous.

The imagery Müller uses to accompany this particular poem reflects the older man's new awareness of everyday things: imagery of simple objects—a box of Christmas tree ornaments, a light bulb—is as visually gorgeous as Jandl's memories and new awareness seem to be. Unlike the poet, however, Müller can actually present this gorgeousness to us directly. Indeed, Müller's film is consistently exquisite and inventive and, like many of his other films, much involved with cinema's ability to model a more intense, appreciative perception of what is normally overlooked (visual details of our everyday surroundings, poems not widely known) in response to the inevitable pressures of mortality. The first film Müller lists on his filmography is *Aus der Ferne—The Memo Book* (1989), which focuses on his process of recovery from losing a partner to AIDS; and *Pensão Globo* (1997) follows a young man losing strength under the onslaught of AIDS as he revisits Lisbon and remembers (imagines?) earlier days. In the wake of both earlier films, *nebel* suggests and demonstrates simultaneously the spiritual effulgence within the everyday *and* the evolution within the filmmaker of a recognition that even our transcendent moments are fragile and momentary—and do not erase the macabre question of mortality and our desperation to escape it.

One of the admirable dimensions of both *Waterworx (A Clear Day and No Memories)* and *nebel* is the filmmakers' obvious commitment to the original poetry they recycle into their films. They don't simply *use,* however honorifically, the work of Stevens and Jandl; they take considerable pains to deliver the poems to us so that we can discover and experience the poets' originality and skill. That is, the filmmakers' creativity is in service of the poets' original contributions, and the (considerable) effectiveness of their filmic manipulations of image and sound is a function of the degree to which these manipulations complement and clarify the poetry. This seems to me an ethical use of the poets' work. On the other hand, both films are distinctive, effective works in their own right. Both makers accepted the challenge of trying to turn poetry into film, and both met this challenge while producing impressive cinema, *without* sacrificing the work of others to their own.

TRAINS OF WINNIPEG—14 FILM POEMS: FEATURE FILM AS POETRY ANTHOLOGY

Whereas Hancox and Müller use cinema to revive relatively obscure works by well-known poets, and bring these works to a new audience, Clive Holden's approach to "republication" is rather different. On one hand, Holden (see p. 141) is interested in enlarging the audience for his writing, but he is also interested in seeing what the impact of new "publishing" contexts might be on particular poems.[56] Each dimension of the "Trains of Winnipeg" project includes a somewhat different set of poems. The book includes far more poems (38) than either the CD (13) or the film (14), but it does not include "Transience," "Grain Train," and "Wind" from the CD or "Hitler! (Revisited)" from the film.[57] And in each medium the poems that

56. Holden's work has been full of poetry/film crossover since before the "Trains of Winnipeg" project. For example, "Hitler!," which concludes *Fury: Fictions and Films* (Winnipeg: Cyclops, 1998), is subtitled a "filmpoem" and includes texts arranged into poetic lines and patterns, and still images of successive phases of actions. *Fury: Fictions and Films,* as the title suggests, is an earlier attempt to meld two media. "Hitler! A Film Poem" is a text/image piece that uses stills from film shots; in several instances, the book includes, in the top right corner of successive pages, frames of image that can be animated like a flipbook.

57. Holden himself is director of Cyclops Press, a micropress specializing in multimedia poetry.

"Hitler! (Revisited)" is based on the earlier film *Hitler!* (1995; a version of this project is also included in Holden, *Fury: Fictions and Films*). *Hitler!* is a somewhat awkward, slightly shorter premonition of "Hitler! (Revisited)." It tells much the same story about Holden's relationship with his older brother Niall, uses the same footage of Niall as in the later piece, and attempts to meld Holden's poetic narration with imagery and sound. In the film/DVD version of *Trains of Winnipeg,* "Hitler! (Revisited)" has no voice-over; as in *Waterworx (A Clear Day and No Memories),* the words are presented entirely by means of visual text.

are included are in an order that bears no particular relationship to the order of the poems in the other media. *Trains of Winnipeg* in its various forms provides a test case for exploring the differences in impact and implication (or the lack of differences) when a particular poetic sensibility, and specific poems, are presented in various media. The project is also an instance of the recent trend among media artists not simply to work in various media but to blend media.

As a book of poetry, *Trains of Winnipeg* is not particularly unusual. Holden is a capable poet, though as in any collection some poems are more interesting than others. The CD records the poet reading his work, accompanied by music—less common than a book of poetry, but not unusual either. The *film,* however, *is* unusual. Indeed, I know no other instance in the history of film, including the multifarious world of avant-garde film, where a poet has used the feature film as an avenue for presenting a collection of poems or, to be a bit more particular, where a feature film has been seen as a means of doing a new kind of poetry reading that includes motion picture imagery (sometimes as complex as the words) choreographed to the reading itself, as well as sound effects, environmental sounds, and music. When I saw *Trains of Winnipeg* at the 2004 Flaherty Film Seminar, it seemed virtually unique; and if there is some unevenness from film poem to film poem, the overall accomplishment and impact of the larger work are considerable.[58]

Like a good many books of poetry (and like Holden's CD), the film version of *Trains of Winnipeg—14 Film Poems* combines individual "film poems" in an order that forms a more or less coherent autobiographical narrative. This narrative takes viewers on a journey across Canada and into Clive Holden's memory. Like a conventional feature film, it develops a story about an identifiable character and moves through a variety of emotional states, from his exhilaration as a happy child ("Nanaimo Station") to his respect for his parents' longevity and high spirits ("Condo" and "Unbreakable Bones"), though the experience is more varied and less confined to narrative than commercial melodramas are. As a narrative of the filmmaker's life, *Trains of Winnipeg* is closely related to Su Friedrich's *Sink or Swim* (1990).

Each film poem has its own visual structure, and the fourteen poems are arranged within the larger structure of the film so that each poem is succeeded by a fade-out and a moment of looped imagery set within a tiny

58. All fourteen film poems included in *Trains of Winnipeg—14 Film Poems* are available as individual works from the Canadian Filmmakers Distribution Centre (see listing of film sources).

frame-within-a-frame in the lower-right-hand corner of the image; the looping image continues until we hear the sound of railroad cars coupling and see the title of the next film poem. The implicit parallel between moving pictures and railroad travel, a commonplace since the invention of cinema, is used not only to suggest a shared technological history but to create an image of the geography of Canada created and held together in Winnipeg, at the center of the Canadian nation, by the railroad.[59]

Trains of Winnipeg—14 Film Poems begins with "Love in the White City," ends with "Trains of Winnipeg," and is punctuated by "Saigon Apartments" and "Bus North to Thompson with Les at the Wheel"—all poems that relate to Holden's life in Winnipeg, the implicit here and now from which the poet flashes back to memories of his early life in the West, in and around Victoria, British Columbia, and of his student days in the East (at Concordia University in Montreal), and to more recent visits to and by his parents. The personal quality of this narrative is considerably enhanced by the fact that, in those instances where a poem is read on the sound track, Holden is the reader. At the same time, Holden is well aware that the poems and the film transform him into a character:

> I'd thought of the fourteen films' connections as being mostly metaphorical, intuitive, emotional, formal and tonal, and didn't see the connection that others would plainly see, that the "I" (or eye) of each piece is the same. Since the accumulation of memories, impressions, and concepts are one artist's, and for others tell a story about that artist, regardless of the accuracy of the biographical facts as presented, it was inevitable that an audience would have this reaction.
>
> For myself (seeing the work from within its process) it's somewhat different. I certainly and consciously use autobiographical elements in these works, but I see these as raw materials, to be worked on, and with, almost as if they're formal materials. I certainly wouldn't hesitate to change so-called factual details, for example, in the service of making a better work).[60]

There is no space here to discuss all the film poems in *Trains of Winnipeg,* but some comment on what for me are three of the more impressive—"18,000 Dead in Gordon Head (A Found Film)," "The Jew & the Irishman,"

59. Cinema and the railroad are two versions of the same technology: both create movement along tracks (railroad tracks, sound tracks, image tracks) mechanically. This connection, and its considerable implications, was historicized and theorized by Wolfgang Schivelbusch in *The Railroad Journey: The Industrialization of Time and Space in the Nineteenth Century* (Berkeley: University of California Press, 1986) and explored in relation to early cinema in Lynn Kirby, *Parallel Tracks: The Railroad and Silent Cinema* (Durham, NC: Duke University Press, 1997).

60. Holden, in an e-mail to the author, November 15, 2004.

and "Bus North to Thompson with Les at the Wheel"—might provide a sense of Holden's approach, range, and style.

"18,000 Dead in Gordon Head" is the longest poem in the book (the 4½-page prose poem is followed by eight stills on four pages) and on the CD, and the second longest in the film.[61] In all three cases "18,000 Dead" is positioned near the beginning: it is the third track on the CD, the second poem in the first section of the book, and the fifth film poem. The printed version of the poem is divided into four sections. The first explains how some film Holden had shot in 1985 was thrown into the garbage by an angry, pregnant roommate; the long second section and the brief fourth section focus on Holden's witnessing the murder of a thirteen-year-old girl (he heard the shot and saw the girl fall as he was arriving at a friend's house, and ran inside to call for an ambulance); and the third section briefly presents six violent events that Holden witnessed during the months after the murder. The first, second, and fourth sections of the text version of "18,000 Dead in Gordon Head" are made up of relatively brief, page-wide paragraphs; the third is organized so that the six brief stories are set in two vertical columns.

In the CD and film versions, this division into sections is less obvious, though the tonality of the reading of the opening section, where Holden explains how his film was thrown into the garbage, does distinguish it from subsequent sections. Holden indicates that during the period he is talking about, he never got mad, even when his roommate, who was "a *tester,*" tested him: his concluding comment on this situation ("then—she—threw my film in the garbage") is wryly amusing, despite the somewhat grim music on the sound track. And it reveals that, whatever the narrator's pretenses of self-control, *this* incident infuriated him, since he was serious about his art. This opening provides background and emotional contrast for the body of the film poem, and it marks a pivotal moment in the evolution of Holden as an artist-filmmaker.

Holden explains that while he was never able to finish that original film, he had made a VHS record of the material for editing purposes (that is, so he could plan the editing using the videotape, before doing a final edit of the fragile, single print of the film he had), which he found nearly twenty years

61. "Hitler! (Revisited)" is nearly the same length; "Trains of Winnipeg," the final section of the film, is just under seventeen minutes; the remaining eleven film poems range from just over one minute ("F Movie") to seven minutes ("Love in the White City"). The CD version of "18,000 Dead in Gordon Head" is listed as 13 minutes, 7 seconds—that is, just slightly longer than the film version.

later. The video, now recycled onto film for *Trains of Winnipeg*, is what we are seeing as we listen to him describe the history of its production. Originally, Holden had attempted to create something like a memorial of the murder and of his witnessing of it: he filmed "the split-levels, service stations, and the air raid siren over the old Gordon Head store" (Gordon Head is a suburb just to the north of Victoria, British Columbia), as well as his friend Andrew doing oil pastels of the crime scene; "I even lay on my side on the road where she died." As Holden tells the story of the murder and its aftermath, and ruminates on his struggle to know how to feel about the girl's death in a world where any young person is a "witness" to eighteen thousand television murders by age sixteen, we see the video of the original footage, presented by means of continual looping: images are looped so that we see them several times, sometimes at one speed, then at an accelerated rate. The sound track (by Christine Fellows, Jason Tait, and Emily Goodden) is also looped, so that we hear much the same musical phrasing and sound effects over and over.

Holden's use of looping throughout much of *Trains of Winnipeg—14 Film Poems* has a variety of effects, and several effects on the experience of this particular film poem. According to Holden, looping seemed a way of bringing something like rhythm and rhyme into the experience of film, and in general the various rhythms created by the looped imagery work in subtle syncopation with the rhythms of the poetic phrasing of the texts themselves and of Holden's reading of them. Each passage of looped imagery is something like a line of poetry, a line defined by particular details of the images and by the specifics of the loop's intersections or lack of them with the music, sound, and spoken poetry. In most cases what we see, over and over, relates directly to what we are hearing: the narrated text on the sound track is the foreground, and the looped images are, like the music, a form of accompaniment (we would understand the narrative Holden is presenting, without any images at all; but without the reading of the poem, the imagery would have little meaning).

The looping of images in "18,000 Dead in Gordon Head" suggests both the intensity of Holden's original experience of witnessing death (an intensity that commercial films have often suggested by slow motion) *and* his obsession in returning to this moment in the following days and months, and, years later, in the poem we are hearing. The looped images move in and out of "sync" with particular moments in Holden's reading of the text of the poem. This is evident, for example, when Holden says, "then—she—threw my film in the garbage": at the sound of "then," the image changes to white Super-8mm leader with its red stripe down the middle in a pulsing rhythm particularly suggestive of a heartbeat, then changes again at "she" (to a looped image of suburban homes), and still again, at "threw my film in the garbage," back to the looped image of Super-8mm leader.[62] The timing of the visual changes provides a confirmation of the emphasis in Holden's reading of the line, and the red stripe on the filmstrip not only suggests that the narrator "sees red" when he learns that his partner has thrown his film away but leads into the story of the murder, which we begin to hear about as Holden cuts to an overexposed, scarlet-framed abstract image. When the poet describes his lying on his side in the street to film where the victim lay dying, we are seeing a side view of the same suburban street that we saw earlier in the film, but now this location has a more particular and complex meaning: it is where a death occurred and where the poet-filmmaker first tried to come to terms in his art with witnessing the girl's death. The sound is also coordinated to the reading; during moments when the narrator is recalling moments of especially powerful stress, the sound—it evokes saws tearing through wood—becomes more abrasive.

The film imagery is clearly several generations away from an original film record of the murder. We are seeing a film (or a DVD) image of a reworked videotape of a Super-8mm film shot a year after the murder; the videotape was made crudely by projecting the Super-8mm film onto the wall of Holden's apartment and recording it with an early camcorder. When Holden rediscovered the VHS and realized its potential, he refilmed the video, focusing especially on the glitches in the original Super-8mm material created when the camera was turned on and off, and digitally enhancing particular frames and moments. The resulting film poem materializes the distance between now and then in a way the textual version of the poem cannot. The film poem provides evidence of the original crime scene in all its banality—throughout the looped material, people are walking into and out of the Gordon Head store, and traffic is moving along the streets—and of Holden's return to this location to make the film at a later moment in his life. The glitches also evoke the decay of Holden's memory of the incident.

62. A print of any film is protected by attaching one or another kind of "leader" at the beginning and at the end. This leader does not include imagery the audience needs to see. The function of leader is to keep various forms of damage movie projectors can do to films—scratching, puncturing a frame when the film is not properly threaded into the projector—away from the print. There are many kinds of leader, which differ somewhat according to the gauge (width) of the film being used. Most viewers are familiar with "Academy leader," the 10–9–8–7–6–5–4–3–2 countdown that sometimes becomes part of the exhibition of a film. In Super-8mm film, leader is generally white with a red stripe down the middle.

"18,000 Dead in Gordon Head" embodies the development of Holden's filmmaking over a period of years. This aesthetic evolution has resulted in a film that expresses the pain of the original moment but also suggests a process of emotional maturation on Holden's part. The original feelings of shock that followed the murder seemed at the time unremarkable to Holden; he says he felt "the same deadness I always felt," despite the fact that those around him can see that he has been traumatized. Even later, around the time when the original footage was thrown away, we know that the narrator was in the habit of suppressing his feelings: "I never got mad back then. I was proud of it. I used to say I could always see the other person's side of the story." But the slow, patient pace of the film poem, its success in returning us to that horrific moment, and to the several grisly events the narrator witnessed in subsequent months, reveals, once and for all, the depth of the trauma. "18,000 Dead in Gordon Head" confirms the filmmaker's early need to simultaneously recognize the power of this extended moment of his life and then to put it behind him, first, by putting a blanket over a dead motorcyclist (in the description of the film poem on his website, Holden calls this the "small, positive action" that "broke the spell" of this period for him); and then, years later, *twenty years* later, by confining the incident of the murder and the violent incidents that followed it within the aesthetic structures of a poem and then a film poem.

Also implicit within the gap between the original crime and Holden's transformation of his memories of it into poetry is his engagement with the history of independent cinema, which seems to have, over time, revealed to Holden possibilities for working cinematically with the particulars of his life. At various moments, *Trains of Winnipeg—14 Film Poems* evokes particular films and filmmakers. For example, the long montage of trains that concludes the film (it is the title film poem of the collection) is a conscious allusion to Bruce Baillie's *Castro Street* (1966).[63] And the looping that is so fundamental to the visual structure of "18,000 Dead in Gordon Head" and so much of *Trains of Winnipeg* is reminiscent of the work of Vancouver-born Canadian David Rimmer, whose breakthrough film, *Seashore* (1971), uses looping as a fundamental figure of style.

"The Jew & the Irishman" is as autobiographical as "18,000 Dead," but quite brief. It is the second film poem after "18,000 Dead in Gordon Head," and its position is significant. The sixth film poem, "Saigon Apartments," continues elements of "18,000 Dead": it provides glimpses of human pain

63. See Holden interview, p. 143. A still from *Castro Street* is included on the *Trains of Winnipeg* website.

and struggle seen outside an apartment house by a pair of lovers watching from inside. After the following transition of auditory train coupling, seen with a looped image of a man inspecting a small plane, "The Jew & the Irishman" changes the trajectory of the film. In it Holden remembers his father becoming furious at guests of the family at a cocktail party when they enjoy a bigoted joke: "My father's face turned from its usual descended black cloud to charcoal red, his mouth opening at last like a thin hidden vent in a volcano, and he actually said something, and they were burned by his words." Holden recalls that after the "White Anglo Saxon Protestants and their reasonable facsimiles" left, he stood looking at the moon with his father, who was "smiling like I'd never seen." The father's refusal to stand for one more conventional Irish and Jewish joke, "after twenty years of those jokes," is a triumph, both for him and for Holden ("and I loved him")—and confirms the possibility of active response to the violence and pain the two previous film poems review.

The visual focus of "The Jew & the Irishman" is a full moon. The moon is seen first through a series of superimposed diagrams (as Holden recalls the guests asking him about his plans for the future); then through panning shots of landscapes and shots from inside a car, as he remembers how he wrecked his first car on a utility pole (when he says the word "wreck," the frame is divided into quadrants in each of which two hockey players collide). When his father responds to the joke, the moon is superimposed with red-tinted imagery of a pulp mill smokestack plume; and, as the guests "filtered away," with a lighthouse, with a looped shot of seabirds flying, and finally, as Holden and his father "gazed together at the free moon," with a shot of a single bird (the shot reveals splice marks and other glitches).

Given the overall trajectory of Holden's reading of the poem on the sound track, the persistence of the moon, which "wasn't owned by any of them," suggests the possibility of freedom and creativity within any social situation and as the underlying reality of life. That the last two images of the film are of birds confirms the father's implicit flight from obnoxious social convention and the son's admiration for his father (this is already clear when, just as Holden is about to remember the telling of the joke, he remembers his "tall, beautiful father" listening to the party conversation, and we see a lovely image of the moon superimposed with two shots of bare late-autumn trees). The combination of the moon, the single bird, and the evidence of the surface of the filmstrip in the final shot (as the film ends, this same image is seen glowing in color negative) suggests that this moment, and this dimension of Holden's father, have helped to lead him into an artistic life, to a life of personal expression, and to the evocation of the memory we have just seen.

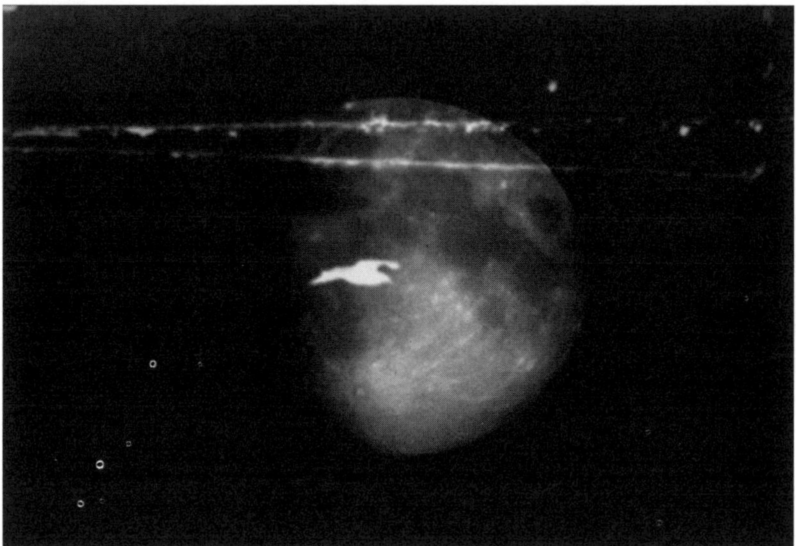

The moon and the single bird from "The Jew and the Irishman" in Clive Holden's *Trains of Winnipeg—14 Film Poems* (2004). Courtesy Clive Holden.

The eleventh poem in *Trains of Winnipeg—14 Film Poems* is "Bus North to Thompson with Les at the Wheel." This brief (2¾ minutes) piece is not an autobiographical flashback but a mini-portrait of an award-winning bus driver, Les Brandt (Brandt is also an artist, and Holden's website includes access to three of his "cow paintings"), filmed on a trip to Thompson, Manitoba, several hundred miles north of Winnipeg, at the end of the main road north. In this instance, the filmed imagery and the music are directly related to the text Holden reads: when he says "Les," we see an image of Les, and the imagery in the film was recorded on the route described in the text. At times Holden wittily interweaves his text and his imagery—when the text describes how a "blood-drunk Manitoba mosquito" weaves across the road in front of Les's bus and is transformed by the windshield into a "circle of red, the size of a Canadian dime," we see a close-up of Les's uniform sleeve and a circular patch indicating his "Safety Years," just below another "Master Driver" patch that commemorates "one million miles"—and throughout the film Holden carefully matches the tone and rhythm of the read text with the tone of the imagery and the rhythm of his cutting. In "Bus North to Thompson" Holden once again uses film to provide what a poem cannot: the poem can evoke the *kind* of man Les Brandt is, but the imagery introduces him to the viewer as a particular, recognizable person, and one of the people who make Winnipeg—as Holden describes it on his website, "entirely flat and the coldest city on earth"—livable, somehow quintessentially Canadian, and *home*.

All in all, *Trains of Winnipeg—14 Film Poems* expands the scope of the "poetry-film" or "film poem" and constitutes a breakthrough in the use of cinema as a means of publishing, or republishing, poetry. It demonstrates the potential of a new, cinematic form of public performance, a new kind of poetry reading, one that has the particular advantage of allowing the poet to "travel" more widely and personally address a more extended audience than might otherwise be possible. The combination of Holden's readings of previously published poems, with a wide range of suggestive, dynamically arranged images and carefully chosen sounds and music, not only extends the expressivity of his words but adds new layers of rhythm, rhyme, and suggestiveness. Whether *Trains of Winnipeg—14 Film Poems* instigates further developments remains to be seen, but for those interested in how poets can come to grips with new media and with our increasingly mediated world, Holden's feature may be of considerable use.

Of course, the fact that avant-garde film has, at least so far, been among the least recognized major contributions to film history, even within academe, makes it unlikely that Holden's, or Hancox's or Müller's, contributions will soon find the audience that I believe they deserve, but perhaps the reader can forgive the hope that a greater recognition of this decades-old, widely ignored intersection between poetry and cinema might allow for a more considerable interpenetration of the somewhat distinct audiences for these two art forms and, in time, help to create somewhat larger audiences for both.

Interview with Clive Holden

In recent years, significant contributions to the history of avant-garde film have tended to come from relatively predictable sources. Certain established filmmakers continue to make noteworthy films, and younger film artists have often come through a relatively small set of MFA programs sponsored by Bard College, the California Institute of the Arts, the School of the Art Institute of Chicago, and a handful of other established institutions in the United States, Canada, the United Kingdom, and Europe, where, in many instances, the more established filmmakers have mentored them. Clive Holden's route to avant-garde filmmaking was indirect. Although he did take college film courses (at Concordia University in Montreal) and, over the years, has been influenced by a number of established makers—Bruce Baillie, Stan Brakhage, David Rimmer, Peter Rose—his move into filmmaking came long after his schooling was finished and from an unusual direction: he had made himself into a writer of fiction and poetry and a desktop publisher and only joined the ranks of independent filmmakers once it was clear to him that he could work not only in both film and video, as well as with writing, but *in between* a wide range of media.

Holden's "Trains of Winnipeg" project and *Trains of Winnipeg—14 Film Poems* (2004) are discussed in the preceding chapter. I spoke with Holden in September 2004 and again in April 2005; the interview was refined via e-mail.

MacDonald: Trains of Winnipeg announces your arrival as a filmmaker. But it's not an early arrival. I'd be interested in knowing something about the life trajectory that brought you to this point in your career.

Holden: I grew up on the West Coast, in Victoria, and I wanted to be an artist from the age of eight when I had an art teacher named Mrs. Kirwin. She was six foot two with a tower of fire-engine-red hair and a pet boa constrictor in a cage. I owe her everything. It was my happiest childhood year; we made a deal where I could paint in the corner if I finished my work early. I think that as a kid I had a natural sense of what it would mean to be an artist one day. But in practice I'd never met one; I was a suburban kid with a fuzzy but strong sense of purpose, and mostly without a clue.

I'm a bit of fringe-dweller by nature. But I think my first official push to the margins was when I was expelled from high school. Later I finished in night school and went on to take university courses, but I never quite got back onto the main highway. And I think I might be a better artist now for developing on a bit of a fringe route. I studied some art and writing on my own. In my early twenties I went to film school part-time in Montreal, at Concordia. To be honest, it was on a whim, and I'd never even heard of experimental films, but at Concordia I had a surprise in store: I held a movie camera for the first time, and it was thrilling.

I also discovered the history of cinema at Concordia. Mario Falsetto taught a life-changing course in experimental cinema, and Tom Waugh was there too. They were both brilliant teachers who had a huge effect on my life.

I never finished university; I left in the mid-eighties without any idea how I'd pay for the kind of films I wanted to make. In school I'd mainly used Super-8mm because it was cheap, but there was no way to screen it anywhere at the time. It was years later when I married Super-8mm with video that it became a truly viable format for me.

But in 1985, since I loved filming and writing equally, I decided to write for a while. Most of my spare time for the next ten years was spent writing my first book, *Fury: Fictions and Films.* It's somewhere between experimental fiction and an artist's book. I included some 16mm film sequences as flip book animations. I loved the years I spent writing *Fury;* I was focused, and it was thrilling to be writing so often. I learned how to write in those years, and, I think, how to make art.

In the middle of that period I saw the growing possibility of working with both film and video at once, and in 1993, I made *Gordon's Head* as a video/16mm hybrid. It's based on a short story in the book, my only film that uses an actor—a young man who talks straight to camera in various sites around Gordon Head, the suburb where I grew up. He tells stories about his schizophrenic older brother—it was semi-autobiographical.

Then I made another film about my brother, Niall. I took a video camera into the mental hospital in Vancouver where he lived. *Hitler!* (Niall used to yell that at passing nurses) was another step forward for me in mixing film gauges and video formats: High 8 video plus Super-8mm film, edited in Digi-Beta, and transferred to 16mm, a crude version of what is now called a "digital intermediate" process. It was a cheap-yet-high-quality method, partly because I did an exhaustive "paper edit" before renting the Digi-Beta suite for an hour for the final cut, and the NFB [National Film Board of Canada] had a really good video-to-16mm transfer machine for the last step.

A lot of celluloid advocates' emphasis is on postproduction. In my own way, I'm just as committed to using film, but I've always been more focused on the shooting, and I've done a lot of exploring of the differences between using film and video cameras, which offer different experiences. I've refined this overall strategy ever since, so I can make films in a process that has some of the freedom of writing. This new ability to synthesize these media with my writing practice—that really got me going, and the "Trains of Winnipeg" project sprang from that.

MacDonald: How did it develop?

Holden: I got the idea for the project beside the river listening to a freight train with rusty brakes crossing a trestle. I'm often drawn to this kind of "ugly beauty."

MacDonald: I assume Winnipeg is an important Canadian railroad town?

Holden: It's exactly halfway between the Pacific and Atlantic, so it was developed as the Canadian railway hub. It has more train yard than any other city in the world; tracks snake through the city in all directions, passing overhead, blocking traffic. They're found sculptures, both kinetic and sound. And almost everyone seems to have an uncle who worked in the yards. Trains are a wonderful blend of romance and kitsch, formalism and abstraction.

MacDonald: You mention on the project website that Winnipeg is totally flat and the coldest city on earth.

Holden: The "coldest city" title has been much debated! Technically, it depends on how you define a city. There's a contender in Siberia that's slightly colder, but with about 150,000 people, I say that's only a large town. Winnipeg, with around 700,000 people, is a city. It deserves the title. And yes, it's flat as a buckwheat pancake.

MacDonald: I take it you took a certain sort of grim satisfaction in being a Winnipeg-ian? Winnipeger?

Holden: Winnipeger.

Well, I was there for eight years, and I do feel proud of that. It was an amazing, lovely place to live. And the weather can kill you, which is exciting. On the worst days there's a beautiful desolation—devastating in every sense of the word. And I think this threat is good for people, psychologically. I mean, while people are obviously good at finding ways to be miserable in nice warm climates too, it might help to be able to point at something outside themselves, like winter, and say, "That's the source of my pain."

The summers are also biblical, hot with tornadoes buzzing the edge of town and the thunderstorms: they create urban flash floods; you have to wait them out in doorways.

I admire Winnipegers because they have to be tough, have a sense of humor, and I also think they make art simply to survive. So the city's full of strong people, eccentric characters, artists, and oddballs. Perfect!

MacDonald: I assume there's a film scene in Winnipeg, that it wasn't just you and Guy Madden.

Holden: Guy Madden's the star, which is obviously well earned. But there's a general arts explosion going on that's partly fueled by semi-outsider artist work that springs naturally from that environment. It's a healthy mix of fuel: semi-isolation, lots of Icelanders, a warped humor coming from hardship, the bizarrely flat landscape, some quality artist facilities, but especially the audiences, who continually show up in big numbers for any kind of strange or esoteric art. And there's the whole amazing history of the Winnipeg Film Group, which Madden helped form but lately has refocused around experimental and hand-processed films sparked by makers like Sol Nagler. There's also the organization that I worked for, Video Pool, which has five hundred media artist members, many of whom are well known in the contemporary art world. The two organizations are down the hall from each other, and in my last years there, it seemed like the younger artists coming in didn't get why you'd be on one team or the other; they were joining both groups and using *all* the equipment.

MacDonald: The idea of crossing media boundaries seems important to you. I became aware of avant-garde film during a moment (the early 1970s) when there was a lot of talk about film purity, the "essential cinema." You seem to have arrived right at the moment when what had been seen as two separate histories, avant-garde film and video art, were no longer separate, at least practically speaking.

Holden: For a time video developed separately; there were very different criteria for what made good video art or experimental films. And as a result, the mixing is now very interesting to watch and be a part of. It's about much more than technology; it's two cultures blending together. The clashes, the problems, the anger even, are part of what makes it exciting. There's always friction, or charge, when cultures clash, and that's an opportunity: you can create something out of that energy.

MacDonald: The most obvious mix in *Trains of Winnipeg*—the film, I mean—is not film and video but, as your subtitle suggests, poetry and film. Over the decades, people have called various forms of film "poetic," meaning different things at different times. What's unusual about your film is that its overall impact is like a poetry reading. How much experience did you have reading poetry before this project started?

Holden: Well, I'd done some public reading before, but a key moment happened at the beginning of the project, when I read the poem "Trains of Winnipeg" to a large audience at Send + Receive, a big sound art festival in Winnipeg. As I was reading (I had train sounds crashing through the room along with electronic accompaniment by Jason Tait and Steve Bates), to my surprise, something happened to me: I'd always thought of myself as fairly shy, but that night I discovered I'm relaxed when on stage. I didn't know this about myself. The other thing that happened was that this voice came out of my mouth that I'd never heard before. Finding that voice influenced all of my work from then on, including my filmmaking. The experience made me think about the experimental films I've loved over the years where the filmmaker creates a vocal persona for a work.

MacDonald: Who are you thinking of?

Holden: Phil Hoffman, and Peter Rose in *The Man Who Could Not See Far Enough* [1981]—that's a seminal work for me.

But I have to say that many of my favorite filmmakers don't use words at all. Bruce Baillie is a tremendous influence on my work. You can't make an experimental film with trains and not be referring to *Castro Street* [1966]. And his use of sound is very strong.

But even though poetry's partly about oral presentation or narration, for me it's more about organic and alternative structures and processes, and these are really the strongest links between poetry and my filmmaking.

I'm very process-oriented, and since writing was the first art form I fully practiced, I tend to think in terms of writing processes. In the case of *Trains*, I decided everything I did would involve what I thought of as a poetic process. This partly involved deciding on a set of poetry-like restraints that would help me focus. A rhyme scheme is just a set of creative restrictions, and this is why I explored some outmoded, even kitschy styles of poetry in the project. Because those structures were interesting, they became new again when applied to film. In each film, I wanted a very tight focus, in concept and expression, and some of the main tools of poetry—metaphor, symbolism, layered meanings, et cetera—can help bring this to a nonlinear film.

MacDonald: Has there been much response to the *Trains of Winnipeg* film from the poetry community?

Holden: Not that much. I think the films are a bit of a head-scratcher for much of the poetry community. And a few people who liked the CD were actually upset with the films, which was surprising at first. Generally, poetry people and indie music fans don't watch avant-garde films, so they don't know what to make of them.

And in reverse, initially at least, the film's less natural narration styles and its use of music were a barrier for some people in the experimental film culture. But there's still a bigger space for me there, because it's more in flux to begin with, and there are more filmmakers using similar strategies now (the music in *Tarnation* [2003], for example). It's generally a more open space than poetry; experimental/avant-garde film orthodoxies do keep trying to form but they're continually subverted, which I think is healthy.

At one Ann Arbor Film Festival a guy in the audience said we shouldn't "fetishize the new," and while I think he's right, I don't want to live in a gated community either. But there's lots of room between the extremes. I think Michele Smith's *Regarding Penelope's Wake* [2002] was a big milestone in this conversation, a work that was so obviously "filmic" in its materials and process, but can only be seen as a video.

MacDonald: You mentioned Baillie and Peter Rose as being important sources for you. When I first saw *Trains of Winnipeg* at the Flaherty, my first thought, partly because you were introduced as being from British Columbia, was David Rimmer.

Holden: Definitely. He came to Concordia and talked to our class in 1982 or 1983, and his use of looping was my first introduction to the technique.

MacDonald: The individual film poems in *Trains of Winnipeg* work very well as isolated pieces, but when I saw the complete film at the Flaherty—and I assume this is one reason why Susan Oxtoby programmed it as the concluding event—it came across as a personal documentary.

Holden: It was an interesting surprise to discover how much of a cumulative narrative is created by the cycle of the fourteen pieces. I worked on each separately, *and* I thought of them as part of an hour-and-a-half feature in a cinema, connected through tone, theme, technique, and the cycle's conceit of a train journey with the coupling sound between each piece. But I missed the most obvious connection: that the audience is following a story about this quasi-fictional character named Clive Holden. Especially with the repeated first-person narrations, the "I" becomes the main focus for many viewers. The cycle does, in practice, become a form of personal documentary because the audience wills it to be so. I think, even with artists who work hard to subvert narrative, the audience will often insist on making story, out the artists themselves if necessary.

But my films aren't fact or fiction; they live somewhere else. I use my own life as a kind of raw material, to be processed with whatever techniques I'm exploring.

Experimental films, and especially the "diary film" semigenre, have been compared to the lyric poem, but with a "first-person eye." And I consciously pushed this analogy further. But that "I," or "eye," isn't factual, in poetry or film.

I don't normally write lyrical poetry, but for this project it was central to the experiment. I wanted to "experiment backward" with some older forms, including narrative and rhyme schemes, but especially by blending these with other media and their cultures and conventions, including avant-garde film's. The dominant "I" is an old convention in poetry, but in film it's still reasonably fresh.

MacDonald: There are particular film poems in *Trains of Winnipeg* that seem more autobiographical than others: "18,000 Dead in Gordon Head," "Nanaimo Station," and "Hitler! (Revisited)."

Holden: In the particular case of "18,000 Dead," I *did* witness this girl being killed, and I went back to the site and lay down with the camera on the spot where she died.

MacDonald: When I first showed Pat [MacDonald's wife, Patricia O'Connor] "18,000 Dead," she said, "There's no way all of that happened to him in one year."

Holden: She's right: those events took place over about three years during my early twenties. I compressed the time to intensify the story, but that *was* still a short time, so I would say the film is true in a broader sense.

I came out of my teens in the early eighties feeling like I was in shock. Part of this was just being a teenager, and some of it had to do with the Cold War: I was waiting for the world to end, suddenly, along with millions of other people at the time—today, it would be the war on terror or environmental catastrophe—but my biggest struggle then could be summed up by a need to wake up. When I was twenty-two, around when the girl was killed, I went cold turkey on all mass media; for years the only books I read were literary or mostly art-focused nonfiction. I never opened a mainstream magazine, didn't watch TV; I even avoided looking at billboards. I'd internalized a collection of ludicrous ideas that I *knew* were ridiculous but that still had power over me, along with a lifetime of deadening and confusing images that made it harder to feel emotion when important things happened, like the girl's death that day.

I think going through that process of "untraining" was a key part of my life, and it did seem to help end the deadness I'd been feeling, just as in "18,000 Dead" my carrying the blanket outside to the motorcycle accident victim was a turning point that "broke the spell."

MacDonald: That's the "small positive action" you mention on the website?

Holden: Yes. That, and looking into the dead man's eyes, looking right *at* the situation.

I have a lot of interest in formal experimentation, but even my work that's less obviously expressive than "18,000 Dead" has a strong emotional component. I don't really think it's possible to make a totally nonexpressive work so I'm not interested in trying; even if people are using machines or mathematical formulas to structure work, it's still an organized randomness, and their choices are still expressive.

MacDonald: What *was* the process of making "18,000 Dead," beginning with the basic video material?

Holden: Originally—this was 1983 or 1984—I thought I was just making a very crude video record of some Super-8mm film footage. I wanted to log the footage without repeatedly screening and potentially scratching it, so I projected onto the wall of my apartment and used a Sony camcorder, one of the earliest on the market, to record it. That Super-8mm footage was then lost, so I reluctantly abandoned the film. But twenty years later I found an old VHS tape while doing some housecleaning and thought, "I'd better look at this before throwing it out," and was shocked to find this footage, or more accurately, the record of this footage. I digitally captured and edited that material, and then finished to 35mm, to complete the work's life cycle back to celluloid.

MacDonald: There are a lot of double exposures.

Holden: That was in the original Super-8mm footage, done in-camera with my Nizo S560. As I've said, I always set up a framework of restrictions when I'm making art, which is part of my interest in old forms of poetry. If you've ever written a sonnet, the strict pattern that's used to determine the structure seems to mysteriously focus your creativity. I don't know why it works, but it can be quite exciting to experience. I think it might help an artist to sidestep the impulse to be clever, which can be very limiting. When I'm shooting, the chosen framework or set of restraints could be almost anything: that everything has to be shot on a Thursday, in a certain neighborhood, or that every shot has to include a dog—whatever seems interesting as a guide. And in this case, I decided that the entire film would have to be made out of that videotape, without any further shooting or film processes. So I didn't add any double exposures, or any other filmic processing; what you see was already on that tape.

I don't know if you've ever worked with Super-8mm . . .

MacDonald: Not very seriously.

Holden: Well, for me, part of the fun of Super-8mm is discovering the little chemical anomalies that happen whenever you pull the trigger or let

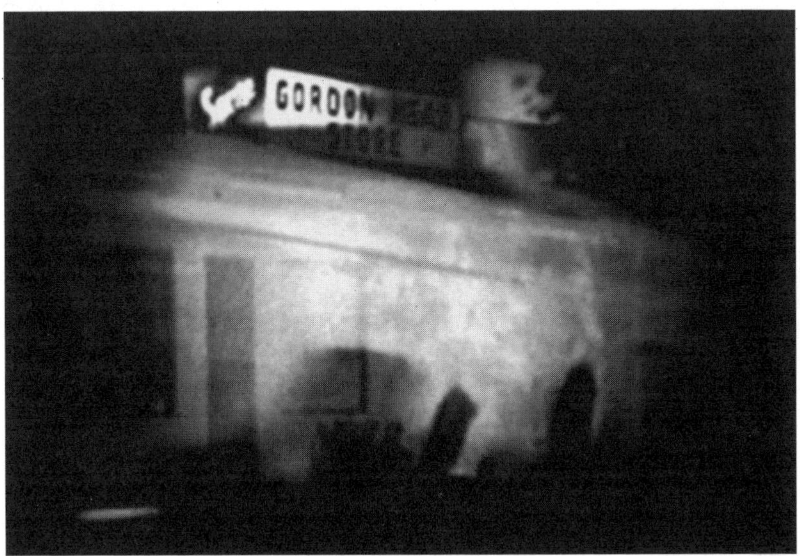

Video record of lost Super-8mm imagery of place where a young girl was killed in "18,000 Dead in Gordon Head" from *Trains of Winnipeg—14 Film Poems* (2004). Courtesy Clive Holden.

the trigger go, and the happy accidents that happen in the darkroom or the semipro lab. Like that "transparent woman" who crosses the road where the girl was shot. The most interesting parts of the taped footage I used in "18,000 Dead" were these little explosions, errors, or chemical blemishes, which I looped.

MacDonald: In a sense the glitches in the otherwise relatively smooth continuity of the Super-8mm are like these violent moments in your experience.

Holden: Exactly. Part of what was remarkable about seeing this tape so many years after the fact is that its washed-out, watercolor-like hues and these violent flaws seemed to echo my memories of that time.

MacDonald: Did the text poem of "18,000 Dead in Gordon Head" come before the film?

Holden: The text poem came out of finding and viewing that videotape.

MacDonald: So the videotape instigated the poem and then the two things instigated the film?

Holden: Right.

MacDonald: Looping is the most pervasive formal trope in "18,000 Dead in Gordon Head" and in *Trains of Winnipeg* as a whole.

Holden: If you're using motion picture imagery, and you're wondering how to work with this in relation to poetry, you start thinking in terms of rhythm, and rhyme, which is just another form of repetition. Visually, you can have color rhymes, or gesture rhymes. If you're more interested in the abstract aspects of footage than in its content, then it doesn't make sense *not* to loop it, and to do all the other things that are done with language beats, or musical notes and phrases, for that matter. I think it's not done more because of the huge, historic dominance of dramatic narrative film, but this is now changing.

MacDonald: You've mentioned that the different film poems began in different ways, some with words, some with imagery. During the period when you were working on the fourteen sections that ended up in the film, were they all in process at once, or did they get done in a particular order?

Holden: I usually had several films going at once, but for practical reasons I'd focus on one or another. I might realize I needed to go to the West Coast to get more footage for a piece, or I'd be waiting for a lab to process something. Early on, I had what now seems a silly plan: I could edit in the morning (when I was fresh, at my best) and then go out and shoot in the afternoon. But I quickly realized that this was an inappropriate attitude toward using the camera. I thought that somehow shooting was just a mechanical process, that the camera/machine would do the work for me. I understand now that I have to *engage* with a camera for it to work, that shooting is an intense, energetic experience that can be quite tiring. If I go out after doing six or seven hours of editing, sure, I may have plenty of daylight left, but I'm depleted and I'm probably going to get crappy footage. Even though it seems like I'm pointing at the same thing in the same way, the results are mysteriously bad. So I learned to stop all other activity and just film for a couple of weeks at a time.

This makes me think about all the current talk about the "death of celluloid," and the attempts to revive its use in new ways, mostly for artists. So much of this is focused on filmic postproduction, but there's a growing problem with film camera usage. They're being used increasingly as if they're video cameras; there's a lot of "recording" instead of filming. Maybe the biggest single difference in shooting film is that you look through the lens. It's more exciting, more visceral, a direct interaction with light. I shoot a lot of video too, but you're looking at a tiny video screen. It's a completely different process, more ephemeral, somewhere between filming and sound recording.

MacDonald: Because there's such passion in your voice as narrator in "Nanaimo Station," the tendency is to assume that that's your family's home-movie footage. Is it?

Holden: Well, yeah, it is. It might not be: at the end of "Unbreakable Bones," where the pigeons are flying around the two people, a common assumption is that those are my parents. But they're just a couple who were at the seaside feeding birds; they become "my parents" in that film. In the case of "Nanaimo Station," a friend of the family took that footage in 1960, which includes my first steps. My parents were new to Canada, and the new home-movie cameras were an exciting part of this techno-utopia they'd come to.

There's this growing semigenre now of experimental films made with home movies. There are tons of them, some more interesting than others, but it's interesting to see how much variation there is in the outcome, even though the actual footage is incredibly similar. I'm certainly not the only one to have footage of my first steps, but part of the interest for me in that piece is the way that nostalgia and irony mix in our minds, even though they're thought to be opposing: we can enjoy nostalgia for that time, but also have the critical knowledge that many of the ridiculous, romantic feelings we have about the fifties or sixties are lies. Of course, it wasn't *all* crap; some people loved each other, and those great big cars, for example, were wonderful in certain ways. With today's lens it's hard to see them as the marvels of human invention that they were.

MacDonald: When I teach *Psycho,* my students are always shocked when Arbogast gets to the Bates Motel and slides across the front seat to get out on the passenger side of his car.

Holden: [laughter] And if you had a date, they'd sit right beside you on the seat, which was great.

MacDonald: Yesterday when you were talking about "F Movie," I realized that the actual image we're looking at has more resonance for you than I'd assumed.

Holden: That piece is made from a tiny fragment of Super-8mm footage that I shot from a hill in Victoria. It looks across the strait, fourteen miles to the Washington State coast. As teenagers, it's where we'd park to look out across the water, hoping the romantic vista would have some wonderful results. It rarely did, but that's part of being a teenager.

When I saw that footage, I connected to those memories, but *then* when I trimmed and looped just a few frames, it created a white flashing in the sky, and the footage was transformed. So I made the whole film from that one tiny clip. The energy that seemed to inform this footage was partly my teenage terror of imminent nuclear war. When I was sixteen, I stopped studying (part of why I was kicked out of school) because I'd read a book that said the world was going to end in 1978, the next year. That made perfect sense because I'd also been reading about how many nuclear warheads there were in the world, and had come to the conclusion that there was no logical hope of avoiding a worldwide nuclear catastrophe. Growing up in Victoria, we knew that across that strait was Bangor, Washington, the largest nuclear submarine base in the world. It would have been one of the main targets for a nuclear strike, included in the first wave of rockets. I fully expected there'd be a giant flash in the sky, coming across the water, and we'd all be wiped out. That was a very real fear in me for years; it gradually dissipated at the tail end of Reagan's time in office.

Now, none of that's described in the film. While it's very important in my editing that I find these charged materials—that charge creates a tension that helps me make a good film—I don't necessarily need, or want, to describe it. Viewers don't need to know all the subtexts; I think they're still there, affecting the work, but it's better for some of them to be submerged; I do have to have confidence that that energy will be there for people who see the work.

MacDonald: I want to go back to the multimedia question for the moment, because I think I remember you saying that there were at least three kinds of film and many kinds of video in *Trains of Winnipeg.*

Holden: There are three film gauges and nine video formats, all mixed together.

MacDonald: What are the video formats?

Holden: The video "production formats" (how I either shot or received the footage) included VHS, Fisher-Price Pixelvision, Regular 8mm, High 8, Betacam SP, MPEG1, MiniDV, DVCam, and Digital Betacam. There was also a layer of "2K" high-res in postproduction.

MacDonald: Did you always assume *Trains of Winnipeg* would be a 35mm film?

Holden: It fit the aims, or metaphor, of the project to use a wide mix of formats *but* to finish in 35mm. It gave me a range of textures and palettes to work with, plus I partly just like the humor in using found footage, Pixelvision, cheap pocket cameras, Super-8mm and then 35mm.

MacDonald: The *Trains of Winnipeg* book is organized one way; the CD, a different way—that is, each includes different sets of poems in a different order—and the film is structured still a third way, with a different selection of poems from either of the other two. I'm assuming that the ordering of the poems in your film is partly instinctive, but it's also clear not only that the film is structured by the little couplings that connect each film poem to the next, but in other ways as well. For example, "Saigon Apartment" comes right after "18,000 Dead in Gordon Head," and it includes a series

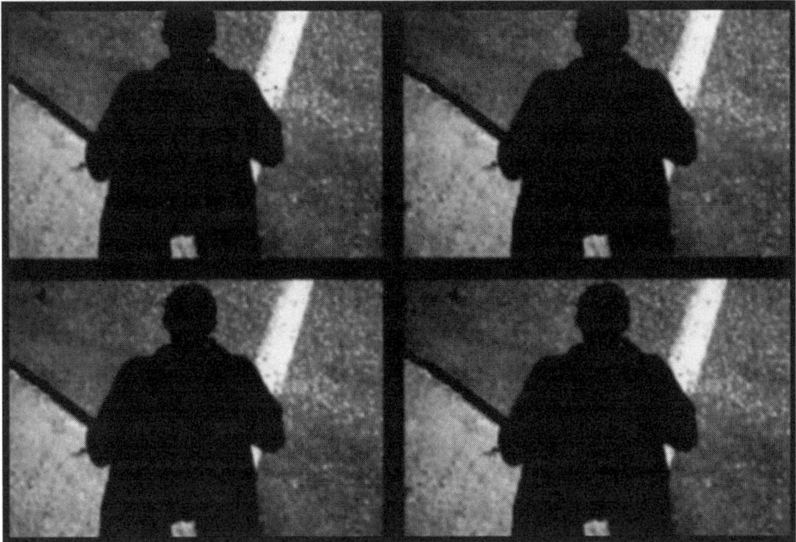

Shadows of Clive Holden on the street filming, in "Love in the White City," the opening film poem in *Trains of Winnipeg—14 Film Poems* (2004). Courtesy Clive Holden.

of vignettes not as violent as those reviewed in the earlier film poem, but painful nonetheless. And right after "Saigon Apartments," throughout which we're looking through a circle with crosshairs, comes "The Jew & the Irishman," which is dominated by a full moon that is exactly the same size as that circle—in this case, a visual transition rather than a narrative one. Can you talk a bit about structuring the film?

Holden: It happened fairly organically. I knew early on that I wanted to end the cycle, and the whole project, with the title piece, with a wordless "poem."

It also became clear early on that I wanted to start with "Love in the White City" because it was emblematic of some of the multimedia aspects, or the multiple viewpoints, of the project, and because it's multichannel *and* made with footage from a pocket-size still camera that I pumped up to 35mm. It may sound like I'm obsessed with technology, but it's actually the reverse. I'm just always thinking, "How can I make some art right now? These are the available tools, let's go!" I try not to identify with a technology, but it's true I've become especially fond of Super-8mm. It's become a part of my life.

To go back to your question, in ordering the films, there were various practical issues. I'd intended the cycle to be enjoyed as a series of individual works but mainly in a cinema, feature-length. That's why I included the twenty-second "bridge films," as a series of rests or palate cleansers. There was also the basic choice to not have all the longer pieces jammed together. And I decided that if one film poem was extra-intense, I'd try to put something after it that was lighter. There aren't any truly light pieces in the cycle, but "F Movie" has some humor, so I put it between "The Jew & the Irishman" and "Hitler! (Revisited)."

MacDonald: "Bus North to Thompson" is pretty light; it follows "Neighbors Walk Softly," which is pretty serious.

Holden: Yes, but it has a subtext too—and that film has a personal connection for me in that I drove a Greyhound bus as a summer job for years.

MacDonald: You collaborated with a number of musicians on *Trains of Winnipeg,* and I assume in different configurations.

Holden: Jason Tait made the sound tracks for "Active Pass," "18,000 Dead in Gordon Head," "Neighbors Walk Softly," "Bus North to Thompson with Les at the Wheel," and "Unbreakable Bones." We worked on these for a few weeks in a makeshift studio above a pool hall. Christine Fellows did the sound for "Love in the White City," "Burning Down the Suburbs," "Nanaimo Station," "Saigon Apartments," "The Jew & the Irishman," and "F Movie." We did most of these in her living room, and by trading files back and forth for most of one winter. Steve Bates did the soundtrack for "Hitler! (Revisited)." It was originally a sound art piece that he made called "winnipeg square (blunderdevelopment remix)," adapted for the film. For the title film ("Trains of Winnipeg"), I worked with Emily Gooden. I mailed her several hours of train recordings I'd collected throughout the project, with a letter describing what I wanted. I decided that getting that letter right would be a writing challenge for me; I wanted to see what would happen if that's all she had to work with. She was living in a house full of musicians and they all took it on as their project. Working with musicians is the main work I do collaboratively, and I'm very grateful to all of them.

MacDonald: One moment in the film that doesn't sit well with me occurs right near the end; there's a shot of you filming that's breaking down into pixels. This moment occurs in the midst of that train footage which is very filmic, cinema-ish, rather than video-ish. It seems out of place.

Holden: Well, in my understanding, that's the conceptual *climax* of the film (and the cycle, and the whole project). There's also an emotional climax a few minutes earlier, during the printing press sequence. The word "climax" is loaded with freight; it's an old-fashioned way of describing the traditional, male-focused, Western narrative, but it's still how most dramatic narrative work is organized. I wanted the cycle to function in an "art cin-

Inside of train in "Trains of Winnipeg," the final film poem in *Trains of Winnipeg—14 Film Poems* (2004). Courtesy Clive Holden.

ema" context, not just an experimental one. So I decided to adapt this core, even corny, organizing conceit from that world. It was another interesting "culture clash" to experiment with.

In general, the seventeen-minute wordless space that is the title film gives the audience a chance to process the verbal intensity that's led up to it; it re-creates something new out of the meditative space that any long journey by train creates, or at least offers.

The printing press sequence seems to initiate an emotional release at about the two-thirds mark. But the scene you're referring to was filmed with a broken Pixelvision camera, the Fisher-Price children's camcorder (ironically, it was operated by my friend Sol Nagler, a passionate celluloid advocate who also taught me hand-processing during the project). In this shot, the camera's tape mechanism was malfunctioning, so you're just barely seeing an image of me kneeling down on the railroad tracks with a camera in the snow (and in what we used to call "snow" in analog video). Along with the sound there's a kind of explosion, as if we're breaking through to the other side of that material: then there's the "denouement" (another old-fashioned concept) combining imagery of power lines, strings of wire accompanied by stringed instruments, which seems to me to be a particularly narrative moment. And there's also the implication that we've pushed through to another era (which we have, we're now postindustrial, postinnocence, post–many things, yet we still have loving relationships with these things called trains and celluloid). The idea was that, after the explosion, things may look the same, but we know they're not.

MacDonald: You mentioned the other day that one of the things that interests you is pixels versus dots of film grain. And that that gap between the two media is one of the places where you're working.

Holden: Throughout the whole project I was thinking about film grain and digital noise and mixing them together in different ways, more obviously in some places than others. The shot of the red freighter in "Active Pass" is my favorite shot in this respect because I caught a dance of film grain and digital noise in an equal mix. I used a high-grain film stock, and this confused the telecine equipment, which produced extra noise in a way that was really attractive.

MacDonald: Trains of Winnipeg is dedicated to your wife, Alissa. Did she have particular input into the film?

Holden: Not usually directly, but yes quite a lot overall. She's a novelist; we work down the hall from each other and have for nineteen years. We constantly talk about our art and our ideas. I don't know if I could be doing what I'm doing if we hadn't met.

MacDonald: What are you working on now?

Holden: I'm well into a new multiyear project called *Utopia Suite.* I chose the name because I think it sounds like an early twentieth-century Scandinavian symphony, with all that that implies. It's a "suite" of experimental film-based works that are being shown equally in galleries and cinemas, and they all involve explorations into moving visuals as music. I'm very excited to be working on these with Oscar van Dillen, a Rotterdam-based composer. I'm learning a lot from him; it's turning into a great relationship.

Each work in the suite explores the meaning of the word "utopia." The project suggests the possibility of a renewed, dynamic utopianism based on organic structures and movement, with avant-garde cinema as a metaphor.

Eventually, there will also be a book to collect the texts that go with each segment of the suite. These texts are by, and about, a quasi-fictional character named "Conn." They alternate between his childhood in utopia/dystopia, and his contemporary life as a forty-eight-year-old avant-garde filmmaker and artist.

Up Close and Political

Three Short Ruminations on Nature Film

A few months ago I saw a film on TV, one of the *Nova* series I think, about spiders. I've never see anything more fascinating, or more visual. How can you possibly ignore such work? I'm delighted it's there, and I've always wanted to show it. And it's always worked very well, in terms of audiences.

Amos Vogel[1]

Probably no substantial dimension of film history that is so widely admired by a public audience and so frequently utilized in academic contexts has been so thoroughly ignored by film critics, historians, and theorists as the nature film (or "wildlife film"): those films and videos that purport to reveal the lives of other species.[2] Indeed, the recent appearance of Gregg Mitman's *Reel Nature: America's Romance with Wildlife on Film;* Derek Bousé's *Wildlife Films;* Cynthia Chris's *Watching Wildlife;* and the beautiful book on the French nature-film pioneer Jean Painlevé, *Science Is Fiction: The Films of Jean Painlevé,* edited by Andy Masaki Bellows and Marina McDougall, with Brigitte Berg, are the exceptions that prove the rule.[3] Until the appearance of these books, there had been a dearth of writing about nature film, at least within the annals of American film scholarship. Most academic film studies

1. Amos Vogel on programming science films, in Scott MacDonald, "An Interview with Amos Vogel," in *Cinema 16: Documents toward a History of the Film Society* (Philadelphia: Temple University Press, 2002), 49.

2. In this particular context, I prefer "nature film" to "wildlife film" because "wildlife film" has come to refer primarily to films about animals, whereas "nature film" more comfortably includes the lives of insects and sea organisms, as well.

3. Gregg Mitman, *Reel Nature: America's Romance with Wildlife on Film* (Cambridge, MA: Harvard University Press, 1999); Derek Bousé, *Wildlife Films* (Philadelphia: University of Pennsylvania Press, 2000); Cynthia Chris, *Watching Wildlife* (Minneapolis: University of Minnesota Press, 2006); and Jean Painlevé, *Science Is Fiction: The Films of Jean Painlevé,* ed. Andy Masaki Bellows and Marina McDougall, with Brigitte Berg (Cambridge, MA: MIT Press; San Francisco: Brico Press, 2000), respectively.

There is also Oliver Gaycken's "'A Drama Unites Them in a Fight to the Death': Some Re-

professionals don't take nature film seriously, either historically or theoretically. Indeed, there are few better indications of the educationally counterproductive gap between the humanities and the sciences.

While one can hope that the three volumes mentioned here—along with the remarkable recent successes of *Winged Migration* (2001, directed by Jacques Perrin), *Deep Blue* (2003, directed by Andy Byatt and Alastair Fothergill), and especially *March of the Penguins* (2005, directed by Luc Jacquet)—will instigate further exploration of this neglected genre, and perhaps increased exhibition of its major contributions, the general attitude of film historians and scholars currently makes such a revival less than certain. The obvious location for serious thinking about the nature film, at least within academic film studies, would seem to be within the history and theory of documentary film. In fact, in the popular mind few forms of filmmaking are more obvious instances of documentary. But historians of documentary routinely ignore the nature film, for reasons articulated by Bill Nichols.[4] For

marks on the Flourishing of a Cinema of Scientific Vernacularization in France, 1909–1914," *Historical Journal of Film, Radio and Television* 22, no. 3 (August 2002): 353–74; and Jan-Christopher Horak's "Wildlife Documentaries: From Classical Forms to Reality TV," *Film History* 18, no. 4 (2006): 459–75. Gaycken's discussion of early French scientific films produced by the Éclair, Pathé, and Gaumont studios, especially the Éclair series called "Scientia," is very useful. Gaycken discusses the distinction between films made in the service of scientific experimentation and films of "scientific vernacularization": that is, films that attempted to make scientific investigations and ideas available to a more general audience; and he examines a number of films involving insects and animals doing battle with one another in ways that are early instances of some of the films discussed in this essay. Horak's essay is particularly useful in its review of early German wildlife films produced by Oskar Messter and others.

Derek Bousé carefully reviews the scholarship on wildlife film in *Wildlife Films*. The British in particular have amassed a considerable body of writing in the field.

4. Lewis Jacobs's seminal anthology *The Documentary Tradition: From* Nanook *to* Woodstock (New York: Hopkinson and Blake, 1971) does include Arthur Knight's brief discussion of Arne Sucksdorff, "Sweden's Arne Sucksdorff," which mentions *Struggle for Survival* (1944), Sucksdorff's study of bird life on a Baltic island; and Bosley Crowther's review, "Cousteau's *The Silent World* [1956]." Erik Barnouw's *Documentary: A History of the Non-fiction Film* (New York: Oxford University Press, 1993) devotes a single paragraph to the nature film (pp. 210–12) in which the early Disney True-Life Adventures and Jacques-Yves Cousteau's film work are mentioned. But none of the recent anthologies focusing on documentary so much as mentions this dimension of documentary history.

Derek Bousé's first chapter includes an extensive consideration of the ways in which wildlife films correspond and fail to correspond to conventional understandings of documentary. In general, Bousé sees the wildlife film as a genre separate from what we usually call documentary. I do consider the films I discuss here documentaries; for me, Jean Painlevé's definition has been particularly useful: a documentary is "any film that documents real phenomena or their honest and justified reconstruction in order to consciously increase human knowledge through rational or emotional means and to expose problems and offer solutions from an economic, social, or cultural point of view." Painlevé, in "Castration du documentaire," *Cahiers du cinéma*, March 1951, reprinted in Painlevé, *Science Is Fiction*, ed. Bellows et al., 39.

Nichols, the capacity of the photographic image to generate indexical representations of the world makes it valuable for scientific imaging, but cinema's very usefulness to science "depends heavily on minimizing the degree to which the image, be it a fingerprint or x-ray, exhibits any sense of perspective or point of view distinctive to its individual maker. A strict code of objectivity, or institutional perspective, applies. The voice of science demands silence, or near silence, from documentarian or photographer."[5] Since documentary requires a "voice of its own," according to Nichols—"voice of its own" meaning a clear or at least identifiable ideological position—nature film is by definition not part of documentary history.[6]

There are several problems with this position, and they grow increasingly evident the more fully modern society comes to terms with the many dimensions of the evolving environmental crisis. Of course, it is true, as Nichols suggests, that nature films (science films in general) have historically pretended to objectivity. There are a variety of reasons for this. Since science is our cultural attempt to find out what aspects of the physical world can be known through observation and experimentation, that is, those aspects of the physical world that are verifiable regardless of ideology or belief, it is hardly surprising that scientific films have an aura of objectivity that is confirmed by the cinema's ability to make indexical, seemingly objective, records of sensory phenomena. But the moment a nature filmmaker begins to construct a particular film, there is no escaping point of view: filmmakers must choose what to show us and why and determine a filmic structure that exhibits a particular set of conclusions, whether they are those of an individual scientist, a group of scientists, or science-interested laypeople. The presumption of objectivity in science film is simply a particular instance of the aura of objectivity that documentary nearly always carries with it, and which, as Nichols has so often made clear in other contexts, must be qualified by the point of view that is explicit or implicit within any specific documentary.

A second reason for the widely held position that nature films are not really documentaries, and therefore not worth serious investigation within a film studies context, is historical, in at least two senses. First, until Mitman and Bousé, no American scholar had described a history of nature

5. Bill Nichols, *Introduction to Documentary* (Bloomington: Indiana University Press, 2001), 85.

6. I am sure Nichols would agree that the films I discuss in this essay *are* more fully documentary than the more strictly scientific use of cinema to collect data, which is his focus in the lines I have quoted. Nevertheless, the position he enunciates confirms the broad tendency not to take the nature film seriously *as cinema*. If I have stretched Nichols's position beyond what is fair, I apologize to him.

film or made an attempt to identify its pivotal moments and landmark contributions—and even the valuable chronology of the wildlife film Bousé includes in *Wildlife Films* is limited in significant ways.[7] It is hard to take a genre seriously if one has no sense of it *as a genre*—and especially since nature films are rarely exhibited as instances of an evolving history. Second, since research into natural phenomena, and other species in particular, is ongoing, and since it is in the nature of new research to make previous research outdated, nature films that may have seemed state-of-the-art at one point can seem outdated in a few years. This tendency is exacerbated by the fact that a good many nature films, especially those designed for use in primary and secondary schools, use strategies that may seem educational to one generation but hopelessly corny to the next: Bruce Conner's recycling of material from outdated educational films into surreal montages (in *Mongoloid* [1978], for instance) has the impact it does because these older educational films now seem more revealing of the absurdities of their era than of scientific information.

This essay makes no pretense of providing anything like a definitive overview of the nature film. I do hope it usefully references a few of the important historical contributions to the genre as a way of foregrounding some of the issues raised in nature films and some aspects of their value in a film studies context. The nature film has, of course, a long prehistory that arguably begins with the dawn of the photographic motion picture: Eadweard Muybridge's breakthrough animal locomotion photographs and Zoopraxiscope demonstrations and Etienne-Jules Marey's chronophotographs used a variety of animal species as their primary subject matter. During the first decades of film history, there was a minor tradition of "animal fight films" that included *A Fight between Spider and Scorpion* (1900, Biograph) and *A Fight between Wild Animals* (1912, Kalem).[8] Films about wildlife, especially hunting films, were important early contributions to the development of the cinema audience: *Roosevelt in Africa* (1910), shot by Cherry Kearton during Theodore Roosevelt's African expedition in 1909, and the more melodramatic and popular fictionalized version of Roosevelt's hunting adventures, *Hunting Big Game in Africa* (1909) by Colonel Selig, instigated a genre of "bring 'em back alive" films that included *Paul Rainey's African Hunt* (1912), William Douglas Burden's footage of the Komodo dragon, and Martin and Osa Johnson's *Trailing African Wild Animals* (1923) and

7. Both Mitman and Bousé focus primarily on American wildlife films, and both tend to exclude films that focus on insects and sea organisms.

8. Gaycken, "'A Drama Unites Them in a Fight to the Death,'" 368.

Simba (1927).[9] And, of course, exotic animals play pivotal roles in such early proto- or pseudo-ethnographic documentaries as Robert Flaherty's *Nanook of the North* (1922) and *Moana* (1926), and Ernest Schoedsack and Meriam C. Cooper's *Grass* (1925) and *Chang* (1927). The mythic version of these early films is, of course, *King Kong* (1933), produced by Cooper and Schoedsack and based on their own and others' adventures filming in the wild.[10]

While the early films about hunting exotic wild animals and about the symbiotic relationships between nonindustrialized peoples and animals provoked, and continue to provoke, widespread debate about what is science and what is showmanship, there were also attempts to use cinema to focus on the life cycles of other species, apart from their interaction with human society. Two particularly significant contributions to this history are the series of films made by Jean Painlevé, beginning with *The Octopus* (*La pieuvre*), *The Daphnia* (*La daphnie*), and *The Sea Urchin* (*L'oursin*) in 1928, and the Walt Disney Studio's True-Life Adventures (in particular, those directed by James Algar), beginning with *Seal Island* (1948), *Beaver Valley* (1950), and *Nature's Half Acre* (1951) and culminating in a series of features, including the commercial breakthroughs, *The Living Desert* (1953) and *The Vanishing Prairie* (1954). The Painlevé films and the Disney films could hardly be more different, especially in their exemplification of two distinct attitudes with regard to the cinematic representation of other species.

DISNEY VERSUS PAINLEVÉ

While Painlevé's pioneering efforts to demonstrate the potential of cinema for scientific experiment and to establish the nature film as a form that combines good science with entertainment and aesthetic awareness precede Disney's True-Life Adventure films by two decades, in the United States there is almost no awareness of Painlevé's contributions, while the Disney films not only are well-known but were formative for several generations of American children, and important for a good many adults as well. The in-

9. Gregg Mitman provides a useful overview of the evolution of the "bring 'em back alive" film in *Reel Nature*, chaps. 2 and 3.

10. The nature film was also an early staple of the ciné-club movement that swept Europe and the United Kingdom in the 1920s and 1930s. For example, at its third public presentation, on December 20, 1925, the London Film Society began the "*Film Society* Bionomica Series," which focused on animal and insect life; and throughout the Film Society's fourteen-year run, a nature film was regularly included within diverse programs that also included avant-garde works, revived classics, instructional films, animations, documentaries of all sorts, and narrative entertainments from around the world. See the London Film Society's *The Film Society Programs, 1925–1939* (New York: Arno Press, 1972).

dependent filmmaker Nathaniel Dorsky, for example, counts the early True-Life Adventures as one of the primary influences on his work: "I had started to make films with an 8mm camera when I was around ten or eleven. I was very influenced by the Disney True-Life Adventure series, like *Beaver Valley* and *Nature's Half Acre.* They were the first time I saw, for instance, flowers growing in time-lapse—very photographic films, held together with music and narration. Both films went through the four seasons, and for some reason, I was very taken with that."[11] I do not remember precisely when or where I first saw the early True-Life Adventures, but such characteristic elements as Winston Hibler's narrating voice and the use of an animated paintbrush to introduce the films remain deeply familiar artifacts of childhood.

Disney began production of wildlife films as a way of dealing with the financial problems created by the high cost of animation. Although the animated features the Disney Studio released during the 1940s were, and remained, immensely popular—*Pinocchio* (1940), *Fantasia* (1940), *Bambi* (1942), *Song of the South* (1946), and *Cinderella* (1949) were the five most popular films of that decade, according to the *New York Times Almanac*—the considerable cost of producing each of these features made them, at first, economically tenuous at best. During this financially stressed moment, the comparable cost of a nature film, even a feature nature film, allowed this new Disney product to be a financial success. While *Bambi* cost $2 million, and lost $1 million during its first run, *The Vanishing Prairie* cost around $350,000, and grossed $4 million.[12]

Furthermore, the True-Life Adventure films were, like the animations, durable: neither the animations nor the nature films aged as quickly as most live-action films tend to. Over the decades, the Disney animated features have done quite well, and they continue to be successful in rerelease, and while the nature films fell prey to changing science and an evolving social awareness (the opening narration of *The Vanishing Prairie,* for example, is patronizing to Native America in ways that have come to seem quite problematic), they too were able to last through their original theatrical runs to become popular television entertainment during the years when Disney was a major force in television programming, and the True-Life Ad-

11. Dorsky, in MacDonald, *A Critical Cinema,* 81. Dorsky's *Hours for Jerome* (shot in the late 1960s and edited in 1982) seems particularly indebted to the True-Life Adventures. Dorsky's film takes the viewer through a year in New York City and at a lakeside retreat in northern New Jersey, not particularly focusing on wildlife but creating a sense of the seasonal cycle, as represented by weather, plant life, and human activity, as a set of events worth contemplating in cinema.

12. Mitman, *Reel Nature,* 111–14.

ventures were ubiquitous in school libraries across the country during the decades when school districts routinely bought 16mm prints of educational films. Several of the feature True-Life Adventures can still be found in video rental outlets.

The popularity of the Disney films was a function of their combination of first-rate nature photography and forms of narrative entertainment developed by the Disney Studio during the decades that preceded the release of *Seal Island.* While the Disney nature photographers were sent into the field without a script to capture the most interesting imagery they could find and ideally, according to James Algar, "those unexpected and unpredictable happenings that cannot possibly be written into a story ahead of time,"[13] Disney made sure that the films that developed out of this cinematic research were as carefully constructed and as entertainment-driven as any film produced by a Hollywood studio. And if the Disney nature films seemed to their first audiences as far from politics or ideology as the early Silly Symphony cartoons, these films were powerful in supporting not only particular attitudes toward family life and gender but a deep complacency about the history of Manifest Destiny and modern middle-class life. Indeed, for all their charm and beauty, the True-Life Adventures can often seem to a contemporary viewer as ideologically motivated as *Animal Farm.*

In *The Vanishing Prairie,* as in so many Disney films, the focus is on the nuclear family, especially on the bond between mothers and children, and in particular on moments within the lives of animals that seem to mirror middle-class American mores and the gender politics of the time. The film begins with birds migrating—beautiful shots that seem premonitions of *Fly Away Home* (1996, directed by Carroll Ballard) and *Winged Migration*—then focuses on various avian courtship rituals and an amusing moment in the domestic life of a pair of grebes: a pie-billed grebe father looks after grebe eggs while the mother grebe is searching for food for several chicks. The father does not see that one of the eggs has gotten caught in his feathers and is pushed out of the nest when he steps out. The narrator comments, "Like most males he's rather careless about domestic chores!" and then mouths the thoughts of the mother grebe when she returns: "Well that's typical! Perhaps if he had to *lay* these eggs, he'd be more careful. I declare, these husbands—always leaving things for someone else to pick up!" The fact that the male grebe is tending to the children and the female grebe is out looking for food runs counter to white middle-class gender roles in the 1950s, but the possible impact of this moment is quickly

13. Algar in an interview with Gregg Mitman, ibid., 119.

suppressed in favor of humorous banter that locates the grebes within conventional family patterns.[14]

A sequence of amusing mating rituals among grouse leads to a passage on buffalo, highlighted by the birth of a buffalo calf, the mother's care of the calf, and the calf's first attempts to nurse; then to a passage on pronghorns and bighorn sheep; then to a long passage of a mother mountain lion caring for and training her cubs; then to a complex passage focusing primarily on a community of prairie dogs and their amusing attempts to deal with interlopers (including a mother coyote, searching for food for her pups, and a male badger that meets a female and falls in love). The climax of *The Vanishing Prairie* is a sequence that begins with buffalo in mating season (no actual mating is shown), followed by a lightning storm that starts a prairie fire, which is put out by heavy rain and a flood. The well-known and much-imitated finale takes us to mountains in winter, where male bighorn sheep battle to the music of "The Anvil Chorus." The film concludes with the narrator's assurance that "Nature preserves her own and teaches them how to cope with time and the unaccountable ways of man. Mankind in turn, beginning to understand Nature's pattern, is helping her to replenish and rebuild so that the vanishing pageant of the past may become the enduring pageant of the future."

It is, of course, a pageant that Disney provides in *The Vanishing Prairie, The Living Desert,* and the other True-Life Adventure films. We are sutured into the Disney vision by the continuous presence of the narrator; by the music, which is carefully and continuously synced with the action so as to create particular, interpretive cinematic moods; and by the film's visual and textual framing of the "adventures" of the animals. Not only do these films create animal characters that are meant to lure children, mothers, and fathers into emotional identification in much the same way as Disney's animated features do, but individual sequences are often fabricated to suggest that the animals, like the spectators in the theater, are interested observers of what is occurring on-screen. In *The Living Desert,* an owl "watches" a burrowing snake, a courtship ritual of tarantulas, and a courting dance of scorpions; and when ground squirrel "Skinny," the "kid from across the way," confronts a Gila monster and chases it away by kicking sand in its eyes, the heroic exploits of the little guy are watched and admired by the neigh-

14. In *Wildlife Films,* Bousé suggests that wildlife films may "entail an ever greater potential [than Hollywood features] for naturalizing ideological values—for example, by 'finding' in nature the predominance of the nuclear family, or the values of hard work, industry, and deferred gratification. Indeed, because wildlife films are about nature, there may be an even greater commitment than in Hollywood films to making things appear natural" (18).

borhood ground squirrels, who realize they have underestimated Skinny (at the end of the sequence, Skinny rides off into the sunset on the back of a desert tortoise). In other words, in these films as in any other Hollywood melodrama, we enjoy the pleasure of gazing at the private lives of characters we can identify with, and we share the characters' gazes at each other.

Originally, the True-Life Adventures provided a new, exotic form of entertainment (after half a century, at least judging from my recent classes on the history of documentary, the entertainment value of *The Living Desert* is still considerable for film students); it combined the conventional pleasures of entertainment film with the sense that the audience was learning something. Of course, the True-Life Adventures do create an expanded sense of the animals that inhabit particular regions, combined with an emotional residue of pleasant nostalgia for the innocent past and an implicit acceptance of the inevitable progress of civilization. The True-Life Adventures may have created in their first audiences a greater awareness of the natural environment, but it was an awareness qualified by a deep complacency. The natural world is valuable and admirable, the Disney films suggest, precisely to the degree it can be understood to reflect and confirm the ideology of contemporary American middle-class family life.

When one comes to the Painlevé films having first experienced the Disney nature films as a formative childhood influence, it is difficult not to feel that they are transformative, at least in terms of what we assume a nature film can be. Whereas the True-Life Adventures were instigated by financial concerns, Painlevé's nature films were an attempt to demonstrate the value of cinema for science (a highly controversial idea for French scientists of the 1920s),[15] and to simultaneously produce good science and good cinema (actually, Painlevé made two kinds of films: research films for use by scientists and films aimed at popular audiences; my focus here is on the latter). In a sense, the pageantry of the Disney films reflects their origins in the studio system: many of the True-Life Adventures were elaborate feature-length extravaganzas, produced within a hierarchical studio system involving many people. The Painlevé films are generally eight to fifteen minutes long and were relatively humble productions, often collaborations with Painlevé's longtime partner, Geneviève Hamon, in which Painlevé, working with technology he himself adapted for filming underwater, did his own cinematog-

15. When Painlevé's early research film *L'oeuf d'épinoche: De la fecundation à l'éclosion (The Stickleback's Egg: From Fertilization to Hatching* [1927]) was screened for scientists at the Académie des sciences in 1928, it was met with skepticism and outrage. "One scientist, infuriated, stormed out, declaring: 'Cinema is not to be taken seriously!'" Brigitte Berg notes (Painlevé, *Science Is Fiction,* ed. Bellows et al., 17).

raphy or worked with a single cameraperson (most frequently, André Raymond early on, and later, Eli Lotar). Like the Disney films, Painlevé's nature films were made in 35mm and were shown in public theaters. Indeed, one of these films, *The Seahorse* (*L'hippocampe,* 1934) was successful enough to support a spin-off: a line of seahorse jewelry designed by Hamon and displayed "in chic boutiques alongside aquariums filled with live seahorses."[16] But *The Seahorse* was the only Painlevé nature film to break even (and even the profits from the seahorse jewelry were stolen). Painlevé was, throughout his life, more a scientist and educator than a capitalist, and his energies were generally directed toward the promotion of science films as an educational tool.

Not surprisingly, given their vastly different production processes and purposes, the Painlevé nature films are very different from the Disney films, both in their scope and in the ideology that seems to underlie Painlevé's choices of subjects: the second of his "Ten Commandments" for filmmakers is "You will refuse to direct a film if your convictions are not expressed."[17] Each Painlevé film tends to focus on a single organism and, because of Painlevé's fascination with and commitment to underwater organisms, usually on a single sea creature. Each film presents, clearly and concisely, the crucial moments in the life cycle of the chosen organism, often beginning by recognizing that this particular organism might not at first seem worthy of being the focus of a film. In general, Painlevé's commitment is to reveal the wonder and the beauty even in organisms that some would consider beneath our notice (the sea urchin, for instance, or the acera, a tiny mollusk). And he is drawn to organisms, or aspects of organisms, that some would find disgusting: the South American vampire bat in *The Vampire* (*Le vampire,* 1945), for example, and the love life of the "cephalopod, horrifying animal" in *The Love Life of the Octopus* (*Les amours de la pieuvre,* 1965). Though the body of each film focuses on in-close examinations of an organism, Painlevé often makes clear how this organism relates to human society—in a simple practical sense. *The Vampire,* for example, introduces its examination of the vampire bat with a brief reminder of the pervasiveness of vampires in the arts and in our imaginations—a shot from Murnau's

16. Brigitte Berg, "Contradictory Forces: Jean Painlevé, 1902–1989," in Painlevé, *Science Is Fiction,* ed. Bellows et al., 25.

17. Painlevé's ten commandments were written in 1948 for a program called "Poets of the Documentary" and are reprinted in Painlevé, *Science Is Fiction,* ed. Bellows et al., 159. Commandment four, "You will seek reality without aestheticism or ideological apparatus," suggests that what Painlevé means by "convictions" in his second commandment is not *political* convictions in the contemporary sense but convictions that develop from an exploration of natural reality from an unbiased position.

Nosferatu (1922) is included; and *Shrimp Stories* (*Histoires des crevettes,* 1964) begins with imagery of men and women fishing for shrimp in ocean shallows.

While the True-Life Adventures tend to reconfirm, in live action, attitudes and ideas evident in Disney's early animated features and cartoons, the Painlevé films can be seen, at least in part, as related to Painlevé's interest in art and, in particular, surrealist art. Painlevé (the son of the distinguished mathematician and French prime minister Paul Painlevé) studied mathematics, then medicine, then biology and zoology. In 1923, at the age of twenty-one, he coauthored a scientific paper with one of his professors and presented it to the Académie des sciences, and in 1924, he graduated from the Sorbonne with a degree in physics, chemistry, and biology. By the time he graduated, he had become fascinated with the then-thriving French avant-garde art scene in Paris and soon was friendly with a number of the surrealists; he was one of the publishers of, and a contributor to, the single issue of the journal *Surréalisme.*[18] Painlevé also became involved with the ciné-club movement, which was sweeping through France and the rest of Europe, making available to public audiences a wide variety of forms of cinema not regularly screened in commercial theaters. Through ciné-club activity he became close friends with Jean Vigo, and in 1927 he finished his own short surrealist film, *Methuselah* (1927), which is reminiscent of René Clair's *Entr'acte* (1924). Painlevé's engagement with surrealism would continue; for example, he supplied the remarkable text for the narration of Georges Franju's *The Blood of the Beasts* (*Le sang des bêtes,* 1949).

The defiance of social convention implicit in Painlevé's early movement between the worlds of science and surrealist art is frequently evident in his nature films, especially in his (usually implicit, but clearly evident) reasons for focusing on particular organisms. While the Disney nature films focus on animals whose activities can be seen as analogous to or sentimentally reminiscent of the activities of the largely middle-class families who were their primary audience, Painlevé's choices often seem, at least in part, a function of the ways in which particular organisms offer a challenge to conventional societal assumptions and values. For example, in a conversation with Brigitte Berg, Painlevé makes clear that one of the reasons for his early

18. Painlevé's contribution to *Surréalisme* was a bit of prose that may well be coherent biology, though it reads like surrealist fantasy. The piece begins, "The plasmodium of the Myxomycetes is so sweet; the eyeless *Prorhynchus* has the dull color of the born-blind, and its proboscis stuffed with zoochlorellae solicits the oxygen of the *Frontoniella antypyretica;* he carries his pharynx in a rosette, a locomotive requirement, horned, stupid, and not at all calcareous." The entire contribution is included in Painlevé, *Science Is Fiction,* ed. Bellows et al., 117.

choice of the seahorse as subject was the way the male and female seahorses collaborate on raising their young: the abdomen of the male seahorse has a pouch into which the female lays her eggs; once the eggs are fertilized, the male nourishes the eggs and, in time, gives birth to the baby seahorses in a manner reminiscent of female human labor. As Painlevé explained to Berg, "The seahorse was for me a splendid way of promoting the kindness and virtue of the father while at the same time underlining the necessity of the mother. In other words, I wanted to re-establish the balance between male and female."[19] Painlevé uses his cinematic report on seahorses to do what he sees as progressive gender politics; he wants us to learn not only *about,* but *from* this strange fish.

Painlevé's interest in the acera mollusks in *Acera or the Witches' Dance* (*Acéra ou le bal des sorcières,* 1972) seems to have two motivations: one of them obvious and the other more subtle. Of obvious interest is the acera's way of finding a mate; as suggested in the film's title, the acera do a kind of ballet, during which the cloaks that encircle their bodies fly open, evoking tutus. A substantial portion of the film is devoted to shots of this dance, which is fascinating and lovely—and reminiscent of moments from films by Oskar Fischinger and from Disney's *Fantasia.* A brief shot of what appears to be Michèle Nadal doing an imitation of Loïe Fuller's "Serpentine Dance" is edited into the sequence of acera doing their witches' dance, Painlevé's way of recognizing a connection between this lowly species and humanity.

Once the acera have found mates, we learn that their means of sexual reproduction could not be further from anything even implied in a Disney film: each acera is bisexual and can function sexually as either male or female, or, as is demonstrated in *Acera or the Witches' Dance,* as simultaneously male *and* female: we see in one instance a chain of five acera in which each of the three middle partners in the sexual act is fertilizing the eggs in one acera and, at the same time, having its own eggs fertilized by another acera. For Painlevé the beauty of the acera does not depend on its mimicking conventional Western assumptions about sexual morality. One can only imagine the repercussions if this lovely film were shown in high school biology classes!

The Vampire, the best-known Painlevé film, at least in this country, makes its politics more specific and more overt. During the German occupation of France, Painlevé was persona non grata for a variety of reasons, including his activities in helping immigrants on the run from fascism to obtain work visas and French citizenship. Painlevé spent the Occupation years in hiding,

19. Ibid., 23.

and is said to have escaped to Spain underwater, using scuba diving gear. Just before the war, Painlevé had seen, for the first time, the Brazilian vampire bat (*Desmodus rotundus*) and had begun work on what would become *The Vampire*. His interest in the creature and the film seems to have been closely related to his hatred of Nazism: the bat, which could be a scourge to its animal and human neighbors, was, like the Nazis, a "brown pest." Near the end of *The Vampire*, soon after we have seen how the bats can transmit disease, Painlevé reveals "the salute of the vampire": "When I was finishing the film, I noticed how the vampire bat extends its wing before going to sleep. I thought it looked like the Nazi 'Heil-Hitler' salute."[20] In this instance, the bat is used overtly as a political metaphor in a way that is not particularly characteristic of Painlevé's work—though, as usual, the film is good science.

Throughout his career, Painlevé's primary commitment was to support the creation of first-rate science films and the development of public audiences for these and other forms of cinema that might function to energize and inform the public. Soon after the war, Painlevé became president of the French Federation of Ciné-Clubs, and he continued to promote the use of cinema as a way of popularizing science through his work with the Institute of Scientific Cinema, which he had founded in 1930, and by helping to found the International Association of Science Films, which held conferences where science films from around the world were screened. He was also among the first science filmmakers to work with television and in time would experiment with new video techniques. While for Disney, the nature film was one small part in the construction of an empire, for Painlevé, filmmaking always remained a means of democratizing scientific research and of using cinema to work across theoretical and cultural distinctions to share information about our remarkably complex, sometimes terrifying, but always wondrous world.

INADVERTENT ENVIRONMENTAL POLITICS IN NATIONAL GEOGRAPHIC'S *SONORAN DESERT, A VIOLENT EDEN* (1997)

For a number of years, I have spent time in and around the Sonoran Desert near Tucson, Arizona. At first, my visits were brief—spring break escapes from central New York State winters—but in time, the visits got longer. The first version of this essay was written during my fourth full winter and spring living in the desert. I have lived in three locations to the west of Tucson, two of them in the eastern foothills of the Tucson Mountains, the third,

20. Ibid., 33

several miles west of the range, within sight of the western headquarters of the Saguaro National Park and about two miles from the Arizona-Sonora Desert Museum. During these stays I have done a good bit of desert walking and like many locals have often made water and "quail blocks" (solid blocks of seed and grain beloved of birds and rodents) available to the neighboring wildlife. I have read some of the literature the Sonoran Desert has inspired and have talked with park rangers and other more permanent locals about the desert—and have even considered buying desert land while some is still available.

I had already developed an affection for and a fascination with the Sonoran Desert when, during one of my winters in central New York State, I noticed that a National Geographic documentary, *Sonoran Desert, a Violent Eden,* was about to air on television. I watched the hour-long piece with considerable interest and found the film stunning and informative—but came away troubled by its impact. Indeed, in the days after watching the film, I found I was questioning whether I wanted to spend the following winter in the Tucson area, as I had planned—a feeling that hovered in my near consciousness for quite some time. This experience helped to instigate a deeper interest in nature filmmaking and has caused some revisions in my courses in the history of documentary. What is interesting to me is how a seemingly scientific film about a specific place can create various contradictory levels of impact, and how some of this impact may well have subtle political effects that the filmmakers may not have foreseen.

Sonoran Desert, a Violent Eden was produced and written by Sean Morris and, in its video release, is part of a series of films, "World's Last Great Places."[21] In general, it is a perfectly competent, relatively conventional nature film, beautifully photographed (by Morris, Keith Brust, and a number of assistants), well edited (by Barry Nye), and contextualized by a traditional voice-of-god narrator (Richard Kiley). Indeed, whereas the True-Life Adventures use footage collected by first-rate wildlife photographers

21. Other titles include *Antarctica, the Last Wilderness; Arctic Kingdom, Life at the Edge; Baja, Mexico's Cactus Forest; Belize, a Tropical Kingdom; Everglades, Secrets of the Swamp; Galapagos Islands, Land of Dragons; Hidden Congo, Forest Primeval; Lake Tanganyika, Jewel of the Rift; Namib Desert, Africa's Hostile Dunes; Panama Wild, Rain Forest of Life; Tanzania, Thorn Tree Country.*

I do not have particular enough memories of my first viewing of *Sonoran Desert, a Violent Eden* to remember whether that viewing was identical to the one provided on the VHS of the piece available from National Geographic. On the VHS, it is preceded by two advertisements for other National Geographic pieces: *Nature's Fury* (1994; the advertisement presents a series of images of relatively horrific instances of "nature's fury") and *The Photographers* (1996), an encomium to the people who gather images for National Geographic television films.

within a context that has at most the aura of science, the science in *Sonoran Desert, a Violent Eden* is, so far as I have been able to determine, relatively accurate, at least in the sense that the creatures are not anthropomorphized in ways that tend to obscure the realities of the biota of which they are a part. Indeed, one naturalist at the Desert Museum told me that Sean Morris and his collaborators were able to capture events he had never seen during a lifetime of studying the desert: the horned lizard squirting a coyote with blood from a pouch in its eye socket, for example. Nevertheless, the filmic exploration of the Sonoran Desert in *Sonoran Desert, a Violent Eden* is problematic.

Sonoran Desert, a Violent Eden opens with a visual précis of what is to follow, then the National Geographic identification logos and an indication that Richard Kiley is the narrator. The tone is set by the subtitle *a Violent Eden* and by the opening lines of the précis: "This is a stern and unforgiving land, a withering desert, tormented by the sun; only the most superbly adapted creatures can survive here and the blink of an eye can separate life from death." These lines are accompanied by a sequence that begins with an image of a Gila monster, followed by shots of an antelope squirrel running and being struck by a rattlesnake, a deer sensing danger, another shot of the Gila monster, a battle between a deer mouse and a centipede, bees seemingly attacking something, and a tarantula darting out of its hole to strike a roach. The body of *Sonoran Desert* follows, moving the viewer roughly through a calendar year, beginning in late winter and ending after the late summer monsoon has allowed life to burst forth, "a sign of triumph and a time of celebration."

After the passage of landscape shots that follows the précis and opening credits, during which the narrator provides information about the Sonoran Desert's geologic past, the film develops a consistent rhythm: sequences focusing on particular creatures are intercut with short, time-lapsed passages of landscape and skyscape that function as transitions through time and from topic to topic. Roughly, the topics covered include snakes and Gila monsters coming out of hibernation at the end of winter, mating, and searching for and finding food ("for their prey, the desert is a death trap"); cactus bees harvesting the blooms of prickly pear cacti, mating, providing food for their offspring, becoming exhausted, and being eaten by ants, birds, and lizards; a family of thrashers protecting their nest from a king snake; nectar bats finding their way to saguaro blooms; sand scorpions becoming cannibals during the heat of midsummer and being eaten by a shovel-nosed snake; a battle between a grasshopper mouse and a ten-inch centipede (one of the "terrible monsters that are on the prowl" during summer nights); plants and animals enduring or succumbing to the brutal heat; the saguaro producing fruit; coyotes taking advantage of a weakened javelina; a horned lizard eating ants and a coyote trying to kill the lizard; a late-summer lightning storm causing a fire; monsoon rains creating flooded washes and ponds in which spadefoot toads live, breed, and die; and the desert covered with poppies after the rains.

As may be evident from this description, *Sonoran Desert, a Violent Eden* is focused primarily on the struggle for food and on desert creatures mating to survive—basically the same foci as in the Painlevé films and the Disney True-Life Adventures. In some ways, the National Geographic film is more like the Disney than the Painlevé films: for instance, it pretends to cover an entire region, rather than a single species. But, like the Painlevé films, it is more candid about what the creatures actually do. Indeed, *Sonoran Desert, a Violent Eden* focuses on what Disney tends to suppress: open depictions of the deaths and the sex acts of the creatures. Early in the film we see, in extreme close-up, rattlesnakes having sex and, soon after this, an expanded version of the scene in the précis during which an antelope squirrel runs from a Gila monster only to be struck and engorged by a rattler; then a Gila monster eating, first, the eggs of a Gambel's quail, then the babies of a white-footed deer mouse—a counter to the Disney tendency to romanticize and suburbanize animals (the narrator explains that "the white-footed deer mouse is a diligent, successful mother" of her week-old "pink babies" just before the Gila monster arrives to eat them). In general, whereas the Painlevé films are brief, witty, poetic science lectures, and the Disney True-Life Adventures, somewhat slapstick comedy-romances, *Sonoran Desert, a Violent Eden* is an action-adventure drama that exudes something of the aura of the early "bring 'em back alive" films.

While all the events depicted certainly do occur, with various degrees of frequency, like any typical action-adventure film, *Sonoran Desert* tends to temporally condense the activities depicted into what becomes an extravaganza of the violent and the bizarre; basically, it constructs a fiction from nonfictional elements.[22] Indeed, the assumption of the film seems to be that it is precisely the unending series of violent events revealed in the film that renders the Sonoran Desert distinctive, one of the "Last Great Places." But all natural environments are full of predators of one kind or another; preda-

22. The tendency of nature films, particularly those hoping to appeal to a general audience, to focus on battles between animals and insects is evident in some of the earliest films that depict insects and animals. See Oliver Gaycken's discussion of *Le Scorpion languedocien* (Éclair, 1912), in which a scorpion attacks and kills a rat, in "'A Drama Unites Them in a Fight to the Death,'" 362–70.

tory "violence" is no more frequent in the Sonoran Desert than in a lake in the Catskills or on a Wisconsin dairy farm: creatures prey on other creatures everywhere, and in ways that, if we saw them in the kinds of close-ups cinema can provide, might seem as impressive as what one sees in *Sonoran Desert, a Violent Eden.*

Further, and more precisely relevant here, the moment one walks into the Sonoran Desert, one experiences a radically different sense of the place from what the film suggests. *Sonoran Desert* excludes much of what might cause a viewer to feel the serene beauty of this environment, where bird life seems to dominate (it is a favorite haunt for birders), and the animals most in evidence are the cottontail rabbit (not represented in the film) and other, smaller rodents. It is true that the Sonoran Desert is home to several poisonous species—several kinds of rattlesnakes, the bark scorpion, and the Gila monster—but the actual danger of these creatures has always been exaggerated by conventional cinematic depictions of the region, and it is exaggerated in *Sonoran Desert.* According to a local Tucson hiking guide, the overwhelming majority of rattlesnake bites are "incurred while someone [often someone under the influence of alcohol], usually a fifteen- to twenty-five-year-old male, is playing with the snake"; no human deaths from scorpion bites have occurred in thirty years; and to get bitten by the rarely seen Gila monster, "you would practically have to fall near one and surprise it."[23] The biggest danger in the Sonoran Desert is probably skin cancer. Indeed, Craig Ivanyi, a curator at the Desert Museum, took particular umbrage at the implication in the film that the Gila monster was an aggressive, dangerous creature: "The Gila monster is the gem of our desert, and if you should be so lucky as to see one, you should treasure the experience."[24]

The documentary effectiveness of *Sonoran Desert, a Violent Eden,* for anything beyond somewhat sensational entertainment, is particularly compromised by the film's refusal to recognize that the human being is now the most visible species in much of the Sonoran Desert (and of course has been part of this environment for centuries); indeed, some of *Sonoran Desert* was shot near the Desert Museum, which is the second most popular tourist attraction (after the Grand Canyon) in Arizona. The only indication in the film that the relatively recent arrival of millions of human beings may have had an environmental impact on the region is the narrator's mention, over footage of the desert wildfire created by the lightning storm, that "wildfires are new to the Sonoran. Plants introduced by man are what make the brush dense

23. Betty Leavengood, *Tucson Hiking Guide* (Boulder, CO: Pruett, 1991), 9, 10–11.
24. I spoke with Ivanyi on the phone on April 8, 2005.

enough to burn." The film's remarkable erasure of human settlement from the Sonoran Desert, while not unusual for a nature film, is a convenient way of avoiding the fact that this "Last Great Place," this "Eden," is, for all the symbiosis of its flora and fauna, endangered.[25] In other words, the film provides a way of entertaining an audience in part by creating a sense that the audience is learning about reality, while at the same time enforcing the audience's complacency about the fragility of the environment depicted.

All in all, the impact of the Sonoran Desert in *Sonoran Desert, a Violent Eden* is somewhat similar to the impact of "If It Bleeds, It Leads" news shows. If one watches this kind of news coverage long enough, one can hardly fail to become frightened. I am sure that the makers of *Sonoran Desert* found the desert beautiful and fascinating—why else would they devote so much time and energy to making the film?—but the impact of their depiction seems more likely to alienate their audience from the desert than to engender respect for it. And this alienation is particularly a problem, given the fact that the southern Arizona climate continues to attract new residents at record-setting rates. If these new residents arrive with deep-seated fears of the natural environment of the region, they are all the more likely to be drawn to forms of residential development that eliminate direct experience of the desert, and they are far less likely to see what remains of the desert as worth protecting. The Sonoran Desert may be one of the "Last Great Places," but given the grotesqueness of what goes on there, the film inadvertently suggests, maybe it is just as well that it *is* disappearing in the face of suburban development. While the makers of *Sonoran Desert, a Violent Eden* may not have wanted to make a pro–suburbia / urban sprawl film, the

25. On March 22, 2005, I spent an hour with Rick Brusca, executive program director, and Mark A. Dimmitt, director of natural history, of the Arizona-Sonora Desert Museum outside Tucson, and both confirmed my sense of the depiction of the Sonoran Desert offered by *Sonoran Desert, a Violent Eden*. Both agreed that the film was well done, and in some cases provided remarkable imagery of rarely seen desert events (some of them filmed at the Desert Museum), but they found that the film's overall sense of the desert was exaggerated and for all practical purposes a fiction. Craig Ivanyi responded the same way in my conversation with him (note 24).

Despite the misleading title, *Namib Desert, Africa's Hostile Dunes* (made in 1977 by David Saxon and David Hughes and finished as *Creatures of the Namib Desert*, another film in the Last Great Places series but not released as part of the series until 1998) avoids the exaggerations and distortions of *Sonoran Desert, a Violent Eden*. Its focus, as its original title suggests, is on the adaptations of those species that live in the Namib desert, which includes, of course, some species preying on others. But this film does not exaggerate the predatory nature of the environment it depicts; further, it does not ignore the lovely serenity of the place or the history of human presence in this environment; we meet men and women researchers who love the Namib. The irony is that the Arizona-Sonora Desert Museum, where much of *Sonoran Desert, a Violent Eden* was shot, is far less remote than the research center shown in *Namib Desert, Africa's Hostile Dunes*.

subtle impact of the film might well confirm a fear of the desert and a desire for protection from it. For all practical purposes, *Sonoran Desert, a Violent Eden* transforms one of the world's most beautiful environments into a problem to be overcome by modern consumer society.[26]

THE NATURAL WORLD AS PARALLEL UNIVERSE: *A DIVIDED WORLD* (1948) AND *MICROCOSMOS* (1996)

One of the problems with the failure of academic film studies to seriously explore the nature film is that even landmarks in the genre have gotten lost, at least for the overwhelming majority of viewers—sometimes when such a loss was easily avoidable. A particularly good example is the Swedish director Arne Sucksdorff's remarkable short *A Divided World.* During the postwar explosion of the film society movement in the United States, the Sucksdorff film was celebrated. It was shown at Cinema 16, accompanied by program notes written by the distinguished critic Arthur Knight. During the following decades, when public, school, and university libraries were buying 16mm films, *A Divided World* was often part of these collections. In recent years, however, as many academics have abandoned 16mm, these libraries have closed, and many of what were considered film classics a generation ago are no longer available to audiences. This seems particularly the case with nature films, including *A Divided World,* which is no longer in distribution in the United States.[27]

A Divided World begins with an organist playing a Bach fantasia, as we see shots of a marsh and a snowy forest, lit by a full moon. A small church and a cemetery and several houses in a small village are visible; then, slowly, the camera moves back into the snow-covered forest, where we see the eyes

26. An interesting comparison and contrast to *Sonoran Desert, a Violent Eden* is provided by the recent *Secrets of the Sonoran Desert* (2004, photographed by Gilbert Urias, written by Marcia Hall and Jean Henderer). A thoroughly conventional documentary (with a voice-of-god narrator: Russell Buchanan), *Secrets* covers much the same ground as *Sonoran Desert, a Violent Eden.* It is less coherently organized and less impressively photographed than the earlier film—and sometimes confirms stereotypes included in *Sonoran Desert, a Violent Eden* (creepy music is used with reptiles, for example). But the makers place much less emphasis on violence and melodrama and much more on celebrating the beauty of the area. They do not demonize the Gila monster; and they do not entirely ignore the presence of human beings and the fact that the growing human population in the American Southwest is having negative impacts on animal habitat and species diversity.

27. I have a decent 16mm print of *A Divided World* only because a public library in northern Minnesota gave away its collection of 16mm films. Over the years I have often presented "Cinema 16 shows" at colleges, universities, and other organizations interested in film history, and the nature films that Cinema 16 audiences saw and admired have consistently been the hardest to locate.

of a distant owl, and the music becomes subdued as the night cries of animals and birds become audible. A tiny white mink is eating the carcass of a bird, but it runs and hides from a fox, which eats what remains. A white rabbit is seen running through the woods (the church is seen in the distance at one point), as wind blows through the trees, making eerie shadows on the snow. The eyes of the owl are again seen in the distance. The owl then flies across the woods and confronts the fox, which has apparently killed the rabbit. As the weasel watches, staying carefully out of reach, the owl and fox battle over the carcass. The owl flies off with the carcass, and the fox is seen nursing an injured paw. At the end of the film, as Arthur Knight suggested in his program notes, "when the camera turns back to the snug little house on the edge of the forest, civilization takes on new meanings. The music of Bach suggests the sublimation of primitive instincts through art and man's creation."[28]

Much of the impact of *A Divided World* comes from Sucksdorff's recognition that the two parts of our "divided world" are in very close proximity, that indeed they exist in virtually the same place and time. In *A Divided World,* one world is visually the background of the other and vice versa, and the Bach fantasia and the sounds of nature interweave throughout the film. While the action in *A Divided World* is reminiscent of both *Sonoran Desert, a Violent Eden* and the Disney True-Life Adventures—like *Sonoran Desert,* Sucksdorff's film focuses on a series of predatory encounters between animals; and as in *The Vanishing Prairie* and *The Living Desert,* humor is added by the presence of the tiny white mink—its impact is very different from that of these other films, in large part because of Sucksdorff's way of combining reality and fantasy.

It is a fundamental tendency of the nature film to use long shots of real landscapes to cover up the fact that the in-close shots of animal or insect life are fabricated within carefully controlled environments.[29] While the kinds of events we see may be part of the real existence of the creatures depicted, the particular depictions are constructed, either by setting up a situation that would be impractical to wait for (when a giant saguaro falls in *Sonoran Desert, a Violent Eden,* we recognize that while such an event is inevitable for every saguaro, this one was toppled specifically for the film),

28. Scott MacDonald, *Cinema 16: Documents toward a History of the Film Society,* 144. Cinema 16 was the most successful and influential of American film societies for more than sixteen years.

29. As Gaycken explains, even in the earliest nature films, the movement from long shot of real environment to close-up of fabricated environment "is deployed in order to enhance the believability of the ethological fiction that the observations are of animals in their natural habitats" (364). He describes a number of such instances, pointing out that match-on-action shots are the primary tool for accomplishing this illusion.

or by creatively editing events (the rattler striking the antelope squirrel at the beginning of *Sonoran Desert* was clearly constructed in the editing). Both methods are used in *A Divided World.*

However, while the animals and their actions in *A Divided World* are clearly real—and, as in most nature films, are made reasonably convincing by careful control of mini-environments and creative editing—the scintillant, gorgeously lit long shots of farm and woods *and* the close-ups of the animals (all of which are beautiful specimens, seemingly unmarked by life in the wild) create an aura of fantasy, and as a result, the film seems more a parable than an exercise in stark realism. The houses and church appear to be models. No people are ever visible, though during the final shot of the farmhouse at the end, smoke is coming out of the chimney. This is a fairy-tale town. Ultimately, the two levels of Sucksdorff's divided world recontextualize each other, each making the other seem less solid, less complete, less "real." The ambiguity of the film is confirmed by what is perhaps the most obvious deviation from the conventional nature film in *A Divided World:* Sucksdorff's refusal of direct commentary or explanation. There is neither text nor narration, and the result is a sense that both human nature and nonhuman nature are beautiful and powerful mysteries.

A related approach is evident in the remarkable French feature *Microcosmos: Le peuple de l'herbe* ("The People of the Grass") by Claude Nuridsany and Marie Pérennou. In making *Microcosmos,* Nuridsany and Pérennou were at great pains to combine science and art as a means of avoiding some of the implications of more conventional nature films. According to Pérennou, "We try to engage the imagination of the spectator. We tell the story of this world as if it were an opera, not simple biology. We are right in the middle of art and science; we put these two fields together—people have a tendency to separate them."[30] As is true in *A Divided World* (and in some of the Painlevé films as well), in *Microcosmos,* the focus is not on a distant, exotic, vanishing "Last Great Place" but on dimensions of the everyday world we normally ignore: in this case, the life of insects in a meadow during the summer.[31] And, like Sucksdorff, Nuridsany and Pérennou do not pretend to explain what they show us but, rather, confront us with the essential mystery, beauty, and wonder of our natural surround.

While the overall organization of *Microcosmos* is similar to the organization of *Sonoran Desert, a Violent Eden*—each begins with a précis, followed

30. Pérennou, in an interview with Charles Wright, in Phoenix.com archives, 1996.

31. Of course, sometimes Painlevé does choose to focus on exotic creatures—in *The Vampire,* for instance—but, at least in the films I have seen, his more frequent choice is to explore the lives of organisms that most of us would normally consider beneath our notice.

by a bit of general commentary, followed by the body of the film, during which we move back and forth between often beautiful landscape shots that purport to be the environment being considered and close-ups of the lives unfolding within this environment—the two films could hardly be more different in tone and impact. Whereas the narration in *Sonoran Desert* is virtually continuous and is meant simultaneously to explain what we are seeing *and* to communicate the filmmakers' sense of the Sonoran Desert as a violent and dangerous (although sometimes beautiful) place, *Microcosmos* uses only two brief passages of narration during its eighty minutes (both spoken by Kristin Scott Thomas). Each is an attempt to promote a form of spectatorship unusual for a film with a scientific bent.

During the précis, we move from airplane shots of cloudscapes down to a helicopter shot of a meadow and then *into* the meadow grass and into microscopic cinematography that makes the grass stems look like tree trunks. And we hear the first of the two passages of narration:

> A meadow in early morning, somewhere on earth.
> Hidden here is a world as vast as our own,
> Where the weeds are impenetrable jungles,
> The stones are mountains,
> And even the smallest pond becomes an ocean.
> Time passes differently here.
> An hour is like a day;
> A day is like a season;
> And the passing of a season is a lifetime.
> But to observe this world, we must fall silent now and listen to its murmurs.

And the filmmakers do fall silent, at least verbally, until nearly the end of the film.

Nuridsany and Pérennou's decision to back away from words and to allow what they show us to speak for itself reflects their confidence in both their subject matter and their cinematic skills in communicating what they feel about the world they are depicting. And it reveals a very different attitude toward the natural world from that revealed in *Sonoran Desert*. For Nuridsany and Pérennou, the natural world is an astonishing, not a fearful, place. As Pérennou explains, "Insects are so often portrayed as little robots who are always killing each other, like [in] science fiction movies. To us they are like mythological creatures, creatures of great beauty."[32] This attitude is

32. Pérennou interview.

evident in the decision both to have a soft-spoken female voice speak the two brief passages of narration that are included and to use language that is poetically evocative, rather than, as in *Sonoran Desert,* blunt and definitive.

Of course, in *Microcosmos,* as in most nature films, music and sound effects do function as indirect forms of narration. In general, Nuridsany and Pérennou use various combinations of sound effects, sometimes by themselves, sometimes along with one of several forms of music (the sound design of the film is by Laurent Quaglio; the original music, by Bruno Coulais). At times, it is not entirely clear whether a sound *is* a sound effect or a musical imitation of insect sounds, while at others, imagery is accompanied by orchestral, sometimes operatic music. The mood created by the sound effects and music depends on the particular subject matter, but the filmmakers are at great pains to avoid using music that might confirm conventional clichés about insects being creepy and dirty. While the use of Bach in *A Divided World* emphasizes the gap between the civilized world and the goings-on in the forest, in *Microcosmos,* music and other sound are used to create a respect for the insects.

During the body of *Microcosmos,* we are presented with a considerable variety of insect life, organized roughly into the cycle of a typical summer day, beginning with early morning and ending, after an evening rainstorm, with night.[33] Imagery of insects (and in one instance a pheasant), based on fifteen years of research and three years of shooting (in some cases with equipment designed by the filmmakers), is presented at appropriate moments during the daily cycle. It is, of course, one of the inherent dimensions of theatrical cinema that the combination of camera and projector magnifies whatever is shot, and in this particular instance, cinematic magnification powerfully confirms the stunning microphotography by Nuridsany, Pérennou, Hugues Ryffel, and Thierry Machado. What is most notable about *Microcosmos,* however, is that the directors choose to place particular emphasis on astonishing dimensions, not of exotic creatures we are relatively unacquainted with, but of the most common insects, and often insects conventionally considered pests.

One of the early sequences in the film begins by following a ladybug crawling onto a stem where ants are tending to a colony of aphids. The ants repel the ladybug, which goes on its way, and we watch as the ants harvest

33. Because narrative development, especially controllable narrative development leading to climax, is difficult to find, or even to orchestrate, in nature films, it is common for longer nature films to include either fires or dramatic rainstorms, or both—often just where a commercial dramatic feature would present its climax.

the honeydew the aphids are producing.[34] The clarity of this imagery negates the need for narration, allowing us to confront the astonishing spectacle of one insect species domesticating another, protecting it, and caring tenderly for it. In another of the film's most remarkable sequences, two snails are apparently having sex. They are filmed in gorgeous, extended, glistening visuals, accompanied by operatic music. The visual beauty of the sequence and the operatic track seem perfectly matched. The film's final sequence powerfully confirms the filmmakers' tendency to invest the mundane with deep significance: after the second passage of narration, an insect—most viewers, I would guess, are not clear at first what insect this might be—emerges from water, undergoing several astonishing and beautiful transformations, to the accompaniment of orchestral music. At the climax of the passage, we realize that the amazing process we have witnessed was the growth of a common mosquito.

While visual beauty is an aspect of many nature films—the True-Life Adventures are full of beautiful shots, and the long shots of the Sonoran Desert in *Sonoran Desert* are lovely—in *Microcosmos,* the filmmakers are at considerable pains to confirm their respect for the insect world by consistently creating lovely visual compositions and a sumptuous palette of color. But often it is the mythical dimension of "the people of the grass" that seems to determine the directors' decision to include the images they choose. The sequence of a dung beetle pushing its ball along the ground, only to have it get stuck on a thorn, and then struggling to free the ball until it can once again continue on its way is reminiscent of the mythological character of Sisyphus; the pheasant that attacks the ant colony, seen sometimes from inside the anthill, is reminiscent of many mythological giants, from the Cyclops to King Kong; and the emergence of the mosquito at the end of the film evokes, as Pérennou has indicated, the mythological Venus, "rising out of the water."[35] Indeed, it is this mythological character of the world of insect life that justifies the loving attention that the filmmakers have dedicated to the film. As in some of the Painlevé films, in *Microcosmos,* it is as much what we can learn *from* the activities in this "underworld" as it is what we can learn *about* them that seems crucial for Nuridsany and Pérennou.

The implication of the National Geographic series title "Last Great Places" is that the subjects of these films are among the few remaining

34. Aphids suck the sugars produced by plants, but they cannot digest all of what they imbibe and release some of it through their anuses in the form of liquid, or "honeydew," which is eaten by the ants.

35. Pérennou interview.

Dung beetle as Sisyphus in Claude Nuridsany and Marie Pérennou's *Microcosmos* (1996). Courtesy Claude Nuridsany and Marie Pérennou.

"Edenic" wilderness environments on earth—"Edenic" meaning, apparently, not interfered with by humanity. And yet, to maintain what is essentially a fantasy, the director, Sean Morris, needs to go to great lengths to hide the human presence in the Sonoran Desert. Nuridsany and Pérennou, on the other hand, do not participate in the kind of romantic fantasy promoted by Morris and National Geographic; they are interested in using cinema to rediscover the complexity of the real life that surrounds us, to alert us to a world "beyond anything we could imagine / And yet almost beneath our notice," as they explain in the narration that leads into the final sequence of *Microcosmos.* The life forms they reveal to us have clearly adapted to life as successfully as we have, and in a "neighborhood" they share with human beings. The message here is not one of fear and disgust but one of empathy, respect, and appreciation.

One context for thinking about the two very different attitudes reflected in the films discussed in this essay is postcolonial theory. The Disney films and *Sonoran Desert, a Violent Eden* are similar in their refusal to allow the creatures they depict anything like their own voice. In both, narration and interpretive music are relentless. That is, in these films the creatures are treated like colonial subjects, subjects that are fully understood by the experts who have come to record them and whose exotic lives must be, and can be, explained to the viewer. Further, the creatures are understood within a set of stereotypes supplied by those who have come to document their lives: the filmic interpretations of many of the actions of the animals and insects in the Disney films are clearly projections of stereotypical middle-class American family experiences; and many of the events in *Sonoran Desert* reflect conventional stereotypes of the brutality of the exotic animal and insect life depicted.

A different sensibility is evident at many moments in the Painlevé films and throughout *Microcosmos.* Painlevé often allows the creatures he records to "speak for themselves": for example, we are allowed to watch the acera dance without continual textual comment intervening; their dance is seen as fundamentally similar in function to the dances we do—though the acera are more graceful than most of us. In *Microcosmos,* the activities of the insects are seen not as exotic and implicitly inferior to human activities. Rather, the activities of these generally familiar creatures are magnified and mythologized, and we come to understand their lives as different, effective, fully evolved strategies for living in the real world.[36] Nuridsany and Pérennou remind us that human life needs insect life more than insect life needs us. Who knows, they imply, what the remarkable adaptive strategies we can see around us every day might teach us during coming decades as we confront our growing environmental crisis and new challenges to *our* adaptability?

A few final conjectures. In her video *The Head of a Pin* (2003), Su Friedrich intercuts between long and medium shots documenting a vacation near the Delaware River in northern New Jersey (Friedrich and several others live in a small cabin and walk to the river to enjoy swimming and picnicking) and in-close shots of a spider subduing and wrapping a wasp or a mayfly that has gotten caught in its web.[37] During the shots of the spider and its prey, the vacationers discuss the strange, grisly spectacle and at one point admit to each other that "what we know about nature" would fit "on the head of a pin." Near the end of the video, the final in-close shot of the spider and its now wrapped and stored prey concludes when the camera pulls back and up, and we realize that this tiny saga of predation has been occurring

36. Sucksdorff's view seems more ambivalent. He does suggest that our world is divided between a fallen creation and a human realm to some degree secure from the brutalities of nature as a result of a spiritual connection with God—and yet, in *A Divided World,* both realms seem equally real and unreal. The natural world seems sensually more beautiful than the human world, just as the colonial world often seems more sensual than the "more civilized" colonizing world—and yet, at least in *A Divided World,* the human realm seems comparatively empty.

37. I have not been able to determine whether the insect is a wasp (Braconidae or Ichneumonidae) or a stem sawfly (Cephidae). Thanks to Dr. William H. Gotwald Jr., professor of biology at Utica College, for his assistance in narrowing the possibilities.

Cathy Quinlan identifying flower in Su Friedrich's *The Head of a Pin* (2004). Courtesy Su Friedrich.

underneath the kitchen table in the cabin. As in *A Divided World,* we see that what can seem to be two different worlds are simply two aspects of the same space; but whereas Sucksdorff emphasizes the differences between two mysterious realms, Friedrich's concluding gesture suggests the relationship between what is going on below the table and what normally occurs on top of it: both spiders and humans live by means of periodic exploitation of other life forms, and intelligence lies in recognizing the intricate relationships between what may at first seem separate worlds.

In the present context, *The Head of a Pin* can serve as a metaphor for the gap that has formed between the humanities and the sciences in the current American academic environment. Although educators generally recognize that anything like a sensible liberal arts education requires experiences with both the sciences and the humanities, the tendency for many faculty and students is to see one of these areas as primary and the other as, for all practical purposes, a strange, hidden world. This gap has produced one of the more remarkable paradoxes of modern intellectual life: the seemingly contradictory nature of crucial recent conclusions and discoveries in the humanities and in the sciences.

The primary conclusion of many scholars working across the humanities during recent decades has been that the categories that earlier generations assumed were biological givens—gender, race, sexual preference, even individual identity itself—are in fact social constructions, that our ways of understanding the world around us and of coming to terms with each other are not biologically intrinsic to us, not *essential* dimensions of us, but the social fabrications of postmodern capitalism. On the other hand, among the most remarkable conclusions of many scholars working across the sciences during recent decades is that our physical being is mapped, from the moment of conception, by our DNA, and that this mapping is so distinct for each of us that anyone with the tools to read it can distinguish each human individual from every other, and various classes of humans from each other, on the basis of even the tiniest molecule of the human body, living or dead. In other words, however much our socialization constructs predictable, conventional, often-problematic patterns of action and thought, there *is* an essential identity within each of us.

Of course, I recognize that I am oversimplifying very complex issues, but I cannot help but wonder whether the tendency on the part of the first generation of academic film teachers and scholars to ignore the history of nature film might be, at least in part, a reflection of a repressed fear of confronting those dimensions of the physical world around us that might frustrate our desire for an unambiguous, stable political consciousness, and for definitive theoretical solutions to complex social questions. Obviously, the humanities and the sciences need each other more than they sometimes realize, and the wide world of cinema, including the long history of films devoted to depictions of the natural world, remains one of those dimensions of culture that may yet help us come to terms with this need.

In any case, I hope it is evident that bringing nature film, and science film in general, into the mainstream of film-historical thinking and teaching has a variety of potential benefits. Most obviously, of course, it would help us become more aware of the full range of cinematic accomplishment. Certainly, the best nature films—of course, we need to develop definitions of what "best" means in this genre—should be recognized alongside the best dramatic narratives, the best animations, the best avant-garde films, the best films of any kind. And we can learn from, and enjoy, the ongoing evolution of this genre. Just as the modern histories of the horror genre and film noir can help us think about the developing power of women to deal with their societal marginalization, the evolution of the nature film can help us think about our relationship to other species and to the environment we all share and perhaps, as suggested earlier, can help us consider the complex, puzzling relationship between our biological nature as individual instances of a species and our psychological and sociological development as members of particular societies.

At its best, the evolution of the nature film—and here there can be no better example than *March of the Penguins*—reveals, at least as fully as any other strand in the weave of film history, an astonishing level of filmmaking courage and persistence, as well as commitment not only to the audience but to a species other than Homo sapiens and to ways of living that may have things to teach us. Luc Jacquet's feature has received generally grudging accolades from serious film critics, many of whom are understandably put off by the film's overuse of sentimental music and narration—and perhaps by the Disney-like marketing of *March of the Penguins* in the United States, where it was touted as *the* family film of the summer of 2005. Of course, *March is* a family film, but as much in the Painlevé sense as in the Disney sense (once the emperor penguins mate, they are monogamous, and focused on producing an egg and raising a chick—but only for one year; for nearly every emperor penguin couple, each year brings a new monogamous relationship).

The advertising for *March*, and many of the critiques of it, also ignore the film's implicit environmentalist politic. Jacquet and his collaborators create considerable empathy for one of many forms of life placed in danger by global warming (the film's official website—http://wip.warnerbros.com/marchofthepenguins—makes the danger of global warming to emperor penguins explicit). But the reticent critics and the sentimental advertising campaign do not entirely obscure what I expect is evident to most viewers—especially those who watch the film's final credits. Throughout the body of the film, the filmmakers are resolutely invisible, entirely in service to the emperor penguins and to the viewers who will see the finished film. But during the final credits, we see imagery of the filmmakers and their utterly unimposing equipment and realize that, like these penguins, the filmmakers have created something fascinating and memorable with very humble means. It is a realization that has any number of ideological implications.[38]

38. As yet, I have not been able to find out exactly what equipment was used to film the penguins. Presumably, the Dumont d'Urville base in Antarctica is well equipped and made its facilities available to Jacquet and his colleagues, but the emphasis in the imagery we do see of the filmmakers during the credits is on the simplicity of what they were working with.

Of course, for us to be able to see the imagery and sound of the emperor penguins in local theaters, the filmmakers needed to create alliances with marketing entities that have considerable resources. But the various steps in the distribution of *March of the Penguins* should not obscure the core of the experience: the filmmaking that Jacquet and his collaborators did in Anarctica and subsequently, in composing the story of these remarkable birds.

I am grateful to my Hamilton College colleague Patricia O'Neill for reminding me of how similar *March of the Penguins* is to Flaherty's *Nanook of the North*.

Interview with Claude Nuridsany and Marie Pérennou

Every cineaste knows that some films require big-screen projection while other films communicate quite effectively on a small screen. In the United States, most nature filmmaking is seen on television; indeed, during nearly the entire history of cinema, it has been rare to see a nature film in commercial theaters. Of course, there have been exceptions: the Disney True-Life Adventure films were hits on the big screen before becoming ubiquitous on television and in classrooms. And in 1971 *The Hellstrom Chronicle*, directed by Walen Green and Ed Spiegel, made its way into commercial theaters. Nevertheless, few could have predicted the theatrical success of a recent series of feature-length nature films, especially *Winged Migration* (2001, directed by Jacques Perrin) and Luc Jacquet's *March of the Penguins* (2005), which has become one of the most successful documentary features of all time and has spawned no end of penguin-philia.

The feature that led the way into the recent fascination with seeing nature films on the big screen is the Claude Nuridsany and Marie Pérennou feature focusing on insect life, *Microcosmos: Le peuple de l'herbe* ("The People of the Grass," 1996). I first saw *Microcosmos* at Film Forum in New York City; I remember entering the theater and realizing with dismay that I was surrounded by very young children. I had read about the film and knew it had no narration, and I could not imagine young children having the patience for it. To my amazement, the children remained in rapt silence throughout the film, as did I. Seeing the tiny worlds revealed by Nuridsany and Pérennou projected large was a revelation that transformed the world normally beneath our feet into mythic proportions. Not only did I find the imagery of insects astonishing, but I was deeply moved by the filmmakers' attitude toward their subjects, and especially by their willingness to allow viewers to *see* what insects do, rather than simply hear an explanatory lecture illustrated by imagery. Of course, Nuridsany and Pérennou's choice of music provides a kind of commentary (most noticeable perhaps during the sequence when two snails appear to make love, accompanied by an aria sung by Mari Kobayashi—an astonishing, amusing, deeply intimate moment), but as is true of the visuals, the musical accompaniment seems thoroughly respectful of both insects and viewers.

Nuridsany and Pérennou began as science students, then transformed themselves into accomplished nature photographers, publishing a series of books: *Photographier la nature* ("Photographing Nature"; Paris: Hachette, 1975); *Voir l'invisible* ("Seeing the Unseen"; Paris: Hachette, 1978); *Insecte* ("Insect"; Paris: La Noria, 1990); *La planète des insectes* ("The Planet of Insects"; Paris: Arthaud, 1983); *Eloge de l'herbe* ("Praise of the Grass"; Paris: Adam Biro, 1988); and *Masques et simulacres* ("Masks and Pretenses"; Paris: Du May, 1990). In 1986–87 they decided to try their hand at 16mm filmmaking, producing three films for French television: *Les habitants du miroir* ("The Inhabitants of the Mirror," 1986), *Le jeu de l'insecte et de la fleur* ("The Game of the Insect and the Flower," 1987), and *Voyage au pays de l'invisible* ("Journey to the Invisible Country," 1987). The success of these films and Nuridsany and Pérennou's increasing discomfort with the restrictions of television led to their decision to make a feature. *Microcosmos* was finished in 1996; it was followed by *Genesis* in 2004; a third feature, *La clé des champs* ("The Key of the Country") is in progress.

As a result of my experiences seeing *Microcosmos* and other recent nature films in theaters, and talking about these films with my students, I have become increasingly impressed with the courage and persistence, and the implicit environmentalist commitment, of nature filmmaking; it has come to seem to me a new kind of cinematic avant-garde. And like the varied history normally designated by "avant-garde film," this work has been largely ignored by those who chronicle film history. Despite their cinematic accomplishments and their recent successes, nature filmmakers are rarely accorded the respect they deserve. Often their films are met with cynicism and their accomplishments as *filmmakers* are ignored. This interview began in March 2007 as an attempt to develop a more complete understanding of theatrical nature features and the backgrounds of those who make them. With the assistance of my Hamilton College colleague Professor Martine Guyot-Bender, Nuridsany, Pérennou, and I exchanged questions and answers via e-mail during 2007–8.

MacDonald: I'm very curious about how you two became nature filmmakers. What moved each of you into filmmaking, and into this particular kind of filmmaking?

Nuridsany/Pérennou: When we met, both of us were students in biology at Paris in the Pierre and Marie Curie University. Before we met, we had both come to feel something like loneliness, because most of our fellow students were interested only in science. We were interested in science too, of course, but also in literature, theater, music, poetry . . . and cinema. As we got to know each other, we discovered that, after all, it was not so "bizarre" to be interested in things other than science.

We had decided to study biology because, ever since our childhoods, both of us had been very interested in animals and in nature, but we were also interested in philosophical issues: for example, what does it mean "to be alive"? This is the main theme of our most recent movie, *Genesis.* As students we were asking ourselves many questions about life, and not only about the lives of animals but also about our own lives. We were full of questions about our correct place in this world.

We earned master's degrees, then worked on our Ph.D.'s. Our original plan was to become researchers in biology, but we were very disappointed with our first contacts with research laboratories—maybe we had too romantic an idea about research work. We decided to leave the university and become "freelance" researchers.

For several years, we took photographs of nature and enjoyed writing about nature, trying always not to do "pure science" articles or books but to mix science and more personal expression. Very soon, we wanted to make films about nature and animals, thinking it would be the best way to combine what had become our two primary passions: cinema and nature.

MacDonald: Was nature film an important part of your growing up? What films and filmmakers were most important to each of you, and why?

Nuridsany/Pérennou: When we were little children, of course, we were enthusiastic about films like Disney's *The Living Desert* [1953] and Jacques-Yves Cousteau's *Le monde du silence* ["The World of Silence," 1956], but later we were much more impressed by the fiction films of the great directors.

Nuridsany: My first shock, the film that showed me that cinema can be an art, was the Eisenstein movie *Ivan the Terrible* [1944, 1946], which I discovered as a fourteen-year-old. The gorgeous images (the lighting, the composition) and the director's dramatic sense enchanted me. When I was in high school, my best friend, who was a film lover like me, and I discovered Alfred Hitchcock's work, Orson Welles's *Citizen Kane* [1941] Alain Resnais's *Hiroshima mon amour* [1959], and Luis Buñuel, Fritz Lang . . . We went very often to the Cinémathèque française, where I continued to go once I became a student . . .

Pérennou: My first shock was the Robert Bresson film *Pickpocket* [1959].

Later, I saw the films of Ingmar Bergman, and Luis Buñuel, Eisenstein, Orson Welles, Fritz Lang . . .

Nuridsany/Pérennou: The Cinémathèque was like a second university for both of us. Once we were together, we discovered or continued to explore Carl Dreyer, Bergman, Bresson, Buñuel, Resnais, Kenji Mizoguchi, Ozu, Satyajit Ray, Robert Altman (*Short Cuts* [1993]!), Terrence Malick (*Days of Heaven* [1978]!), Stanley Kubrick, Eric Rohmer, Fellini, Max Ophüls, John Cassavetes, and Murnau: *L'aurore* [*Sunrise,* 1927] may be the most beautiful film in the world! And we discovered one of our favorite "cult films," Charles Laughton's *The Night of the Hunter* [1955]. And so many other films and directors we're forgetting to name.

Our favorites? Murnau, Bresson, Dreyer, Ozu. Why? We are not very attracted by realism in any form. We feel that an auteur's "duty" (and for us a filmmaker *is* an author) is to make his or her unique voice heard, to explore it in depth: it is through deepening one's knowledge of oneself that one can legitimately talk to others. All these filmmakers have reinvented cinema. They were never afraid of calling upon new formulas, and creating their own tools, in order to build a world of their own.

After seeing one of their films, one is profoundly "changed." The films live on inside us, and we sometimes reinvent the films as we remember them, often by imitating shots that remain very present in our memory. The "labor" (as when one speaks of the labor of childbirth) that these works perform inside of us, remaking our way of seeing, is the sign of their value.

These favorite filmmakers also have in common a seeming effortlessness, a simplicity: as is sometimes the case in theater, major filmmakers manage to give birth, in front of our own eyes, to extraordinary images, using a decor reduced to almost nothing. They do not encumber our eyes with an overload of images. Economy, simplicity of visual means, is used to invite spectators to engage the experience that is proposed to them. This participation is so intense that, at the end of a screening, we spectators may feel a sort of exhaustion.

Of course, one of the great aporias of cinema, its founding "contradiction," is that it uses a quasi-scientifically-objective recording tool—the movie camera—to create a universe that reveals a unique, personal vision of the world.

MacDonald: Were there nature films that were important to you, other than the Disney True-Life Adventures and Cousteau's work?

Nuridsany/Pérennou: The French feature called *Le territoire des autres* ("The Territory of the Others," 1970), directed by François Bel, Gérard Vienne, and Michel Fano, was, for us, a revolution in wildlife filmmaking.

It had no commentary, no music, a very original sound track, and the editing was very free. They shot for seven years! That was the *only* nature film that made a great impression on us. We hoped it was the beginning of a new era for wildlife films, but it remains a unique case (we were not enthusiastic about their second film, *La griffe et le dent* ["The Claw and the Tooth," 1976]). We do not know if *Le territoire des autres* was distributed in the USA; nobody speaks about that film in France—it's been forgotten. Orson Welles was enthusiastic about the film.

MacDonald: In recent years, Jean Painlevé has been rediscovered in the United States. I admire his films very much, and I wonder if you knew him, and if his films had importance for you.

Nuridsany/Pérennou: We are sorry to say that we have never been too excited by Painlevé's films, except maybe his novel use of jazz. In any case, his films created nothing of the magnitude of the shock we felt when we saw *Le territoire des autres.* To be honest, it is hard for us, except for that particular movie, to think of documentaries we have actually enjoyed. We have always preferred fiction.

After seeing *Microcosmos,* Godard suggested we watch the documentaries of Arthur Peleshian, which we did; and we have admired his precise editing and the poetic tone of his films—for us, probably the most important aspect of a film.

MacDonald: Were you filmmakers separately before becoming collaborators? How did your collaboration evolve? And how does it work? Does each of you take charge of particular dimensions of your films, or do you work together on all aspects of the process?

Nuridsany/Pérennou: We became filmmakers together, and our collaboration has always been the same: we work together on all aspects of the process. When we started to make nature and animal films, we talked together about what exactly we wanted to do and not do. We were not convinced by the animal films that were shown on television. Some showed surprising and interesting things about animals, but in a very academic way. There was always the voice-over commentary, almost interchangeable from film to film, that dictated to the spectators what they should understand from the images that were presented to them. The music was often overbearing, and the editing was there to invent an artificial story line, to create events that actually never happened in real life. And we didn't like that the animal world was always presented through a natural science bias, as if, for example, human love stories in films should be based entirely on reproductive biological discourse.

The systematic scientific tone so characteristic of these films sounded fake to us. In those movies we did not find the emotion that *we* felt when we watched animals in real life. Everything was enlightened by Mister Know-It-All. There were no dark areas, no mystery, no ambiguity. During our childhoods, before we were shaped by the bible of science, we saw animals as accomplices, peers, monsters, fairies, divinities, and it is this vision that we maintain as adults—though our relationship to the universe has never been as intense as it was then.

MacDonald: Being interested in making films about wildlife is one thing, but being able to actually make the films is another thing. Could you talk about *Les habitants du miroir, Le jeu de l'insecte et de la fleur,* and *Voyage au pays de l'invisible?* How were you able to get financial support to make these films?

Nuridsany/Pérennou: Regarding our first three shorts, we owned a Beaulieu 16mm camera, complete with all its accessories, but were waiting for the opportunity to use it. Marlyse de la Grange, the person in charge of the then well-known television program *Les Animaux du monde* ("Animals of the World"), had contacted us because she wanted to shoot a program on our work as photographers (we had already published several books). We offered to complete her program with some microcinematographic shots of our own. She asked to see what we had already shot, but we had absolutely nothing to show her! We asked her to trust us, which she did after much hesitation, which we fully understood. Finally, we showed her some work, and she liked what we shot and integrated our images into her program. Soon after that, we offered to shoot several twenty-six-minute shorts for her program, and she agreed. She gave us total freedom. So that is how the public television channel Antenne 2 produced our first three films.

We were shooting images, writing and recording commentaries, composing and interpreting music, creating sound effects. It was a lot of fun, and it taught us a lot. Unfortunately, Antenne 2 did not have much of a budget for this type of film: we were paid for three weeks of work, while we actually spent between four and five months behind our camera (which means that we mostly worked for free). More important, the twenty-six-minute frame, along with our own self-censorship, prevented us from expressing what we really had in mind and from trying to work in an innovative style.

MacDonald: You've mentioned that these films now seem "antediluvian" to you. How do you mean?

Nuridsany/Pérennou: The films didn't fully express our sense of the worlds we were filming. They were much too close to the traditional animal documentaries we have always been so critical of. In the end, we decided to abandon our collaboration with television and began to consider a feature-length piece for movie theaters.

Moving from short films to features was a major step for us. It allowed us to liberate ourselves from television's limiting time frame and from its old-fashioned documentary style. The project we had in mind as we started what became *Microcosmos* was to make a film based on nature and animals, but also to trade the usual pedagogical tone for an "evocation" of a distinct world. We often say that what we create are "natural fictions," or "natural tales." We find it strange that speaking about animals can be done only within the frame of natural science. Whatever our respect and interest for the scientific register, it does not seem to us adapted to "spectacle," and a film is, before anything else, a spectacle. And as we've said, the presence of a commentary tends to overwhelm films about the natural world; to us it's as unbearable as commentaries by tour guides during organized guided tours of exhibitions: they limit your imagination and your sensibility, alienate your liberty, and, as far as we're concerned, spoil your pleasure.

MacDonald: What did you hope to accomplish with *Microcosmos?*

Nuridsany/Pérennou: With *Microcosmos,* we wanted to project the spectator onto an unknown planet, Planet Earth rediscovered at the centimeter scale (humans only know it at the meter scale). On the other hand, in order to film the inhabitants of that planet, we wanted to use the same tools as are used to film actors and actresses in fiction films: traveling shots, cranes, et cetera, so as to give the insects the stature of real characters. For that, we had to conceive new tools, since the ones that already existed could not function satisfactorily on such a small scale. The elaboration of a sophisticated "motion control," able to function satisfactorily at this scale with no noticeable vibration (precise to one-tenth of a millimeter), was extremely laborious. We wrote out a list of goals and missions and started to think about the motion-control tools of the machine we needed, which we wanted to use ourselves without the intervention of a technician (the motion controls on the equipment that then existed required a specialized technician).

A producer, Romano Prada, who had an engineering background (he has since passed away), got interested in the project and started to build a prototype, which, unfortunately, did not work really well. We knew Jacques Perrin, who had produced *Le peuple singes* ["The Monkey People," 1989] by Gérard Vienne. Together we decided to contact Perrin, who decided to call on engineers and computer scientists specializing in robotics. Ultimately, they created a trustworthy and user-friendly machine (this took two years!).

In France, there are very few feature films on animals. The most famous is probably *Le monde du silence* by Jacques Cousteau and Louis Malle, which received the Palme d'or at Cannes, and the two films by François Bel and Gérard Vienne. There are also films by Frédéric Rossif: the television series *L'opéra sauvage* ["The Wild Opera," 1975–79] and *Sauvage et beau* ["Wild and Beautiful," 1984]. In spite of these films, however, quality nature filmmaking remained a rare event.

MacDonald: For *Microcosmos,* you shot for the better part of four years. How fully did you know what you might shoot before you began shooting?

Nuridsany/Pérennou: Our project was written as precisely as a scenario. The action in each sequence was carefully described, and so was the ordering of sequences. This is why we call it a "fiction naturelle." We had observed insects for decades, writing out in journals behaviors that appeared interesting (our descriptions were more like theatrical notes than like the notes of entomologists). For example, one day, we caught sight of a group of ants around a minuscule pool of water. We saw that scene only once, and decided we really wanted to integrate it into our movie. Waiting for the scene to reproduce itself was unrealistic, so we organized circumstances in the hope of making it happen again.

We chose a large, flat rock in the middle of which we carved a hole, which we waterproofed with a special varnish. We placed the rock in a basin full of water, leaving only the top of the rock dry. We filled up the small cavity with sweetened water (which ants love), and we moved a couple dozen ants onto the rock. After a few minutes of excitement during which they ran all over (without being able to escape the rock because of the surrounding water), they formed a perfect circle around the sweetened water.

What we are looking for in such arranged sequences (obviously, we always prefer when things happen naturally) is to find the memory we kept of a particular scene, to present a sort of mental image and, on the other hand, to confront the spectator's imagination by showing him scenes of nature so that he too can mentally create a particular comparison, or metaphor, or mythological episode: in other words, so that he actively uses his mental powers, rather than passively swallowing flatly realistic images.

MacDonald: All in all, how much material did you shoot for the film? Four years of shooting for a seventy-five-minute film suggests a very high shooting ratio.

Nuridsany/Pérennou: For *Microcosmos,* we shot about forty times the length of the movie (about fifty hours of rushes), which is not that enormous if you take into consideration the length of time we spent shooting. In fact, in some cases, we did not shoot at all (in spite of all our efforts) for weeks. Since we know exactly the effect we want to get and what is useful

Ants and sugar water in Claude Nuridsany and Marie Pérennou's *Microcosmos* (1996). Courtesy Claude Nuridsany and Marie Pérennou.

for the film, we avoid filming so long as the scene we are expecting is not happening in front of the camera. And, when it finally happens, we shoot the scene as much as possible, trying to improve the framing, the light, the camera movements . . . sometimes thirty times in a row. Of course, the order of some sequences was modified during the editing process, but without major upset. Very few sequences we shot were actually eliminated.

MacDonald: In *Microcosmos,* the structure of the composite day is a useful device for arranging a very wide range of material. The result is that *Microcosmos* is structurally much like the city symphonies of the 1920s. Using this organization allows you to do away with a narrator; there are just the two brief narratorial interventions, spoken in the English version by a woman (Kristin Scott Thomas), which is unusual for narrations of nature films [Jacques Perrin supplied the narration for the French version].

In *Genesis,* your choice of a kind of double chronological organization (the chronological history of the development of life on earth, and the chronological development of particular creatures in the womb/egg and in the world) is held together by the use of Sotigui Kouyaté as narrator. For me this is something of an unhappy compromise: the near elimination of narration in *Microcosmos* is refreshing and focuses the viewer's attention on the visuals, whereas here, the visuals sometimes seem to be illustrations of the narrator's lecture. What led to the decision to use Sotigui Kouyaté?

Nuridsany/Pérennou: We developed *Genesis* exactly as we developed

Microcosmos: the scenario, the sequences, the casting of animals, the text and the role of the storyteller were written beforehand. The storyteller's text was written with Sotigui Kouyaté in mind (without knowing if he would accept the role). We shot pretty much according to the initial plans. In other words, we did not write the commentary after we shot, as is usually done, in order to give coherence to the pictures we had.

We wanted to experiment with something different from the near absence of narration in *Microcosmos,* while at the same time trying to stay away from the ordinary, scientific commentary in animal movies. We started our project with this question: "What does it mean to be alive?" This is an existential question—at once very simple and vertiginous/unsettling; everyone asks it. We needed the presence of a person on screen to personify the question and some of its answers in the form of daydreaming. We decided to use a griot.

For us, the griot is not a conventional narrator. Griots are African storytellers-musicians-genealogists who work for royal families and transmit their status from father to son. They were quite numerous during the ancient empire Mandingue, which corresponds to today's Mali and Burkina Faso. In *Genesis,* Sotigui Kouyaté represents humankind and the questioning of all human beings. We chose an African man because Africa is the cradle of humankind and also a land of storytelling, a place where oral tradition is still very much alive. However, our storyteller does not tell an *African* story; he shows us the way in which a person today can answer questions on the origin of our "being," the origin of life in general, of the earth, of the universe, all those themes that, since humans have been on earth, have belonged to mythology.

As soon as we imagined the character of the griot, we thought about Sotigui Kouyaté, who is the descendant of a famous family of griots from Burkina Faso. We admired him as a theater actor when he worked with Peter Brook, whose work we have always loved (his Shakespeare's *Tempest,* for example). Kouyaté's figure, tall and thin, his long, thin fingers, his wide and controlled movements, his calm and warm voice make us see many things.

Today, science pretends to answer most of the questions we wanted to confront: Darwin tells us the origins of humankind, and the big bang theory tells us the origin of our universe. The sciences fulfill the role of mythology. Our intention was to allow today's knowledge to be heard in the form of traditional tales. The African griot is there to give these tales the flavor of ancient myths of origin. He is a human being who questions life; his questions are as much about his own origin as they are about the universe or animals.

MacDonald: The credits for *Genesis* indicate that you two wrote the screenplay; does that refer to the text the narrator speaks, as well as to the

The griot, Sotigui Kouyaté, in *Genesis* (2004) by Claude Nuridsany and Marie Pérennou. Courtesy Claude Nuridsany and Marie Pérennou.

imagery we see? What is the source of the opening quotation: "Life is a story that unfolds between a beginning we can no longer remember and an end we know nothing about"?

Nuridsany/Pérennou: We wrote the scenario, the storyteller's text, as well as the sentence at the beginning. The original text in French was: "Etre, c'est tisser une histoire entre un début dont on ne se souvient pas et une fin dont on ne connaît rien." The translator from French to English worked with us and did a good job (he usually translates Godard's films).

MacDonald: Here, as in *Microcosmos,* you mix music with sound effects. At what point is the sound recorded for your films? And how much of it is the actual sound of the creatures we are seeing when we hear those sounds? There are many instances when I wondered about this, including the sequence of the walking fish, the sequence of the Galapagos tortoise, and the sequence of the dancing spiders.

Nuridsany/Pérennou: For both *Genesis* and *Microcosmos,* we mixed real sounds with sounds we created in a studio with a sound designer, Laurent Quaglio. The sound in our films seems to us as important as the visuals, and we spent a lot of time (eight months!) on sound editing. For us, working on the sound track is like working on the viewer's imagination. We feel more freedom with sound; we can forgo realistic concerns more easily than with images. Sounds represent the secret life of images. They allow images to penetrate more deeply into the labyrinth of the viewer's mental space. Sounds reach us as bootlegged merchandise: always hidden behind the almighty images, filtering through the border of our perception. That is why their power on the viewer's imagination is so strong. They travel straight into the heart of the unconscious.

The soundtrack is often made of several strata: one realistic layer is created by mixing different real sounds (*témoin*), sounds we have recorded as witnesses, to which we add sounds we create artificially (*bruitage*), in one or more metaphorical layers that we hope will suggest a variety of associations. The "giant" sounds in the sequence of the turtle in the Galapagos were entirely created in a studio. All the sounds in the spider sequence were made with musical instruments; they were composed by Bruno Coulais. The sounds of the walking fish were also enhanced in the studio.

MacDonald: At one point the narrator says, "We are all born of love." When *March of the Penguins* was being reviewed in the United States, many critics objected to the use of "love" in connection with penguins, and I'm sure these same critics would also object to the idea that insects and crabs and frogs can "love." When you use "love" in *Genesis,* how do you mean the word?

Nuridsany/Pérennou: One of the most basic questions in making nature films is the question of anthropomorphism. From our point of view, refusing any type of anthropomorphism is to assume that humans and animals have no commonality, and that human beings are absolutely unique (if not divine). That is of course questionable. On the other hand, using an excessive anthropomorphism plays on the viewer's feelings by betraying the true nature of animals, turning them into zoomorphic puppets; this is artistically indefensible.

Can we speak of "love" between animals? "Love" is a very ambiguous term that designates both a feeling and an act. *Genesis* attempts to convey to the viewer that we do have some kind of familial link with the animal kingdom (and not only to animals, but also to mountains, clouds, and stars . . .). If you spend time observing the very subtle preliminaries that precede lovemaking (and sometimes the *devouring* . . .) between pholque spiders [*Pholcus phalangioides,* commonly known as daddy longlegs], it is difficult to think that these are merely little robots whose behavior is entirely genetically programmed. Do they have feelings? We may have to find another term. In any case, placing all the animals on one side of a line and humankind on the other is artificial; reality is much more complex and mysterious.

MacDonald: What led to your beginning the film with the vitamin C crystals?

Nuridsany/Pérennou: For a long time we had known the polychrome patterns that vitamin C produces when you look at it under a polarized light. We took many photographs of this phenomenon during the 1970s and 1980s.

A medusa (a stage in the life of a jellyfish) in *Genesis* (2004) by Claude Nuridsany and Marie Pérennou. Courtesy Claude Nuridsany and Marie Pérennou.

Their form against a black background gives them a cosmic appearance, and their rapid growth gives them an organic feel. They are neither too figurative nor too abstract; they are just enough to capture the viewer's attention and create some intrigue. They create a "beginning of the universe" and "beginning of life" atmosphere.

MacDonald: I do not remember *Genesis* showing in New York in commercial theaters, the way *Microcosmos* did. Was *Genesis* as financially successful as *Microcosmos?*

Nuridsany/Pérennou: We do not know how *Genesis* was distributed in the United States by Thinkfilm. There were probably only a few prints made. The film was shown in many countries (just as *Microcosmos* was), but the revenues were far lower than for the earlier film.

MacDonald: How long did you shoot to get the material for *Genesis?* And how long did the editing take?

Nuridsany/Pérennou: For *Genesis* we shot for thirty months, almost nonstop. The editing took eight months; the mixing, one month.

MacDonald: May I ask you about the film you're shooting now? What is its focus?

Nuridsany/Pérennou: The writing and other preparations for our new film *La clé des champs* were done during 2006 and 2007. The shooting should last for twenty-four months (from March 2008 to August 2010). This year [2007], we spent a fair amount of time finding locations and making technological preparations.

La clé des champs will be a natural fiction. Here is the synopsis: in a small village in the French countryside in the fifties, a taciturn young boy is on vacation at his cousin's home. He is lonely and is trying to kill his boredom. He finds an abandoned pond outside the village. He goes there day after day and discovers an unknown world, inhabited with strange creatures. As he explores this new realm, he enters a sort of initiation journey where beauty and violence, harmony and chaos, life and death mix. One day, he finds out that someone—a little girl who is on vacation in the village with her parents—has visited "his" pond. Little by little, the person whom he first considers a trespasser becomes his accomplice. The two children, walled up in their silence and solitude, have actually chosen the same place as their paradise and have recognized each other as companions. Far from the enigmatic adult world, by observing nature, they gradually come to a reconciliation with life.

The Attractions of Nature in Early Cinema

(for Tom Gunning)

When I first realized that during the early decades of the history of cinema, there was a genre that might be called "landscape film," I was surprised.[1] The early actualities and trick films that circulated through most academic film courses at least until the mid-1990s had not suggested that the "cinema of attractions" included films that focused on natural vistas.[2] However, once I learned that there were films that, as Iris Cahn put it, "showcased the beauty and attractions of natural landscape," and took the time to examine some of these films at the Library of Congress, I realized that this generally neglected genre was, simultaneously, an ironic culmination of developments that had been going on for nearly a century before the Lumière Brothers unveiled their *cinématographe* in Paris in 1895 *and* a premonition of a distinguished group of avant-garde films produced nearly a century after the Lumières and Edison began marketing photographic motion pictures.[3]

Early in the nineteenth century, the American painter Thomas Cole became the crucial figure in a new fascination with American landscape, especially the landscape of the Northeast. For Cole, the accelerating exploitation of American forests as a result of the expanding population and the arrival of the industrial revolution required an artistic response. We might still be in Eden, as Cole claimed in his "Essay on American Scenery," but unless we restructured American society, we would soon expel ourselves from the remarkable reward God had given those willing to cross

1. I learned about these early nature films from Iris Cahn's "The Changing Landscape of Modernity: Early Film and America's 'Great Picture' Tradition," *Wide Angle* 18, no. 3 (July 1996): 85–100. Cahn, a student of Tom Gunning's, was the first person I am aware of who explored this material.

2. Here, as in my title, I am referring, of course, to Tom Gunning's definition of early cinema before the evolution of narrative, as a "cinema of attractions." See his "The Cinema of Attractions: Early Film, Its Spectator and the Avant-Garde," in *Early Cinema: Space/Frame/Narrative*, ed. Thomas Elsaesser (London: BFI, 1990), 56–62.

3. Cahn, "The Changing Landscape of Modernity," 85.

the ocean to find the Promised Land.[4] In his paintings, Cole used several strategies to argue for the importance of landscape, some more direct than others.

In what has become one of the most discussed American paintings of the nineteenth century, *The Oxbow* (the full title is *View from Mount Holyoke, Northampton, Massachusetts [The Oxbow]*, 1836), Cole provides an overview of the environmental problem facing Americans. *The Oxbow* divides roughly in half: on the left is what looks to be undeveloped wild land; on the right, in the distance, we see the checkerboard of farms in the Connecticut River valley. The framing of the river itself, which divides the image, causes the oxbow to look like a question mark, as if Cole is asking us which side of the divide we are on, or at least how far we will allow the development of wilderness to proceed before we recognize the need to conserve some of it. The painter seems to demonstrate *his* loyalty to wilderness by including himself, painting on the wilderness side of the image, in the foreground—though his parasol crosses the line between the wild and the cultivated, demonstrating Cole's awareness of his own complicity in the developments that concern him.[5]

Other Cole paintings confront the issue of wilderness and industrial development in less obvious ways. In a number of paintings focused on the Catskill Mountains, Cole offers viewers a sense of what is being lost through industrial development. In *The Falls of Kaaterskill* (1826) and *The Clove, Catskills* (c. 1827), Cole depicts the seemingly untouched original beauty of the Catskills; in *View on the Catskill, Early Autumn* (1837) and *River in the Catskills* (1843), he reveals the pastoral beauty of the Hudson River, with the seemingly untouched Catskills in the distance beyond. Even the locomotive visible in the middle distance in *River in the Catskills* seems to harmonize with Cole's landscape. In both sets of Catskill paintings, Cole depicts nature not so much the way it looked at the time he was painting but the way it once looked or perhaps the way it *should* continue to look—in the hopes of convincing the city art buyers of his time that a new respect for original American landscape was in order.

Cole's influence on American painting was substantial, though it sometimes moved other artists in directions counter to those suggested by Cole's paintings. On the one hand, Frederic Church, Albert Bierstadt, Thomas

4. Cole's "Essay on American Scenery" is available in *A Hudson River Valley Reader*, ed. Bonnie Marraca (Woodstock, NY: Overlook Press, 1995), 373–85.

5. For a recent reading of *The Oxbow*, and probably the culmination so far of the discussion of the painting, see Angela Miller, *The Empire of the Eye: Landscape Representation and American Cultural Politics, 1825–1875* (Ithaca, NY: Cornell University Press, 1993), chap. 1.

Moran, and others extended Cole's assumption that wild nature was essentially divine—God's original creation—into what came to be known as the "Great Picture." Beginning in the American Northeast, these painters moved westward with American expansion across the North American continent and to places beyond (Mexico, the Caribbean, South America, the Arctic), often painting large, epic landscapes that drew considerable audiences. Particularly noteworthy are Church's *Niagara* (1857), *The Heart of the Andes* (1859), and *The Icebergs* (1861), Bierstadt's *Storm in the Rocky Mountains, Mt. Rosalie* (1866), and Moran's *Grand Cañon of the Yellowstone* (1872). For these painters the divinity of American landscape was obvious in its grandeur; and by drawing attention to the wonders of the American West, and of other more distant frontiers, they simultaneously played a role in what became a society-wide mission to protect Yellowstone, Yosemite, and other natural wonders *and* in the movement of industrial development across the continent: railroad builders used growing awareness of the wonders of the West to attract travelers.

Other painters took different tacks. The Luminists asked viewers to meditate on those moments of serenity in comparatively ordinary natural scenes when the world seems bathed in a spiritual light.[6] The lovely but unimposing paintings of Martin Johnson Heade, John Frederick Kensett, Fitz Hugh Lane, and the other Luminists provide a counterpoint to the epic grandiosity of the Church, Bierstadt, and Moran Great Pictures, as do the paintings of the Tonalists—Ralph Albert Blakelock, George Innis, Albert Pinkham Ryder—who created nocturnes, masterful evocations of moments of subtle visual transition, often working in more self-reflexive and abstract ways, and sometimes on very small canvases.[7]

Another form of painting relevant to the early American "landscape films" is the panorama, which evolved alongside more conventional forms

6. John Baur apparently coined the term and explored "Luminism" in "American Luminism, a Neglected Aspect of the Realist Movement in Nineteenth-Century American Painting," *Perspective USA*, no. 9 (Autumn 1954): 90–98. Ila Weiss reviews discussion of the topic in chapter 1 of *Poetic Landscape: The Art and Experience of Sanford R. Gifford* (Newark: University of Delaware Press; Cranbury, NJ: Associated University Presses, 1987); and the term is debated throughout *American Light: The Luminist Movement, 1850–1875*, a collection of overviews edited by John Wilmerding and published in 1980 by the National Gallery of Art in Washington on the occasion of a major exhibition.

7. In *The Color of Mood: American Tonalism, 1880–1910* (San Francisco: M. H. De Young Memorial Museum, 1972), Wanda M. Corn describes the Tonalists: They "confronted Nature as a private and extremely personal experience. . . . They were not interested in the grandiose drama of nature, but were attracted to its most suggestive moments—when burnt with the hues of autumn, at the break of dawn, in a clearing mist after rain and snow had bleached out sharp contours, or under the magic pall of night illuminated by gaslamp or moonlight" (1).

of painting throughout the century.[8] Originating in Europe, the panorama took two forms: the still panorama was a 360-degree circular painting viewed from a central platform; the moving panorama was a very long painting that was unrolled through a frame set up in front of an audience, from right to left or left to right. Both forms of panorama drew substantial audiences, though in the United States, where distances between cities were considerable and transportation slow, the moving panorama, which (like a film) could tour from city to city, became more popular and influential. Usually, moving panoramas took viewers on trips up and down major rivers. For a time, St. Louis became the Hollywood of the moving panorama, where different studios offered increasingly epic journeys along American waterways, especially the Mississippi.[9]

By the time the photographic motion picture arrived on the scene, it was probably inevitable that at least some fledgling filmmakers, looking for moving images that might appeal to audiences, would exploit the widespread cultural memory of these various forms of painting focused on landscape. And, indeed, when one looks at the earliest film depictions of landscape, the influence of these earlier developments is obvious in a variety of ways. Two of the earliest of what we might call "landscape films" are *Waterfall in the Catskills* (1897) and *Falls of Minnehaha* (1897), both by the Edison Studio, and both of them single shots (eighteen feet long). The Catskill waterfall is not identified, and could be either the upper Kaaterskill Falls or nearby Haines Falls—an ambiguity that echoes the debate as to the identity of the lower waterfall in *Kindred Spirits* (1849), Asher B. Durand's famous painting depicting Thomas Cole showing William Cullen Bryant the beauty of the Catskills.[10]

Whichever waterfall we actually see through the foliage in *Waterfall in the Catskills*, the decision to film a *Catskill* waterfall is clearly an attempt to evoke the depiction of the region in painting (Kaaterskill Falls and nearby waterfalls were painted by many Hudson River painters) and in literature (Kaaterskill Falls is where Rip Van Winkle falls asleep; and in James Feni-

8. The most extensive history of the panorama is Stephen Oettermann's *The Panorama* (New York: Zone, 1997), translated from the German by Deborah Lucas Schneider.

9. For discussion of the St. Louis panoramas, see John Francis McDermott, *The Lost Panoramas of the Mississippi* (Chicago: University of Chicago Press, 1958); and Angela Miller's "'The Imperial Republic': Narratives of National Expansion in American Art, 1820–1860" (Ph.D. diss., Yale University, 1985), sec. 2.

10. The F. Z. McGuire & Co. Catalogue (March 1898) claims the waterfall is Haines Falls, "a picturesque and almost inaccessible mountain cataract in the Catskills." While I have no reason to doubt that it *is* Haines Falls, the scene looks as much like the better-known upper Kaaterskill Falls as it does like Haines Falls. The waterfall in *Kindred Spirits* is widely assumed to be a fabrication combining aspects of two different waterfalls.

Thomas Cole (in hat) shows William Cullen Bryant the wonders of nature, including Kaaterskill Falls, in a fictionalized, composite version of Kaaterskill Clove, in Asher B. Durand's *Kindred Spirits* (1849; oil on canvas, 44 × 36 in.). Courtesy Crystal Bridges Museum of American Art, Bentonville, Arkansas.

more Cooper's *The Pioneers,* Natty Bumppo calls Kaaterskill Falls the most beautiful place he has ever seen). The titles of other early films confirm this attempt: *In the Haunts of Rip Van Winkle* (American Mutoscope and Biograph, 1906), for example. Similarly, the decision to record the falls of Minnehaha in Minnesota evokes Henry Wadsworth Longfellow's depiction of Minnehaha in *Hiawatha.*

Not surprisingly, the most filmed waterfall in the early American nature films is Niagara Falls, the most frequently painted waterfall during the nineteenth century.[11] In order to confront the immensity of Niagara as a visual subject, the earliest filmmakers make use of strategies familiar from paintings of the falls. While some films—*American Falls, Luna Island* (1903) and *American Falls, Goat Island* (1903), both by American Mutoscope and Biograph (AMB)—depict a portion of the Niagara Falls area in brief shots (both eight feet long), most films of Niagara attempt to provide a sense of the immensity of the scene by panning slowly across the vistas of the falls. The most effective of the extant Niagara Falls panoramas I have seen, *Panoramic View of Niagara Falls* (1903, AMB), shot by F. S. Armitage, seems almost an homage to Church's *Niagara:* its leftward pan from the rapids just before the Horseshoe Falls, across the falls themselves, echoes the angle and sweep of the Church painting. Other films—*Circular Panorama of Horse Shoe Falls in Winter* (1904, Edison), *Crossing Ice Bridge at Niagara Falls* (1904, Edison)—are 360-degree pans of Niagara scenes, which for the viewer sitting in the movie theater echo the kind of motion created by the moving panoramas of the previous century.

Still from the Edison Studio's *Waterfall in the Catskills* (1897). The entire film can be seen online at the Library of Congress's American Memory site.

Waterfalls may have appealed to early filmmakers because nineteenth-century painters had trained audiences to appreciate them, but an even more obvious reason why waterfalls are the most frequent natural subject in the early films has to do with the fact that waterfalls are in constant motion. Most natural vistas and most of the particular beauties of landscape are largely a function of their stillness. Indeed, the quiet respect accorded landscape by Cole, the Rocky Mountain painters, the Luminists, and the Tonalists was an attempt to interrupt the high energy of commerce and industrial development. As viewers contemplated the serene moments offered by

11. As early as 1896, both James White, Raff & Gammon and Thomas Edison produced series of films of Niagara Falls. None of the James White, Raff & Gammon films survive, and of those by Edison, only *American Falls from Above, American Side / American Falls from Top of American Shore* survives.

Of course, I am generalizing from a view limited by the fact that much early cinema is no longer available to us.

Cole or Kensett or Innis and/or explored the wealth of particulars in one of Church's or Moran's grand landscapes, the depth of their appreciation was presumably a function of their willingness to step away from the busyness of their normal activities out of respect for the painters' evocations of the divine-in-nature. However, while the traditional respect for landscape may have led filmmakers to the conclusion that there might be a *film* audience for such spectacles, the simple fact that waterfalls continually move made them one of the few natural subjects that a motion picture camera could capture. Under most circumstances, after all, a mountain, a canyon, or a forest offers a filmmaker nothing that cannot be depicted at least as well in a still photograph. And even a waterfall offers only a limited form of motion: indeed, the motion itself is a form of stasis; it does not evolve, at least not within a time frame relevant to conventional cinema. This might explain the tendency of early films to place the particular motion of Niagara within the additional movement of the panning camera, so that the waterfall itself becomes the climax of the "narrative" of the panorama.

The representation of waterfalls in these early films is full of paradox. The desire to film waterfalls may well have been inspired by the painters of the previous century, but *filming* a waterfall and presenting the result to audiences seems likely to create an impact opposite to that sought by the painters. On one level, a film image of a waterfall might be a fuller representation of the essence of the scene—the *motion* of the water—and yet the *experience* of a few seconds of a moving waterfall could hardly be expected to create anything like a moment of serenity, especially since the waterfall film would likely have been presented as one among several attractions. One of the effects of the nineteenth-century Great Picture was to reduce the number of paintings that might be exhibited in any particular instance; but early cinematic representations inevitably made views of nature only a portion of a larger presentation, minimizing their individual importance.

The incorporation of nature within larger technological systems was increasingly a characteristic not only of turn-of-the-century America but of turn-of-the-century film. In fact, nearly all the early films that, judging from their titles, focus on nature and landscape are in fact more fully concerned with representing the spread of technology than with depicting the natural wonders mentioned in their titles. The subjects of such films as *Canyon of the Rio Grande* (1898, Edison), *Panoramic View of Albert Canyon* (1901, Edison), *Gap Entrance to Rocky Mountains* (1902, AMB), *Frazer Canyon* (1902, AMB), *Panoramic View of Mt. Tamalpais* (1902, Edison), and *Panoramic View of Mt. Tamalpais between Bow Knot and McKinley Cut* (1906,

AMB) are the railroads that have been built through these natural spaces. In general, the movie camera is mounted on the front of the train and focuses consistently on the parallel lines of track receding before the camera. Whatever the natural beauties of the named canyons and mountains, they must be imagined from the limited portions of the scenes that roll by to the right and left of the railroad tracks. At times, the camera does pan across vistas—in *Panoramic View of Mt. Tamalpais,* for example—but the function of these pans is less an evocation of the beauty of whatever vistas are offered by the train trip on the mountain than an attempt to create a thrill for the spectator along the lines of a roller-coaster ride in an IMAX film. If the panoramic vistas of nineteenth-century painting were designed to move spectators into a deeper appreciation of the wonders of American nature, the "panoramas" in these early films move spectators through American nature by means of visual experiences that are paeans to the technological development epitomized by the modern railroad and modern cinema.

This is certainly not to say that these films are never inventive. American Mutoscope and Biograph's *In the Valley of the Esopus* (1906, filmed by Billy Bitzer), for example, at first seems a relatively standard trip on a railroad built through a Catskill valley, filmed by a camera mounted on the front of the engine. The trip itself is framed, at the beginning and end, by distant shots of the Catskill Mountains, but during the film the focus is on the movement of the train, which speeds up considerably after leaving town. This train trip includes a surprise, in the form of a man fishing off a railroad trestle (the Esopus has long been famous for its trout). The fisherman seems not to notice the oncoming train, which is forced to stop to avoid hitting him. Two men then grab the man and *throw him off the trestle,* after which the trip continues, finishing pretty much as it began. The sudden intrusion of an obvious bit of enacted fiction within what has seemed to be a straightforward document makes the experience of *In the Valley of the Esopus* memorable.

I have only begun to explore early American nature film, but even my limited foray into this body of work reveals that early filmmakers found a variety of ingenious ways of representing, if not nature, at least the exploitation of nature in a modern technological society. Two films are particularly memorable: *Captain Nissan Going through Whirlpool Rapids* (1901, Edison) and *Down the Hudson* (1903, AMB). The earlier of these films documents Captain Nissan's successful voyage through the infamous Whirlpool Rapids below Niagara Falls in a strange, submarine-like craft. Early in the film, Nissan's boat is towed into the center of the river; and then, cameras on shore follow Nissan down the rapids in three successive shots. On the most obvious level, the film records the triumph of human ingenuity and technology, as exemplified in Nissan's craft, over the forces of nature. At the same time, however, the film draws attention to a second level where this theme is evident. During the succession of shots that follow the boat through the rapids, we cannot ignore how quickly the camera—and whatever vehicle is carrying it—is moving. Various poles, and spectators too, flash through the frame in the foreground, drawing attention to the velocity of the camera as it keeps up with Nissan's speedy voyage down the river. The implicit parallel between the movement of the boat and the movement of the vehicle recording the boat is confirmed by the visibility of the cuts between shots 2 and 3 and shots 3 and 4. The momentary interruptions in the smooth flow of the film echo the interruptions in the movement of Nissan's craft created by the rocks in the river. It is obvious in *Captain Nissan* that the technology for recording the captain's voyage was carefully coordinated with the voyage itself, in order to produce not simply a victory over nature but a filmic record of that victory that could be exploited later. Indeed, the technology of the recording seems at least as complex as the technology of the boat.

In *Down the Hudson,* technology "triumphs" over nature in a different sense. What makes *Down the Hudson* (actually what we could call a voyage *up* the Hudson, from Haverstraw to Newburgh, New York) unusual is that this voyage through the Hudson River highlands—a frequent topic of painters during the nineteenth century—is filmed not in a manner that might emulate the many paintings that record the serene beauty of this section of the river but so that the spectator experiences the river at a speed impossible in real life. By pixilating at various rates, the filmmakers turn this voyage into a visually spectacular amusement park ride that emphasizes not the river itself but the many transportation and industrial technologies arrayed on and along the river. Locomotives hurtle by as the boat holding the camera negotiates its way through a variety of river craft. If most paintings of the Hudson depict the river as natural fact and resource, *Down the Hudson* transforms the Hudson into a background for an engaging cinematic trick.

The momentary interest in nature (or at least in legendary natural wonders) as the focus of motion picture experiences quickly moved into the background as film itself industrialized and developed increasingly popular narrative forms. With relatively few exceptions—Robert Flaherty's *Nanook of the North* (1921) and Merian C. Cooper and Ernest P. Schoedsack's *Grass* (1925), for example—filmmakers were content to fabricate faux nature as background for melodramatic action. Of course, in time, the hunger for representation of beautiful natural places did reassert itself—in the Western, most obviously—but few filmmakers other than John Ford allowed place to speak in any but the simplest ways. Even the early history of alternative forms of cinema reveals limited interest in nature as subject. Indeed, I can think of only two filmmakers working in the United States who were exceptions: the photographer and sometime filmmaker Ralph Steiner and Henwar Rodakiewicz, an Austrian émigré who has generally been identified with the social documentary.

Steiner was an accomplished still photographer who had become interested in the potential of the motion picture camera for producing "a visual poetry of formal beauty."[12] As the title of his *H_2O* (1929) indicates, Steiner was not concerned with portraying a particular *place;* rather, he was determined to see what his camera could reveal about an elemental reality—water—as he found it in a variety of common locations. During the thirteen minutes of *H_2O*, Steiner depicts water, first, under a variety of forms of technological control (gushing out of pipes, being regulated by pumps); then, increasingly, he focuses on the ability of water—specifically, quiet water near some piers—to create a multileveled reality of surface and reflection. Ultimately, the film produces a phantasmagoria of light and shadow that renders its simple title almost ludicrous.

While *H_2O* is heavily edited, it is structured so that the more complex the composition, the longer we have to see it. Early in the film, the shots are quite brief, but the final twenty-two shots of the film are on-screen for an average of eleven seconds each. In other words, Steiner's structure argues that viewers not only need to look more carefully at everyday visual realities but also need to slow down when doing so. Except for the editing itself, Steiner's technique in *H_2O* is quite simple: the increasingly complex visuals of the film are the result of his careful observation and skillful composition and nothing more. Essentially, his is a democratic urge: for Steiner, the world *is* a motion picture, and his mission is to demonstrate how much is visually available to all people with an interest in refining their perceptions of the everyday realities that surround them.

Basically, Steiner's interest was less in landscape than in perception. Though he followed *H_2O*'s exploration of the visual qualities of water with *Surf and Seaweed* (an exploration of the movement of water, plant life, and light along an ocean shore), his third film, *Mechanical Principles* (1930), focused on the movements of machinery, and by the mid-1930s he had be-

12. Ralph Steiner and Leo Hurwitz, "A New Approach to Film Making," *New Theatre*, September 1935, 22.

gun to focus more fully on the social realities of the Great Depression. Steiner did not return to his interest in nature until the 1960s. Of course, even *H_2O*'s apparent focus on elemental nature needs to be seen within the context of Steiner's time. While his exploration of the intricacies of chiaroscuro created by water in a quiet moment seems related to Luminist painting, his use of a montage structure for *H_2O* is part of the increasing mechanization of cinema during the silent era. *H_2O* may be a meditation on an aspect of the natural world, but it is a highly energetic "meditation" that seems serene only in comparison with the pyrotechnics of action and emotion that had become usual in commercial films by the mid-1920s.

Like Steiner, Rodakiewicz collaborated on a number of important documentary projects. He wrote the screen treatment for *The Wave* (*Redes* [1936], directed by Fred Zinnemann); he wrote the scenario for *The City* (1939; directed by Ralph Steiner and Willard Van Dyke); he directed *One Tenth of a Nation* (1940); and during World War II he worked with Alexander Hammid, Irving Jacoby, and Willard Van Dyke at the Office of War Information. Also like Steiner, before this collaborative work, Rodakiewicz had made a very different kind of film: his *Portrait of a Young Man,* which was finished in 1931 but shot sporadically over a period of six years in Bermuda, New Mexico, Arizona, Colorado, and British Columbia. Using a Bell & Howell 16mm camera, Rodakiewicz shot at sixteen frames per second (and in some cases at sixty-four frames per second: slow motion), exposing the film—according to a page of notes on the film he wrote in 1969—often "in the reverse of then accepted practice: i.e., exposed for highlights instead of shadows." At forty-nine minutes, *Portrait of a Young Man* is substantially longer than the Steiner films and is the result of a somewhat different sensibility.

Rodakiewicz explains his approach in a text that follows the opening credits: "As our understanding and sympathy for the things about us must reveal our character, so is this an endeavor to portray a certain young man in the terms of the things he likes and his manner of liking them: the sea, leaves, clouds, smoke, machinery, sunlight, the interplay of forms and rythms *[sic],* but above all—the sea." We never see the young man, presumably Rodakiewicz himself, but may deduce his sensibility on the basis of what he focuses his camera on and how he presents the results of his cinematic observations. *Portrait of a Young Man* is divided into three "movements" of approximately equal length (sixteen to seventeen minutes). Each explores somewhat different visual events. The first movement focuses on ocean surf, though Rodakiewicz interrupts his varied visual impressions of moving water and reflected light with a passage focusing on close-ups of moving machinery and, later on, with an exquisite passage focusing on smoke. The second movement's foci include moving water again (in this case, a stream), trees and leaves in the breeze and in the light, and clouds. The final movement returns to the sea, exploring the motion of surf and of reflected light, interrupted by very brief passages of tree trunks (twenty-six seconds) and moving machinery (twenty seconds). Rodakiewicz's imagery is often beautiful and reveals a photographic sophistication that accounts for the fact that it was, according to Rodakiewicz's notes, the only film ever shown at Alfred Stieglitz's An American Place (*Portrait of a Young Man* premiered at the Julien Levy Gallery in New York City).

Rodakiewicz's introduction to *Portrait of a Young Man,* along with his title, suggests a somewhat different audience-film relationship from that developed by Steiner for *H_2O*, though in some ways the two filmmakers do reveal parallel attitudes: both are interested in using the motion picture camera in a manner that is quite unusual for the twenties—that is, for meditations on nature—and both make clear that their fascination with the visuality of the natural world and natural process is not to be understood as being in opposition to the human world of industry. Indeed, Rodakiewicz's inclusion of imagery of working machinery in the first and third movements of *Portrait of a Young Man* suggests his sense that the motion of machines is beautiful in part because it is an extension of the more primal motion of the sea (in all cases, his imagery of machinery is surrounded by imagery of surf). While Steiner's title focuses the viewer on the perceptual richness of water (and on the camera as a means for revealing this richness), Rodakiewicz focuses more fully on the person using the camera. And this particular perceiver's "manner of liking" what he likes is, in at least one sense, more radical than Steiner's manner of presenting water. Rodakiewicz's shots are not simply long in comparison with the montage editing so characteristic of the late 1920s; they are consistently long enough to test most viewers' patience, almost always lasting at least ten seconds and sometimes as long as a minute. That is, Rodakiewicz seems to have understood that the camera can provide a form of meditative mindfulness entirely in contrast to mainstream film, that cinema can be dedicated to achieving not just momentary excitement but serenity.

If Rodakiewicz went further than Steiner in exploring the possibilities of the motion picture camera vis-à-vis the perceptual world, the arrival of the Great Depression seems to have had the same impact on his filmmaking as it had on Steiner's. Despite the accomplishments of *H_2O* and *Portrait of a Young Man,* it would not be until the final decades of the twentieth century that other filmmakers would explore the potential of cinema to provide viewers with experiences analogous to (and in some cases, specifically inspired by) nineteenth-century painting. In many cases, the filmmakers who would build on what Steiner and Rodakiewicz accomplished in the late twenties would return to the beginnings of cinema, before film editing had evolved, for inspiration. There is no space here to survey what has become a major contribution to independent film history, but some discussion of one particular filmmaker, Peter Hutton, might usefully represent this tendency.[13]

By the time he was hired to teach film at Bard College (located on the Hudson River just across from the Catskill Mountains, and a short drive from Shady Grove, Cole's home in Catskill, New York) in 1985, Hutton had developed an approach to filmmaking that looked backward rather than forward: "I reference a time when there hadn't been a sophisticated history of cinema."[14] Hutton's films present individual images (often filmed in black-and-white and nearly always presented silent), separated from one another by moments of darkness. Hutton extends the duration of the shots so that viewers can explore each image. Once at Bard, Hutton began to explore the surrounding area and made two films as a conscious homage to Hudson River painting and to Thomas Cole in particular.

The first of these films, *Landscape (for Manon)* (1987; Manon is Hutton's daughter) evokes Cole's Catskills again and again, in a series of twenty-two shots. The film opens with a twenty-five-second shot in which a train moves across the image: at first the train seems to be filmed from a great distance, though just at the end of the shot a slight movement of the freight cars reveals that the train itself is a toy. This miniaturization of the locomotive has much the same impact as Cole's depiction of the locomotive in *River in the Catskills.* Hutton's subsequent shots are presented (with two exceptions) one at a time, and the lengths of the shots invite the viewer into a meditative experience of landscape very close to that created by the Luminists and the Tonalists. Indeed, *Landscape (for Manon)* reverses the conventions of film history by beginning with comparatively extended shots (the first six are 25, 27, 11, 27, 18, and 27 seconds long) and then *slowing down* (midway through the film each shot lasts nearly 50 seconds, the length of the original Lumière Brothers' films). Hutton's second Hudson Valley

13. Other filmmakers whose work is particularly relevant in this context include Larry Gottheim, especially *Fog Line* (1971) and *Horizons* (1973), and James Benning. See my discussions of Gottheim in *The Garden in the Machine: A Field Guide to Independent Films about Place* (Berkeley: University of California Press, 2002), chaps. 1 and 2. Benning is interviewed about his recent films—those most relevant to this discussion—in this collection.

14. From my interview with Peter Hutton in *A Critical Cinema 3* (Berkeley: University of California Press, 1998), 246.

Thomas Cole's *River in the Catskills* (1843; oil on canvas, 27½ × 40⅜ in., Museum of Fine Arts, Boston; gift of Martha C. Karolik for the M. and M. Karolik Collection of American Paintings, 1815–65, 47.1201). Photograph © Museum of Fine Arts, Boston. Note train in left middle-ground.

film, *In Titan's Goblet* (1991)—named for Cole's painting *The Titan's Goblet* (1833)—is a closely related study of landscape and skyscape, particularly reminiscent of the Tonalist fascination with nocturnes.

In more recent years, Hutton has turned his attention to the Hudson River itself. *Study of a River* (1996) is a stunning, contemplative evocation of the Hudson in winter, shot from various positions along and on the river. For years, Hutton worked as a merchant seaman and has used his charm and his connections to gain access to commercial craft working the river. A second river film, *Time and Tide* (2000), is prefaced by *Down the Hudson.* Hutton's use of the early film is both respectful and ironic, since the perceptual experience of *Time and Tide* runs directly against the grain of the modern, accelerated lifestyle embodied so effectively in the earlier film.

Like *Study of a River, Time and Tide* reveals both Hutton's concern for the river *and* his fascination with industry, as embodied by the vessels on which he travels up and down the Hudson and by the many industrial structures that measure his trip down the river into New York Harbor, then up the river as far as the Albany area, then back down through the Hudson highlands. The movement of the various vessels on which Hutton rides the river is generally as serene as Hutton's pacing, and it allows for frequently

Catskill landscape in Peter Hutton's *Landscape (for Manon)* (1987). Courtesy Peter Hutton.

impressive views of the landscape that slide by (only two images in *Time and Tide* are clearly filmed from land). Even more fully than in *Study of a River,* the many factories, power plants, and bridges Hutton passes are impressive; the shots recorded in New York Harbor are a paean to the shipping industry. It is obvious in Hutton's imagery how fully the twentieth century continued the exploitation of the Hudson so evident in *Down the Hudson.* While there are shots that reveal no industrial exploitation (other than the always implicit presence of Hutton filming), they are exceptions rather than the rule—exceptions that periodically remind us of the natural magnificence of this waterway. And for those viewers who are familiar with recent environmental battles along the Hudson (two of them within the area of Hutton's home), some of the industrial imagery has particular, contemporary relevance.[15]

In Hutton's films, it is as if the river of time that brought full-scale industrialization to the United States during the nineteenth century is reversed so that one of the quintessential products of the industrial revolution, cin-

15. The still-ongoing debate between the Environmental Protection Agency and General Electric about the proposed cleanup of a layer of PCBs in the riverbed of the upper Hudson has been on the minds of many who live near the river, including Hutton. GE has contended that the river is fine as it is and that to dredge the Hudson to remove the buried PCBs will

ema, can not only sing the power of technology to transform nature, as most of the earliest "nature films" do, but also model a sensitivity to the perceptual world around us that confirms the best efforts of the proto-environmentalist Cole and those other nineteenth-century painters who came to see industrialization as both gain and loss. Cole's paintings and Hutton's films are a kind of aesthetic parenthesis around a century and a half of industrial development.

---

recontaminate the river; those who support the cleanup are not content to allow the buried PCBs to continue to move through the river's food chain and believe that, while dredging the river will release PCBs currently buried, in the long run the river can only return to full health once the PCBs are gone. Hutton's inclusion of a fifty-five-second shot of a GE light sign near Schenectady that lights up, goes dark, lights up, goes dark . . . is a conscious reference to this controversy; indeed, the fact that this image is the only one of forty-six shots *not* filmed along the Hudson (the Schenectady GE plant is several miles to the west of the Hudson, on the Mohawk River), and one of the two not filmed from a vessel, suggests the importance of the GE reference for Hutton.

A second controversy, this one focusing on plans for an immense new cement plant, has also been much in the news in the upper Hudson area; indeed, as one drives to Bard College along the river, signs announcing "Support the plant" and "No to the plant" are ubiquitous. The countryside along the Hudson has long been a producer of cement; *Time and Tide* includes several images of cement facilities along the river. The plan for the proposed new facility includes a smokestack so tall that it may interrupt views from Olana, Frederic Church's home above the river across from Catskill, New York, a state historical site; some locals (including Hutton) fear the new plant will create enough dust pollution to be a health concern. Obviously, it could be argued that without specific references within the film to these current controversies, only viewers from the Hudson Valley would be likely to get these references. But in the annals of American avant-garde cinema, particular films have often, even usually, been presented with the filmmakers present, and when Hutton is present these environmental controversies are never far from conversation about the film.

Interview with Peter Hutton

Over the past thirty-five years, Peter Hutton has developed an approach to filmmaking that distinguishes him from virtually all filmmakers of his generation. Hutton has devoted his filmmaking to rigorously silent (and, from 1970 to 2000, black-and-white), meditative representations of a very wide range of places: New York City, Budapest, Thailand, the Hudson Valley, the Skagafjörður region of northern Iceland, the Yangtze River in China, and, most recently, a Korean shipbuilding operation and a ship-dismantling operation in Bangladesh. Hutton's depictions of place often evoke the earliest motion pictures, as well as the assumption on the part of the Lumière Brothers that each shot was a separate film. Hutton does not make single-shot films, but from early on he has generally separated each shot from the next with a moment of darkness, his way of emphasizing the integrity of each individual image. Hutton's films also continually evoke the history of photography; indeed, at first, many of his shots appear to be still photographs, then gradually reveal a variety of subtle changes. In general, Hutton has abjured conventional approaches to editing: his individual shots often do not seem arranged with any aim other than allowing his quietly dynamic compositions to reveal themselves.

While Hutton's approach has remained relatively consistent for thirty-five years, there have been several important developments. In his 1970s films, Hutton combined normal shooting with moments of time-lapse; in more recent years, he has avoided time-lapse and has tended to lengthen his shots, so that the viewer experiences subtle alterations of light and texture entirely in real time. Indeed, he has tended to avoid all forms of cinematic manipulation other than the careful framing of his imagery; even a brief zoom or a superimposition is rare in Hutton's recent work. And beginning with *Time and Tide* (2000), Hutton began to incorporate color, at first using a very restrained palette, though in his newest film, *At Sea* (2007), he uses a broad range of color. Throughout his career, the pleasures offered by Hutton's films have remained relatively consistent—though in my experience as a programmer and as a teacher, recent audiences have become gradually more appreciative of his work. Perhaps it is not surprising that in a society increasingly characterized by media overload and multitasking, Hutton's films allow viewers to have what, in my earlier interview with him, Hutton called "a reprieve . . . , a moment to study something that's not fraught with information" (Hutton in MacDonald, *A Critical Cinema 3* [Berkeley: University of California Press, 1998], 243).

At their best, Hutton's films are both unusually beautiful and full of visual magic; and while they are never overtly political, the images Hutton shows us, and the experience his films create, have subtle political implications. The recent *Skagafjörður* (2004) and *At Sea* are among Hutton's most remarkable films, exemplifying two somewhat different tendencies in his work. From the beginning of his filmmaking, Hutton has been drawn to the visually marginal: to the subtlest changes in the quality of light, and often to the edges of visibility. *Skagafjörður*, like *New York Near Sleep for Saskia* (1972), *Florence* (1975), *In Titan's Goblet* (1991), and *Landscape (for Manon)*, is evocative of American Tonalist painting and, particularly, Albert Pinkham Ryder and Ralph Albert Blakelock. *Skagafjörður* is made up of thirty-seven shots of various lengths, from less than ten seconds to nearly two minutes, which reveal the sweep and sensuality of the Skagafjörður region. *Skagafjörður* is full of magical compositions, many of them made in weather conditions and at moments in the day that challenge the limits of film stock and camera, but that surprise and reward the patient and perceptive viewer over and over.

Making beautiful images comes easily to Hutton, and periodically this very facility seems to trouble him, to seem self-indulgent and politically oblivious. As a result, Hutton regularly initiates projects that reveal something of his environmental politics and historical awareness: *Budapest Portrait (Memories of a City)* (1986), *Lodz Symphony* (1993), *Time and Tide*, and the recent *At Sea* are instances. *At Sea* is closer to a narrative than any of Hutton's previous films, except for *Time and Tide* (see the description of this film on pp. 211–12). The three sections of *At Sea* visualize the "life" of a seagoing ship. The opening section depicts a high-tech, brightly colored Korean shipyard in the process of constructing giant container ships; the second section records moments from a voyage across the Atlantic on a loaded container ship; the final section documents workers on the beach at Chittagong in Bangladesh, breaking down now-aged vessels in order to recycle usable metals and other materials. While *Skagafjörður* is primarily a feast for the eyes that reflects Hutton's fascination with a deeply romantic landscape and seascape, *At Sea* is, at least implicitly, a reflection on the implications of transnational capitalism and on the impact of industry on the environment.

Moonlight (c. 1885–93; oil on canvas, 16 × 24 in., Henry Art Gallery, University of Washington, Seattle, Horace C. Henry Collection, Acc. 26.9; photo by Chris Eden), a Tonalist nocturne by Ralph Albert Blakelock (top); and a cine-nocturne in Peter Hutton's 1991 film *In Titan's Goblet* (courtesy Peter Hutton).

Fundamentally, however, it is the nature of the experiences Hutton creates in all of his films—their construction of a contemplative viewing experience and their modeling a deeper, more careful awareness of the world around us—that is the best evidence of Hutton's politics. Hutton's films help us to respect perception itself, and to enjoy an experience of cinema that seems to lie outside the conventional world of hysterical consumption.

This conversation with Hutton was begun at Harvard University in early October 2007 and was refined during the following months in phone conversations.

MacDonald: When we talked before, the last film you had made was *Study of a River* [1996]. A lot has happened in your filmmaking since then. For people who have followed your work, the most obvious change is your use of color (the earliest film you distribute, *In Marin County* [1970], is color, but for three decades your films were in black and white). What finally led you to embrace color?

Hutton: A combination of things. About fifteen years ago, trying to print reversal became very problematic. *Shooting* reversal was not a problem, but *printing* it was. I had used black-and-white reversal for all my early films because it had a particular quality that I couldn't get with black-and-white negative. I got addicted to those qualities, and then, when working with the labs became problematic, I thought, well, maybe it's time to switch over to negative stocks, which the labs are more familiar with. And since the endgame *was* in sight, I thought, why not kick it up a notch and go to color? It also had to do with living in the Hudson River Valley and growing more sensitive to the nuances of color as a response to my exhilaration with what I was seeing in Hudson River School painting and in the work of other landscape painters.

When I was younger, I saw *Red Desert* [1964, directed by Michelangelo Antonioni] and other commercial films that worked with color. How can you *not* be astounded by the color? But early on in my filmmaking, using color was financially prohibitive. I wanted to be able to shoot as much as possible, to shoot all the time, so working in black and white made more sense. The cost of working in color has decreased. A roll of color stock costs forty-five dollars; a roll of black and white is eighteen dollars, but the development and the subsequent lab work have become comparable. In any case, it just seemed time to expand the palette. As I'm getting older and more stable, it's come to seem like a worthwhile investment, just as a way of expanding the potential of what I'm doing.

When you switch from black and white to color, you're going from a palette that supports the abstraction of reality, which in itself is exciting, to a palette that's more familiar with reality. I found this a challenge; the fact that I'm color-blind didn't help matters.

MacDonald: How does your color blindness affect what you see?

Hutton: I can differentiate between primary colors. It's more the nuances of color that confuse me. A light blue can easily become a light green, and a warm green can become a brown. I think it's very common for people who have blue eyes to have problems differentiating color. You go to a store and buy a pair of brown pants, and when you get home, it's like, "I didn't know you like green!" "I *don't* like green!" "Well, those pants are green." "You're kidding me!"

With color, there are *so* many possibilities, and it's difficult to make color really distinct. You have to explore and you have to work with it. I played around a lot with polarizing filters to try and transcend the more familiar range of colors, tones, and values.

MacDonald: Another thing that changed in your work in recent years is that your films have gotten longer. *At Sea* is sixty minutes. Was there a specific decision to make longer films?

Hutton: No, not at all. In the case of *At Sea,* instead of a single piece, I ended up doing a triptych; the subject needed more breadth to illustrate what I was interested in, but each of the three sections is similar to my usual length. And the pace of my films has remained pretty much the same.

Years ago, when I switched over to an electric camera, I was superconscious of the fact that the velocity of the culture was being ramped up by MTV, by the introduction of computers in the home, by a variety of developments. Even Hollywood films are cut with a shorter and shorter sense of time and duration; there's a tendency to try and cram more and more "information" into a certain concept. When you feel that your culture is being overaccelerated, there's a tendency to want to go against that tide.

Also, in observing landscape, sometimes it takes a lot of time to comprehend what's actually changing. In a shorter shot you can't perceive details, subtleties. In my films each shot becomes its own small film. This was the case even in my earlier films; though the durations were shorter, each individual shot became its own separate moment in time, isolated from the subsequent moment, even though sometimes there are relationships. In fact, in shots of longer duration there's a tendency to form even closer relationships with the surrounding shots, because you can comprehend what you're seeing.

MacDonald: What you're describing is evident as early as *July '71 in San Francisco, Living at Beach Street, Working at Canyon Cinema, Swimming in the Valley of the Moon* [1971], which is a mix of several kinds of recording. Unlike many of your films, this one is full of people, often people interacting with you and the camera. Who are these people?

Hutton: Mostly art students. I lived in a sort of a commune with a half dozen people, many of them people I met at the San Francisco Art Institute. Someone had found an old abandoned space down on Fisherman's Wharf; first, it had been a metal shop for someone and then it was used as a studio; finally, it was turned into a living space. Rent was seventy dollars a month! I used a little hut out in the backyard as a kind of crash pad—I didn't stay there full-time. I was also living in other places.

MacDonald: At one point in that film, you pixilate a screening at the Canyon Cinematheque. The film we see is *Riverbody,* the Anne Severson [now Alice Anne Parker] film of images of nude men and women, each dissolving into the next.

Hutton: Which I was in, by the way. That moment in the late sixties was like *The Whole Earth Catalog.* A lot of people were living out utopian ideas, building geodesic domes, doing yoga, living communally, cooking meals, baking bread—this was my foray into an alternative lifestyle, and it was really fun.

We never spent any time in the Haight Ashbury; we lived over in North Beach, near Fisherman's Wharf. I didn't really like the Haight scene. A lot of people there were like lemmings. But I liked the alternative ideas.

MacDonald: What was your experience at the San Francisco Art Institute?

Hutton: All my undergraduate work was in sculpture. I studied with Robert Hudson, William Wiley, Bruce Nauman—Nauman was the first artist out there doing minimalist conceptual art, which was very interesting.

Alan Kaprow came to the Art Institute, and I got immersed in his work and with the idea of happenings. That was a time when everybody was trying to reinvent their art form, to break down traditional barriers, to get our studios out into the street. I started doing happenings and making little 8mm films to record them (video wasn't available yet), and then I became fascinated by how beautiful the little films were, how much more interesting they were than the actual events!

MacDonald: You still have the films?

Hutton: I had probably five hours of 8mm stuff and lost it all. I left it with a friend in Marin County, and when he and his wife divorced, she threw it out when she was cleaning up. I also made a long film, black and white, silent, 8mm, on a train trip from Oakland to Detroit. It was almost a precursor of what I'm doing now.

MacDonald: Did you study with filmmakers at the Art Institute?

Hutton: I took a class with Bruce Conner; he didn't really teach us anything practical. He just showed us all about *Bruce,* which was interesting in itself. He'd come in and play his harmonica or read reviews of his latest show. I think Bruce Baillie was probably an influence on me, because of his lyrical idea of landscape and of a sensual camera. Of course, I was seeing Brakhage too. And Robert Nelson. In *my* mind Nelson was the most interesting filmmaker of that period; he was so involved with his work and with working collaboratively with other artists: William Wiley, Nauman, and Robert Hudson. Plus Bob's a really great person.

I don't know if I've mentioned it to you, but *July '71* ends with aerial shots of the Valley of the Moon in Napa, shot from a glider; and the first image of *New York Near Sleep for Saskia* is a shot looking down at the city, matted to look as if I'm still in the air and am landing in New York. I used to have each new film begin with a shot that recalls the last image of the previous film. *New York Near Sleep* ends on that raft spinning around, and *Images of Asian Music* starts with the images of the water from the ship. I don't do that anymore, but at the time I wanted to suggest that each new film was just a continuation of one long, ongoing film.

MacDonald: There are shots in *July '71* that are recognizably Peter Hutton shots, but there are many shots that seem very different from what you typically do. *New York Near Sleep,* made just one year later, seems completely yours.

Hutton: That's partly the difference in the two environments. For me, New York was very interior. Most of *New York Near Sleep* was shot inside—I was living in a basement—but *July '71* is *California:* it's all over the place, like the state itself and like I was when I lived there. Moving to New York changed things for me: when the Whitney decided to show *July '71,* I thought it would be good to go to New York for the screening, and then I just decided to stay. I was burned out on California anyway.

I had always thought, "My work will be recording my environment, wherever I am." My whole philosophy is that truth is stranger than fiction, so if you just keep a record of what you do, the result will, in time at least, come to seem strange and interesting. But in New York I did get much more formal, and more focused on the language of cinema.

I started working as a cameraman for Red Grooms, and I met Rudy Burckhardt and Jonas [Mekas] and P. Adams [Sitney], and got connected to the New York art scene in a way that made me feel, "Oh boy, here I am in this mythic city, and I'm an *artist*!" I was relatively young, twenty-seven, and had grown up in Detroit; it was great to confront this new environment.

I made *New York Near Sleep* as a present for Red and Mimi Grooms. It's called *New York Near Sleep for Saskia,* after Saskia, their young daughter. Red and Mimi inhabited this colorful, cartoony, happening-like world; and I was shooting the colorful, zany, almost vaudevillian stuff that Red was doing at the time. But on my own, I was doing austere, minimalist studies of light and shadow. I think I wanted Red and Mimi to know who *I* was.

To come back to your original question: about my beginning to include color. At some point in the sixties, I just decided to shoot black and white for a while and get to know it, but then I got addicted. When you take an art class and you start drawing with charcoal, you think, "This is so limiting!" Then you realize that you *can* learn to draw really well in charcoal, though it requires a lot of discipline—and that the results can look interesting and distinctive. I always saw working with black and white as learning to use a difficult, but fundamental visual vocabulary. Also, you have to understand that at that time, *everybody* was shooting color: supervibrant, psychedelic color was the language of the sixties. Going against that grain seemed more interesting.

A lot of my interest in black and white comes from a period in the early sixties when I was living in Hawaii and watching a lot of early Japanese films. While in Hawaii, I took a course in Chinese brush painting.

MacDonald: Time and Tide was your first color film in thirty years, and I've written about it as a kind of environmentalist film, but last night when you were talking about the final section of *At Sea,* it occurred to me that, without your saying something about it, I don't know if your environmental awareness would be evident—at least not from the films themselves.

Hutton: Inherent in my practice of wandering around the world making these records of things—landscapes, urbanscapes, ships—information is inevitably going to emerge that speaks of that time and that place. I've spent many years working on ships and have learned that these industrial machines are inherently dangerous to the environment. A ship, even without a cargo, is like a toxic time bomb. One of the jobs you have when you're working on a tanker is to clean out the tanks. When you switch cargoes, go from crude oil to molasses, for example (which is commonly done, even though it's a little hard to imagine), you have to do "butterworthing": you bring these high-powered hoses into the cargo tanks way down in the bowels of the ship and clean the tanks out as best you can; then you scrape up the shale at the bottom. That material is often permeated with industrial chemicals. Where does all that waste go? Right over the side, into the ocean. Ships are constantly cleaning themselves when they're at sea and ridding themselves of chemical residue. So ships are inherently vessels of pollution. The Environmental Protection Agency is employing more safeguards on ships—they can't discharge waste water in harbors any longer—but despite the new safeguards, there's the recent phenomenon of waste water from one part of the world being discharged in another part of the world and introducing alien species of plants and sea life into that water.

When I made *Time and Tide,* however, I wasn't focusing entirely on environmental issues. I was excited about the revelation of traveling on tugboats and barges up and down this landscape that had been painted so much in the nineteenth century, but rarely from the point of view I was using—even though in the nineteenth century, there was much more river traffic on the Hudson than there is now. I thought it was interesting to create an aquatic perspective on the landscape and also to record the beauty of motion and movement and the different sense of time you have when you travel by boat.

I did purposely put an image of the General Electric logo in the middle of the film, just to say, "There *are* other issues inherent in this very beautiful bucolic landscape; there is something underneath this surface that's not so beautiful." GE polluted the Hudson River with PCBs for many years, within legal limits, of course, but with terrible consequences.

MacDonald: The GE logo is the one shot in *Time and Tide* that was not made on the Hudson River, but in Schenectady, to the west of Albany.

Hutton: Yes, though the PCBs were discharged into the Hudson at a now-abandoned factory at Fort Williams, further north on the river from Albany.

So, the film resulted from a desire to be involved in a new kind of pictorial relationship to this particular landscape, *and* I had an intention to draw attention to environmental issues. I didn't make the film as an environmental film, but drawing attention to the issue is for me an inevitable consequence of making a filmic record of that place.

MacDonald: James Benning often mentions that filmmaking and photography are very dirty industries, so on some level filmmakers and photographers are complicit in environmental damage.

Hutton: That's totally true, and not so thrilling to realize. And if you're making films, you're dealing with animal products: the film base itself is made from animal bones. I tell that to my vegan students and they wince. But it's not just *film,* of course: I'm sure that inherent in video there's some horrible, environmentally damaging thing. Even in oil painting there are problems. There are environmental consequences in the origins of the Hudson River School—granted, not of the magnitude that would cause major environmental damage—but consequences nevertheless. It's as if we humans can't help ourselves.

It's interesting to consider the cycles of environmentalism. In the

The Statue of Liberty through the window of a boat, and up the Hudson River on a barge, in Peter Hutton's *Time and Tide* (2000). Courtesy Peter Hutton.

mid–nineteenth century, there was the clear-cutting of the Catskills, a fact that's revealed in many of the Hudson River School paintings. If you study the early history of representing this area, you're constantly reminded of other cycles of environmental damage, even when painters weren't trying to create what we could call an environmental awareness. I've never wanted to deconstruct those paintings to the extent that art historians do, but when you're making paintings or films, it's almost impossible not to include elements that trigger interpretations. I've often talked about the fact that I struggle to free my films of signifiers that speak of specific moments and places.

As you know, my interest in thinking about the history of the Hudson also led me to include, at the beginning of *Time and Tide,* the short film *Down the Hudson,* produced by American Mutoscope and Biograph in 1906 (it may have been shot by Billy Bitzer). It was called *Down the Hudson,* though in fact the trip is *up* the Hudson.

MacDonald: What drew you to make *Looking at the Sea* [2001]?

Hutton: Given that I'm part Irish, I guess I always wanted to go back to the old sod and all that stuff. Of course, you should be able to make a film anywhere, in even the most mundane location. Part of the delight of being a filmmaker is to be able to turn any situation into something wondrous or amazing.

I used to just wander around and respond to things with my camera. Always at the core of my filmmaking was an idea that came from being a painter and a sculptor, where every day you go to the studio and pace around and come up with something. When I got into film, I thought it was important to always have a camera with me, to maintain a very close relationship to my work on a daily basis. Of course, as I've gotten older, I've used a project-oriented working process. But in all my films there's a mixture of very spontaneous responses to the environment and more contemplative studies.

MacDonald: Do you have a stockpile of material that you've never used?

Hutton: Not a stockpile, but a lot of films I've never finished.

MacDonald: I was thinking about this because when Leonard Retel Helmrich was at Harvard recently, he mentioned that he accumulates a lot of material, out of which, from time to time, he pulls a film. That was also, maybe still is, Jonas Mekas's working method.

Hutton: When I make a film, I want it to have a loose sketchbook form, rather than be a finished piece. For me, the raw material is inherently what is interesting about this work, not how it's fused or shaped or crafted into a specific "finished" piece. The process of collecting images is my primary interest; always when I start on a project I find an incredible validity to the entirety of what I shoot, and I've always struggled against the more formal implications of making finished pieces.

When I've collected a couple of hours of material, I'll look at it over and over, eventually boiling two hours down to twenty minutes or so, hoping that the essence of the material will emerge. When I look at images over and over and over, I finally lose interest in some of them; they fall away because they're not communicating as effectively as other images. At the end of the day, you realize that distilling what you've collected benefits the audience, gives them a more concentrated hit.

When I was shooting the material that ended up in *Looking at the Sea,* I was standing on these cliffs on the west coast of Ireland, looking west into the sun and thinking of the immigrants who wanted to leave Ireland because of the famines and were confronted with that same perspective. They must have seen the sea as this huge complicated obstacle. I was struck by how alluring, how seductive the light on the sea was, and also how, when you're standing on shore, there's something utterly incomprehensible about the sea. I remember being reminded of a piece written by Henry David Thoreau in *Cape Cod,* about a ship that crashed at Cohasset, an amazing meditation on the aftermath of the ill-fated *St. John,* which had come from Galway.

MacDonald: Was part of *Looking at the Sea* shot on the Aran Islands?

Hutton: Yes. Of course, when you go to the Aran Islands, you can't help but think of Flaherty and *Man of Aran* [1934]. I wasn't thinking of making any commentary on Flaherty's project, yet his film was a reference point for me. Certainly, Flaherty has been an important influence.

MacDonald: I visited the Cliffs of Moher when I went to Ireland for my niece Amy's wedding; did you shoot there?

Hutton: Yes, though the images I made at the Cliffs of Moher were edited out. I shot a ton in Ireland, because I was struck by how familiar it all felt to me—as if I'd been there before, as if I'd experienced it in a dream. After shooting at the Cliffs of Moher, I did a little research and realized that there are even higher cliffs up in Sligo. I spent a week with Kiki Smith and an interesting writer, Susanna Moore, visiting these cliffs. A lot of the images in the film where the camera is looking down at the surf, and that one long, protracted, rich, and sensual image of the waves crashing on a rock, were made in that area. The film ends with images from the Aran Islands.

MacDonald: I remember you saying you weren't happy with that film.

Hutton: That was a technical issue; I was unhappy only in that I had the lab print the black and white and the color material together, and the black and white ended up having this somewhat bluish tint, which I wasn't excited about. Now I print black and white separately and just splice it into the film, so that what I've shot keeps its black-and-white quality.

I had become intrigued with the idea of mixing black and white and color—perhaps an outgrowth of my sense that collecting imagery is doing a kind of sketchbook. I like shooting color and black and white side by side, and I like mixing things up in an antiformalist way. But it's problematic technically for a lab to deal with that, so I'm mixing black and white and color less and less.

MacDonald: Your next project was *Two Rivers* [2002], which focused on the Hudson River and the Yangtze. It's not in distribution through Canyon Cinema.

Hutton: Two Rivers is a film I've rarely shown—though it was a big project and I like it. Minetta Brook, the organization that funded the film, presented it as a single-channel piece, but I've never really shown it in the same way that I've shown the other films. It was the most ambitious thing I'd done, which had a lot to do with the fact that I wasn't paying for it. I was able to afford the luxury of taking another person with me to China to help out and to translate. Diane Shamash, who ran Minetta Brook until she died, was a fairy godmother to me and to a lot of other artists. She'd say, "What do you want to do? We'll make it possible." Whoa!—do you know how rarely that happens! I really miss her.

The *Two Rivers* project came out of my interest in the Hudson River and in Hudson himself and the various recollections of his journeys to the New World. Robert Juet, Hudson's pilot, was an Englishman who kept a very extensive diary of their journey up the Hudson. Hudson himself had kept a rather extensive diary, most of which is lost, though there are fragments of it in the Maritime Museum in Rotterdam. After he explored the Hudson River, Hudson went back to Europe, got another crew together, and went north into the Hudson Bay region, looking for a northern trade route to China through the ice. In the end his crew mutinied. They were so fed up with his relentless quest for this passage that they set him adrift in a small boat. That was the last anyone saw of Hudson.

I thought it was interesting that Hudson's imagination was conjuring up these images of China, and I thought it would be great to create a film that was essentially about Hudson and the Hudson. At first I thought of intercutting the Hudson River and the Yangtze River material, but then decided it would be best as a two-projection piece where on one wall you would see the Hudson and on another you'd see the Yangtze as a kind of imaginary continuation of Hudson's voyage.

There's an environmentalist backstory to the project. When I wrote the proposal for Diane Shamash, I commented on the environmentalist issues facing both rivers: the Hudson was very much in the news because of General Electric and the PCB controversy; at the time, I thought the dredging of the Hudson would be part of the film—though that dredging still hasn't begun. There was also environmentalist resistance in China to the damming of the Yangtze and the resulting damage to the Three Gorges. So in addition to the imaginary historical connection, both these rivers were/are in peril.

I also thought this was a very interesting idea because my imagery of each river was preceded by a great painterly tradition: I thought it would be interesting to think about how these specific landscapes influenced particular aspects of Chinese and American painting.

MacDonald: I know you've struggled over the past ten years or so, trying to figure out whether your work fits into the gallery context. Sharon Lockhart has shot photographs in tandem with her films—as separate but related projects—and has been very successful: the sale of the photographs has provided her with additional filmmaking options. Gallery exhibition seems like logical possibility for you, though galleries and museums tend to rely on DVDs and to avoid 16mm projection.

Hutton: It's ironic. For the past ten years or so there has been a novelty interest in referencing this older, 16mm technology within the context of the digital age. When Chrissy Iles did her "Into the Light" show ["Into the Light: The Projected Image in American Art, 1964–1977," Whitney Museum of American Art, 2001], young people were fascinated that the 16mm projector had a place in the gallery. Chrissy was professional enough to bring in good equipment, so they could loop things without degrading the films.

Filmmakers from my generation are looking for other options for presenting their work because of what seem to be inherent limitations within avant-garde film culture in terms of accessibility. Finding avenues for my work within the art world certainly makes sense, but it's easier said than done with film. I have made a DVD of *In Titan's Goblet,* which was exhibited by Shoshana Wayne (a gallery in Santa Monica) in a show with Kiki Smith. They sold it to collectors, and I could see that there was the potential for doing that kind of thing, but I never liked the way the film looked on that DVD; it wasn't a high-end transfer.

A good thing the gallery did was to make a separate room for people to view the film, with chairs. A big issue for me is how to present your work in a gallery space and allow the viewer to actually stay engaged with its timing. I frequently go into an installation and see that people are just walking through it, not really giving the work the time it needs. My work needs to be experienced from the beginning to the end, *as a duration.* You can walk through it and get a glimpse, but you're not really getting what I'm trying to give you. So gallery exhibition is a conundrum for me.

MacDonald: MoMA's installation of Kiarostami's *Five* [2004] in conjunction with their retrospective of his work ["Abbas Kiarostami: Image Maker," Museum of Modern Art, March 1–May 28, 2007] is an instance of this. Each section of *Five* was set up in a small gallery, as a separate DVD projection. The problem was most evident in the last room and Kiarostami's beautiful, thirty-five-minute nocturne of the moon reflecting on water, with subtly changing light and sound. There were no chairs in that room, and I couldn't imagine that anyone would stand there for thirty minutes.

Hutton: If you arrive at a certain stature within a culture, as Kiarostami has, your work can be taken seriously on less formal terms because it's already imbued with a certain mystique. Once you become sufficiently sophisticated and successful in a medium, you are liberated do almost anything, like Picasso doing ceramics or neckties. We should all be so fortunate as to have the freedom to dabble that way, and to have our work actually be seen.

Having seen the tremendous range of Kiarostami's narrative films, and then seeing him distill his work into a shot of the moon reflecting in the water, suggests to me that after being involved in the big theater of cinema in a more traditional way, he's become aware of the quietude, the subtlety, the nuance of understatement; and by dedicating *Five* to Ozu, he references another who worked in a different form of cinematic time. But while this new sense of time may reflect a personal evolution, Kiarostami's use of it in *Five* isn't revelatory within the history of cinema; there are so many precedents.

I've been thinking of making a film called *One (for Kiarostami),* a single killer shot.

MacDonald: Skagafjörður is full of magic.

Hutton: We [Hutton and his wife, Karolina Gonzales] went to Iceland during the summer of 2002 and shot preliminary stuff, then went back the following summer and shot a lot more, so I had the luxury of going there and scoping the place out and then having time to think about exploring the potential of that place and of the first material I shot there. Of course, Iceland is such an extraordinary, dazzling landscape that it would be hard *not* to make an extraordinary film there. I was able to spend time in a patient mode, waiting for weather conditions to come together and for light to change—though the resulting film is still my usual mixture of spontaneity and careful searching.

Landscape and seascape from *Skagafjörður* (2004) by Peter Hutton. Courtesy Peter Hutton.

There's never been an occasion when I haven't gotten something unplanned when I've gone out to shoot. I used to have this little plaque on the back of my Bolex that said, "The Whole World Within Reach," which was the logo of Star Films, the production company started by Georges and Gaston Méliès. Film continues to be so conceptual in many filmmakers' minds that they tend not to practice the craft of just shooting and looking and shooting and looking.

MacDonald: The third shot, of the light moving across the mountainside, is amazing.

Hutton: The way the light gradually evaporates from that hillside is a perfect metaphor for what my films are about: just taking the time to let something naturally evolve and astound you with how beautiful it is, rather than manipulating or crafting something through editing. I think it all goes back to those first Lumière projections, or at least to what must have been the original audiences' reactions to those early films.

MacDonald: For me it goes even further back than that, because descriptions of the Louis Daguerre Diorama shows in the early nineteenth century [see Richard B. Altick's *The Shows of London* (Cambridge, MA: Harvard University Press, 1978)] suggest that they had much in common with your way of handling imagery: they reflected an interest in the gradual movement of light as an entertainment, as an experience that people could share.

Hutton: The movement of light is the core phenomenon of the moving image. It's interesting that this initial manifestation of cinema was completely eclipsed by other concerns. Western culture is so much about waving your hands at the viewer and shouting, "Pay attention to me! Look at me!" As a result of this, people tend to lose the discipline necessary for really seeing things; they come to films with the expectation that the filmmaker is going to feed them. This is very different from what I think of as a more classical Eastern orientation to looking, whether it's at a rock garden in Kyoto or a piece of calligraphy, where you must learn to feed yourself.

Recently I was in London and spent a lot of time in the older Tate, looking at Turner's work. Turner has always been a great reference point for any mariner; he's the painterly equivalent to Conrad, someone who spent a lifetime devoted to issues of the sea and weather and atmospheric conditions. In the Turner Wing there was this little show of Turner's watercolors. When you look very carefully, you see the way he used white as subtle highlights, in almost calligraphic gestures. It amazed me that such simple gestures could create representations of ships, that he could reduce painting to such simple brushstrokes. I hope that my way of working in some sense emulates that.

MacDonald: I know you flirted with the idea of having music with *Skagafjörður* and that Sigur Rós played with the film at the premiere in Reykjavík. Is using music still something you think about?

Hutton: I love to listen to music when I'm editing and when I'm studying the footage and trying to see what I have. It's often painful when the time comes to say to myself, "Okay, I've got to sober up and get back to reality and look at the imagery silent." More and more people are interested in showing my work with musical accompaniment. That's become a thing with classic silent film, and since my films are silent, people ask me about it.

I just had a retrospective in Portugal. Two different groups played music to two sets of my films. Quite honestly, I wasn't thrilled with how it was done. I'd sent them tapes so they could rehearse, but you know, you get so addicted to looking at the work silent, and music gives the experience a different velocity, a different frame. Good things can come out of collaboration, but there are also things that negate one another. It's like poetry and film. A lot of students have a fantasy that putting a poem into a film is interesting, but in fact the words and the imagery often cancel each other out.

MacDonald: Could you talk about how the tripartite structure of *At Sea* evolved? The film is different from earlier work in that you're cutting directly from one image to another, not exactly in a narrative way, but often in ways that are closer to narrative than the cutting in earlier films.

Hutton: There was a conscientious effort to edit in a more conventional manner, just to reference the connectivity within this vastly complex mechanized world I'm observing. Because of the size of each of the activities I'm showing, it was impossible to visualize what is going on in single, inclusive shots, so you get almost a cubist rendering of the spaces.

MacDonald: The Chittagong material reminds me of the wrecked ship in so many nineteenth-century American paintings.

Hutton: Yes, true, but when I think of that section, I think mostly of Turner. In Turner, you see explosions and other disasters unfolding. There's an amazing painting called *Slavers* [1840]; it's horrific: slaves are being cast over the side of a ship, and there are explosions and conflagrations.

For most of my maritime life I've been aware of ship-breaking, even though it's a relatively new industry. And I've seen photographs by Sebastião Salgado and various Magnum photographers who make a career of going around the world and showing the amazing things happening in these different landscapes. Also, I was once a sculptor, and I love looking at objects in space. Ships are fascinating objects—not unlike beached whales, which reminds me of a piece by Barry Lopez, "A Presentation of Whales," about a pod of whales that gets beached in Oregon.

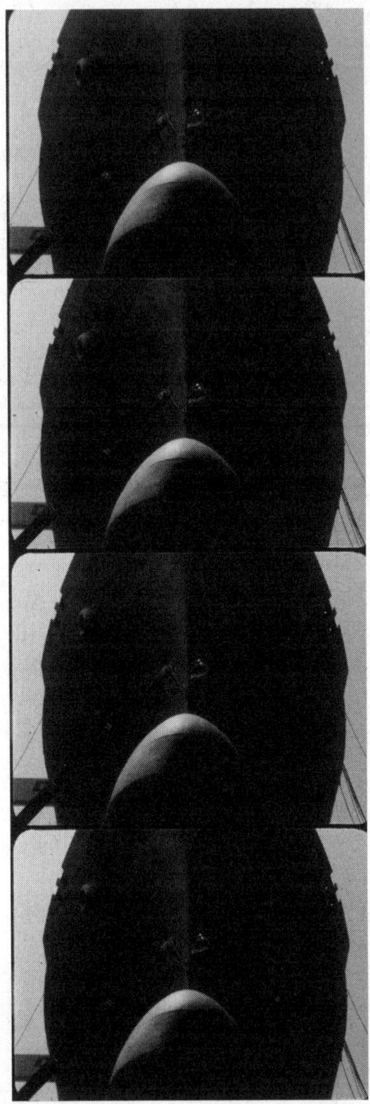

Prow of ship in Korean shipyard in *At Sea* (2007). Courtesy Peter Hutton.

That beach in Chittagong is an interesting art park, an apocalyptic dystopian kind of tableau. Before going to Chittagong, I'd made *Skagafjörður*, which is all these superclean, clear, pristine, almost fantasy landscape images. I wanted to collide that experience with something industrial, to avoid creating the impression that I spend my life somewhere up in the ether. I went to Chittagong with the idea of making an entire film about ship-breaking, but they pulled the plug on me after a couple of hours of shooting: they thought I was making an environmental film, which I *could* have been making. But my interest was also aesthetic, which I know seems somewhat perverse, though there *is* a considerable aesthetic tradition of photographing old factories as a reminder of the past and of the consequences of industrialization, a more recent version of the way the landscape painters of the nineteenth century painted ruins or old ships.

Instead of admitting defeat after being prevented from doing what I wanted to do in Chittagong, I thought, well, maybe this experience and the material I did shoot should be a part of something bigger. The next summer, I went to Korea and shot the shipbuilding, and then the following year, 2006, I did the voyage across the Atlantic. In my film I wasn't interested in aestheticizing these environments, but in documenting them as facts of life. At the time I was thinking of the title "How the World Works." We may see shipbuilding as modern, sophisticated industrial stuff, but then what happens is that it often ends up back in the third world, as garbage or as toxic waste.

There's a metaphor inherent in the three parts of *At Sea*—a metaphor for my own interest in always taking cinema back to its origins. I thought that by ending the film with black and white and with the portraiture of people in awe of the camera, I could take us back in time.

MacDonald: To *Workers Leaving the Lumière Factory* [1895]?

Hutton: Exactly! The ending references the original phenomenon of the motion picture apparatus.

MacDonald: There seem to be echoes in part three of things that happen in part one. How much thought went into relationships between the sections?

Hutton: I had looked at the Chittagong material a lot by the time I went to the DSME shipyard in Okpo, Korea (it's part of Daewoo), but while I was there, I wasn't thinking about what I had shot earlier. There are a couple of shots in Bangladesh where people are working within a cross section of a ship, and in the Korean shipyard you're also seeing cross sections of ships, slices, that haven't been connected to the other sections yet; echoes are inherent in observing those two processes of construction and destruction.

MacDonald: Was there any resistance to your filming in the Korean shipyard?

Hutton: In Korea I had an amazing amount of freedom—I had a car and a translator and Karolina as my assistant—but the circumstances of that intense industrial environment prevented me from doing portraits of people. Certain red flags were raised by the public relations people when I met with them. I told them that I'm fascinated with ships and that there really wasn't much more to what I was doing beyond my artistic interest in the process of how ships are made. But for reasons of insurance and whatnot they didn't want me to get too investigative with the camera.

And the heat was intense; it was like 110 degrees in this steel shipyard and there were fumes, which you don't get a sense of in the footage. It was one of the most intense shooting experiences I've ever had. After a couple hours, I would have to go into a dark, cool space and let my brain readjust.

You're confronted with so much stuff that you can't begin to make sense of it. It would have been appropriate to do an even more cubistic rendering of that space than I ended up doing, because it was so bewildering. It was very hard to get far enough back to be able to look at what was happening.

MacDonald: How did you decide where you wanted to voyage from and to in the middle section?

Hutton: It was just based on convenience. A friend of mine in Charleston said, "I can get you on a Russian reefer ship"—a refrigeration ship (not to be confused with the other sense of "reefer"!)—and got me connected with

Seascape in *At Sea* (2007). Courtesy Peter Hutton.

a shipping agent who worked for a company called East West Trade that transported food all over the world. I wanted to cross the North Atlantic in the winter, because when I was a kid—and I'm sure you remember this—the first nautical films we saw were episodes of *Victory at Sea* [an NBC series that originally aired in 1952–53, directed by M. Clay Adams and accompanied by music by Richard Rogers], great newsreels about American ships going to Europe with troops and merchant seamen carrying food and armaments and whatnot. *Victory at Sea* included heroic images of these battleships plowing through what's called "the Great Circle" in the North Atlantic, which in wintertime is one of the most treacherous seas in the world. I wanted to cross the Great Circle in winter on this Russian ship, which was to carry a load of frozen chickens from Jacksonville, Florida, to St. Petersburg, Russia. We would have cut the corner on the Great Circle, and I was preparing for a really incredible ride—and then the whole thing fell through.

It was an American-Russian corporation, and the Russian side must have caught up with some of the e-mails that the shipping agent was sending me, or he might have let it out of the bag. The week before I was supposed to leave, he called and said one of the Russian owners found out there were going to be Americans on his ship, and he didn't want anything to do with it. I had just seen *Darwin's Nightmare* [2004, by Hubert Sauper], an extraordinary piece that turned into a massive exposé about Russian planes flying armaments into Africa and then leaving with the Nile perch from Lake Victoria; and I wondered if these corporate guys were concerned that we might be doing a film about their frozen chickens.

Ironically, after my involvement in the voyage was canceled, the avian flu hit Russia and the market for frozen chickens collapsed, so the ship actually left Jacksonville and sat out in the Atlantic for a couple of weeks waiting for another market to open up. Another market never did open up, so they had to haul the cargo to St. Petersburg anyway, where they were frozen out: it was the coldest winter in twenty years and the river was rock solid; they had to get icebreakers to clear a channel for ships to get into port. I can only imagine what that voyage would have been.

I went on the Internet and found a company in California that booked passengers on freighters and picked one that was going across the North Atlantic, but by the time I actually took the voyage, it was the beginning of spring and the seas had settled down. I didn't get the drama I wanted, even though the opening of the sea leg of *At Sea* is sailing into a snowstorm, which I thought was kind of interesting. In all the years I'd been on ships, I had never encountered a snowstorm.

MacDonald: Where did you go from and to?

Hutton: We went from Montreal to Hamburg. The bridge you see as we're leaving port is in Quebec City. It was a great voyage. What's interesting about reencountering the maritime experience after twenty or thirty years of not being on an oceangoing ship is that the nature of shipping has changed dramatically. I was planning to do a lot of shooting on the trip, but because of the design of the container ship I was actually very limited. During the storms I couldn't even go out on deck; I was stuck up on the bridge shooting through the windows. Fortunately, I got some interesting images of the storms. When the weather settled down and the sun came out, I was able to go out, but it turns out that there's a very limited deck on a container ship. The ships I used to work on were much smaller and more traditionally shaped; they *looked* like ships. This was surreal, to say the least, like going to Europe on an industrial quilt.

The ship was crewed by Indians, and they were fantastic. I was the only passenger. I ate Indian food for ten days, and the captain was a great cook. He would come down and whip up this killer prawn curry, which was about the hottest thing I've ever ingested. I'd eat with the officers every day, and they would always watch me eating to see how I was going to react.

MacDonald: How did you do?

Workers at Chittagong, in Bangladesh, in *At Sea* (2007). Courtesy Peter Hutton.

Hutton: Not bad, though I think I had the runs all the way from Montreal to Hamburg—though I guess we don't need to talk about *that.* It was great being back on the sea; that in itself was worth the trip.

The footage was different from anything that I'd ever filmed before. For example, there were no portholes on the ship—all the windows were square with round edges. The circular porthole had always been a cool framing device in the films I shot on ships, but it's archaic now. I always love shooting through things to give the viewer a different way to see. I did make a few shots through parts of the ship, referencing the earlier work, but in the end I thought it would be better to do something completely different.

MacDonald: So in all three parts of this film your vision was constricted in ways it usually isn't.

Hutton: And that's why the film feels more documentary. In shooting, I couldn't be contemplative; in each case, it was, "Whoa, I've got to grab all this stuff as quickly as I can!"

MacDonald: Do you know what your next project will be?

Hutton: I think I'm making a film in Detroit. Last year, I went to Media City, a nice little festival in Windsor, Ontario, and met a young guy who runs the Detroit Film Center. He was interested in having me come and do some shows and a workshop and whatnot, so we visited with him and he ended up driving us back to the airport in Detroit. I asked him if he would drive along the Detroit River so I could revisit some of the areas that I had experienced when I first worked as a merchant seaman on the Great Lakes. The industrial environment of the river was always fascinating to me.

Along the river I saw this amazing steel mill that I'd remembered, on what is called Zug Island. There were Do Not Enter and Forbidden signs posted everywhere, so we just looked at the mill from West Jefferson, the boulevard that parallels the river. I thought, "Wow, I should come back and do a film about Zug Island!" When I was in Poland doing *Lodz Symphony*, some Poles asked, "What are you doing here?" I told them I was fascinated with nineteenth-century industrial architecture. They asked where I was from, and when I said, "Detroit," they said, "What about Detroit!" and I realized that I had never thought of Detroit that way: it was always too close to me to seem exotic.

In fact, I can see now that Detroit is probably one of the more interesting landscapes around. This new project will reference Vertov and *Three Songs of Lenin* [1934], all those workers' films, as well as Charles Sheeler's fascination with industrial spaces.

Why *is* that stuff so fascinating? I've always wondered about that.

MacDonald: We both grew up when industry was the most exciting thing in the environment. My parents had been powerfully affected by the Depression and were so happy that factories were working again. I think that in some way, the decay of that architecture is the decay of our generation.

Hutton: That's true. When I showed *At Sea* at the Walter Reed, I mentioned that the smells of these industrial environments were fascinating. And there were these amazing machines in Toledo and Ashtabula, big hydraulic lifts that would take fully loaded coal cars and turn them upside down so the coal would flow into a chute and end up in the hold of a ship. Then this giant hydraulic claw would set the coal car back down on the tracks and would pick up another. You could do a 360-degree pan and see one of the most amazing visual spectacles, fraught, of course, with all this pollution and coal dust and funky residue. It felt apocalyptic.

MacDonald: At one point you thought that *Study of a River* [1997] was going to be one part of a seasonal Hudson River piece. Is that an idea that you've put behind you?

Hutton: I still think about it. Maybe because the Hudson is so just-outside-the-door for me, I'm unconsciously saving it. Deep down maybe I think I'll do this when I can't go to faraway places. I'm still very drawn to traveling.

I don't know if we've talked about this, but in the late 1950s my father used to take me to the Detroit Art Institute, where once a month or so, there was a program of travelogues. My father was a bit of a wanderer when he was young, and he got a lot of pleasure from these films. The travel film is a genre that for politically correct reasons no longer exists: travel and politics are hard to separate these days. *Mondo Cane* [1962, by Paolo Cavara and Gualtiero Jacopetti] was the grand manifestation of the tradition of the travel film, but the films we saw at the Art Institute were made by individuals, primarily in 16mm. Sometimes they would single-frame things and do interesting visual tricks with double exposures and whatnot. It was an amateur form and one of the first influences on me as a film viewer. Looked at one way, what I've been doing most of my filmmaking life is keeping a diary of my travels.

MacDonald: Tell me about your parents.

Hutton: My father edited and published a couple of magazines. One was a commercial magazine that told people about the city of Detroit, the kind of thing you'd find in a hotel. Another was about our hometown, a little cultural magazine. My father wrote stories and he had his friends write things and he'd interview local artists. He also had his finger in the advertising business, which is where he actually made money. He also started his own film society with a friend, and frequently showed Jacques Tati. One time he received a letter from Tati.

My father went to the University of Michigan—I don't think he ever graduated—but he was a great Michigan fan. He published the programs for the Michigan games. We would go to the stadium, and my father would give my brother and me fifty copies of the program and we'd sell them in the parking lot; something that cost two bucks once you got into the stadium might bring ten dollars from people having tailgate parties and getting drunk by the time the games started. It was a great source of money for a couple of years.

MacDonald: Did your mother work?

Hutton: She was a homemaker, but she and my father were involved with amateur theater and got a lot of work at a theater associated with the Cranbrook Academy of Art. My mother was an amateur painter, and my father was a silversmith: he had a little workshop in the basement, where my brother and sister and I would go down and make things. He also made very elaborate model ships. Because of my parents' connections I was able to do apprenticeships with several regional artists, which began my love affair with art.

Part of my youth was spent making models. Later when I got into sculpture, I made little rooms, simple architectural tableaux. I can see some of this in *At Sea.* I'm always interested in obscuring the scale of what I film, which has a lot to do with my not putting people in a lot of films.

MacDonald: This play with scale is evident as early as *In Marin County* [1970], where you use pixilation to transform construction machinery tearing down a neighborhood into giant insects.

I remember our getting in a wrestling match in the projection booth at Hamilton College because you wanted to show *Skagafjörður* and the Korea and Chittigong material in *At Sea* with a lens that made the image substantially *smaller.* You wanted to show that immense shipbuilding process in Korea as a miniature! I didn't believe the audience would stay—they did, actually.

Hutton: I like to see how the films play in different circumstances. I thought the films looked good, very crisp, in that smaller image. Shooting on Zug Island will allow me to work with unusual scale again.

Oh, here's an interesting image: when I was due to go onto my first Great Lakes boat, my father said, "I'll drive you down"—he was remembering his own experiences when he was young and traveled on ships, I think. We stopped in a bar in the western section of Detroit and had a few beers and then he dropped me off at the gate. I walked about a quarter of a mile to the waterfront, carrying my duffle bag. I remember these two gigantic piles of coal, several stories tall. I walked between them to the river. It was completely dark and I kept turning around, thinking, "Am I in the right place? This feels like the end of the earth!" And suddenly, out of my peripheral vision, I saw a light, a searchlight from a ship that was coming in, looking for the various mooring points.

(When ships dock in the Detroit River, they don't tie up to a pier, but to hooks in the river; the crew goes over the side to hook up the cables that then draw the ship closer to the shore. It's an interesting maneuver to observe.)

This was my ship docking and the first evidence was the searchlight beaming through the dusty hot summer night, followed by this monstrous bow moving out of the darkness.

They got the ship tied up, and then this long Jacob's ladder came over the side and I thought, "Holy shit, I've got to carry this heavy duffle bag up *that* ladder?!" I looked at the top and saw four or five guys looking down, so I climbed with my duffle bag and by the time I got to the top, felt about ready to die. I thought for sure someone would grab the bag and pull it over the edge as I clambered onto the deck, but they just stood there and watched me. It was the first test of an ordinary seaman.

But I what I remember best is standing between those two giant coal piles, and seeing that light coming out of the darkness.

Putting All Your Eggs in One Basket

The Single-Shot Film

In 1995, cineastes around the world marked the centennial of the invention of the *cinématographe,* and the Lumière Brothers' accomplishments as inventors and as filmmakers were celebrated. This celebration included the production of a compilation film for which forty noted directors were asked to produce single-shot films fifty seconds long: *Lumière and Company* (1995, directed by Sarah Moon). It seemed clear in *Lumière and Company* that, generally speaking, the notable directors who agreed to participate (including John Boorman, Peter Greenaway, Spike Lee, David Lynch, Arthur Penn, Wim Wenders, and Zhang Yimou) had little feel for the single-shot form; indeed, those forty films did little more than remind us that Louis Lumière and the cinematographers who carried the *cinématographe* across the globe during the first years of cinema history were often remarkably adept with the new camera and the limited time frame it offered them.

Once narrative had replaced the early cinema of attractions, the single-shot film came to seem "primitive"; it would be more than half a century before a young generation of filmmakers would come to see the formula one shot = one film as a valuable opportunity. While many of the memorable avant-garde films of the 1960s were calculated attempts to energize a new audience by highlighting subjects considered outrageous in new frenetic visual and auditory styles, by the mid-1960s, some avant-garde filmmakers were critiquing the increasing tendency of both independent and popular cinema (and, of course, television) to barrage audiences with overloads of visual and auditory stimuli. This critique took a number of forms. Some filmmakers made long, slow, boring (or "boring") films: Andy Warhol's *Sleep* (1963), *Empire* (1964), and other films opened the way for this development. Another dimension of this critique came at the hands of a number of young filmmakers, many of whom were just finding their way into cinema: in an effort to confront the increasing tendency toward hysterical consumption (of images, of other consumer goods), they revived the single-shot film.

For our purposes here, a single-shot film is, or appears to be, exactly one continuous shot long and is meant to be seen as an individual work of cinematic art. Of course, the original "single-shot films" produced in the 1890s by the Edison Studios and by the Lumières were certainly not made in reaction to commercialism—quite the contrary. For Edison, the Lumières, and other early filmmakers, the one-shot film was a means of generating excitement and profit, a goal clear in the frequent decision of early programmers to "edit" several diverse films together for public programs. These protomontages were as fully the ancestors of the commercial barrage avoided by the avant-garde filmmakers I am discussing here as their individual films were the ancestors of modern single-shot cinema. For the generation of filmmakers that produced the single-shot films discussed in this essay, however, the Lumières in particular were almost romantic figures: the simplicity of their filming methods was seen not as a primitive step on the ladder to feature-length commercial narrative but as an approach worth emulating for its clarity and simplicity, an approach worth exploring precisely because it was what the commercial industry had left behind.

Any chronicler of avant-garde cinema, of any strand in the weave of film history, is always in danger when claiming that one or another specific film was the first instance of a trend. I do not know what the first significant modern single-shot film was. It is clear that beginning in 1963, and especially in 1964, 1965, and 1966, Andy Warhol made hundreds of what came to be called *Screen Tests* (early on, they were called "stillies," as opposed to "movies"): single-shot portraits of women and men.[1] All the *Screen Tests* I have had a chance to see have been one shot long; they were filmed at twenty-four frames per second, and screened at eighteen frames per second. The *Screen Tests* are, of course, single-shot films, but they are also part of a series and are usually seen in series. But there is also Warhol's *Mario Banana (No. 1)* (1964), a funny, sexy single-shot film in lush color in which Mario Montez eats a banana. Other early instances of single-shot film include Bruce Baillie's *All My Life* (1966) and *Still Life* (1966); and several films included in the 1966 single-reel *Fluxfilm Program* assembled by George Maciunas: *Disappearing Music for Face* by Chieko Shiomi, *Smoking* by Joe Jones, and *Eyeblink* and *Match* by Yoko Ono.

All My Life is a single, continuous, three-minute, steady (but handheld) tracking shot along a rose-covered fence and finally to the blue sky, with the accompaniment of "All My Life" (1936), sung by Ella Fitzgerald, per-

1. In her *Andy Warhol Screen Tests: The Films of Andy Warhol Catalogue Raisonné,* vol. 1 (New York: Abrams, 2006), Callie Angell lists, contextualizes, and illustrates 472 Warhol *Screen Tests,* all shot with a silent Bolex. Angell describes the production and context of the *Screen Tests* and extensively annotates her listing.

forming with Teddy Wilson and his orchestra. At times, the fence seems to be a staff, and the red flowers the notation of Fitzgerald's singing. *Still Life* is a stunning, classically composed two-minute "still life" image of a portion of a room (with table, vase of flowers, ashtray) within which several men and women socialize. All three of the *Fluxfilm* single-shot works were filmed by Peter Moore at two thousand frames per second, but in each the extreme slow motion has a different effect. In Ono's *Eyeblink* (I have not yet seen *Match*), the sixty-second slow-motion shot transforms the eye so that it suggests other body parts and functions in a manner reminiscent of Willard Maas's *Geography of the Body* (1943). In *Disappearing Music for Face* a change in the expression of a mouth, "from smile to no-smile," as the *Film-makers' Cooperative Catalogue* puts it, occurs so slowly (the shot is more than ten minutes long) that one cannot actually see it happening, though at any given point in the latter part of the film one can see that a change has been occurring. *Smoking* is a stunning four-minute, thirty-second shot in which a man's ever-so-slow exhalation of smoke causes his face to seem continually transformed.[2]

Whatever we ultimately decide were the first single-shot films in this 1960s revival of the form, it is clear that during the past ten years, the new digital technologies have, in a certain sense, rendered the form obsolete. When rolls of film came in specific lengths, there was always the option of extending a shot to the full length of a roll; but now, as Leonard Retel Helmrich demonstrated in *Jemand auf der Treppe* ("Somebody on the Stairs," 1994) and Alexander Sokurov in *Russian Ark* (2002), remarkable single-shot moving-image works of virtually any length and level of production are possible. However, while the single-shot films discussed in this essay are no longer radical in terms of their length, they do remain interesting and evocative on their own terms, variations on a form of cinematic haiku that are worth experiencing and exploring.

It should also be mentioned that a number of remarkable single-shot films, close in spirit to the late 1960s and early 1970s single-shot films, have been produced in recent years, including two by Sharon Lockhart: *Teatro Amazonas* (1999) and *NŌ* (2003). For *Teatro Amazonas,* Lockhart organized an audience to fill the opera house in Manaus, Brazil (the opera house made famous by Werner Herzog's *Fitzcarraldo* [1982]); for thirty minutes the audience watches the stage, where Lockhart is apparently filming, and

2. A fourth single-shot film in the *Fluxfilm Program* is by George Landow: after the title, *The Evil Faerie,* a director credit, and the designation "starring Stephen M. Zinc," we see a three-second shot of a man goofily flapping his hands at his shoulders "like a faerie."

listens to a chorus sing a continuous chord that gradually lessens in volume as voices drop away, one at a time; at the conclusion, once the singing has stopped, viewers seem to share a visual and audio environment with the audience. In *NŌ*, we see two farmers covering a field with hay. During the thirty minutes of the film, our understanding of what we are seeing gradually transforms: at first we may assume that the film is a candid, spontaneous document of the man and woman working, but as it gradually becomes clear that that they are covering only that portion of the field recorded by the camera, we realize that in fact these farmers are performing for the filmmaker. Both the Lockhart films required an adjustment of conventional technology: the 35mm *Teatro Amazonas* was shot in "three-perf," so that Lockhart's single shot could last longer than the normal ten-minute limit for 35mm shooting; *NŌ*, shot in 16mm, is only the illusion of a continuous shot; in fact, it includes one nearly invisible edit. Abbas Kiarostami's digital video *Five* concludes with a nearly thirty-minute, black-and-white shot (actually the illusion of a single shot): a nocturne during which the moon's appearance and disappearance behind clouds and a brief rainstorm seem to instigate a variety of variations in the sounds of frogs and dogs within the environment.

SINGLE-SHOT FILMS AS MEDITATIONS: *THE AWFUL BACKLASH* (1967) AND *BLUES* (1969)

The Awful Backlash must have seemed the ultimate put-on to those who saw it in the 1960s. Certainly, little in the raucous, busy Robert Nelson films that had preceded *The Awful Backlash*—*Plastic Haircut* (1963), *Oh Dem Watermelons* (1965), and *Confessions of a Black Mother Succuba* (1965)—would have prepared an audience to watch, in close-up, a man's hands slowly untangling a remarkably knotted fishing reel for fourteen minutes—little, that is, except the two-minute meditation on a watermelon, set on a football field like a football ready for a kickoff, that opens *Oh Dem Watermelons* (for Nelson this shot was a means of building tension in the audience so that "when the movie finally got going, it would be like a release").[3] I assume that the title *The Awful Backlash* refers not only to the "backlash" William Allan—a good friend of Nelson's at the time—created for the film but to the backlash against conventional expectations that Nelson felt it was time to produce.

3. Scott MacDonald, "Interview with Robert Nelson," in *A Critical Cinema* (Berkeley: University of California Press, 1988), 265.

While the single-shot tactic of *The Awful Backlash* can be understood as another instance of the tendency of Nelson's early work to create humor through outrage, the film can be seen in other ways. Most obviously, perhaps, the film is a documentation of Allan's considerable patience and skill in untangling fishing line. Nelson's fascination with Allan's skill is suggested by the fact that the film's length appears to have been determined not by the formal precondition of the standard length of a roll of film, as is the case in many single-shot films, but by the length of time it takes Allan to finish the job: the film begins a few seconds before Allan starts untangling the line and fades to black a few seconds after he finishes. Nelson's meditation on Allan's skill is implicitly a statement of his respect, reminiscent of those early Lumière films where certain kinds of physical labor are seen as filmically interesting simply for themselves.

However, while *The Awful Backlash* does document Allan's completion of a particular task, it is not strictly speaking a documentary. Nelson added a sound track on which someone is heard periodically mumbling, as though talking to himself while working to untangle the backlash: we hear phrases, bits of stories. We also hear the sounds of the reel as Allan winds inches of untangled line onto it.[4] The mumbling on the sound track moves the film in the direction of fiction by transforming the person untangling the line into a character. Nelson's idea seems to have been to create a first-person protagonist. The framing of the image confirms this implication. The camera is mounted looking down so that the reel is seen in close-up; Allan's hands enter the image from the sides (we never see more than the hands): we share, as nearly as possible, the point of view of the character at work on the reel.

When one takes into account Nelson's long interest in Taoism, one can see that *The Awful Backlash* may also have been an attempt to create a meditative experience that functions on at least two levels. First, regardless of the frustrations experienced by some viewers early in the film (I am basing these observations on responses to the film in classroom situations), by the end of a few minutes, Nelson's essential seriousness about Allan's skill seems obvious and well founded: Allan is able to finish a job many of us would never have begun. *The Awful Backlash* is a meditation on Allan's pa-

4. Nelson has sometimes felt that the sound track is technically a failure; the transitions between silence and sound are very noticeable, due to Nelson's limited knowledge of film sound at the time. See the interview in *Critical Cinema*, 267. Perhaps it is not surprising, then, that not long ago, Nelson—at a moment when he had decided to remove his films from distribution—sent me a print of *The Awful Backlash* on which the sound track had been literally scratched out. The film with the original sound track is currently back in distribution.

William Allan untangling the fishing reel in Robert Nelson's *The Awful Backlash* (1967); the bowl of blueberries in Larry Gottheim's *Blues* (1970). Courtesy Robert Nelson, Larry Gottheim.

tience and, simultaneously, a gauge of the patience—or impatience—of those in the audience who see the film through to its conclusion.

Second, since Allan's task is suggestive of the medium within which it is revealed, the film can also be seen as a meditation on cinema, on its conventional history and its possibilities. *The Awful Backlash*'s ending, a long fade-out soon after the fishing line is untangled and reeled up, suggests the projector's progressive winding of the unspooling film onto a take-up reel; further, the untangling of the knotted line can be read as a joke on the tradition that all the narrative "twists" in a conventional film plot must be unraveled before the film can end.

The use of single-shot filmmaking to encourage a more fully meditative film experience is consistent in a series of one-shot films Larry Gottheim made between 1969 and 1971: *Blues; Corn* (1970); *Fog Line* (1970); *Doorway* (1971); and *Thought* (1971, previously called "Swing"). Unlike Nelson, however, Gottheim was not interested in documenting a particular person's skill or in creating a character. Gottheim used the single-shot form to create or capture images of subtle visual beauty and dense conceptual suggestiveness. *Blues* does focus on a simple human action—eating a bowl of blueberries and milk—but the image is framed so that the bowl fills the screen, and a hand and spoon periodically enter to remove spoonfuls of the fruit: our consciousness of a person eating is minimal. While the act that *Blues* captures is mundane, Gottheim's presentation of the act transforms it, both as a visual experience (*Blues* is silent and, ideally, projected at sixteen frames per second) and as a metaphor.

Given good projection, the image in *Blues* is full of subtle color harmonies and rhythmic pulses. A mottled blue bowl containing a portion of dark blue and black berries in milk rests on a blue tablecloth. Within each blueberry is a tiny, rounded dot of white light. As the film proceeds, the harmony of the image is punctuated by the repeated entry of the spoon, by a regular slight lightening of the image (this was caused during the shooting by a defective motor, but Gottheim ultimately decided that the accidental effect was appropriate for the finished film), by the dance of the film grain in certain sectors of the image (since *Blues* was originally shot in Super-8mm and enlarged to 16 mm, the grain is especially visible), and—if the film is projected at silent speed—by the subtle projection flicker visible in the white milk. *Blues* ends with the flare-outs at the end of the roll.

The experience of *Blues* is suggestive in a number of ways. The fact that eating a bowl of blueberries does not seem enough to sustain an 8½-minute film fuels what I see as an implicit polemic. Not long before making *Blues,* Gottheim had moved to rural central New York State, and his increasing involvement with the land is evident in his reverence for the simple but beautiful and healthful act his first one-shot film portrays: eating the berries is a synecdoche for living a more healthy life in general. Or, to put it another way, *Blues* can be understood as a "health food" alternative aimed at a society endlessly urged by film and TV to overconsume both food and imagery. On the level of the act portrayed and of the medium within which the act is revealed, Gottheim asks that we slow down and appreciate. And, just as the fishing reel in *The Awful Backlash* can be read as a metaphor for the projector mechanism that reveals the film to us, the bowl of blueberries being eaten can be read as parallel to the act of watching the film: blueberry by blueberry, frame by frame, *Blues* measures out a film experience, the basic elements of which are visible in the grain and flicker of the imagery. This parallel is confirmed at the conclusion of the film, when the end-of-roll flares begin precisely as the final blueberry is removed from the bowl.

While *The Awful Backlash* asks a level of viewer patience akin to, and perhaps inspired by, meditation, Gottheim's interest in meditation seems a bit more direct. As the berries are removed from the milk, continually altering the mandala-like shape of the basic composition, the subtle flicker becomes increasingly evident in the milk until, at the conclusion of the film, the bowl vanishes, reappears, and vanishes in the lovely color and light of the flares. Gottheim suggests that meditation on the simple things of the world (healthy foods, the basic materials of cinema) may be a means to a higher consciousness, to illumination.

Each of Gottheim's single-shot films offers a different meditative experience. Probably the most engaging is *Fog Line,* a nearly eleven-minute contemplation of a pasture on an early summer morning as fog clears, to reveal a lovely green landscape and, for a few seconds, two horses grazing; *Fog*

Line recalls the Louis Daguerre Diorama shows of the early nineteenth century that fascinated spectators with gradually changing scenes.[5] The most straightforward of the Gottheim single shots is *Corn,* during which ears of corn are shucked and cooked, as the afternoon light gradually changes.

SINGLE-SHOT FILMS AS VISUAL DISCOVERY: *SNOW* (1971) AND *PATENT PENDING* (1976)

Most of the single-shot films I am aware of can be said to provide meditations of one kind or another on the subject matter we see and ruminations on the kinds of film practice these films are alternatives to. The assumption that the viewer will (or can, or should) use the film experience as a kind of meditation takes a variety of forms, another of which is allowing the apparatus of filmmaking to discover its own imagery. This approach is evident in Robert Huot's *Snow* and Alan Berliner's *Patent Pending.*

By the late 1960s, Huot, who had made a name for himself as an accomplished young minimalist and conceptualist painter, was being increasingly drawn to film. Hollis Frampton, whose (faux) single-shot *Lemon* (1969) is dedicated to Huot, taught his friend how to make a splice, and Huot immediately began to apply minimalist tactics to filmmaking. In 1969–70, Huot finished the single-shot *Black and White Film* and the two-shot, single-roll *Nude Descending the Stairs* (for both of which Frampton did the camera work) and the diary film *One Year (1970)* (1971). *Rolls: 1971,* a second diary film, was finished in 1972. Both diary films include roll-long shots. *Rolls: 1971* begins with the roll-long single shot that Huot subsequently put into distribution under the title *Snow.*

Snow is a one-hundred-foot, roll-long shot, during which the mounted 16mm camera looks out on a barn and on heavily falling snow. Because of the framing of the image, the particulars of the composition are somewhat mysterious: we can see we are looking at a landscape, but the details around the edges create a frame within the frame. Within this inner frame, the primary visual drama is created by the snow. When I look at *Snow* (and others I have spoken with have the same experience), my eye is drawn back and forth between the flutter of the snowflakes in the foreground and the flakes nearer the barn that seem to move more quickly, creating a visual plane reminiscent of a waterfall. But once we become mesmerized by the "waterfall" in the background, we are distracted by the flakes drifting down in the foreground; they

5. A good description of the Diorama shows is available in Richard B. Altick's *The Shows of London* (Cambridge, MA: Harvard University Press, 1978), chap. 12.

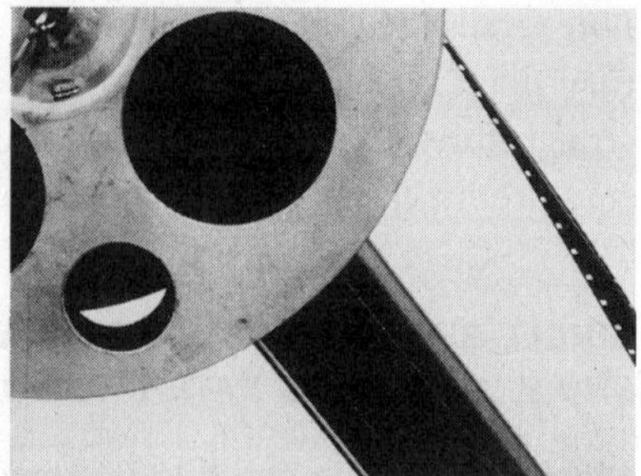

Snow in Robert Huot's *Snow* (1971) and the take-up reel in Alan Berliner's *Patent Pending* (1976). Courtesy Robert Huot, Alan Berliner.

hold our attention until the waterfall effect distracts us again, and so on. The process becomes regular, almost rhythmic, and reminiscent of certain op art works.

This visual experience (*Snow* is silent) is entirely dependent on Huot's decision to extend the shot.[6] The combination of restricted framing and the extended length *discovers* a visual experience that exists solely within the film. If one were actually to look out that window at a snowfall, the experience would not exist with anything like the particular rhythmic intensity it has in Huot's film. In fact, my guess is that Huot meant only to document the snow, which must have seemed nearly perpetual during his first winters in central New York State, and only discovered the visual experience the camera and projector had made available, as a viewer, once the film was shot.

In Alan Berliner's *Patent Pending* the single-shot method is also a means of discovery, but here the ostensible focus is not on the outer world but on cinema's "inner world": the movie projector in the projection booth or, more precisely, on the visual discoveries generated by the interface of a 16mm camera and a 16mm projector. For some years, Berliner was a student and, to make money, a projectionist at the State University of New York at Binghamton (now Binghamton University), where Gottheim was chair of the cinema department. *Patent Pending* developed out of Berliner's many hours sitting in the projection booth watching films unwind and preparing for reel changes.

For eleven minutes (the length of a four-hundred-foot roll of 16mm film), the camera records a portion of the feed reel of a projector: a quarter of the

6. I have heard Huot say that the film's title is a reference to Michael Snow, that *Snow* can be considered an homage. I assume the particular reference is to Snow's tendency—in *Wavelength* and other films—to extend a relatively minimal gesture well beyond conventional time expectations.

reel fills most of the left side of the image; the arm holding the reel cuts through the right side of the image to the lower right corner. At first, the image is still; then the projector is switched on, and the film, which we can see through the holes in the reel, begins to wind off the reel. *Patent Pending* seems to be going nowhere; the reel turns, film unwinds. But as the core of film shrinks, the feed reel gradually spins more quickly, and those viewers who have remained attentive discover a series of visual effects peculiar to cinema. First, the outer edge of the reel seems to take on something of a third dimension; it seems thick rather than flat. Later, the interaction of the camera's shutter speed and the graphic rhythm created by the holes in the reel as they spin though the image creates that reverse-motion effect we are familiar with from stagecoach wheels in Westerns. Finally, the holes in the reel are moving through the image so quickly that their round images tend to double up on the viewer's retina and become animated in a manner reminiscent of some of Oskar Fischinger's abstract animations from the 1920s. When the film finally runs out, the reel stops so we can read "Pat. Pend." (according to Berliner, this was "totally fortuitous").[7]

SINGLE-SHOT FILMS AS PROPOSITIONS ON CINEMA HISTORY AND PRACTICE: J. J. MURPHY'S *SKY BLUE WATER LIGHT SIGN* (1972) AND MORGAN FISHER'S *CUE ROLLS* (1974)

Like Huot and Berliner, J. J. Murphy has used the single-shot form to discover film experiences. In fact, his *Highway Landscape* (1972) and *Ice* (1972) are particularly interesting attempts to set up parameters within which the cinematic apparatus can take over and generate its own imagery and sound. Murphy's most ingenious single-shot film, however, goes a step further: *Sky Blue Water Light Sign* can be understood as a tiny, dense cinematic theorization about elements of film history and prehistory.

The simplicity of the film's production belies its considerable conceptual

7. Letter to author, May 17, 1988. *Patent Pending* was Berliner's first sound film. The primary sound is simply the projector running, though Berliner modulated this sound by moving the microphone around. At times, the sprocket-hole rhythm made by the film moving through the projector is reminiscent of the sound track Tony Conrad created for *The Flicker* (1966). When the projector is switched off—after the take-up reel spins for a while, flapping the tail of the film—I am aware of a secondary sound, that of the camera running. In one sense, in fact, the middle of *Patent Pending*—the long passage when the projector is running—tends to separate the "still," "silent" passages that frame the film so that its closing moments discover details in the image (scratches and dust on the print), as well as the sound of the camera on the sound track that were not perceptible to me at the beginning of the film, presumably because at that point my attention was directed toward the motion I was sure was about to start.

density. To make *Sky Blue Water Light Sign,* Murphy merely filmed a light sign in an Iowa City bar, an advertisement for Hamm's Beer. The sign was constructed so that a continuous image of a woodsy landscape with creek, campsite, and waterfall moved through a rectangularly shaped frame from the right to left. Murphy, who had enjoyed the sign as a graduate student in film studies at the University of Iowa, filmed it so that we cannot see the sign's location or even its physical structure: Murphy matched the camera's framing with the frame around the sign's moving image. The camera was allowed to run for 8½ minutes, long enough so that between the moment when the image fades in and fades out we see slightly more than one entire revolution of the bar-sign landscape, accompanied by sounds Murphy recorded at a real "babbling brook."

Sky Blue Water Light Sign is fascinating both to experience and to think about. Most viewers tend to be a bit mystified about what they are seeing. While there is evidence that the moving imagery is not a photographed scene—the sign has a nonfilmlike texture; various portions of the scene seem obviously contrived—many viewers are convinced, or convince themselves, that a real scene was filmed and subsequently manipulated: the reality of what is presented is not questioned. On its most obvious level, *Sky Blue Water Light Sign* demonstrates our hunger to believe what we see in a theater, often regardless of its absurdity. The water in the *Sky Blue Water Light Sign* scene, for example, seems to be flowing toward us throughout the entire pan!

The ability of *Sky Blue Water Light Sign* to fool viewers has a good deal to do with Murphy's use of the transformative powers of the film medium. By aligning the camera's frame with the inner light-sign frame, he transforms the right-to-left movement of the imagery into an apparent left-to-right panning of a camera. And by filming and projecting the sign's imagery, he enlarges it so that most viewers are unlikely to realize the origin of what they are seeing, even if they have seen similar signs in bars (of course, those familiar with this particular Hamm's ad have a different experience of the film). And his use of the sound of a real brook implicitly argues with whatever doubts viewers have about the reality of what they are seeing.

The film is more than an audience conundrum, however. Once one knows what the imagery is and how the film was made (the title, after all, does indicate precisely what we're seeing, and "Thanks to Hamm's Beer" is flashed during the credits), its conceptual dimensions become more available.[8] When

8. *Sky Blue Water Light Sign* was made as a class assignment, so most of its original audience might not have been in doubt about the original source of the imagery; the transformative powers of framing would most likely have been the subject of discussion.

I have taught with *Sky Blue Water Light Sign,* I have used it to demonstrate the fragility of our conventional distinction between fiction and documentary. Murphy's film is reminiscent of both the Lumière and the Méliès traditions: it is simultaneously fantasy and reality. Murphy presents an unedited image of a real object, but because of the placement of the camera, we are mystified by the nature of the object and by the imagery it presents. Murphy's film reminds us of the truism that the film frame fictionalizes *any* real space, depriving its subject of its physical and ideological context; *and* that recording fictionalized scenes not only *documents* the enactment of the fiction but also confers an illusory level of reality on what is documented.

Murphy was originally drawn to the Hamm's Beer sign because of its parallels with the cinematic apparatus: the imagery of the sign is printed on a strip of plastic, which is lit by a light source that shines through the strip and is moved through a rectangularly shaped frame. Whether consciously, unconsciously, or accidentally, however, *Sky Blue Water Light Sign* also seems to encapsulate certain precinematic developments that played a historical role in the development of the audience that flocked to cinema shows in the wake of the Lumières' perfection of the *cinématographe.* One of the most popular of the protocinematic entertainments of the century preceding the Lumières' first projection of single-shot films was the panorama. The panorama developed in two phases: the "still panorama," a 360-degree painting observed from a central platform, and the "moving panorama," a long painting unrolled through a rectangular frame (for further information on this history, see pp. 200–201). *Sky Blue Water Light Sign* evokes both panoramic forms. The experience of seeing *Sky Blue Water Light Sign*—the feeling of a 360-degree pan of the landscape—is reminiscent of the still panoramas that preceded the moving versions. And the Hamm's Beer light sign itself—like the cinematic experience that recorded it and presents it to us—evokes the moving panorama.

Certainly one of the options offered by any cinematic form is defiance, and there are instances where the single-shot film has been used in a way that defies its own parameters. Several of the most notable instances of such defiance are by Morgan Fisher, who has revealed a penchant for single-shot filmmaking since the beginning of his career. Several of Fisher's films are one shot long or facsimiles of single shots. In some cases—*Documentary Footage* (1968), *Phi Phenomenon* (1968), *Screening Room* (1968), and *The Wilkinson Household Fire Alarm* (1973)—the use of a single, continuous shot has mostly to do with Fisher's interest in documenting a single, continuous performance or event. In the case of *Production Stills* (1970), *Cue Rolls,* and *Standard Gauge* (1984), however, the idea of single-shot film-

The camp in J. J. Murphy's *Sky Blue Water Light Sign* (1972); the synchronizer in Morgan Fisher's *Cue Rolls* (1974). Courtesy J. J. Murphy, Morgan Fisher.

making is itself questioned and, in different ways, defied. Both *Production Stills* and *Standard Gauge* use a continuous, unedited shot as a space for presenting a series of discrete events.

In *Production Stills*, Fisher presents a series of Polaroid snapshots, one at a time, that together document the process we are watching—the filming of the Polaroids with an industry-level camera (a Mitchell)—and hearing (the film was made sync sound). In other words, Fisher uses the single-shot form to create an essentially edited experience (we see the filming in several "shots") and to redirect an industry apparatus into an avant-garde approach. *Standard Gauge* presents a scrolling text that reminds us of the decision that determined that 35mm would become "standard gauge," and then, during a thirty-five-minute continuous shot, Fisher presents and provides often-witty, deadpan commentary on a series of pieces of 35mm film he has collected over the years as he has worked in and around the Hollywood industry. His commentary foregrounds many of those who work, uncelebrated, in the margins of the commercial industry.

Cue Rolls differs from the other single-shot Fisher films in that it is a facsimile of a single shot, like Frampton's *Lemon*, Joyce Wieland's *Dripping Water* (1969), and Sharon Lockhart's *NŌ*. Unlike these films, however, *Cue Rolls* fabricates the illusion of a single shot as a way of offering a proposition or a set of propositions about the relationship between avant-garde film practice and Hollywood filmmaking. At the beginning, we think we are seeing a continuous 5½-minute shot of a synchronizer, a piece of equipment used in the industry: that is, an avant-garde procedure seems to meditate on an ordinary industry mechanism. But as we listen to Fisher, as narrator, explaining how synchronizers work, we realize, slowly but surely, that what we have been seeing as a single shot has in fact been edited—for no purpose other than to reveal that editing has occurred.

To be more precise, in making *Cue Rolls,* Fisher "analyzed" a forty-foot shot of four strips of leader moving through the synchronizer into ten-foot segments that were subsequently A and B rolled so that the segments could be resynthesized into a convincing illusion of the original, uncut shot.[9] The leader moving through the synchronizer was a plan for the negative cutter who would edit (or who, by the time we see the film, *has* edited) *Cue Rolls.* Each of the four cue rolls used white leader to designate those sections of the A and B rolls that would be (and now have been) used by the negative cutter. As one ten-foot segment of white leader on one cue roll passes through the synchronizer, it is followed by a segment on the cue roll to its right, and so on (the synchronizer holds four cue rolls). Since the leader moves through the synchronizer at the same speed as the finished film moves through the projector, the movement of the leader is visible only at the moment when one kind of leader replaces the other in the synchronizer.

Once the sound track has explained that there *are* cuts in the finished film, the changes from one cue roll to another within the image signal the almost imperceptible jumps in the finished film that indicate that the cuts have been made (before this explanation, our attention has been drawn away from any consciousness of the minute movements that signal the edits by the sudden "drama" of the white leader moving through the synchronizer). An industry method for making cuts as unobstrusive as possible, and rendering human intervention in the printing and editing process invisible, has been redirected so that the primary subject of the resulting film is the process of human intervention that took place during the time between the original shooting and our seeing the film. *Cue Rolls* proposes that the particularity of cinema is its interface of rigorous mechanical equipment and fallible human process—an interface encoded by those moments when the cuts interrupt the otherwise continuous shot and dramatized by the juxtaposition of the precision mechanics of the visuals and Fisher's somewhat halting narration.

Like most of his films, *Cue Rolls* demonstrates Fisher's belief that, to be interesting and productive, avant-garde film practice (including the use of the long, continuous shot) should function as more than a set of alternatives to mainstream cinema, as more than a means of adding forms of view-

9. A- and B-rolling is used to avoid the appearance of splices: "The shots of the negative (or sometimes positive) are staggered in alternate spaces on two rolls of film of the same length with black leader between the shots on each roll—the shots on one film correspond with the black leader on the other. The odd-number shots on the A roll and then the even-number shots on the B roll are printed in consecutive order." From the definition of "A and B printing" in Ira Konigsberg, *The Complete Film Dictionary* (New York: New American Library, 1987): 1.

ing experience ignored by the commercial industry to the articulation of film history. For Fisher, the importance of avant-garde filmmaking rests in its potential for providing cinematic critiques that help us go beyond our sense of the power, the prestige, and the technological primacy of the industry and its dream factory approach to a more progressive, more democratic, more materially aware sense of both the fantasy and the reality of both commercial and avant-garde cinema. *Cue Rolls* is an early theoretical statement of this position; *Standard Gauge* more fully articulates its implications.

Some interesting single-shot or faux single-shot films not mentioned in the preceding discussion: *9-1-75* (1975) by James Benning; *Saturday Morning* (1979) by Dan Curry; *Behind the Scenes* (1975) and *Untitled* (1977) by Ernie Gehr; *Metamorphosis* (1970) by Barry Gerson; *Harmonica* (1971) by Larry Gottheim; *Kiri* ("Mist," 1972) by Sakumi Hagiwara; *Necrology* (1970) by Standish D. Lawder; *Apotheosis* (1970) and *Film No. 5 (Smile)* (1968) by John Lennon and Yoko Ono; *Tosca* (1978) by Dominique Noguez; *Say Nothing* (1965) by Andrew Noren; and *Stream Line* (1976) by Chris Welsby.

Interview with James Benning

James Benning established himself as an important contributor to American independent cinema in the mid-1970s with *11 × 14* (1976) and *One Way Boogie Woogie* (1977), formally inventive and visually engaging representations of American landscape and cityscape. That the places in Benning's early films were midwestern gave notice that what was sometimes called the cinematic "flyover zone" (the territory between the centers of film production in New York and Los Angeles / San Francisco) not only could be the focus of interesting independent films but also could produce an important avant-garde filmmaker. Benning's move to New York City in 1980 and then to California in 1987 (he has taught filmmaking and mathematics at CalArts since 1987) expanded his horizons and fed his filmmaking. Given the considerable body of work he has produced and the continuing focus of so many of his best films—including the recent *13 Lakes* (2004), *Ten Skies* (2004), *RR* (2007), and *casting a glance* (2008)—it seems fair to say that Benning has become the foremost filmmaker of American landscape and cityscape.

Benning's work has always been challenging. His *11 × 14* and *One Way Boogie Woogie* were made during the aftermath of Andy Warhol's long, slow films and of the "structural films" (see pp. 27–30) that followed. Warhol and Michael Snow, Ernie Gehr, J. J. Murphy, and others used extended duration and repetitive structures to confront not only the commercial cinema and its reliance on conventional narrative but also the various forms of personally expressive cinema that had dominated the 1950s and early 1960s film avant-garde (most obviously, Stan Brakhage, Kenneth Anger, and Jack Smith). Benning's roots in structural film have remained evident throughout his career and have informed his filmmaking in a variety of ways. Early on, Benning used depictions of place as the backdrop for witty formalist games (for a full minute, an off-screen sound in *One Way Boogie Woogie* seems to approach, but never enters, the frame) and for redirecting conventional narrative expectations: early in *11 × 14* a pair of lovers is introduced; not only do they not meet again during *11 × 14*, but by the end of the film, they seem to have become different characters.

By the 1980s, Benning was growing increasingly fascinated with aspects of American history. *American Dreams* focuses on Hank Aaron's quest to break Babe Ruth's home run record and on Arthur Bremer's quest to assassinate a political figure, within a context of the politics and popular culture of the 1950s and 1960s (see pp. 69–72 for more information on *American Dreams*). *Landscape Suicide* (1986) offers a comparison and contrast of Ed Gein and Bernadette Protti: one, a murderer and grave robber from a rural Wisconsin town (and the prototype for Norman Bates) who sometimes wore his victims' body parts; the other, a young high school student who murdered a cheerleader classmate in a posh San Francisco suburb. Each murder is seen within its physical and social environment; the film asks us to consider how environment relates (and does not relate) to violent crime. *North on Evers* (1991) is Benning's *Easy Rider;* it records identical motorcycle trips from Benning's home in Val Verde, just north of Los Angeles, across the Southwest and the Deep South, then up to Washington, D.C., and New York and back to California via a northern route, taken in two successive years, the first presented in a crawling text that moves across the bottom of the frame, the second, in imagery and sound recorded a year later in the same locations. The trip evokes Benning's experiences of the places he visits and the ways in which these places have played into the history of that generation of Americans who, like Benning, came of age during the 1960s.

Benning's first two "Westerns," *Deseret* (1995) and *Four Corners* (1997), explore the geography and history of the American Southwest: specifically Utah ("Deseret" was the Mormons' original name for the territory) and the Four Corners areas, where Utah, Colorado, New Mexico, and Arizona meet. *Deseret* juxtaposes a series of nineteenth- and twentieth-century *New York Times* stories that reflect the evolution of what was considered important about Utah during different eras (e.g., polygamy in the nineteenth century, environmental damage in the late twentieth century) with imagery recorded throughout the state; the history of Utah becomes a cinematic synecdoche for the evolution of American empire. *Four Corners* is divided into four identically structured sections; each uses image along with spoken and visual text to reveal a different aspect of the complex interplay of cultural groups that has characterized the Four Corners region during recent centuries. For *Utopia* (1998), Benning recycled Richard Dindo's sound track for *Ernesto Che Guevara: The Bolivian Journal* (1997), using it as the audio for his exploration of California's Imperial Valley and the border with Mexico, simultaneously demonstrating the region's visual distinctiveness and the relevance of Guevara's life and final struggles for this region where the first and third worlds meet.

Since 1999, Benning's fascination with place and his commitment to rigorous formal organization have been directed more fully into an implicit environmental politics. His California Trilogy—*El Valley Centro* (1999), *Los* (2000), and *Sogobi* (2001)—and three of his most recent films—*13 Lakes, Ten Skies,* and *RR*—confront the hysterical consumption modeled and sold by American commercial media, and they attempt to retrain those who come to see the films, testing viewers' patience in order to reinvigorate their perceptual capacities. The three California films use an identical structure (thirty-five rigorously composed, 2½-minute shots) to map the state, visualizing both its beauty and its environmental and ethnic politics. *El Valley Centro* focuses on California's central valley, where a considerable percentage of America's food is produced; *Los,* on Los Angeles; and *Sogobi* (the title means "earth" in the Shoshone language), on what remains of wilderness California. Benning develops a web of interconnections between the three films; during early screenings, he asked that all three films be shown during a single extended presentation with breaks for conversation and dinner.

The formal rigor of the California Trilogy is expanded in several remarkable recent films. *13 Lakes* presents thirteen ten-minute, tripod-mounted shots of thirteen American lakes, each shot composed so that the film frame is rigorously divided between the surface of the lake and the land and sky. By the second or third shot, it has become clear that the film will be an extended sequence of ten-minute durations, and further, that these durations will be, at least compared with nearly all moving-image experiences in film and on television (even with nearly all avant-garde experiences in film and on video), unusually minimal: almost nothing will be happening. Once this realization has come, viewers must decide either to leave the theater or to accede to Benning's durational challenge. The fact that, at least in my experience, nearly all of those who come to see *13 Lakes* do stay for the entire experience is something of a victory for Benning's artistry, demonstrating that though Benning has refused to provide what most people go to the movies for, what he *has* provided is not only endurable but engaging enough to sustain a 130-minute experience.

What is it that Benning provides? The composition of the individual images in *13 Lakes* and the slow, steady revelation of lake after lake create a kind of spatiotemporal grid within which the audience can measure the subtle changes over time within each shot and the distinctions between one lake and another. While some of the images of lakes are more visually engaging than others (Benning is certainly capable of stunning imagery but generally resists easy "beautiful" shots) and while some of the transitions from lake to lake are more dramatic than others, it is the audience's growing awareness of their own perceptiveness that replaces character and narrative within this film. By the time the end credits identifying the thirteen lakes roll up through the frame, Benning has transformed his audience by modeling and demanding a more perceptually active sensual awareness of the world. This awareness argues that our culture's tendency toward relentless distraction and hysterical consumption (and their planet-damaging implications) need not be the inevitable product of modern life; it reminds us, as Thoreau reminded us in *Walden,* that slowing down and appreciating the moment-by-moment incarnation of the physical world can transform our sense of what we are and what we—as individuals and as a culture—need. *Ten Skies* (ten rigorously composed, ten-minute shots of different skyscapes) is a companion to *13 Lakes.*

RR (as in "railroad") is somewhat less spare than *13 Lakes* and *Ten Skies;* it presents a series of forty-three shots of trains moving across the American landscape, each shot as long as the train's journey through the frame. Here, Benning's concern with the issue of overconsumption is more direct (the railroad system, after all, remains a crucial element of modern capitalism)—though the tendency to confront the issue of overconsumption by means of testing, and hopefully expanding, the viewer's patience is consistent with the earlier films. While in American avant-garde circles, Benning remains identified with the 1970s, his ongoing productivity and the consistent quality of the films he has made since 1990 have placed him in the pantheon of contemporary independent filmmakers, and his influence as both teacher and filmmaker is widely evident, both in the United States and in Europe. Reinhard Wulf's *James Benning—Circling the Image* (2003), chronicles Benning on the road shooting images for *13 Lakes.*

This interview began in April 2007, following the American premiere of *RR* at Colgate University. At the time, Benning was in the process of editing *casting a glance* (2007), his film on Robert Smithson's *Spiral Jetty* (1970). Our conversation continued by e-mail during the following months.

MacDonald: I think of you as an international person. You're often at film festivals, especially Rotterdam and Berlin. And you've taught in Korea and in Mexico. Austria is hosting a major Benning retrospective this fall. But in all these years, you've stepped outside the United States only three times to make shots, and then only to look *at* the United States. What's this about?

Benning: I have to know a place before I film it.

MacDonald: But you know Berlin and Vienna, and you've not shot there.

Benning: Going to a festival to present your films and staying in a hotel room and drinking beer isn't knowing a place. I do know Vienna a little—I go there a lot. But I wouldn't make a film there. If I made a film in another country, no matter how hard I'd try to be honest about what I was shooting, I'd accidentally misrepresent things because there's so much I *don't* know.

Of course, there *are* good filmmakers who make films in other cultures. Peter Hutton has filmed in China and Iceland, and in Bangladesh, Korea, Thailand, and Poland. Sharon Lockhart has filmed in Japan and in Brazil. They've both been able to negotiate those different cultures. Sometimes they get criticized for doing that, which I *also* think is silly: I don't see their films as forms of misrepresentation or imperialism. We're all citizens of the world, after all.

There's also the practical problem of traveling with film, getting films through airports and all that goes along with it—I have no idea how to do that.

MacDonald: Your recent films, *13 Lakes* and *Ten Skies,* are unusually minimal—each uses only a series of rather spare ten-minute shots. What led you to this strategy? And what did you have in mind for viewers?

Benning: Duration has been part of my work from the very beginning; in *11 × 14* I used a four-hundred-foot magazine (eleven minutes) to record the Evanston Express going to downtown Chicago. *One Way Boogie Woogie* used sixty one-minute shots to contain mini-narratives I created or found in Milwaukee's industrial valley. But it wasn't until making the California Trilogy that I really began to understand that place can only be understood over time; that is, that place is a function of time. And while filming the Trilogy I could see that even a shot length of two-and-a-half minutes (the length of each shot in those three films) didn't always do the job.

I should also mention that I was very much challenged by Sharon Lockhart's *Goshogaoka* [1997]. I saw the film right after she completed it and was very taken by her connection to structural film (Warhol's work, and Frampton's, and mine), but I was even more impressed by how she radicalized structure, pushing duration to a new aesthetic level. After I saw *Goshogaoka,* my own work became more radical.

As for audience, this new strategy is asking them to work harder; you can't experience something subtle if you don't look more closely than we're accustomed to looking, and looking more closely isn't easy. At first I was worried that audiences would be bored, but the contrary seems to be true. These films have been successful with many different audiences.

MacDonald: Your shots always seem very carefully composed. Could you talk about the factors you consider as you frame one of these long continuous shots? Also, are you always conceiving the sound simultaneously as you frame your images?

Benning: Talking about framing is difficult. The answer will be different for each film, even for each shot. For instance, with *13 Lakes,* I wanted the frame to include the same basic information for each of the thirteen shots: that is, half sky and half water. But the real problem was to find a frame that would reveal the uniqueness of each lake.

Finding a frame is a spontaneous and fluid event. Now, in no way do I want to describe this process as "intuitive." I do admit, however, that when I'm working on framing, the little voice in my head is quiet; it doesn't say, "No, no, more to the right; no, not that far." I find each frame in a purely visual way—considering symmetry, negative space, meaning, color, texture, balance. . . . By *not* using language I can communicate with myself much more efficiently. It's not intuitive, but rather a kind of fast thinking based on years of experience.

Sound is considered when I choose a location, and sound may affect the final framing. But while I'm looking for a frame, I'm thinking only in visual terms. Once the frame is arrived at, I might reconsider what I've decided on if it doesn't correspond to my concerns for the sound. For example, I might move the frame left or right to make a sound on-screen or off-screen, depending on how I want the sound to work with the imagery.

MacDonald: How did you choose the thirteen lakes we see in *13 Lakes?*

Benning: First, I made a list of the thirteen largest lakes in the U.S., but five of them turned out to be in Alaska, and four of those were frozen year-round. Still, I wanted to do large lakes and knew I wanted to do at least one of the Great Lakes; I decided on Superior. And I wanted to film Pontchartrain, a large urban lake, and Okeechobee, which is in a swamp.

I also wanted lakes that have interesting histories, like the Salton Sea, which was created accidentally in 1903 soon after they started farming in the Imperial Valley using a crude irrigation system coming off the Colorado River. When the Colorado flooded in 1905, it broke the irrigation gates, and the river was diverted into what was called the Salton Sink; for two years the water from the Colorado River ended up in that basin, which became the Salton Sea. Of course, this diversion of the Colorado River ruined all farming for the Mexicans downriver. Over time the lake rose, and in the 1960s resorts were built around it. In 1976 and 1977, hurricanes caused the flooding of most of the resorts, including the western edge of Bombay Beach, where all these trailers are now mired in sand and salt. I've filmed Bombay Beach several times.

I chose Lake Powell, created by a dam on the Colorado River, because it covered a lot of the Anasazi culture that interests me. I also wanted to film in an out-of-the-way place in the East, and I chose Moosehead Lake up in Maine. Crater Lake came to mind because it formed inside a volcano: its water remains relatively warm because there's still thermal activity at the bottom of the crater. I chose Jackson Lake, the smallest lake I filmed, because of the Grand Tetons (I wanted some mountains in the film) and Upper and Lower Red Lake because it's surrounded by the Chippewa Nation, who refuse to allow any development.

MacDonald: Did you need to get their permission?

Benning: Well, I probably should have. A peninsula divides Upper from Lower Red Lake, and a two-lane blacktop public road goes out to the end of that peninsula. I filmed there in the morning and then drove all the way around the two lakes looking for another vantage point only to realize that that peninsula *was* the best place, so I went back in the afternoon to film there again. I drove down a little gravel road off the main road, made a shot, and was getting ready to leave when I noticed a car going to the end of the blacktop road and coming back, kind of watching me. Just as I closed the trunk, that car drove down the gravel road and blocked me in. I got into my car, a little bit afraid. Two very large Chippewa men got out, knocked on my window, and said, "Let's talk!" I rolled the window down, and they said, "What do you think you're doing here?" in a threatening way. I said that I was making a film and had just made a nice shot, but that since it was starting to rain, I was going to go. They said, "No, no. Get out of the car, let's talk some more." So I got out.

"Why did you come *here* to film?" they asked. I said that I knew this was the Chippewa Nation and that since they prided themselves on keeping development away, the lake would be very pristine; and the one guy said, "Pristine?! Bullshit! All the whitefish in this lake died fifteen years ago! And you know why? Because of *your* paper mills." I had thought I was going to be robbed, but when they started talking like that, I knew this was political. They kept at me for a good half hour. Finally, one of them said, "What are you gonna do, write one of those fuckin' *books?*" And, out of nervousness, I laughed. I think they respected that I laughed, because finally they said, "Let's let him go." I said, "'Let him go!' What were you going do?" And the one guy said, "You don't wanna know."

When I got back to California, I learned that the Chippewa had recently restocked the lake and that there are whitefish in there again. They sued to get the paper mills to stop the pollution and worked with some whites who were sympathetic with what was happening to them.

So, yeah, I probably should have gotten permission. But one of the nice

Jackson Lake, Wyoming (top); Lake Winnebago, Wisconsin (bottom); and Moosehead Lake, Maine (facing page), in James Benning's *13 Lakes* (2004). Courtesy James Benning.

things about making films is how much you learn from the experience. When I watch *13 Lakes,* I remember the narrative that happened around each particular shot, and I hope some of my experience comes through for viewers. Because you have ten minutes to look at each shot, you have time to think about a lot of things, including what might have gone into the making of the shot you're seeing.

MacDonald: How does what *you* know about a place get conveyed via the shot? Is there an attitude or a compressed idea that gets injected into the setting? Does the landscape become your psychological reflection?

Benning: These questions have different answers, depending on the film we're talking about. On the sound track of my film *Deseret* [1995], a narrator reads ninety-three news stories about Utah taken from the *New York Times* from 1852 to 1992. Each story is made up of six to ten sentences, and in the film each sentence is illustrated with a shot of Utah. The number of shots in each section equals the number of sentences in that story. Now, I spent a good part of several years in Utah making that film; I know Utah well, both from roaming around and from doing research. During the film, the viewer learns about Utah from both the *New York Times* texts I decided to use and from the images I collected to illustrate those texts. One of the shots in that film is of the site of the Mountain Meadows Massacre, where a wagon train of Arkansas pioneers were killed by Mormons dressed as Paiute Indians. Everyone who could talk was murdered, over 180 men, women, and children. The *Times* article you hear in voice-over is very direct in providing the information about the massacre, but the current peacefulness of the place, which is evident in the image and sound, helps to convey a fuller meaning. In other words, the meanings we get from these different sources combine and hopefully create a complex response.

Or take the shot of Lower Red Lake in *13 Lakes*. The water is gently lapping toward the shore. The sun, which is at a low angle, is coloring the water gold. Birds fly across the frame from left to right and right to left. It is extremely quiet. But in the distance at the horizon of the lake the sky is dark. Occasionally, thunder can be heard. There's a tension in the frame between the golden, lapping water and that violent sky; that tension captures aspects of the uniqueness of that place and of my experience of it.

MacDonald: Let me take this a little further. Is it your expectation that, after seeing the film, the viewer will investigate the history of these places and come to realize what the Salton Sea might signify to you, or what it would mean for you to drive into Chippewa territory in order to get your shot of Lower Red Lake, and that that research would then further enrich the viewer's experience of *13 Lakes?* In other words, do you think of the film operating in two different ways: as an almost purely formalist experience on first viewing *and* as a springboard for the viewer's active exploration of place after the fact?

Benning: Well, there are many different ways to enter one of my films. Certainly the formal and aesthetic level is the most apparent, and perhaps the most immediately challenging. From the very beginning I tried to define a new film language, a new way of giving information (or telling a story). When I first showed *11 × 14*, I lost half of my audience because they didn't know how to watch the film, but it always pleased me when people would tell me they'd *almost* left, but instead had stayed with the film and felt that the experience had taught them to look differently, to pay more attention and become more proactive as viewers, to look around the frame for small details and not wait for the film to come to them.

I have a very simple definition of an artist; the artist is someone who pays attention and reports back. A good artist pays close attention and knows how to report back. I teach a course called "Looking and Listening." The class and I practice paying attention. I take them to many different places, often for a full day, and we look and listen. Sometimes we go to an oil field in the Central Valley, or to a mountaintop to watch the sky brighten as the sun begins to rise, or to a homeless neighborhood in downtown Los Angeles, or to the port at Long Beach. We gradually learn that our looking and listening is coded by our own prejudices, that we filter what we see through our own particular experiences. And we learn that we need to confront our prejudices, and to learn more about what we do see, if we want to see and hear more clearly.

I do think people want to know more about things after they learn how to really hear and see. Yes, I do hope they will go on to interrogate not only what I show in my films but what they see and hear in their everyday lives. Paying attention can lead to many things. Perhaps even a better government.

MacDonald: I think of many of your films, including the recent ones, as part of a long tradition of landscape depiction that includes American landscape painting of the nineteenth century, and the larger history of landscape representation. What relationship do you see between your films and art history, particularly landscape painting?

Benning: I studied mathematics in school, so when I first decided I wanted to try to make a film, I had little knowledge of film or art history. I began by buying a few how-to books on photography and filmmaking, and taught myself. I've never formally studied art history, though of course my filmmaking led me to be more and more curious. I did get an MFA in filmmaking from the University of Wisconsin in 1975. When I lived in New York City in the 1980s, I went to many galleries and museums to see both art and films. The relationships between my films and painting developed pretty quickly as I grew as a filmmaker. *One Way Boogie Woogie* (1977) was conceived as a tribute to Piet Mondrian and Edward Hopper.

For the past few years I've been copying the paintings of Bill Traylor. He was born a slave and continued to work on a plantation until he outlived everyone. At the age of eighty he moved into town and started painting. He painted on the streets of Montgomery, Alabama, mostly from 1940 to 1943, completing over fifteen hundred drawings and paintings during that time. I've learned a lot about framing from studying his paintings.

You mentioned nineteenth-century American painting. At this point in my life, I am very familiar with the Hudson River painters: Frederic Church and Thomas Cole in particular. And I'm interested in other approaches to landscape during that era. Currently, I'm building a replica of Thoreau's Walden Pond cabin near my home in the mountains, to see what that might teach me.

MacDonald: When you were making *13 Lakes* and *Ten Skies,* did you think of them as a diptych?

Benning: I thought of them as companion films, but not as a diptych; a diptych implies a closer relationship. The two films are very different. For example, in *13 Lakes,* everything was shot in sync. Additional sound was taken before and after each shot, so that I could manipulate the sound and make it more real than the production sound would have been: in the original recording I'd sometimes get noises that would have been distracting in the finished film. In *Ten Skies,* all the sounds come from earlier films. I tried to make that process obvious in the eighth shot: those gunshots are the same gunshots you hear in the Crater Lake shot in *13 Lakes.*

MacDonald: Another way in which the two films are different is that in *13 Lakes* you traveled across the United States and you flew to Alaska, whereas at least according to the end credits, *Ten Skies* was filmed in Val Verde, where you live.

Benning: Not exactly. *Ten Skies* was shot within 150 miles of Val Verde, which I think of as my "backyard." There are three or four shots that were made within a mile of Val Verde, but nothing was actually shot in the town itself. The fire of the second shot, for example, was filmed in October 2003, about a mile down the road from where I live; that fire came very close to my home. Three shots were made in the Sierra Nevada mountains where I have a little house—that's part of my "backyard" also. The shot made furthest from Val Verde is the smokestack filmed in Trona, which is located one valley west of Death Valley. Kerr McGee owned the town for many years, and then it went to American Chemical, and now somebody else owns it. Searles Lake is right next to Trona; half of the elements known to earth can be found in that lake bed, but mainly they mine borax, which is used for all sorts of things: soap and napalm.

MacDonald: I understand that you've called *Ten Skies* an antiwar film (meaning, I assume, that natural beauty and contemplativeness are an antidote to belligerence and destruction)—but would you expect a viewer to think of the film in that way?

Benning: Ten Skies was conceived as an antiwar film. It was (and still is) hard for me to ignore the arrogance of the George W. Bush administration and their violent so-called solutions, so the film began as a response (or an antithesis) to that. I wanted the shots to be peaceful and serene.

But quickly the film became something else. The very first shot I made was of the sky above the wildfire, which was accidentally started by two guys mishandling a welding torch. The fire raced up and down the local hills, creating its own weather system. Large white clouds rose thousands of feet into the air and then turned orange from the fire below. This made me realize that the look of the sky was very much a function of the landscape below. But I'm still hoping there are enough shots that suggest peace so that the film implicitly calls for an end to war.

MacDonald: After the premiere of *RR* the other night at Colgate University, I was a bit surprised to hear you talk primarily about the political ramifications of the film, and especially about the realities of overconsumption. During that first viewing, I was primarily aware of *RR* as a landscape film.

Benning: I stood along train tracks for two and a half years, filming 216 trains—there are 43 in the film—and during that process, I could not *not* think about consumption. You probably remember the double train shot, where the first train is hauling SUVs. You can tell they're SUVs because they're too big for the traditional auto carriers and require the new AutoMax carriers. So that first train pulls through the image for a good three or four minutes hauling SUVs, and then when the second train, going the other way, passes, we realize that half of that train is oil cars. For me *not* to see this film as about overconsumption would be a surprise.

Now I know *RR* is anchored in a certain aesthetic and also in the kind of nostalgia that trains tend to create, but trains have a complicated economic and political history that constantly plays into this film. The railroad system was built through massive land and bond fraud; the process made some people very rich. In 1980, the train system almost went out of business in this country, but right now it's in great shape because of containerization. This is reflected in the film: you see more and more container trains near the end.

Of course, I also decided to make a film about trains because when I was a kid, I liked trains; I had a train set, and grew up aware of the romantic side of railroads. In 1900, the train was the fastest thing on earth.

I wanted the film to function on all these levels.

MacDonald: I grew up in the 1940s, when the sound of trains seemed to suggest security; as a child, I loved the sound of trains chugging around at night, coupling in the distance, tooting.

Benning: Formally, *RR* is all about sound-image relationship. If you watch the film a number of times, you'll discover that different trains and different cars make different sounds. The sound a particular car makes when it's loaded is different than the sound it makes when it's empty. Standing on the side of railroad tracks for years, I became very aware of these sounds. I shot everything in sync, and then did a lot of work on Pro Tools to refine the sound track. I'm very proud of the way the sound of each train in the film is unique to that train.

At the beginning, I had the idea of using quotations from the Bible throughout the film. It might have been interesting to do that, but I got so caught up in the train sounds that, in the end, I allowed myself only a very few intermittent sounds that don't come from the trains: a baseball game, an advertisement for Coca Cola, a quote from Revelation about raping the earth, and a bit of Eisenhower's farewell speech, warning about the military-industrial complex (you hear that over a coal train that's three miles long). Each of these additions has a political dimension that hopefully is not overstated.

MacDonald: How fully did you try to reflect the geography of the American train system?

Benning: In a sense, *RR is* a landscape film, where the landscape contour is described by the railroad tracks. Trains can't ascend at more than a 2 percent grade, so they have to fit into the landscape. If the land is flat, you have this straight track going into the Z axis, but if the terrain is mountainous, the train will need to loop over itself.

MacDonald: We see that looping in one shot, though it takes a while to realize that it is the same train.

Benning: That's the Tehachapi Loop, just east of Bakersfield.

I shot *RR* at two different times. When I began the film, I was already filming *casting a glance.* For a year, I'd always take a different route back from Utah to film trains in Utah, Nevada, and California. Half the film comes from that year. The other half comes from a trip I took last summer, when I drove to New Orleans and filmed in Louisiana, Mississippi, Alabama, Kentucky, West Virginia, Pennsylvania, New York, Pennsylvania again, Ohio, Indiana, Illinois, Wisconsin, Iowa, Nebraska, and Wyoming. I tried to represent lakes and rivers and mountains and deserts. The result is less about mapping the U.S. into the film than about mapping different kinds of landscape into the film.

MacDonald: To what extent do you think of your filmmaking as an antidote to contemporary consumer culture?

Benning: Oh, this is a loaded question. How can any of us escape consumerism? I drove over fifteen hundred miles to shoot *13 Lakes.* I've traveled extensively for many of my films. And filmmaking isn't a clean industry. As Pogo says, "We has met the enemy and he is us!" When I lived in New York City, SoHo was an artists' neighborhood. Look at it now. Artists have been one of the main catalysts for gentrification and capital investment. And look at the art world and its relationship to money.

But, yes, my films are an antidote to consumerism. They're made as cheaply as possible—most of the time for less than $20,000—and they're not about consuming more; they're about seeing and hearing more of what's already around you. I don't work to transform my films into consumer products. You can't buy DVDs of my films, and while the films do tend to pay for themselves, they're certainly not making me wealthy. *13 Lakes, Ten Skies,* and *One Way Boogie Woogie / 27 Years Later* [in 2006, Benning finished a shot-by-shot remake of *One Way Boogie Woogie*, called *27 Years Later*; the films are shown together] recently ran for a week at Anthology Film Archives in New York, and I didn't make enough money to cover the costs of wear and tear on the prints!

MacDonald: The Center for Land Use Interpretation is your LA neighbor. Are you familiar with the organization? Do you see any connections or similarities between their explorations of American geography and your own?

Benning: Well, yes, Matt Coolidge [Matthew Coolidge has been director of programming for the center since 1994] is a good friend of mine. I think the Center for Land Use Interpretation is a landmark in today's art world, and yes, we are both interested in studying place from many different perspectives: social, political, physical, economic . . .

I would also like to include William Least Heat-Moon here as another colleague. His book *PrairyErth* [1991] is a great model for seeing a place in a wide variety of ways.

MacDonald: I know your films are often shown on German television. Do you have an ongoing contract with German TV to buy your films?

Benning: It's film-to-film. WDR Cologne has been very good to me; they've financed my last ten films, either by giving me start-up money or by buying finished films. I'm really grateful to Reinhard Wulf and Werner Dütsch for their belief in me.

MacDonald: What are your goals for *casting a glance?*

Benning: I want people to know the *Spiral Jetty*, and especially how it changes over time. The first time I went to shoot material, the water level was almost exactly the same as when the *Spiral Jetty* was built; it was May and the water had washed away the salt, and the *Jetty* was black and pristine, as if it were brand new. Over the following two years, I was able to simulate the *Jetty*'s entire thirty-seven-year history. I have it when it's full of salt, when it's completely out of the water, and when it's completely submerged (it was entirely underwater from 1973 until 2000), that is, doing what Smithson originally wanted it to do: change over time. In the film, I give the dates, not of when I shot, but when, over the years, the water was at exactly the level as when I shot.

The sound there also changes continually. There are different birds at different times of year, and the air varies, so noises travel differently.

Recently, the state of Utah has gotten involved in making the *Jetty* a tourist attraction, and I guess they must have realized that when people went down there, they saw not just the *Spiral Jetty* but an old trailer, an amphibious boat, an old steam shovel—all this junk mired in muck and covered in salt within a quarter of a mile of the *Jetty*—and also a commercial

Three views of Robert Smithson's *Spiral Jetty* (1970) in James Benning's *casting a glance* (2007). Courtesy James Benning.

jetty nearby that goes far out into the lake and makes just a slight curve (it was used for oil exploration). In his writings Smithson eloquently describes the area as "giving evidence to a succession of manmade systems mired in abandoned hopes." He was very interested in building the *Jetty* next to these buried man-made systems; that was part of the original experience. But recently the highway department, or someone—I'm assuming it's the state—hauled all that junk out of there.

MacDonald: You've mentioned that *casting a glance* might be your last 16mm film.

Benning: I would say my use of 16mm is going to end soon. It's become so stressful to finish a film and go to the lab and try to get good prints. Then it's even more stressful to go to screenings, because I'll get a good screening, an appropriate screening, one out of every five times, and three out of five will be god-awful. The projector will have a lot of movement in it or it won't focus across the image, or the sound will be garbled, or the gate will be all dirty, or it'll scratch my film. A print lasts about five or six screenings now, which is expensive and frustrating. On the other hand, once in a long while, a screening will be perfect, as it was the other night at Colgate. I see that and I think, "Well, 16mm is still *possible.*"

MacDonald: You'd move to digital?

Benning: Yeah. I am depressed about feeling forced out of my craft, but I'm also excited to try to learn a new trick, at my age. The change will make me contemplate a whole different way of image-making. I'm sure I'll be frustrated, and who knows, I could come back and make a film once in a while. But I suspect that soon 16mm just isn't going to be there.

The Mohawk Valley Journey to *The Journey*

Early in January 1983, I was surprised to receive a phone call from Sweden; it was the film director Peter Watkins. "Do you think," he asked, "that the people in the Utica area who have been so supportive when I've shown films there over the years might be willing to help me produce a section of a new film? It's likely that I'll work in several countries, if there is broad enough support, but part of the film will be shot in the Mohawk Valley. I know you're very busy, but is there any chance that you would have time to organize a support group for this new project? The support group would need to raise money and organize the shooting."[1] I hesitated: the idea of raising money for a documentary film did not seem particularly attractive or feasible, and I had no idea what would be involved in organizing a film shoot. But Watkins is an Academy Award–winning director (his remarkable and controversial *The War Game* was Best Feature Documentary in 1966), and I was a college professor who regularly lectured on Watkins's films and believed that some of them—*The War Game, Punishment Park* (1971), and *Edvard Munch* (1974)—were landmark contributions to film history. I could not imagine saying no. I agreed to form a support group.

At the time of the phone call, I was teaching English composition, American literature, and film history at Utica College and curating a Thursday evening film series that presented classics, new films from other cultures, visiting filmmakers, experimental films—whatever seemed cinematically interesting but was not available in local theaters. Watkins had been a regular visitor to this series, and to other area colleges, ever since Joseph A. Gomez had first brought him to Mohawk Valley Community College in the early 1970s.[2] Watkins had

1. Of course, I was one of many—dozens, perhaps—of people who received this call from Watkins. Basically, he had decided to see if he could mobilize the network of those who showed independent film to local audiences across this country, and in other countries, to do something besides *showing* films. I know of no other instance within the annals of independent cinema where a filmmaker has reenvisioned film exhibition in this way.

2. Gomez wrote the first book on Watkins: *Peter Watkins* (Boston: Twayne, 1979); it remains the most useful exploration of Watkins features up through *Edvard Munch*. James

visited central New York to present *Punishment Park* at the First Utica Film Symposium, "Focus on Contemporary Film," in 1973; in 1975 the Third Utica Film Symposium presented *Culloden* (1964), *The War Game, Privilege* (1967), and *Punishment Park*, along with two discussions with Watkins; and in 1976, a grant from the George E. Upson Fund of the Utica Foundation made possible a two-week Watkins visit that included a retrospective of his feature films, the local premieres of *Edvard Munch* and *Fällan* ("The Trap," 1975), as well as several discussions with the director.[3] Watkins was back at Utica College in February 1977, and again in February 1979, to present *Edvard Munch*, and he lived in the area for several months in 1983, during a moment soon after the collapse of an attempted remake of *The War Game*—the tentative title was "The Nuclear War Film"—in the United Kingdom.

These frequent visits had resulted in a number of personal connections with professors and students at local colleges and with local artists (especially those working at Sculpture Space), and Watkins's films had developed a considerable following. Some of the enthusiasm generated by his visits to the area was a function of Watkins's international reputation and influence as a politically rebellious director. For a time, *The War Game* was among the most widely screened documentary films in the world, not only because of its intelligence and power but because its envisioning of nuclear holocaust was politically controversial. Though it had financed *The War Game* and had scheduled its first television transmission for the week of August 6, 1965,

---

Michael Welsh's *Peter Watkins: A Guide to References and Resources* (Boston: G. K. Hall, 1986) includes an overview of Watkins's career, a critical survey of writings about Watkins, a detailed filmography, and a listing of all publications about Watkins's films and career in general up through 1985. Insofar as I am aware, no one has provided an overview of Watkins's work that goes beyond the early stages of *The Journey*.

In 1991, Ken Nolley, professor of English and film at Willamette College, who had been much involved with the Salem, Oregon, support group for *The Journey*, edited a special issue of the *Willamette Journal of the Liberal Arts*, suppl. ser. 5, devoted to *The Journey*. The issue includes Watkins's own "*The Journey:* A Voyage of Discovery"; my "Process Is Product; Product Is Process: Peter Watkins' *The Journey*"; James Welsh's "An Arduous *Journey*"; Mary Ann Youngren's "*The Journey:* An Analysis of Symbolic Imagery"; Gregg B. Walker's "*The Journey:* A Conflict Resolution Perspective"; Catherine Collins's "A Narrative Analysis of *The Journey*" and Nolley's "Do You Need a Space? Here Is a Space: Notes toward a Reading of *The Journey*."

I interviewed Watkins about the project, in Utica, in November 1983. The interview appeared first in the *Independent* 7, no. 9 (October 1984): 28–34, and then, along with an earlier interview, in *A Critical Cinema 2* (Berkeley: University of California Press, 1992). *A Critical Cinema 3* (Berkeley: University of California Press, 1998) includes the edited transcript of a contentious discussion of *The Journey* with Watkins and others involved in the production, following Richard Herskowitz's presentation of the film at the 1987 Robert Flaherty Seminar.

3. All of these events were cosponsored by Mohawk Valley Community College and Utica College of Syracuse University and were co-organized by Gomez and myself. Watkins may have visited the area in 1974, but I have been unable to confirm such a visit.

the twentieth anniversary of the bombing of Hiroshima, the British Broadcasting Company, concerned about the potential political ramifications of the finished film, postponed the television premiere indefinitely and, in the end, banned *The War Game* from television broadcast anywhere in the world.[4] Watkins was furious and took the issue to the British press. The revelation of the suppression of *The War Game* created enough negative reaction that, as a compromise, the forty-seven-minute film was released as a feature and toured art cinemas in the United Kingdom, Europe, and the United States during 1966 and 1967 (the BBC's television ban was not lifted until 1985).[5]

Boy's eyes burned in Peter Watkins's *The War Game* (1965). Courtesy Peter Watkins.

Watkins's willingness to confront those who wanted to suppress *The War Game,* and to rally those concerned about the nuclear arms race, had broad impact. Certainly, *The War Game,* which continued to be widely exhibited during the 1970s, especially in educational institutions, played a role in the global antinuclear movement, and in general, Watkins's work seems to have affected many individuals. In *The Ballad of John and Yoko,* compiled by the editors of *Rolling Stone,* John Lennon is asked, "Was there any one incident that got you into the peace campaign?" He responds:

> Well, it built up over a number of years, but the thing that struck it off was a letter we got from a guy called Peter Watkins, who made a film called

4. *Culloden* (a carefully researched film about the final major battle between the Scottish and the British and the subsequent destruction of the Highland clans as a political force) and *The War Game* were Watkins's first professional films, but he had also made a number of amateur films. His *Diary of an Unknown Soldier* (1959) won an "Oscar" in the Ten Best Amateur Films Competition in England; *The Forgotten Faces* (1961), another amateur "Oscar." See Gomez's useful discussion of the amateur films, and their relationship to Watkins's later career, in the first chapter of *Peter Watkins.*

5. My first experience with *The War Game* was in Gainesville, Florida, I believe in 1966, when I was a graduate student at the University of Florida. One afternoon, I attended a one o'clock screening of the film at the local art theater and was—as were so many of those who saw the film—deeply moved by its unflinching examination of the issue of nuclear war (to my knowledge, *The War Game* was the first film to attempt to show what the results of a nuclear strike might look like and feel like). As I was driving home after the screening, I was puzzled when more than one clock indicated that it was not yet 2:00 P.M.—an hour earlier than it should have been. Only then did I understand that Watkins's film had been so powerful that at first it seemed much more temporally substantial than it actually was.

> *The War Game.* It was a long letter stating what's happening—how the media is controlled, how it's all run, and it ended up: "What are you going to do about it?"
>
> He said people in our position and his position have a responsibility to use the media for world peace. And we sat on the letter for three weeks and thought it over and figured at first we were doing our best with songs like "All You Need Is Love."
>
> Finally we came up with the bed event and that was what sparked it off. It was like getting your call-up papers for peace. Then we did the bed event.[6]

At local colleges, Watkins's introductions to his films, his question-and-answer sessions, and his lectures consistently revealed a filmmaker's passion for using cinema to engage crucial cultural and political issues.[7] And his appearances often revealed the same confrontation of complacency that Watkins's letter to Lennon and Ono had exemplified. When an audience member in a crowded Macfarlane Auditorium at Utica College would ask what Watkins considered a flippant question, a question that suggested that the questioner was more interested in being entertained or entertaining than in engaging serious issues, Watkins might pause for thirty seconds, standing quietly in the front of the auditorium, looking directly at the questioner, seeming to think through the ramifications of the question, rubbing an index finger slowly back and forth along the edge of the podium, before responding—usually by turning the question back on the questioner and back toward the issue at hand. Watkins's appearances in the Mohawk Valley, and elsewhere, were a form of theater, where the filmmaker acted the way he felt other filmmakers would act if they understood that their primary responsibility was not an entertaining reconfirmation of the status quo but the use of media as a means for rethinking and engaging the many social

6. *Rolling Stone* editors, *The Ballad of John and Yoko* (Garden City, NY: Doubleday, 1982), 66. The "bed event," of course, is the Lennon-Ono Bed-In in Montreal in 1969, which was documented by Lennon-Ono in *Bed-In* (a.k.a. *Bed Peace,* 1969).

Watkins's attention to the political implications of popular music was evident in *Privilege* (1967), a feature that focuses on the power and influence of rock musicians during the 1960s and suggests that popular music and the near-religious fanaticism surrounding it had become means of redirecting energy that might have been used to confront pressing political problems into a harmless and sterile but, for some, very profitable avenue. Near the end of the film, Watkins draws a parallel between the modern rock concert and Leni Riefenstahl's *Triumph of the Will* (1934).

7. The interest among local artists was solidified, I believe, by their admiration of *Edvard Munch,* which Jack Kroll, in *Newsweek* (September 27, 1976), had called "the best film I've seen in its depiction of the artistic process. A welcome event, the cinema's most intelligent attempt to probe and dramatize the mind and methods of a great artist." A June 2005 rerelease of the film in New York garnered rave reviews.

problems of modern society, including the social complacency created and endlessly confirmed by commercial entertainment film and television.

Watkins's local appearances were impressive and, for many, engaging—even charismatic. Over the years, the many local screenings of his films revealed again and again that Watkins was that unusual film artist whose cinematic means are as subtle and sophisticated as his politics are direct and politically defiant. If the films that followed *The War Game* did not have quite that film's impact, all of them were passionate and intelligently made, demonstrating that this was a remarkable and innovative director. That Watkins wanted to work in Utica and surrounding communities to make a new film, and—judging from that January phone call—perhaps a new kind of film, seemed to me, and to those I talked with during the following days, an exciting prospect.

In the months before Watkins called me to see if he could enlist the support of Mohawk Valley residents, he had been primarily engaged in trying to fund "The Nuclear War Film" in the United Kingdom. At first, this project had seemed to garner considerable support. Member of Parliament Frank Allaun had formed a Peace Film Fund to help raise money for the film, and London's Central Television had agreed to cover the behind-the-camera costs; research teams had been organized, and Watkins was scouting possible shooting locations throughout the United Kingdom.[8] Whereas *The War Game* had focused on a single location and had been funded entirely by the BBC, Watkins had conceived the "remake" as a more fully national undertaking that would be funded in large part by grassroots contributions from peace groups and average citizens.[9] Above all, Watkins wanted to avoid any larger financial entity that might have the power to suppress the new film, the way the BBC had continued to suppress *The War Game* from television broadcast.

As the concept for "The Nuclear War Film" expanded, so did its proposed budget, and by mid-1982, both Allaun and Central Television had become concerned. Allaun decided to use the money raised by the Peace Film Fund for a low-budget film directed by someone else, and while Central Television did not withdraw, Watkins was told that it would be up to him to raise the additional financing for the now-larger project and that, since it *was* a larger project, "The Nuclear War Film" would require more involvement and control by Central Television.[10] Watkins, always fiercely jealous of his indepen-

8. See Welsh, *Peter Watkins*, 18–20.

9. By a single location, I mean that once the atomic attack has begun, the town of Rochester in Kent, six miles from the site of one detonation, becomes the focus of the film.

10. I am indebted to James Welsh for the history of "The Nuclear War Film" project. See his introduction to *Peter Watkins: A Guide to References and Resources*.

dence, rebelled and made an extended visit to Australia to try to raise funds there for an entirely independent "Nuclear War Film" and to develop an international movement that might provide financial support for the project. In October 1982, I received a letter from Watkins, including both a nineteen-page overview of the thinking behind "The Nuclear War Film" and a shorter summary of that thinking, asking that I copy the letter and the attached materials and distribute them to anyone who might be willing to contribute.

In retrospect, it is clear that even as Watkins worked to keep "The Nuclear War Film" project alive, his concept of this project was changing. Of course, all along, the issue of nuclear war was for Watkins, and for anyone thinking seriously about it, one of the quintessential *international* issues: any nuclear war would be a global war, if not in actual combatants, certainly for those who would suffer as a result of the conflict. Watkins's international appeal for funding to make "The Nuclear War Film" was predicated on this understanding. During 1982–83 Watkins was beginning to feel that a film about *the* international issue of the moment should itself be as international as possible, not just in terms of who financed the film, but in terms of who participated in its production. The summary statement about "The Nuclear War Film" that was circulated in late 1982 made clear that the project was expanding, at least conceptually: "The film will concentrate on sequences made with a number of real families in the United States, the Soviet Union, West Germany, Sweden, Denmark, Norway, Finland, France, Australia, Japan, Mexico, India, Micronesia, and one African country. One (or possibly two) family sequences will be shot in each of these countries, providing a unique opportunity for those in each area to express themselves within an international context." It was this new sense of a truly international filmmaking process and a truly international finished film that Watkins had become committed to when he called me to enlist central New York support. And it was this *international* dimension of the project that made it unusual and attractive, and that would allow those of us who were interested in being part of Watkins's effort to create excitement around it. Not only were we going to assist an accomplished filmmaker to make a new film; we were going to be part of an exploratory filmmaking process that would connect us with like-minded people across the globe.

Another major change in Watkins's thinking was confirmed by the announcement that *The Day After* would be broadcast by ABC television on Sunday, November 20, 1983. *The Day After* is, in its broad outlines, a remake of *The War Game,* though the Robert Papazian and Stephanie Austin production is quite different from the Watkins film: *The Day After* is a relatively conventional melodrama, whereas *The War Game* is a polemic that addresses the audience *directly* in a wide variety of ways, in the hope of enlisting those who see the film in immediate political action to prevent the terrifying future it portrays.[11] By the time of the broadcast of *The Day After,* Watkins had concluded that his hope of using a dramatization of the realities of nuclear war to create a powerful and effective intervention in the complacency promoted and modeled by commercial television had been thwarted not just once, by the BBC, but again by ABC. "The Nuclear War Film," as originally envisioned, now seemed impossible—it would be seen as just another *The Day After*—and more important, would contribute to the development of an even deeper complacency about "the Bomb": the more frequently mass media provided imagery of nuclear detonations, the less impact and importance this imagery would have, and the more inevitable nuclear detonations would come to seem.

I do not remember with any precision, and so far as I am aware, there is no paper trail that can help in detailing the first meetings of what would grow into the large and effective Mohawk Valley support group (as I remember, Sonia Tarlin, who taught English composition at Utica College, was an early chair of the group). I do recall that at the very beginning, the small group of people who met with me seemed more interested in a free-form discussion of their frustration and despair about the nuclear issue in general than in taking practical action to work toward the production of a specific film. At first, this was, no doubt, because the nature of Watkins's project was rather ambiguous. But as Watkins developed his ideas for what would become *The Journey*—at the beginning, we called it "The War Game 2 Project" (and "The War Game II Project"); Watkins called it "The Peace Film"[12]—the focus and effectiveness of the support group evolved as well.

During the spring and summer of 1983, Watkins lived with Patricia

11. A fundamental dimension of Watkins's films, throughout his career, had been the direct engagement of the viewing audience by the filmmaking process itself. There are a number of aspects of this, but one of the most notable is Watkins's commitment to breaking down the implied wall between the characters on-screen and the audience in the theater. The people portrayed in Watkins's films often look directly at the camera, at us, as if to draw attention to their connection with us. In *The War Game,* for example, the horribly injured people we see in the aftermath of the nuclear strike on Britain look out of the screen at us, from this imagined future, implicitly pleading with us to make sure that *this* future does not occur. Watkins's characters know *we* are interested in the issue that is affecting them—we have attended this film—and they know we have the time to assist in changing the future: we clearly have time to go to the movies! In every sense, *The War Game* and Watkins's other films are not simply grim entertainments or warnings but direct calls to action.

12. Our original name was a wry comment on the then-new proliferation of Hollywood remakes—and also a way of connecting the new project to the film that had established Watkins's reputation, at least in this country (*Culloden* had established Watkins's reputation in the United Kingdom), and was best known locally.

O'Connor and me and our children in New Hartford, making regular visits to colleges, universities, and public schools to present films and discuss them with audiences, while he worked to develop the international network that would, in the end, make *The Journey* possible. Watkins's calls to international film and peace communities for support for the new project produced additional contacts and a range of responses, including a letter from Harry Belafonte and Performers and Artists for Nuclear Disarmament (PAND). Dated October 7, 1983, the letter indicates that at the PAND international convention in Hamburg, Germany, "the member nations representing the will of some of the most renouned *[sic]* artists in the world . . . unanimously voted their approval of Mr. Watkins' film" (PAND later supported Watkins's project in a variety of ways in Norway and in the United States). Word of the project was getting around.

The Mohawk Valley support group gradually became more and more serious in its consideration of ways to raise money for the project; in September 1983, it announced a benefit screening of *The War Game* at the Stanley Theater to be held on Sunday afternoon, October 30.[13] The function of this benefit was twofold: to raise money that could be used for further fund-raising and to solidify area support for the new film. In terms of numbers, the benefit was not as successful as the support group had hoped it would be, but it did net $2,035.78 (general admission was $10.00; students and senior citizens, $3.50) and, more important, produced a considerable group of volunteers who signed up to be part of various War Game 2 Project committees: an International Dinner Committee, chaired by the Reverend Rick Krause-Neale; an Art Sale Committee, chaired by the teacher-artist Susie Wadsworth; a Garage Sale Committee, chaired by the artist Georgia Deal; and a Publicity Committee, chaired by the photographer Don Tracy. These committees would themselves evolve during the following months.

By 1983, Watkins was working with Catharina Bragee and Lena Ag at the Stockholm-based Svenska Freds och Skiljedomsföreningen / Film för Fred (the Swedish Peace and Arbitration Society / Film for Peace). The organization had become a crucial financial supporter of *The Journey* and was supplying Watkins with an organizational base for coordinating support groups around the world. American support groups had emerged in three areas: in the Mohawk Valley; in Seattle, Washington; and in Oregon (separate groups

13. In advance of the benefit we applied to the Film Fund, a New York State Council on the Arts organization that functioned as a fiscal agent for nonprofit enterprises. On November 1, 1983, we received word from the fund's executive director, Carmen Ashcroft, that the War Game 2 Project had been approved. The Film Fund would serve as our fiscal agent throughout the fund-raising and the shooting.

Peter Watkins (left) and Scott MacDonald during the production of *The Journey* (1987).

had formed in Portland and in Salem). The mission of each group was to raise enough money to shoot with at least one family. Additionally, Watkins hoped that the more financially successful support groups would be able to assist with the shooting in those locations where raising money for the film would not be possible: in fact, the European support groups did supply money for the shooting in Mozambique, and the Portland group helped fund the shooting in Mexico.

When Watkins arrived in Utica at the end of January 1984, it was clear that the new film would be shot in as many locations around the globe as possible, and that in each location, shooting would focus on a family discussion about the issue of nuclear war. In those locations where enough money could be raised, Watkins would also engage larger groups in dramatizing dimensions of a nuclear war scenario as it might involve the families. Watkins was no longer interested in dramatizing a nuclear strike itself, but he *was* determined to demonstrate that government civil defense planning, here and abroad, was basically a charade. As it turned out, the Mohawk Valley group was the only American support group to raise enough money to dramatize crowd scenes (crowd scenes were filmed in Norway, Scotland, and Australia), and Watkins became intent on dramatizing the evacuation of an African American neighborhood under the threat of a nuclear attack. Robert Baber, a lifelong Utican then teaching journalism at Utica College (currently dean of the Munson-Williams Proctor Arts Institute School of Art in Utica), had arranged for Watkins to interview several local African American families during the winter visit. After conversations with these families over a period of months, the William and Elizabeth Hendricks family agreed to be the focus of the local portions of the film.[14]

Once the groups in the various locations committed to the project,

14. The Glen Simmons family and the Bill Phillips family were the other two families Watkins talked with. Baber remembers that while the Simmons family were Watkins's first choice, they were unable to commit the necessary time and energy to the project. Fortunately,

Watkins made clear that he would work, as best he could, with however much money each support group could raise, but he did suggest a practical figure for the Mohawk Valley: "It is really impossible to say at this early stage how much money we might raise in the New York State area, and I imagine that probably a larger part of our US total will come from the North-West, so perhaps we might not be talking about a total in New York of more than, say, 30,000–50,000 dollars."[15] While this amount might seem a pittance compared with the extravagant costs of Hollywood features, it was a sobering and daunting figure for our group, especially since it was Watkins's assumption that the fund-raising itself should, insofar as possible, reflect the ideals of the proposed film: that is, whatever we did to raise money should involve ordinary citizens, people not connected with commercial media; it should reflect the project's internationality; and whenever possible, it should help to raise consciousness about the dangers of the arms race and the many issues related to it. In a tape he recorded in November 1983, just after the Stanley benefit, Watkins made clear that the public process of raising money was not just a means of helping to make the War Game 2 Project possible, but was an essential part of the project and its fundamentally educational and activist goals.

The Stanley benefit and Watkins's visit to meet with the prospective families energized the Mohawk Valley support group and drew increasing attention to our efforts. In February, the Central New York Community Arts Council granted us the $750 that would support Watkins during his visits to the area leading up to and including the shooting, which was scheduled for fall. Also in February, the Edith Barrett Art Gallery at Utica College hosted a show of antinuclear posters designed and printed by Robert Huot, a local artist, during the previous years, including a new poster, "Utica—This Is Ground Zero," copies of which were offered for sale as a benefit for the War Game 2 Project, for twenty dollars.[16]

---

the Hendricks family were interested in the project and remained committed and thoroughly engaged throughout the process.

At one point, there were also discussions about Watkins filming a gathering of African Americans at Bill Phillips's Ten Pin Tavern on Eagle Street, talking about the situation of African Americans in Utica, but this idea did not get beyond the discussion stage.

15. This letter is not dated, but judging from the details, it must have been written in late 1983.

16. Huot had designed another No Nukes image that appeared first as a poster that hung in New York City subway stations for some months, then reappeared as a large pin that could be worn. Huot was, and remains, an accomplished painter and filmmaker (see "Putting All Your Eggs in One Basket: The Single-Shot Film" in this volume); until his retirement he taught at Hunter College in New York City. Huot lives on a small farm near New Berlin, New York, about thirty miles south of Utica.

THIS IS
GROUND ZERO
© Robert Huot 1984
THE MOHAWK VALLEY, LUSH GREEN, UTICA, EARLY WINTER
SNOWS, CHURCHES, 4th of JULY AT THE PARKWAY, TREES
THE CRUISE MISSILE, CANNOLIS, GENESSE STREET, THE
WEST END BREWERY, LATE SUMMER SWEET CORN,
UNION STATION, A DRIVE IN FROM PARIS, B-52 BOMBERS
WEST CANADA CREEK, THE FESTIVAL OF NATIONS, LAKE
DELTA WALLEYES, CORTLANDS AND MACOUNS, OCTOBER
IN OLD FORGE _ _ _ _ _ THIS IS GROUND ZERO.
SPONSORED BY ARTISTS FOR A SANE ENVIRONMENT AND
THE WAR GAME 2 PROJECT, P.O. BOX 538, NEW HARTFORD, NEW YORK 13413

Poster designed by Robert Huot as fund-raiser for shooting *The Journey* (1987) in the Mohawk Valley of central New York State.

By April, the efforts of the various committees were coming to fruition, and the Friday, April 13, issue of the Utica College *Tangerine* devoted its entire front page to "The War Game 2 Project," listing some of the upcoming benefit events on and off campus, including an "End of the World Beerblast," sponsored by the Gamma Sigma Sigma sorority and the Phi Beta Sigma fraternity on April 13; "War Game II Day at Utica College," featuring four local bands plus screenings of *The War Game* and *Punishment Park,* sponsored by WPNR-FM and the Alpha Phi Omega fraternity (April 28); a combined flea market and antique sale (May 26); and an art auction (June 16). Benefit screenings of Watkins films were held at Hamilton College during April (Professor Richard W. Werner helped organize these screenings) and at Colgate University (thanks to Professor John Knecht).[17] Of the various spring benefits, the most financially successful were the international community dinner, held on May 10 at Saint Basil's Church in east Utica; the art auction; the flea market; and the sale of benefit tickets to the Broadway revival of Arthur Miller's *Death of a Salesman,* starring Dustin Hoffman.

John Zogby, then the local representative of the Arab-American Anti-Discrimination Committee (now the nationally known pollster), was a driving force behind the international dinner, which was coordinated by Suzanne Parson and supported by a number of local restaurants, including Symeon's, the Phoenician, and Casa Too Mucha. The dinner drew 150 people, many of whom brought dishes representative of their cultural heritages, and netted about $1,400. The art auction, held at the Barrett Art Gallery at Utica College, netted $3,100. It was organized and run by Suzie Wadsworth, who took donations of artworks from dozens of local artists—including Jane Bair, Mary Beach, Joan Blanchfield, Edward Christiana, Vincent Clemente, Georgia Deal, Sylvia de Swaan, Joanne Elias, Bill Evans, Francis Fiorintino, Lisa Gregg, Christine Heller, Heidi Jost, Margaret Kelly, Carol Kinne, Jonathan Kirk, John Knecht, Lorraine Kreimeyer, John Loy, Mary Loy, Marc Mancini, Clyde McCulley, Debbie Pappenheimer, Easton Pribble, George Ray, Marge Salzillo, Keith Sandman, Lynn Schwarzer, Penny Simon, Jon von Bergen, Al Wardle, Shirley Waters, and Su Yurewicha—and arranged for a professional auctioneer to oversee the bidding. The flea market, run by Georgia Deal and Patricia O'Connor, with the assistance of Roland Randall, Ralph Zammiello, Anita Morris, and Dickie Lynn Gronseth, netted $750 and produced a spin-off garage sale, coordinated by Anita Morris.

17. I have no record of the dates of the screenings at Colgate.

Only one of the benefits took place outside of the Mohawk Valley. According to Don Tracy, Harry Belafonte, who had expressed his support of Watkins's efforts early on, knew Dustin Hoffman, then appearing as Willie Loman in a revival of *Death of a Salesman* on Broadway (the revival, directed by Michael Rudman, costarred John Malkovich, Stephen Lang, and Kate Reid). Apparently, Belafonte was able to interest Hoffman in the project and, through a representative, Lee Gotsagen, Hoffman made it possible for the War Game 2 Project to sell a number of tickets to the May 31 performance of the play and keep the markup cost of each ticket. The benefit ticket price was set at $100; and Tracy and Dickie-Lynn Gronseth placed ads in the *New York Times* and *Village Voice* (Dick Loomis, a professional graphic designer for Evans, Garber and Page, designed the ad). They also plastered the Times Square area with a poster and mailed flyers to potential theatergoers. In the end, we sold fewer tickets than we had hoped, but it was enough to pay for the ads and to net approximately $3,000.

As of the end of July, the several spring and summer benefits, plus donations from individuals, added up to $12,000. In August, we were able to announce that the Film Bureau of the New York State Council on the Arts (NYSCA) had decided to respond to our March application for funding with a $20,000 production grant. B. Ruby Rich and Deborah Silverfine, of NYSCA, were in Utica on August 8 to make the announcement. While Watkins had made it clear that, regardless of the amount of money we could raise, there would be a Mohawk Valley family in the film, the addition of the NYSCA grant allowed us to make final plans for several sequences, each of which would place the Hendricks family within a moment during the panic that might follow an announcement by the federal government of an immediate nuclear threat to Griffiss Air Force Base in Rome, New York, and the need to evacuate the city of Utica.

Plans for shooting the evacuation sequences had developed over the previous months. Early in the year, a research committee, headed by Robert Baber and including Kim Landon, a journalism professor at Utica College, and Utica College students Larry Platt and Roxanne Blatt, had obtained a copy of the "Crisis Relocation Plan for Oneida County, New York State," studied it (along with comparable documents from other local counties), then conducted interviews with Dick Griffith, the Oneida County civil defense officer, and other individuals who, according the plan, were to be in charge should an evacuation be ordered. This research confirmed what might have seemed obvious, at least to cynics: that the government "plan" was, at best, partial and ambiguous, even to those who were supposedly in charge of it;

and that it was completely unknown to many of those who were supposed to play important roles during a crisis.[18]

As the time for Watkins to direct the Mohawk Valley sequences approached, the research group focused on specifics. They discovered that, should an evacuation be ordered, the Hendricks family and their neighbors in the Cornhill section of Utica—all thirteen thousand of them—were to drive nine miles down the Mohawk Valley to the Remington Elementary School in Ilion, where they would be assigned to private homes in the Ilion area. The researchers made contact with those teachers in Ilion who, according to the civil defense plan, were to handle the influx of evacuees, and many of the teachers agreed to enact this role during the shooting. Grace Osborne organized those in Ilion who wanted to be involved.

Throughout the summer, Don Tracy, who had been involved with the project from its inception, assembled a crew to work with Watkins during the shooting, now scheduled for Saturday, Sunday, and Monday, September 29 through October 1. From the beginning, Tracy, an area native himself, made every effort to hire experienced professionals who were local residents or who at least had local connections, and who were committed to the thinking behind the project. Skip Roessel, the cinematographer, had graduated from Hamilton College and was working for Paisley Productions, a film production house that had moved from Utica to New York City not long before planning for the Watkins film began. His wife, Karen Morse, a Utica native who had also worked for Paisley Productions, served as art director. Tom Trovato, another Utica native, was gaffer and key grip. Once Tracy had found capable people to do the more technical work during the shoot—all of them agreed to work for minimum pay—he and they filled out the crew with local volunteers. Joan Olsson agreed to serve as location manager; Debbie Benzer, David Gislason, Dickie Lynn Gronseth, Jonathan Kirk, Margit Morse, and John von Bergen were the art department; Krista Perry Dunn, Lorna Lentini, Maura Macnulty, and Pat Spear were production assistants; Roxanne Blatt did continuity; and Sylvia de Swaan made production stills. Watkins was back in Utica at the end of June to meet with the crew and to spend time with the Hendricks family.

By early September, the fund-raising had drawn to a close, the research committee had made its report to Watkins so that he could make his final plans for the Mohawk Valley shoot, and Tracy had finished organizing the

18. Baber was particularly struck by the fact that the civil defense plan was woefully out of date. The plan mentioned a number of bomb shelters around Utica, one of which was in the Mutual Distributors Building on South Street—a building that, at the time of Baber's research, no longer existed.

crew. On September 8 a meeting was held at Utica College to coordinate a support system for the shoot. Volunteers agreed to house out-of-town members of the crew and visiting scholars (Joseph Gomez and James Welsh had decided to be witnesses to the shooting; Ken Nolley, who had been a prime mover in the Salem, Oregon, support group, became an active part of the Mohawk Valley support group during the shooting), to supply food for the crew during the filming, to transport cast and crew from one location to another, and to be on call should unforeseen problems arise. Further meetings were scheduled for late September so that Watkins himself—fresh from shooting in Moscow—could meet with the Mohawk Valley crew and support staff, and with those who were interested in being part of the cast. A sizable and energized group showed up at the Saint Francis de Sales School auditorium on the evening of September 27 to listen to Watkins explain the nature of the scenes he planned to shoot, to find out what to wear and what to do in the crowd scenes, to learn what to expect during the filming, and to get a schedule of shooting locations and times.

In general, the process of preparing to shoot the new film had gone reasonably well, but there was one frustration that would cause considerable anxiety during the shooting itself. We had, of course, made an effort to be in touch with the city throughout our planning. Sometime during 1983, as the project was getting under way, Mayor Stephen Pawlinga indicated that we would have the full support of his office. During Watkins's visit to the area in January–February 1984, he and Robert Baber met with then-new mayor Louis LaPolla to talk about the project. As Baber remembers, "Watkins explained in detail the thinking behind the project and what we would need during the shooting, and when Peter was finished, the Mayor said nothing for a while, then, 'We'll do whatever Robert wants [LaPolla and Baber had known each other for years].'"[19] The Utica Common Council made clear its support in a May 2, 1984, resolution put forward by Councilman Robert DiBrango:

> WHEREAS, The issue of nuclear weapons and the arms race is of vital concern to all Americans and it is of special importance that citizens learn as much as possible about this issue, and
>
> WHEREAS, the Common Council of the City of Utica voted unanimously in 1983 with over 100 municipalities and states in the United States to endorse a bilateral and mutually verifiable nuclear freeze between the United States and the Soviet Union, and

19. Phone conversation with Baber, June 2005.

> WHEREAS, internationally acclaimed and Oscar-winning film-maker Peter Watkins has chosen the City of Utica as one of the sites for the filming of a movie on the impact of the arms race on families and neighborhoods, and
>
> WHEREAS, this film serves to broaden public awareness and makes Utica part of an important international film,
>
> NOW, THEREFORE, BE IT RESOLVED: That the Utica Common Council endorses the War Game II Project of Peter Watkins and extends our warmest welcome to him, and encourages all Uticans and neighbors to become involved in this project.[20]

As time for the shooting drew closer, Don Tracy and I felt it would be a good idea to get back in touch with the mayor's office, and at some point during the late spring or summer, we took a 16mm film projector and a print of *The War Game* to city hall to demonstrate the quality and seriousness of Watkins's work; we wanted to be sure that the new mayor would reconfirm his predecessor's support. Mayor LaPolla seemed somewhat taken aback by the film—as most first-time viewers are—but Tracy and I left assuming that we would have the assistance of city hall during the shooting. We met again with LaPolla on September 5 to reconfirm our need for assistance with crowd and traffic control at particular times and places.[21] We also asked for permission to borrow police uniforms and riot helmets (a local outfitter had offered to loan us Utica police uniforms, free of charge, upon receipt of a letter from the proper authorities releasing them to us). When I did not hear back from the mayor's office, I wrote to LaPolla on September 13 to ask for a response. None ever came. The mayor had apparently decided to ignore the project entirely. Ironically, in 1987, when *The Journey* was finished and had made a splash at several international film festivals, and the Utica premiere had been announced, we finally heard from the mayor's office: apparently, Mayor LaPolla wanted to give Watkins the key to the city. Perhaps it was impolitic of us, but we declined.[22]

20. I believe John Zogby contacted Councilman DiBrango and asked for this resolution.

21. I have no way of determining exactly when Tracy and I screened *The War Game* for LaPolla, though there is no question that we did. I do not believe it could have been as late as the September 5 meeting, which I do have a record of, since showing the film would have made much more sense earlier on, and since there is no indication in my letter to LaPolla after the September 5 meeting that a screening had occurred.

22. In time, I came to regret this decision, and to wish that I had agreed to be part of the ceremony the mayor had in mind—so that I could confront him publicly with his original refusal to offer our project even minimal support. Such a confrontation might have made news and helped to spread the word about *The Journey*, and it would have been representative of the film's goal of confronting conventional politics and media.

As a result of Mayor LaPolla's lack of support, we needed to improvise makeshift uniforms and riot gear, and we were forced to block off several streets, and one intersection, for several hours at a time. Fortunately, we had scheduled the Utica street scenes for Sunday, September 30, when there was comparatively little traffic, and since the Sunday *Utica Observer-Dispatch* had run several substantial articles about the project, including a Sunday morning story on the front page of the regional section by Padraic D. Riley that focused on the Saturday shooting in Ilion ("'Lights, camera . . . chaos,' he shouted" was the headline), many people in the neighborhoods where we shot did have some idea of what we were doing. (Throughout the process of raising money for "The War Game 2 Project," during the shooting itself, and later on, when *The Journey* was premiering, the *Observer-Dispatch* provided regular coverage; Jonas Kover showed particular interest.)

For most of us, I would guess, the shooting itself was the most surprising dimension of the *Journey* experience—among other things, it was remarkable how quickly the nearly $35,000 we had raised over the previous two years disappeared! On Saturday morning I led a caravan of cars full of cast members, from Saint Francis de Sales School to Remington Elementary in Ilion, where we met up with the crew and the cast members from Ilion. The bulk of the day was spent psychodramatizing the Hendricks family's arrival in Ilion during the evacuation and the chaotic process of checking them in and finding a home for them to live in. I say "psychodramatizing," rather than "dramatizing" because, in this project as in most of his earlier projects, Watkins was not primarily interested in "good acting." Though he himself had studied theatrical acting (at the Royal Academy of Dramatic Art in London in 1954), as a filmmaker he had become more interested in the process of average people imagining what a certain possible future might feel like and then working with him to demonstrate what they have imagined. That is, at the Ilion shoot, Watkins was looking primarily for individuals' honest expressions of their concerns and fears about what could happen to them, and their willing participation in a kind of cinematic warning about one frightening moment during one possible dangerous future.

Filming the Hendricks family and the other Utica area cast members and the Remington Elementary schoolteachers working together was also Watkins's way of demonstrating how government planning ought to work. It was obvious from the research of Robert Baber's committee that the civil defense planning *for* the public had not been done on the basis of any communication *with* the public. In contrast, Watkins was using media not simply to report to average citizens what others had done or had decided for them but as part of an interactive educational process through which average citizens would learn what the government had planned for them and could explore their own feelings about these plans. Before the shooting was over, Watkins organized a recording session with the Ilion teachers during which they talked about how frightening the small-scale dramatization at Remington Elementary had been, and how it had demonstrated to them that there was no way they could function effectively in the roles the civil defense plan assumed they would fill.

Once the chaotic scene at Remington Elementary had been shot, a more intimate scene was filmed on Prospect Street in Ilion. Here Robert Baber and Patricia O'Connor played a frightened couple asked to house the Hendricks family for the duration of the evacuation. From the beginning, Watkins had been interested in working with an African American family, in part because he knew from his research on *The War Game* that ethnic differences were rarely taken into account in evacuation planning. This was certainly the case in Utica: it was assumed that the Hendricks family and thousands of their neighbors in the largely black Cornhill neighborhood would willingly drive to a small, nearly all-white town, and could expect to be accommodated there.

On Sunday morning, the crew and selected cast members met at Ray Ferrone's Mobil station at the corner of Rutger and Albany Streets in Utica at nine o'clock in the morning to dramatize—or, again, psychodramatize—a gas station overwhelmed by the Hendricks family and other Uticans rushing to fill their gas tanks before leaving town during the evacuation, as local police worked to keep some semblance of order. Shooting the scene, which involved many cars honking their horns incessantly, certainly disrupted the quiet Sunday morning, though no one came out to complain. Ferrone, who seemed happy to cooperate with the filmmaking, was later to say that, if anything, Watkins had underestimated what such a scene might look like were a real evacuation to be ordered.

The entire cast and crew had been asked to gather at noon in Watson-Williams Park, near the Hendricks's home, to participate in the second large crowd scene, during which many people from the neighborhood would refuse to evacuate, on the assumption that they would be as safe in Cornhill as in Ilion, a mere nine miles down the Mohawk Valley in the direction of prevailing winds, and for fear that their homes would be looted once they were gone. When Don Tracy and I arrived at Watson-Williams Park, we joined those who had shown up, a smaller group than had participated at Remington Elementary, and awaited Watkins and the crew.

The moment Watkins saw the relatively small, largely white group that had gathered, he asked, "Where are the people from the neighborhood?" I

Peter Watkins (in center, with microphone) shooting crowd scene for *The Journey* (1987) at Remington Elementary School in Ilion, New York. Production still by Sylvia de Swaan.

said, "We put out a casting call and these are the people who showed up." Watkins was adamant: "We can't fake this. We need *the people of this neighborhood* in the film; go get them onto the street while we get ready to shoot." Tracy and I looked at each other, dumbfounded; how were two middle-aged white men supposed to get this largely African American neighborhood onto the street and involved in an experimental documentary film? But saying no to Watkins had come to seem inconceivable, so we strode down High Street as though we had some idea of what we were going to do—and began knocking at doors.

A child opened the first door I knocked at, and I asked for her father or mother. A man came to the door, and I said something like, "Good morning, sir, sorry to bother you on a Sunday. We're working with film director Peter Watkins to make a film about a nuclear attack on America, and we're getting ready to dramatize part of the evacuation of this neighborhood, which according to local civil defense plans will be expected to go to Ilion. We'd be very grateful if you and your family could spare the time to participate in the shooting. It might take a couple of hours." I will never forget the man's response: "*Ilion!*" he said. "*Ilion!* I ain't going to no fuckin' *Ilion!* Give us a minute, we'll be right out." Within an hour, what seemed like the entire neighborhood was on the street, dramatizing their resistance to the evacuation plans with considerable passion. What surprised me was that so many of the citizens of High Street were more involved with the *issues* Watkins had meant to confront than they were with the idea of being in a film. In the end, while this scene did not find its way into *The Journey* proper, it certainly functioned effectively as community psychodrama and was as valuable a part of the *process* of the film as those scenes that did become part of the final version.[23] After the shooting on High Street was completed, the cast and crew moved to nearby Calvary Baptist Church on South Street, where Watkins filmed a group of people huddled in the basement, designated as a shelter in the civil defense plans. This material also did not find its way into *The Journey* proper, though similar imagery from other parts of the world was included.

The remainder of the shooting, on Monday and Tuesday, was more intimate: Watkins filmed William and Elizabeth Hendricks and their four children—Tonya, Tamara, Sonya, and Billy—around their kitchen table (this was a motif in *The Journey;* all the families sit at their kitchen tables), discussing the issues that are the focus of the film. Watkins had realized that there was another way to include the reality of nuclear holocaust in the film without attempting to dramatize it. Since a nuclear holocaust would be merely a larger, more devastating version of what had already happened in Hiroshima and Nagasaki, Watkins made blow-ups of a series of horrific images of the aftermath of the atomic bombing of Japan, and in *The Journey* these images are passed around each kitchen table as a means of beginning a new kind of dinner-table conversation during which families discuss not only their personal experiences of that day but the real political issues that are threatening their lives. That is, Watkins was using the family sequences to reenvision how the modern family functions: for Watkins, the assumption that politics and painful political issues cannot be a subject of conversation for a family with young children is a way of putting one's head in the sand and teaching children to do the same. If the family is as powerful a social unit as we say it is, why shouldn't families talk about politics, especially with an eye to considering what action they might take, *as families,* to ameliorate what they decide are the most serious social and political problems facing them? How better to empower children in the long run? The families presented in the finished film become models for a more mature form of family interaction.

23. The effectiveness and usefulness of this footage were marred by the presence of several adolescent boys who were so excited by the presence of the cameras and crew that they simply could not be serious. Watkins tried to work around them, but to no avail.

By Wednesday the Mohawk Valley shooting was complete, and by the end of the week, Watkins had left for Mexico (the local photographer Sylvia de Swaan, who has lived in Mexico, had helped to establish contacts for Watkins there). For us in the Mohawk Valley, "The War Game 2 Project" was over, at least for the moment, but for Watkins, it was to continue for three more years, as he finished shooting and then edited the hundred-plus hours of film he had shot, at the National Film Board of Canada in Montreal (the NFB had agreed to donate its postproduction facilities). During 1983–84, Watkins had been in virtually perpetual motion, circling the globe, first, to develop interest in the project; then, to meet with those who were interested in collaborating on it; and finally, to shoot in twelve different countries.[24] By the time he arrived at the NFB in early 1985, he had already demonstrated that a global film, a film involving the active participation of everyday people in a wide range of cultures, was, in fact, possible. Watkins's individual achievement in getting the film shot was his way of suggesting that all of us, whether we are involved in media or not, can and must do a good bit more than we tell ourselves we can do—if we truly care about delivering a more humane and progressive world to our children and grandchildren. The editing was another sustained labor; it required as much time as the fund-raising and shooting.

The final chapter of the Mohawk Valley's participation in *The Journey* would not be possible until the editing was complete. On October 29, 1986, Robert Baber, Roxanne Blatt, Patricia O'Connor, and I drove to Montreal to meet with Watkins and with those who had been working with him at the NFB to see a nearly final version of *The Journey*. I think it is fair to say that all of us who gathered in Montreal had assumed that *The Journey* would be a long, perhaps even an epic, film (the television version of *Edvard Munch* had been 3½ hours long), but none of us expected that its epic scope would reach 14½ hours. We saw *The Journey* in a small screening room at the NFB, on two successive days, approximately 6½ hours the first day, the remaining eight hours, the second day. Watkins had fashioned a film that asks viewers to continually circle the globe: *The Journey* moves from nation to nation, from family to family, so that hour by hour the circle of humanity revealed by the film expands. While the visuals are quietly paced, they are dense with information, especially because of the complexity of the sound

24. In 1983–84, Watkins organized and filmed in three American locations (Portland, Oregon; Seattle, Washington; the Mohawk Valley); in Canada; in the Hebrides Islands and Glasgow, Scotland; in France; in several locations in West Germany; in several locations in Norway; in the Soviet Union (Moscow); in Mozambique; in at least two Japanese locations; in several Australian locations; on the island of Tahiti; and in Mexico.

track: sometimes the audience is hearing sound from two or three different locations simultaneously while seeing imagery from a fourth.[25]

As wide-ranging and complex as *The Journey* is, however, it is also deeply meditative. Watkins refused to edit within the individual shots that recorded the comments of the families; each person is given space and time to say what he or she has decided to say, without interruption (and without the implicit judgment that comes when one edits a conversation: *this* is interesting, but *this* is *not*). That is, as one listens to the families considering the Hiroshima photographs and the many other subjects that are raised, one experiences the temporal duration of the original conversations—generally uncomfortable conversations, with extended silences, since these families, like most families around the world, have never talked with each other at any length about such topics (and especially not in front of a film crew). Though the pacing of the family sequences would be the most controversial dimension of *The Journey,* Watkins's determination to show his respect for the families by not reducing their comments to sound bites was in keeping with the thinking about media that had instigated the project. As he explained in an interview in 1981, "When I talk to people now, I ask them to think about the way these rhythms [the fast-paced rhythms of conventional film and television editing] cut up the time continuum, like a chip fryer slicing French fries. I try and have people think about that as breaking up, slicing through, our psychic continuity. I mean if we normally relate to things, or should relate to things, in gentle curving flows as we progress and grow, this is the opposite. It fragments our learning process, and our psyches."[26]

I cannot speak for the others in the Utica delegation, but I remember that the night after the first day's screening, I was so exhilarated by what I had seen that I lay awake for hours. I was astonished by what Watkins had done and knew that, indeed, we *had* been part of film history—though of a very different and more experimental kind of film history than we had anticipated. During the second day's screening (four hours in the morning and four hours after lunch), the strain of seeing so much film in so short a time became more pronounced, as did the sense among some of those who had been working with Watkins that he had made a serious mistake in allowing the film to be so long, and especially in including the family discussions so completely. The question now was who would be willing to actually watch

25. I have discussed the structure of *The Journey* in more detail in "The Filmmaker as Global Circumnavigator: Peter Watkins' *The Journey* and Media Critique," *Quarterly Review of Film and Video* 14, no. 4 (August 1993): 31–54; and in Scott MacDonald, *Avant-Garde Film/Motion Studies* (New York: Cambridge University Press, 1993), chap. 15.

26. From my interview with Watkins in *A Critical Cinema 2*, 410.

such a long, slow film? Watkins had been considering this issue throughout the editing and was assuming that the film would have, first, a theatrical life; then, a television life (14½ hours is not unusual for a miniseries or for a reality show); and, most important and long-term, a pedagogical life: *The Journey* is divided into approximately fifty-minute chunks, so that it can be used as a classroom text in schools and colleges. The release of the film would be followed by an extensive study guide designed to help teachers and students come to grips with the many issues raised. As we drove back to Utica, we wondered how *The Journey* would fare at its upcoming premiere in Berlin, and at the Utica premiere we were planning for the following fall.

At the Berlin Film Festival in February 1987, *The Journey* was, according to the festival organizers, the main event of the Forum (the Berlin Film Festival is divided into two sections: the Panorama, which focuses on commercial releases, and the Forum, which focuses on all other forms of cinema). The film was shown three times in three different theaters, to sizable audiences; it was scheduled so that each audience could see the film in three sections. Postscreening discussions with audiences were held at each of the theaters. At these discussions, the film was represented by Watkins and by a number of those who had worked on it in Germany, Sweden, France, and Canada. Patricia O'Connor and I were the Mohawk Valley representatives. Not surprisingly, response to the film seemed mixed: many festival-goers seemed impressed; many others were frustrated by the film's length and its refusal of most forms of entertainment. What *was* clear, clearer than it had been when we were collaborating with him in the Mohawk Valley, was that Watkins was esteemed as one of the world's major political filmmakers. This was obvious from the respect given him by the festival and from the comments even of those who expressed disappointment with the film.

The Utica premiere, which took place on April 24 through 26 at the Stanley Performing Arts Center, was announced by an *Observer-Dispatch* story, "'The Journey' Begins in Utica," by Jonas Kover, on Sunday, February 15. The announcement was accompanied by a picture of the Hendricks family and Kover's interview with them.[27] Tickets went on sale in March. *The Journey* was presented in five sections: opening night was Friday evening; Watkins was present to introduce the film. The film continued on Saturday afternoon, Saturday evening, Sunday afternoon, and finished Sunday

27. In the interview, Elizabeth Hendricks remembers the family "walking up to a man's house in Ilion where they [the Hendricks family] were supposed to stay. 'I never felt so afraid. . . . The man had a rifle. His stomach was out. It was so real.' Her son, Billy, 10, yelled, 'Don't go in there. That guy's crazy,' she said. 'It was one of those times I was thankful it was a film.'"

evening. Six hundred were in the audience for opening night; 295, 305, 185, and 300 attended the remaining screenings—not what we had hoped, but certainly a good turnout for a long, demanding, highly political documentary.

The Journey concludes with an unusually extended credit sequence—fitting, since so many people in so many places had played a role in the production. For thirty-five minutes, the credits for each of the many groups that had raised money and/or hosted the filming are interspersed with the images and sounds of people from the various family groups and community dramatizations: one child playing the piano, another singing a song, still another sleeping, families expressing relief once their part in the filming was complete, bits of on-screen text, and so on. At the final screening of the Utica premiere, I remember waiting to see how those in the audience, many of whom had been part of the production process, would react to the Mohawk Valley support group credit sequence—the longest in the film.

Of course, even during the Utica premiere and the other premieres (at Berlin; at "30.Dok," the international festival in Leipzig, in what was still East Germany; at the Festival of Festivals in Toronto; at the Robert Flaherty Film Seminar), *The Journey* was *not* complete—at least not conceptually. In retrospect, it is quite clear to me that Watkins saw the entire multiyear, global production of *The Journey* as merely the first part of what could be an ongoing process. The film was conceived as a means of instigating a "horizontal" form of global communication: that is, communication between citizens of disparate nations that did not require hierarchical media or government structures. Watkins could see that forms of direct engagement between people from all over the world were being made ever more possible by new media technologies, and I believe he hoped *The Journey* would energize peace-loving people from many nations who would continue to share information and experiences and to collaborate internationally on grassroots media projects that would help them educate themselves and their fellow citizens about crucial international issues. Watkins was using filmmaking to create a new kind of global community.

Though a number of us did talk about how we might continue to utilize the Mohawk Valley support group once the local premiere was over, how we might develop lasting contacts with the other support groups, and how we might stay in contact with those people from other cultures we had been in contact with during the fund-raising and shooting (and though Don Tracy and I worked with an attorney to set up a nonprofit organization to handle money from presentations of *The Journey* and other, related activities), not much came of these efforts. Basically, we allowed the most crucial aspect of the opportunity Watkins had provided us to pass, and moved back into our lives as teachers, photographers, artists, insurance salespeople. In other words, while the film was to become part of *film* history, it did not continue to function as a cinematic process, except in isolated instances: the Peace and Conflict Studies Department at Colgate University, for example, has often used *The Journey* as a text in college classes; and in recent years, the film has been revived here and there in response to the powerlessness so many have felt in regard to the war in Iraq.

But even if the final part of Watkins's dream for *The Journey* did not materialize, if in fact most all of us who worked with him to produce the film failed to use it as a way of developing an ever-larger global grassroots network, certainly the process of getting the film made was a tremendous education for many of us, especially about the arms race and related issues, and about the way in which media organizations and educational institutions function in relation to such issues. And our efforts on behalf of the film were full of small but meaningful successes. That was obvious to me that Sunday evening in the Stanley Performing Arts Center as I watched the final section of the *Journey* from the balcony and heard—as the Mohawk Valley credits began to roll—a thrilling, full-bodied cheer welling up from the theater below.

Interview with David Gatten

In the program notes he composed for *The Great Art of Knowing* (2004), the second film in his planned nine-film project *Secret History of the Dividing Line, a True Account in Nine Parts,* when it premiered at the "Walking Picture Palace" series at Anthology Film Archives, curated by Mark McElhatten, David Gatten included this statement: "An antinomian cinema seems possible. A gentle iconoclasm?" These lines are particularly revealing of Gatten's sense of the *Secret History* project and of his identity as an avant-garde filmmaker. "Antinomian" has two relatively distinct meanings: on one hand, the word refers to those Christians who believe that faith alone is necessary for salvation; on the other, it refers to forms of contradiction or opposition between principles that seem equally reasonable and necessary. Both senses of "antinomian" seem relevant to Gatten and to the *Secret History* project.

Gatten's reference to religious tradition is his way of situating himself within that community of avant-garde filmmakers and videomakers who have seen their filmmaking as a spiritual practice: Stan Brakhage, Bruce Baillie, Kenneth Anger, Jonas Mekas, Nathaniel Dorsky, Larry Gottheim, Leighton Pierce, and others. In both *Reminiscences of a Journey to Lithuania* (1972) and *Lost Lost Lost* (1976), Mekas imagines a community of media-makers devoted to the primacy of the human spirit and sees filmmaking as a way of participating in the age-old quest for spiritual connection. Both within his films and within his life as a working artist, Gatten sees himself as a part of such a community. All four completed sections of *Secret History of the Dividing Line, a True Account in Nine Parts*—the title film, *Secret History of the Dividing Line* (2002); *The Great Art of Knowing; Moxon's Mechanick Exercises, or the Doctrine of Handy-works Applied to the Art of Printing* (1999); and *The Enjoyment of Reading, Lost and Found* (2001)—are silent, serenely paced, spiritually evocative film experiences; the earliest of these films to be completed, *Moxon's Mechanick Exercises,* focuses specifically on the production of the Gutenberg Bible as a pivotal moment in world culture.

It is clear in *Moxon's Mechanick Exercises* that Gatten sees cinema as a way of paying homage to Gutenberg's achievement in simultaneously "fixing" and "unfixing" spiritual texts (after Gutenberg, individual hand-copying of biblical texts gave way to the fixity of mechanical reproduction, *and* mechanical reproduction allowed for more general access to biblical texts and new opportunities for "unfixing" traditional interpretations of these texts). To make his film, Gatten literally unfixed bits of text from the pages of reprints of several Bibles and painstakingly transferred the texts to celluloid, simultaneously refixing them by printing the filmstrips, a process that is reminiscent of the spiritual practice of hand-copying the Bible that Gutenberg's printing press rendered out-of-date, *and* "unfixing" the texts in a new, modern way, by transforming them into animated visual fireworks.

The other, nonspiritual sense of "antinomian" is equally important for understanding Gatten's films. Like much of Su Friedrich's work, the *Secret History* project accommodates filmmaking approaches that have often been understood as oppositional. During the late 1960s and early 1970s, a set of approaches to filmmaking that P. Adams Sitney called "structural film" seemed to abjure the forms of personal expression evident in the psychodramas of the 1940s and 1950s and in the films of Stan Brakhage after the late 1950s (and films by filmmakers influenced by Brakhage: Carolee Schneemann and Nathaniel Dorsky, for example). Michael Snow, Hollis Frampton, Ernie Gehr, Paul Sharits, and others identified, at least early on, as structural filmmakers seemed to critique personal cinema, to question the very idea of the personal, and to be bent on replacing "the personal clutter / the persistence of feelings / the hand-touch sensibility / the diaristic indulgence / the painterly mess / the dense gestalt / the primitive techniques" (Schneemann's description of early objections to her work in *A Critical Cinema* [Berkeley: University of California Press, 1988], 143) with rigorous, formal, highly intellectual approaches to shooting and editing, approaches that allowed for in-depth theoretical considerations of the nature of cinema itself.

The films in Gatten's *Secret History of the Dividing Line* incorporate both approaches. For example, the title film of the series is rigorously structured *and* it incorporates a "hand-touch sensibility." Like each of the subsequent films in the project, *Secret History of the Dividing Line* is made up of a brief introduction and three sections, each of which is organized mathematically (Gatten describes the details in our interview). The first section begins with what appears to be a hand-scratch down the center of the filmstrip (it was actually made by tearing the filmstrip in two, then reassembling it), which leads into a series of visual texts: dates of important historical and cultural events leading up to and away from the life of William Byrd II of colonial Virginia, who founded the city of Richmond; led the surveying party that drew the original boundary (the "dividing line") between Virginia and North Carolina; wrote one of the first detailed descriptions of American nature, *History of the Dividing Line* (written soon after the surveying expedition but not published until 1841); and assembled one of the two largest libraries in colonial North America. After the sequence of dates, the "scratch" divides the frame in two, revealing on one side passages from Byrd's official *History* of the drawing of the Virginia–North Carolina boundary and, on the other, comparable passages from his secret history of the same events, written before the official history and circulated privately to other colonial gentlemen. Gatten's work with visual text, along with his precise, mathematical organization, recalls Frampton's *Zorns Lemma,* while the ongoing "scratch" is reminiscent of those filmmakers who have worked expressively directly on the filmstrip (Douglas Crockwell, Len Lye, Harry Smith, Brakhage, Schneemann, Robert Huot, Jennifer Todd Reeves).

The middle section of *Secret History of the Dividing Line* confirms this combination of intellectual organization and handcrafted self-expression: Gatten presents a series of film splices, made in black leader with a defective splicer, magnified by an optical printer. These splices are arranged in groups of fifty-seven and are presented first at high speed and then one by one, for several seconds each, so that we can see that each splice is different from the next. The abstract nature of this imagery, particularly within the context of the earlier information about Byrd's expedition to draw the boundary line between two colonies, tends to lure viewers into reading the splices as wilderness scenes. The final section of *Secret History of the Dividing Line* is an "Appendix": a rolling text of Byrd's listing of fifty-seven landmarks along the Virginia–North Carolina borderline, measured in miles from the ocean as the surveying party moved west. The listing of the fifty-seven locations is simultaneously a detached presentation of an aspect of Gatten's research into the Byrd saga and, at the same time, quite personal for Gatten, since during his childhood and youth, he often visited a number of these locations and remembers them fondly: the most frequently mentioned location in Byrd's list is the Dan River, in which Gatten swam, innertubed, and boated at summer camp.

Throughout the *Secret History* films, Gatten confirms and expands the synthesis of the intellectual and the emotional, of visual text and abstraction, of public and personal history, and of the many accomplishments of avant-garde filmmakers (as well as of poets and painters) that predate and inform his own project. Various *Secret History* films and sections of films recall work by Brakhage and Frampton, and by Ken Jacobs, Michele Fleming, Phil Solomon, Su Friedrich, Nathaniel Dorsky, Larry Gottheim, Tony Conrad, and a good many other moving-image artists; and each of the *Secret History of the Dividing Line* films recycles a variety of other cultural artifacts that Gatten's research has led him to, many of them books that were part of William Byrd's library. The *Secret History* project is not a critique of earlier cinematic accomplishments, the way "structural film" was a critique of "personal cinema," the way feminist filmmaking of the 1980s was a critique of what had been a male-dominated field, and the way the handmade, hand-processed cinema of recent years is a critique of both the formalities of industrial cinema and the formal pretensions of earlier generations of avant-garde filmmakers. Rather, Gatten's project is a "gentle iconoclasm," a celebration of the history and diversity of independent cinema, and, more generally, of the long, troubled, and glorious history of experimental cultural production.

Gatten's individual films, and the *Secret History* project, ask for an unusual sort of film viewer. The *Secret History* films are simultaneously modern and postmodern; they ask viewers to consider the physical processes that resulted in the imagery we see and the ways in which these processes express the filmmaker's engagement with his medium, *and* they offer theoretical considerations of crucial moments in the development of modern culture: Gatten's focus on the Gutenberg Bible and on William Byrd's part in the imposition of European cultural history on colonial America are meant as a rumination on our current moment and the transformations in modern culture instigated by the arrival of new electronic and digital technologies. But, above all, the *Secret History* films ask for a viewer willing to make an ongoing commitment to the pleasures and revelations of Gatten's research. Gatten is less interested in impressing viewers with his technical dexterity, which is considerable, or with conclusions about modern life or about cinema, than with sharing his excitement in retrieving and considering the increasingly complex saga of William Byrd II, itself a microcosm of colonial history and a premonition of the development of modern life. Gatten is, above all, a new form of cinematic researcher, for whom making films is a way of exploring the evolution of cultural history. As we watch his films, we join Gatten in *his* survey of territories that are new for him and for us, and we have the opportunity to enjoy both what he and we learn about the past and how this past continues to materialize into the film-viewing present.

This conversation with Gatten was recorded in August 2006 and has been refined online.

MacDonald: I know you're from North Carolina and that your father is a college professor . . .

Gatten: A biologist.

MacDonald: Which doesn't necessarily predict an art interest, although it's always seemed to me that biologists tend to be closer to the arts than other scientists.

Gatten: I wasn't really aware of it as I was growing up, but my father was also a photographer. When he and my mother were first together, he set up half of the kitchen as the darkroom.

My mother was an English major in college; she was particularly interested in Shakespeare. She and my father met as editors of William and Mary's yearbook. For a while she ran political campaigns, and she's now a city council person in Greensboro.

My parents read to us a lot, almost all of Shakespeare, and Edgar Allan Poe, Arthur Conan Doyle, E. B. White . . .

MacDonald: What were your important film experiences as a kid? Were you and your parents moviegoers?

Gatten: The earliest film experiences that stick out are *Fantasia* [1940] and *Star Wars* [1977]. I think I saw those at about the same time. I was six when *Star Wars* came out, and seeing it in a theater was very exciting. It played in local theaters for at least eighteen months, and then was rereleased before *The Empire Strikes Back* came out in 1981. For about two years, every single birthday party I went to had a *Star Wars* theme; you dressed up as a character, and then you went to see the movie. I think I saw the film seventeen or eighteen times during that period. So *Star Wars* was big, as were the other science fiction films from that time. My dad and I going to see *Close Encounters* is a vivid memory. We did see a lot of movies, certainly all the Disney films.

MacDonald: Your seeing *Star Wars* so many times explains where that opening text in *The Great Art of Knowing* comes from.

Gatten: [laughter] That *has* been commented on!

Once VCRs were available and you could rent films, my father started showing me Hitchcock films. And Kurosawa films—*The Seven Samurai* [1954], one of my dad's favorites, and the films that the Sergio Leone Westerns were based on: *Yojimbo* [1961] and *Sanjuro* [1962].

In high school I went to the regular mall movies that most high school students went to. In eleventh grade, somebody said, "You *have* to see this movie *Eraserhead* [1977]." I had no idea what to make of the film but was certainly intrigued by the sound.

MacDonald: What experiences led you toward avant-garde film?

Gatten: As improbable as it seems, Greensboro had a drama program that focused not on the musical theater productions that you would expect to find in the South but, instead, on sixties experimental theater. Dan Seamen, who ran this program, used experimental theater as a teaching tool; we did adaptations of Jean Claude Van Italie, Joseph Chaikin, the Open Theater. And we did a lot of writing, much of it based on collage, using plays, news, poems, many different sources. During my junior and senior years, I would go to my home high school in the mornings, and then for three hours every afternoon I'd attend this drama program, which was a formative experience in terms of working with history and thinking about bringing disparate material together to create some sort of friction.

I did like performing, but I think by the time I was through high school, what I was being drawn toward was that process of putting things together—though at the time I didn't *know* that was my interest. I went to Chicago and spent a year studying acting at the Goodman School of Drama at DePaul University. During that year (1989–90), I was entranced with Bergman and Truffaut and Tarkovsky, Godard—sixties and seventies international cinema.

During that year, I also became disillusioned with what looked like the life one could eke out as an actor. The people that I knew were excited if they got a fried chicken commercial, and that didn't seem as interesting as what I had been doing in high school. So I went back to Greensboro to reevaluate things. I took some classes at the University of North Carolina at Greensboro [UNC-G] as a part-time student and attended the film festival that had just been started there. That festival was intended to showcase industry work from North Carolina, but when the professor who was directing it left to start a program in Singapore, we students took over, and submissions of experimental film instigated some research on experimental work. We heard about Kenneth Anger and found out you could get his films from Mystic Fire Video. In those days very few opportunities to see experimental film existed in and around Greensboro, but in time I was able to see Maya Deren; and *Dog Star Man* [Stan Brakhage, 1961–64]. We were always driving two hours to Chapel Hill or to Durham to see movies or to rent movies. It was a pilgrimage: we'd rent a couple of movies, drive back home, watch them, and go back the next day. Also, Tom Whiteside at Duke University had a semester of programs at a gallery, and there I saw Henry Hills's *Money* [1985], and Frampton's *Lemon* [1969] and *Palindrome* [1969], and Brakhage's *The Loom* [1986]—that was a big experience.

Also, I was encouraged to travel to a festival in Nashville: the Sinking Creek Film Festival, which focused on experimental and independent film.

Mary Jane Coleman, the founder and director of Sinking Creek, presented a program of festival films in Greenboro, and she invited me to visit Sinking Creek, so for four years I went to Nashville every summer. Kenneth Anger was a guest. I spent a week with him. I also met Robb Moss there and saw *The Tourist* [1991] for the first time, and also a lot of animation. I remember being particularly struck by Jay Rosenblatt's *Short of Breath* [1990]—I had never seen a found-footage film. Then there were Craig Baldwin's *¡O No Coronado!* [1992] and *Tribulation 99* [1991].

I was also reading a lot—I read *Visionary Film* around 1994, and the *Critical Cinema* books a bit later—but I couldn't see most of what I was reading about; it was exciting and frustrating to try to *imagine* the films talked about in those books. Then I found Frampton's *Circles of Confusion* [*Circles of Confusion: Film/Photography/Video, Texts 1968–1980* (Rochester, NY: Visual Studies Workshop, 1983)], and *that* was huge for me. Frampton's approach to history and art, the mode of inquiry in his writing, became an operating principle for me. In particular, "Incisions in History / Segments of Eternity," where he tells the story about Craig Breedlove, became my touchstone.

Craig Breedlove built a car to break the world land speed record, a car that crashed, though Breedlove wasn't seriously injured. The crash took exactly 8.7 seconds to occur, and when Breedlove is interviewed immediately afterward about what he thought and did during those nine seconds, he talks for an hour and a half! Frampton does this wonderful conceptual riff with recorded time versus lived experience. And I was *completely* captivated by this—and then did research on Breedlove. I actually got hold of the film footage of the crash (there was a camera in the car). My plan was to try and get the entire interview and slow down the nine seconds of footage so that it lasted ninety minutes. I didn't do that project; instead, I made a three-projector piece using that footage—my first use of 16mm. But that Frampton essay sent me to the library and I've been there ever since.

I eventually enrolled full-time at UNC-G as a media studies major. UNC-G offered some production—they had Bolexes—but generally if you were going to shoot film, you were going to transfer it to video and make a tape for broadcast. I also studied art history. I was at UNC-G from 1990 to 1995.

Then I reconnected to Chicago and to the people who were teaching film production at the Art Institute. I had seen the work of Zack Stiglicz at Sinking Creek, and had met Zack and Shellie Fleming when I visited Chicago to look at the program there, and was really taken with Shellie's work. They were the reason I went to study at the Art Institute. I was also interested in what Tatsu Aoki was doing and Dan Eisenberg. I still had not seen very much experimental film, but the film collection at the Art Institute school was very good, and for three years a group of us put on screenings every Thursday afternoon. A little money was provided by the school so we could also rent some things, and we saw a lot of films in class. And Chicago Filmmakers was going, as was the Film Center—there was a lot to see. I had a very good experience in Chicago the second time.

MacDonald: Hardwood Process made an impact, though I found it rather perplexing, since I couldn't really decide what it *was.* Could you talk about the process that resulted in *Hardwood Process?*

Gatten: When I originally visited the Art Institute to look at the program, Shellie told me there were amazing filmmakers working in Canada and that I should ask them to send their work to our Greensboro festival, and so I did. I contacted Phil Hoffman, Mike Hoolboom, Barbara Sternberg, and Gary Popovich, and they all sent work and we showed a lot of it. During a conversation with Phil Hoffman, he mentioned that he had started this summer independent film retreat: "Would you like to come? It's a week long; we give you a camera and some film, and there's a place to stay." I thought, "Fantastic, I'll move to Chicago, find an apartment, and then pop over to Toronto," which in my southern sense of geography seemed a couple of hours away. Actually, the film retreat wasn't in Toronto, but in Mount Forest, about two and a half hours northwest of Toronto.

I was expecting a film studio and was really surprised to arrive at a farmhouse and a barn, where there were ten Bolexes, ten tripods, ten light meters, some chickens, some cows . . . One corner of the barn had black plastic curtains, a screen and a projector and some folding chairs—that was the screening room; and on the other side was more black plastic and tubs of chemicals—that was the darkroom where we were going to process what we shot. They gave each of us six rolls of black-and-white, high-contrast film with an ASA of about 6; I was used to shooting 200T color negative, 500T color negative, and I thought, "You'd need an *explosion* to expose this stuff!" But the sun was plenty.

We learned to process the film ourselves, and this was certainly not the pristine lab environment that I had been taught to expect, where your film is processed very carefully, transferred to video, and sent back to you as a videotape—so that you never touch the film, because if you *touch* the film, you could *damage* it: you always needed to have an untouched backup negative at the lab. What we were doing at the farm was shooting the six rolls and processing them ourselves in buckets and spraying the film with a garden hose. In the process the film might fall on the rough floor and you might step on it; the dog might come over and chew on it. And we projected the *original.* I'd done that with Super-8mm, but I didn't think you were *supposed* to do this with 16mm!

When my film was projected, I was excited because I could see not only what I'd photographed, which was one kind of record, but also that many of the marks on the surface of the film were *legible.* I knew, "Oh, that's where Arrow came over and chewed the film," or "That is exactly where I stepped on it," or "That's where somebody turned on the light in the darkroom and solarized the image"—those things were readable to me and I thought they were beautiful.

So two layers of experience were recorded: the photographic record and the inscription on the surface of the film of that object's passage through the world—a *completely* new idea for me. At some point during the trip, when Weena [Weena Perry] and I were unpacking the car, I'd cut my hand and was being careful about putting my hand in the chemicals, thinking a lot about the scar that was forming, and talking about it too. I started to think about the surface of the film and the emulsion as very much like the skin of one's body: we have marks on our body that are legible; there are stories we can tell about them.

I generated a lot of material in that week, which when I look back seems like at least eight weeks. Back in Chicago, when I went to class on the first day, I already had eight hundred feet of film I was very excited about. I'd learned a lot about film *in a week* and soon after started experimenting with an optical printer and working in the darkroom at the Art Institute, trying to figure out how to organize that material, along with other things that I had shot and was shooting and a written journal that I'd been keeping sporadically.

MacDonald: There are various kinds of texts in *Hardwood Process.*

Gatten: Yes. The main text is from something I had written. I have very bad handwriting. North Carolina public schools in the seventies went to great lengths on penmanship, but I'm left-handed, and the desks made me awkward (at least they didn't still call you the Devil's Child and put you in the corner!). My handwriting often devolves into a kind of illegibility, even for me. And so part of the work of what became *Hardwood Process* was to take incomplete phrases, things that I could no longer make out but that I knew were important as records of the emotional events that they referred to, and then to find and work with images to complete those phrases. So it's a diary on several levels; it's trying to reach back to emotional events that occurred over a certain period of time, but it's also a record of my working and learning about film.

MacDonald: Why "Hardwood"?

Gatten: Weena and I had this really old apartment; the floors were in terrible shape, *really* scratched up. My first impulse was to get a rug down, but then I got interested in the floor. I thought, "Okay, here's a *third* surface; this floor has been here for a hundred and fifty years and chairs have been moved, things have fallen; a whole history, which is completely *ill*egible to me, is inscribed into the hardwood floor." I could *imagine* into that space. So I could interpret the scars on my body (and on Weena's body), on our hands; I was *creating* the "scars" on the filmstrip and could "read" them; but the ones on the hardwood floor were a mystery.

Also, the whole process of getting that film made was *hard*. It was the first time I'd ever lived with anybody, so some of the interaction with the hands in that film refers to what it's like to negotiate a shared space.

MacDonald: After returning to Chicago from Hoffman's film retreat, how much additional material did you generate for *Hardwood Process?*

Gatten: The material from the farm is in only two of the fourteen sections of the film: that experience became a doorway into making the film, but it's not the bulk of what you see.

MacDonald: I remember first seeing *Hardwood Process*, having heard a lot about it, and finding it relatively opaque in terms of anything like meaning, but the textures were engrossing. Did you have audience in mind as you made it? I assume not.

Gatten: Not really, no. I was excited to be making something. Certainly by this time, I was aware that there was a community and a culture in which a film like this might move, but it was my first year of grad school, and I didn't have any grand expectations for my student work, didn't feel any pressure in that regard. I wanted to make a contribution to the conversation; I wanted to share what I was excited about. The film was intended to be evocative more than to mean something.

Dan Eisenberg suggested that Phil Solomon should see the film. I had heard of Phil but hadn't seen any of his work. I sent an in-progress version of *Hardwood Process* to him, and he showed it to Brakhage; and Brakhage then programmed it in a show at Anthology Film Archives, called "The Avant-Garde Today." That was its first exposure.

MacDonald: Jennifer Reeves was in that show.

Gatten: Yes. It was the public premiere of *Chronic* [1996]; Jenn came over and introduced herself. There was also a Lynne Sachs film [*The House of Science: A Museum of False Facts* (1991)], a Mark Street film [*Echo Anthem* (1991)], and a Luther Price film [*Home* (1999)]. I hadn't been in New York in fifteen years; I'd never been there as an adult, and to show at Anthology—this place I'd read so much about—in a *Brakhage* program was amazing for me.

About six weeks later, *Hardwood Process* played at Ann Arbor and won the Grand Prize, so then people knew about it.

MacDonald: It was not so long after that that you finished what is now the first part of *What the Water Said* [1997].

Gatten: Hardwood Process was about a lot of different processes; it involved a lot of exploration, a lot of experimentation, and then a lot of decision making about how to find a shape for the resulting footage. By the time I was done with the film, I was interested in doing less. I had already said to myself that I was going to make a water film. Seabrook Island and its beach are really important to me; I grew up going there with my parents, and Weena and I got married on that beach. So I wanted to do something with that place and the water. I brought a camera, thinking I was going to shoot and then process the film myself, so it would be scratched up and "watery," but more and more that seemed like what I had just done in *Hardwood Process.*

There are a couple of sections in *Hardwood Process* where I'd taken pieces of Scotch tape and used the sticky side of the tape to pick up dust around the apartment, then used that tape as a negative to make a rayogram. That process was an entry for me into the new film—or, as Maya Deren said, "the crack in the wallpaper" that allowed her to enter the room from a different place. In the finished print there were just these white lines of the white dust flying through the frame, and I thought, "That's the most *documentary* part of this film." In thinking about that experience, I realized that if I just put the film stock I had brought with me into the surf, the results would be completely documentary.

Making *What the Water Said* was a lark. I went and bought a crab trap and some rope, put the film into the trap, and threw the trap into the surf, thinking the film was just going to be a record of what happened on that particular day (January 1, 1997). I used single-perf sound stock, so I knew that whatever happened to the filmstrip would extend past the area of the frame onto the area where the sound track is normally stored and would create a sound record, as well as a visual record, of what happened under the water.

It was an experiment, and of course I didn't know what the results were going to be, but to my surprise, the results were interesting. I've done a lot of experiments in which the results are *not* interesting, but this felt meaningful to me, partly because on that first trip down there, I threw film into the surf on three successive days and each day the results were distinct; it seemed clear that the material and the apparatus *were* responding to differences in the world, and that there was some sort of correlation between what happened in the ocean and what happened on the film.

The second time I did the experiment, the following October, I did one section during a thunderstorm when the ocean was very choppy, and that section is very frenetic; it *sounds* like a storm. I suppose if I had called the film "By the Campfire," we would interpret those sounds as flames; I do think language is incredibly important. My biggest gesture as author of *What the Water Said* is to introduce the idea of water with the T. S. Eliot text that talks about being under the water: that does condition your experience of the material.

I didn't edit the film; I put X amount of footage in the trap, and whatever the ocean gave me back is what I used. Sometimes I got back half of what I put in, sometimes all of it.

MacDonald: I showed *What the Water Said* in Buffalo when I did a "Garden in the Machine" show some years ago, and Tony Conrad was a little impatient with it; in the early seventies, he did a variety of experiments with film stock, frying film, boiling film; your film seemed old-hat to him. Did you know his work?

Gatten: Not when I started the film. I had just done the first two sections when he came to do a show in Chicago. He had the *Roast Kalvar* [1974] and the *Curried 7302* [1973], and we could all smell and taste it. I was very excited by his work.

But I also think the *Water* project is substantially different from Tony's work from the 1970s. The combination of explorations with the film material / projection apparatus along with the use of language (in the form of the T. S. Eliot quote and, in the later films in the cycle, Hawthorne, Poe, Defoe, Pessoa, and Melville) to reference literature's representation of water represent's a different impulse, I think. Certainly I am conducting an experiment with material and process, like Tony, but ultimately with this project I am more interested in the documentary qualities and shifting representations of water: water as it represents itself by inscribing the filmstrip, the representational relationship between the individual sections and the dates that correspond to them, and the way writers tried to represent the power of the ocean in the nineteenth and early twentieth century.

MacDonald: I've always assumed a connection between your major multipartite project *Secret History of the Dividing Line, a True Account in Nine Parts* and Frampton's seven-part *Hapax Legomena,* or perhaps with his Magellan project. I'm thinking about the idea of a multipartite work that reaches out not just to *film* history but to social history, art history, poetic history—all these other realms. And I'm wondering whether you conceived *Secret History* as a multipartite project or whether you did one film and realized you needed to do another, and so on. At the moment the project is conceptually nine films.

Gatten: When I started what evolved into the *Secret History* project, I didn't actually know I was making a film, much less a cycle of films. I didn't know *what* I was doing. The same week I was at the beach doing the first section of *What the Water Said,* I was reading a Susan Howe book, *Frame Structures* [Susan Howe, *Frame Structures: Early Poems 1974–1979* (New York: New Directions, 1996)]. I had been introduced to Howe in 1997 by one of my friends at the Art Institute who knew of my interest in Frampton's *Circles of Confusion.* In *Frame Structures,* which contained reprints of some of Howe's early work, the final section is called "Secret History of the Dividing Line." I found it fascinating. Howe draws mostly from a book her father wrote on Oliver Wendell Holmes.

Also at that time, I was working with black leader in a way that was inspired by Agnes Martin's paintings. I had gone to a show of her work in Chicago, thinking, "Oh, she's a minimalist painter, grid, Sol LeWitt . . . " But I had an amazing experience actually seeing the *paintings,* as opposed to slides or reproductions in a book. From twenty feet away, one of her grids may appear very regular, but from five feet away, you can tell that they're not really regular, and from *twelve inches* away, you can see that the grids on these large eight-foot-by-eight-foot canvases are constructed with a twelve-inch ruler: she's drawing a line and moving the ruler, drawing a line and moving the ruler; and so there are slight discrepancies, "imperfections," in the grid, which, close up, you can see is incredibly irregular and that Martin is in fact *not* simply a minimalist but an abstract expressionist of a certain sort. That was exciting to me.

At the time I went to that show, I was very tired; I remember thinking that her simple, repetitive process seemed so healthy. I wondered, "What might that repetitive process be *in film?*" I was interested in splicing, and was already working with cement splices, and I realized that splices are comparable to Martin's lines. A cement splice is different from a tape splice in that while you can undo a tape splice, once you do a cement splice, it's done. I had edited *Hardwood Process* with all cement splices, but that film uses mostly fades and dissolves; there are very few hard cuts, so the straight cut had been repressed in my work. I was interested in working with direct cuts for a change. I had a cement splicer that was out of alignment, and I remember sitting, watching a Bulls game, tearing a strip of black leader into pieces and then splicing them back together. Every time you make a cement splice, you lose a frame on the head and the tail, so the strip of black leader was getting shorter and shorter, and more and more filled with splices.

Now, if you make a perfect splice between black leader and black leader, you won't see that splice; but since my splicer was slightly out of alignment, my splices weren't invisible; this strip of leader was filled with these very small white lines. If you held the edited strip of leader eighteen inches from you, they looked like very uniform lines, but when I put the filmstrip on an optical printer and looked at the individual splices, they were incredibly varied. I started filming the individual splices on the optical printer, really zooming in on them, and letting them last on screen for seven seconds, ten seconds. Each image was a unique object, as opposed to a uniform machine-made thing. I made hundreds of these images.

Cement splice as evocation of landscape in David Gatten's *Secret History of the Dividing Line* (2002). Courtesy David Gatten.

MacDonald: This is what we see in the third section of the title film, *Secret History of the Dividing Line?*

Gatten: Yes. The white area on screen is the area where the blade irregularly scraped off all of the emulsion or into the celluloid base itself. Also, the cement forms bubbles, which you can see. At the beginning, I thought this was just a completely formal process, just a way of looking carefully at splices.

Six months or so later, I saw that Howe book and thought, "Wow, 'secret history of the dividing line'; the splice is supposed to be invisible; it's what's been repressed. . . . I'm going to steal that title! But maybe I should figure out what *her* title refers to." In the acknowledgments in *Frame Structures,* Howe reveals that the source for her title is two texts by William Byrd II of colonial Virginia: *History of the Dividing Line* and *The Secret History of the Line.* I decided to read these books.

When I read the official history and then the secret history of the drawing of the boundary between North Carolina and Virginia, I realized that I *recognized* some of the areas that Byrd describes. For example, the western part of the line in the Byrd expedition crosses the Dan River several times; as a kid at summer camp, I did a lot of inner-tubing and rafting on the Dan River. Bryd's descriptions of the landscape and the river were so clear that I often knew (or imagined I knew) *exactly* where he was—I have very vivid memories of that river. I continued to read as much about Byrd as I could.

As a grad student in filmmaking at the School of the Art Institute of Chicago, I kept feeling that I was *supposed* to be making a film. Instead, I had thrown some film in the ocean and I was going to the Newberry Library every day! All I did know was that I was following what I was interested in.

In reading the Byrd literature, I eventually got to the story of his library. In his time William Byrd was most widely known for his library and the fact that he let people borrow his books. His four thousand volumes were one of the two largest colonial libraries (only Cotton Mather's may have been larger). Byrd had inherited some books from his father, but every time he went back to England, he would return with many more. Thomas Jefferson ended up with a number of Byrd's books, and *Jefferson's* library became the Library of Congress, so Byrd's library in some way serves not only as the site for the transfer of European intellectual and philosophical and religious thought to North America but as the foundation of our national library.

The fact of Byrd's library was interesting to me, but what *really* hooked me was a 1958 article from the American Antiquarian Society journal by Edwin Wolf, who details his ten-year search to try and find Byrd's books. William Byrd II died in 1744; his son, William Byrd III, squandered the family fortune and committed suicide on January 1, 1777, and in order to pay the debts off, his widow had to auction off the library. A series of auctions began in 1777 or 1778, and in 1777, before the auction, a catalogue was assembled. It didn't just list the books, but preserved the location of the books on the shelves, so we can see not only what Byrd collected but how he organized the books. There was no Dewey Decimal System at the time; Byrd's way of putting things together tells us something about his thinking. I thought that was very exciting.

By this time, all these forms of division, and all these collections and connections, were coming together. There was the division of landscape through exploration, and the various reasons for dividing the two states: the official reason—the efficient collection of taxes by the British government—and the secret reason: the politics of colonies wanting access to intercoastal waterways in order to get around the British trade tariffs for the shipping of tobacco. There were also the library and the auction as sites of collection and division. That library is still together on paper, even though it's been physically divided: the books are dispersed all over the world. And I was thinking about the *cinematic* dividing line (and conjunction): the splice, which defines duration and creates our temporal experience of film. So at that point, I thought, "Okay, I want to do something with all this." I didn't want to just make a formal or a structural film, but to work with the documents and with history and bring all of these things I was excited about into a single work. Frampton's writing was serving as something of a guide.

MacDonald: The splices that you optically printed were the germ of the *Secret History* project and the central section of your *Secret History of the*

Dividing Line, but the film in which those splices appear wasn't the first of these films you finished.

Gatten: No. My working in the library first resulted in *Moxon's Mechanick Exercises, or the Doctrine of Handy-works Applied to the Art of Printing* [1999]. One of the books from Byrd's library, by Joseph Moxon, was the first manual of style for printers. I wanted to let this interesting text rub up against something else, specifically the Gutenberg Bible. The Gutenberg Bible represents that moment where the word and the Word become culturally fixed in a new way; it's a point of transition from scribal reproduction to mechanical reproduction. I decided to use the Joseph Moxon text as a source for instructions on how to recompose the Gutenberg Bible material that I'd collected by using Scotch tape to "translate" text from the pages of books onto a strip of plastic that could move through a projector; and I let Moxon direct: I made an interpretation of Moxon's instructions for a typesetter and applied them to the "translated" material. I thought, "Okay, Moxon says this; that means I should do *this* with these captured texts," and the result would affect the visual layering or the pacing or the size of the translated texts in the film.

William Byrd II bookplate in David Gatten's *The Great Art of Knowing* (2004). Courtesy David Gatten.

Translation, in the most conventional sense and in other senses too, had become a central interest. I looked at and worked with five different translations of the Bible, thinking about those translations alongside the two different Byrd histories, the secret history and the official history: that is, the "translation" of Byrd's experiences into one form, then another. I was also interested in the general politics of translation: the issue of access to the Bible, and how the control of the information in the Bible evolved.

MacDonald: How did you decide on the five particular Bibles you used?

Gatten: I was principally interested in the Gutenberg Bible. I wanted to go back and unfix the Word or fix it in a new way, and it was during the process of making the selections of texts to transfer from a reprint of the Gutenberg Bible to celluloid that I realized that I wanted to know what exactly I was reading, and so I had to go to an English Bible. I was raised on the King James Version, which is such beautiful poetry. It's what my mother always read to us, and even when we went to church, we took our King James with us; it was a Presbyterian church, and they used the New Revised Standard. I would often sit and compare the two versions and feel how much we'd lost in going to the more modern translation.

Once I had decided I wanted to deal with translation and started reading about the history of translation, I knew that I was going to use the Gutenberg *and* the King James. Before starting the project I had found a copy of the Scofield Reference Bible in my studio space and was intrigued by that Bible's attempt to reconcile all the discrepancies that you could find in other Bibles. I can't remember the exact reasons why I chose the Polyglot Bible, except that it put different languages side by side. And finally, the Geneva Bible; I had found a wonderful reproduction of it that had a typography that was graphically somewhere in between the to-me-illegible block letters of the Gutenberg and the English in the King James. The Geneva is the one that has all the descending *f*'s that look like *s*'s; you have to relearn the alphabet to actually read the words. The Geneva Bible was the perfect intermediate space for me, in terms of a visual representation of language that was both abstract and legible.

MacDonald: To what extent does your going back to that Gutenberg moment relate to the current transformation from mechanical printing technologies to all the new digital methods?

Gatten: I see it as a *direct* relationship. I was trying to address that very issue. After the Gutenberg printing press, and the Gutenberg Bible, the *text* was fixed, but *meaning* was *unfixed.* You had the dissemination of texts, and the proliferation of texts gave way to the proliferation of interpretations. Books were still very expensive, but far less so than when they were reproduced by hand, so more people had the opportunity to interpret the Bible and other writings as well. In the late 1990s, similar things were happening; everyone was very excited about digital technology and the ways in which it was unfixing traditional text and texts. This was the moment after analog video, when digital video was starting up, and it seemed as if DV was going to answer everyone's questions about access to the means of reproduction. I thought, "Well, maybe if I can go back to this earlier transition in print culture, I'll be able to learn some things." At that point there weren't specific answers that I was hoping to pull out of the older material; it was just a way of thinking through these huge cultural changes.

MacDonald: A question about a detail in *Moxon's Mechanick Exercises;* within the second section, there's a poem about being halfway up the stairs.

Gatten: Yes, from A. A. Milne. I remembered this poem from childhood (it was something I recited), but I didn't know what it was, and it wasn't until the premiere at the New York Film Festival when somebody asked me why the poem was not listed in my endnotes, that I relearned its author.

Moxon's Mechanick Exercises was the first film that I made from my engagement with the Byrd library, but it has nothing to do with Byrd. He's not mentioned; he's not a character or even a presence in that film. My film simply uses a book that came from his library as a source and a kind of guide. When I started *Moxon's Mechanick Exercises* in 1998, I didn't know that I was making a film about William Byrd or William Byrd's library. *Moxon's Mechanick Exercises* seemed at that point entirely separate from the splices I had made and set aside.

I finished *Moxon's Mechanick Exercises* in 1999. By that point I was committed to the Byrd project because I'd read about his daughter, Evelyn, and her love affair with Charles Mordaunt. That story gave the Byrd saga an entirely new dimension. Some of what has come down to us about Evelyn is the stuff of legend. But it does seem clear that she went to England in 1723 and met this man who was the grandson of the Third Earl of Peterborough, Byrd's main political rival in England at the time. The Peterboroughs were Catholic; the Byrds were Protestant. Evelyn's father found out about what was a budding romance, and Evelyn was shipped back to Virginia, where she refused to see suitors. It turns out that she carried on a secret nine-year transatlantic correspondence with Mordaunt, who eventually travels to the colonies under an assumed name and infiltrates Virginia society. They make secret plans to elope. But they're betrayed by Byrd's secretary. The ship sails with Mordaunt tied up on the ship; Evelyn is prevented from going aboard. And during that voyage the ship goes down; everyone aboard is lost. Evelyn is heartbroken; she confesses to her friend that she feels that she can't go on, and two weeks later she dies, at age twenty-nine, of *heart failure.* And the following spring, in 1738, the first of seventeen recorded sightings of her ghost is reported.

I thought, "Wow!" Here was an epic story and a tragic love story, again about *division*—they're apart for nine years (their only communication is through letters that are carried back and forth by hand); they're divided by the ocean and by religion, but connected by text. It was becoming obvious that I couldn't fit all of what I was learning about the Byrds into the little splice line film I was working on. By this time I'd also decided that the splice line film was going to be about the landscapes of Virginia and North Carolina—because to me the individual splices had begun to look like landscapes. I was realizing that I might need to make a love story film and ghost story film.

Another part of this saga happened when Weena and I were moving from one apartment to another. For years I had had a print on the wall that was done by my first film professor at UNC-G: Joanna Hudson. I had always referred to the piece, which I had never really looked at carefully, as "the handless maiden": in the print a woman has her head turned and her hands are sort of dissolving. As we were packing up to move, I became aware, for the first time, of the actual title of this piece: "Evelyn Byrd, the Ghost of Westover"! Evelyn had been on my wall for seven years without my realizing it, and I'd just spent eighteen months researching her family!

I contacted Joanna, and it turned out that she knew all about the love story and ghost story parts of the Byrd history. Evelyn is mentioned in a lot of ghost story books.

MacDonald: What's the historical record for the Evelyn Byrd story? How does anybody know that this set of events happened?

Gatten: Her father wrote letters that mention the events and also referred to Evelyn in his secret diary. In his private writing, William Byrd often gave people satirical names; Charles Mordaunt was "Erranti." There are also Evelyn's letters. And in 1895 there was a novelization of the events, called *His Great Self* [by Marion Harland (Philadelphia: Lippincott, 1893)]; it's a wonderful florid romance that has only marginal relation to what actually happened. Basically, I was working with many different sources to arrive at my understanding of this history and my imagining into the relationship of Charles and Evelyn.

So at one point, I thought, "Okay, three films." But then even that wasn't enough. I started to think about other aspects of the Byrd history that needed to be addressed if I were going to create some real sense of its many dimensions. I continued and continue to find the Byrd library fascinating. In 1998, a scholarly edition of the 1778 catalogue, meticulously annotated and researched by Kevin Hayes, appeared. It's fascinating reading; I open it up all the time, just to read the titles and descriptions of Byrd's books.

In the summer of 2001 I took a trip to try and find the fifty-seven locations that Byrd lists in the appendix of his *History,* and sure enough, many of them were still there with the same names. The border has shifted—Virginia has steadily gotten smaller; there were later border-drawing expeditions that enlarged North Carolina—so most of the 1728 dividing line is now in North Carolina, but I could find these places, and Ariana Hamidi and I spent three weeks camping along the dividing line and shot a lot of film. There will be two expedition films: the title film of the cycle, *Secret History of the Dividing Line,* and another (it'll be the eighth in the cycle) that will revisit the expedition with actual imagery of those points along the original border that are abstractly envisioned by the splices.

MacDonald: Let's talk about the title film, section by section. The first part begins with the scratch, although I think you mentioned that it wasn't created as a scratch, but by first tearing the celluloid filmstrip and then putting it back together?

Gatten: Yes, that line is the scar of an actual rip right down the center of the film.

MacDonald: How do you *do* that?

Gatten: Very carefully! It took us three weeks to shoot the fifteen hundred dates in that time line. Ariana Hamidi helped me with the research and production for that film. She selected some dates, and I selected others, and then I printed out each date on an 8½ × 11 piece of paper. We spent many days shooting the time line a frame at a time, with *x* number of frames in between each date—everything was scored out. I got the strip of film processed, and then I ripped it in half. I didn't want to rip through the texts, so I had to be very careful to keep the tear in between the dates and the texts. Then taping the strip back together also took quite a long time.

MacDonald: Could you tell me what the first two texts are? They're clearly not there to be read, but just to signal the viewer that some new development in the film is beginning. But where *do* you start your time line of the world?

Gatten: The first date is 14,000 B.C., and the event is the last ice age recedes. I think that date is on screen for two frames. The next one is the building of the Great Pyramids; it flashes for only one frame. You're right, these dates are not meant to be legible, but to cue the viewer that the line might be something more than just this scratch on the filmstock.

MacDonald: It's a very inventive way of slowly focusing in on a particular story. The amount of time that each of the dates and descriptions is on screen depends on how important they are to the particular story of the Byrds. We begin with dates/events that have at most the same general impact on their story as on the stories of most everyone else, but when we get to the crucial events of the Byrds' particular history, the images/descriptions stop for a moment; it's almost as if we're moving from the distance into a particular focus the way many narrative films do—the opening sequence of *Psycho* [1960], for instance—but here we're moving through time, more than through space.

Gatten: That's right. At some level, I was also trying to convey my own sense of poring through history, which is filled with so much information and is overwhelming at times, and slowly narrowing down and choosing a particular thread to follow. It *is* very much like a zoom forward or like the long shot, medium shot, close-up grammar for establishing a location and time for a set of events in narrative cinema.

The time line ends in 1929 with the publication of William Boyd's edition, where Byrd's *History* and *The Secret History* are presented on facing pages, *History* on the left-hand side, *The Secret History* on the right. You can make your way through that edition, reading the official version and the secret version in relation to each other. I was completely fascinated by the fact that the *two* texts came into the world at different times, and in different ways—one circulated officially, one circulated privately—and I had a great experience reading this edition, and wanted somehow to convey that experience. My decision was to print both as scrolling texts, the official history in one typeface and the secret history in another. I shot both; then taped them together, one on top of the other, and did the same thing I did with the time line: I tore down the center, this time a little more recklessly, so that sometimes the tear went all the way to the edge and pieces of the film came completely apart. What I had then was a jigsaw puzzle of sorts. I combined moments from the left-hand side (the official history) on one layer, and passages from the secret history on the other.

MacDonald: You create just enough movement back and forth from one version to the other so that we can see that in *The Secret History,* Byrd is less politically correct than he is in the later, more formal, official history.

Gatten: Yes, the governor had asked him to write up an official account of the expedition, and that's where the *History of the Dividing Line, Run in the Year 1728* comes from.

The "secret history" was a genre at the time. Byrd had other secret histories in his library. He made note in his commonplace book of having read *The Secret History of White-Hall* by David Jones [*The Secret History of White-Hall from the Restoration of Charles II Down to the Abdication of the Late K[ing] James . . .* (London: printed for D. Brown, A. Bell, 1717)]. Works in the secret history genre were almost always parodies or satirical sketches that circulated privately, among friends.

In *The Secret History of the Line,* Byrd names himself "Steddy"; he envisions himself as the steady one, the sensible one. He was very biting in his commentary on the party from North Carolina. There was great rivalry between Virginia and North Carolina, and Byrd thought the North Carolinians were a bunch of buffoons.

MacDonald: That's clear in his naming them "Jumble," "Shoebrush," "Plausible," and "Puzzle."

You mentioned that in section two of the film, we see fifty-seven splices in some detail, although actually that section divides into two parts, the first of which is a kind of flicker film where we see what seem like many dozens of splices, first at the bottom of the frame, then at the bottom and the top, then in the middle. Then you slow down, and we start getting one splice at a time for several seconds each. When I counted these longer shots of splices, I came up with fifty-nine, but I assume that's because in two instances the light radically changes within an individual image.

Gatten: Yes, it is fifty-seven different splices and, yes, in two instances I changed the exposure during the shot—my way of suggesting sunrise and sunset over the landscape.

MacDonald: Since it's almost impossible not to read the splices as landscapes, I wonder to what degree you tried to evoke the terrain of North Carolina–Virginia moving from east to west.

Gatten: Initially, I had made images of about two hundred splices, and for a number of years, I just shifted them around, trying different combinations and different durations. It was not until the summer of 2001, when I took the trip with Ariana to try and find the locations, that I hit on the shape of the film—and it seemed so obvious once I had it: the central section would be fifty-seven of these splices, one for each location. My experience of being in the locations combined with what Byrd wrote about them in 1728 allowed me to find in these Rorschach-like images evocations of certain places and certain descriptions. For each of the splices I used, there is a specific connection; if you went to that location, it might not be a recognizable connection for you, but for me, finding a connection for each splice was the constraint that I used to power the construction of the film.

MacDonald: How, for you, does the early flicker section function? I see breaking ocean waves, maybe because I'm trying to—well, *obviously* because I'm trying to—and partly because I have an affection for the North Carolina coast.

Gatten: In his accounts in *History* and *The Secret History,* Byrd writes about the process of getting to the starting point of the expedition. All of the commissioners from North Carolina and Virginia agreed to meet at Currituck Inlet on the Outer Banks, so there was a process of travel before the drawing of the line could begin. I imagine Byrd and the others rushing to get to the starting place, and I tried to evoke that—I love that you see waves, because that *is* in fact where everything starts. Those splices that create the flicker effect are also in multiples of fifty-seven.

MacDonald: In many of the individual splices that are on screen for a while, there's a very subtle flicker.

Gatten: When I started photographing the splices on the optical printer, I did a roll and processed it myself. The result was really flickery; there were water spots all over everything, and it was sort of frenetic. I thought, "too distracting." Then I did another roll, sent this one off to a lab, and they processed it very cleanly; I got it back and projected it, and it seemed completely flat; it was almost like watching slides. I decided I needed to go back to processing the film myself, and work with the level of water spotting that would occur. In the end, I was able to modulate the rhythm of the flickering light basically by leaving or removing water spots, and deciding on the relationship of the internal rhythm of one shot to the internal rhythm of the next shot became an important part of the editing process. Each shot of an individual splice is not just about duration and composition but also about the way the light is moving in the shot.

MacDonald: Did you find all fifty-seven locations?

Gatten: I found forty-two.

MacDonald: One of the central dialectics in the film is straight lines of either logic or geography versus the curvilinear reality of life. As we read the list of places where the surveying group stops, we cross many winding rivers. It's also interesting how the names on the list reflect a particular historical moment in the process of settling Virginia. There are clearly English names imposed on the landscape at the beginning, then there are Indian names, and then at the end we go back to a preponderance of English names.

Gatten: The surveyors went about 240 miles from Currituck Inlet across North Carolina, about two-thirds of the way across the state as it now exists. In the European-settled areas on the coast, the Native American names had been replaced by European names; then there was an unpopulated area or certainly a much less densely populated area in and around the Dismal Swamp and other areas where the group had Native American guides, so the names they were being told were the ones used by Native Americans. Then when they got further inland, into the Piedmont area, the party just started naming things themselves. Certain places are named for members of the expedition; the Mayo River, for instance, is named after John Mayo.

What you said about the straight line versus the curved line was important to me throughout the film, which begins with the jagged line within the more uniform borders of the film frame and the "lines" of texts. I do love the idea that the surveyors are trying to go straight across something that is not straight and that that is then inscribed in the appendix *list*—another kind of line.

MacDonald: Secret Life of the Dividing Line reminds me of Frampton's *Gloria!* I assume that's a film you know.

Gatten: Gloria! is actually my very favorite film. I adore that movie and find it incredibly moving. But I have never thought about it in direct relation to *Secret History of the Dividing Line.*

MacDonald: Gloria! does with beginnings and endings—literal, historical, material—what you do with the idea of the *line.*

Within the structure of the larger *Secret History* project, at least as you envision it now, *The Enjoyment of Reading, Lost and Found* is the fourth film, but it was the second one you finished. When we showed it at Hamilton College, many of the texts were hard to read. Did you mean for those texts to be right at the edge of readability?

Gatten: I *am* always wanting things to be at different degrees of legibility, to pose different challenges for the viewer/reader, and I did want to start the film with text that was thin—but here it didn't quite work. Part of the difficulty was the font that I chose: it made certain parts of the letters *very* thin, and in some prints of the film and in certain projection situations, maybe too thin. Because I make these films on rewinds, I never know exactly what I'm going to end up with until the film is finished.

MacDonald: In the long first section, are we looking at microfilm?

Gatten: No, again I'm using my Scotch-tape transfer process: lifting text from a book and "translating" it to celluloid. I had gone through the original catalogue of Byrd's library and had copied down a couple hundred titles, and then made a further selection. I made transparency slides of eighty-one splices. I often make slides of images and put them on a lightbox as a way of thinking about how to arrange them. I'd been planning to make traditional titles once I had the slides arranged, but then decided to film the *slides* themselves. I took the gate off the optical printer and put each slide where normally you would have the variable-density filter and then filmed the slide, racking in and out of focus. So, no, they're not actually from microfilm, but I did intend to reproduce something of my experience of sorting through both microfilms and card catalogues in archives: there's so much material, some of which you glance at, some of which you read carefully, much of which you can't absorb, and some of which you first go past, then find yourself drawn back to. The series of descriptions of books in this section of *The Enjoyment of Reading* works in a similar way to the time line at the beginning of *Secret History of the Dividing Line* in that there are certain moments of focus within a wash of information.

MacDonald: In the second section, we get the color passage, "emblems of love, that she made while waiting, always waiting." There are two parts to this passage; a bluish first section that is quite abstract, then a somewhat less abstract section of lovely out-of-focus imagery of light through leaves blowing in the wind. In both sections, your focus creates dots or circles of light. What exactly are we looking at there?

Gatten: In both sections you're seeing a blue, foil-wrapped candle.

MacDonald: We see that candle in clear silhouette during the second section.

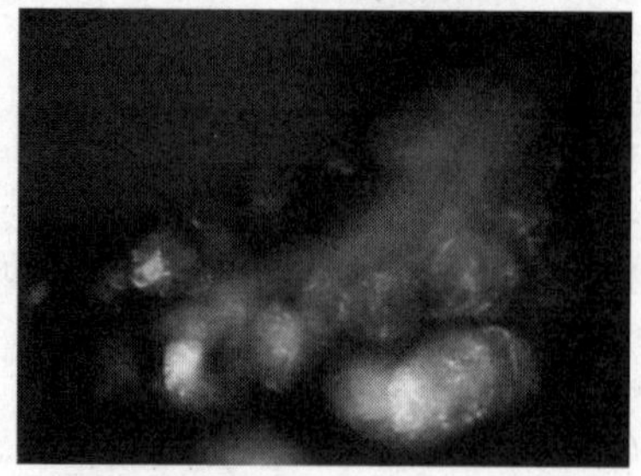

Candlewick and "circles of confusion" in a "text of light" in David Gatten's *The Enjoyment of Reading, Lost and Found* (2001). Courtesy David Gatten.

Gatten: Yes. At the beginning you're seeing, in extreme close-up, the tip of the candle, and there is one flash when the wick actually comes into focus. The tip of the candle was filmed with extension tubes, which magnify imagery; basically you're seeing the sun glinting off the blue foil and creating "circles of confusion." I was moving the camera very slightly, just shaking it basically. For a moment, a bit of cobweb is visible between the wick and the edge of the candle, and then I pull back and you see that the candle is in the window, within more "circles of confusion."

I think of that image as one of the iconic images of a lover waiting: you put the candle in the window to signal to your beloved.

MacDonald: Your alluding to Frampton's *Circles of Confusion* just now is interesting, given that this particular section is very Brakhage-ian. It strikes me that one of the things that you're attempting to do in the larger *Secret History* project is to bring together various supposedly oppositional avant-garde practices. At one point, Brakhage and Frampton were thought to be at opposite ends of at least one independent filmmaking axis: Brakhage was personal and romantic, Frampton detached and intellectual. Did you have both Frampton and Brakhage in mind as you were making this passage?

Gatten: Well, when I was looking through the camera and realized that what was coming and going were "circles of confusion," of course, I thought of Frampton. But further, I had begun *The Enjoyment of Reading* (I already had the title for the film) with a lot of reading from texts that I conjectured were of particular interest to *William* Byrd. For the second section I wanted to shift the focus of the film into *Evelyn's* space, into color and into what I considered to be a different kind of "reading": a reading of "the text of light." I was thinking very specifically about Brakhage's *The Text of Light* [1974] and also about the way the kinds of images in the Brakhage film and in this section of this film might be conditioned by the seven or eight minutes of literary text that have come before them; what kind of new space would open up visually, physiologically, conceptually, when we went from black-and-white letters to a color image—that was very much on my mind.

MacDonald: In the third section of *The Enjoyment of Reading,* little shards of text at the bottom of the frame allude in one way or another to the various stories in the project, and then we see several images of a decaying book; I can't read the title.

Gatten: That's *Religion of Nature Delineated* [1738] by William Wollaston, the first of Byrd's books that I was able to film at the Virginia Historical Society in Richmond, something I was very excited about. This was in 2001, right when I was starting to understand that this was a project about the Byrds. I had made *Moxon's Mechanick Exercises* and had been doing a lot of research in Chicago, but this was the first time I went down to Virginia.

Religion of Nature Delineated is a very fragile book, so fragile that they only let it out of the archive once every five years, so we (Ariana had agreed to assist me) felt lucky to have this opportunity. The staff there, all of whom were very nice and supportive of the project, brought the book out and we filmed it, after which they took it back into the archive, and we thought, "Wow, it's gone for five years!" Then we realized that we'd not removed the 85B orange color-correction filter for tungsten film. We'd been shooting in black-and-white Tri-X, and that meant the exposure had been off by almost a stop and a half. We went back to the counter and said, "Um, can we have that book back one more time?" And they were so sweet, they brought it back out, and we filmed it again—but now nobody will see that book for *ten* years. We were embarrassed about that.

MacDonald: In general, has it been difficult getting to film the various books and texts in the rare book libraries?

Gatten: Oh no; the librarians have been *so* excited. Somebody is making *movies* about *old books!* At the American Philosophical Society, where I shot many of the books in *The Great Art of Knowing,* they were *so* helpful, *so* generous with their time; they even had a conservator on hand to work with me, and they let me move the books to a table so I could get natural light coming through a window. I've never had any problems getting access, which is exactly the way you would hope things would work.

MacDonald: Another book that's focused on in that third section of *The Enjoyment of Reading* is *Robinson Crusoe.*

Gatten: Yes. The publication date of *Robinson Crusoe* is one of the dates on the time line in *Secret History of the Dividing Line,* and it will come into play again later, in regard to Charles Mordaunt's shipwreck, which is alluded to already in *The Great Art of Knowing* and a little bit in *The Enjoyment of Reading.*

MacDonald: Did you choose the particular sonnet from Michael Drayton because you know that Evelyn read it?

Gatten: I chose that particular sonnet because it fits the theme of the

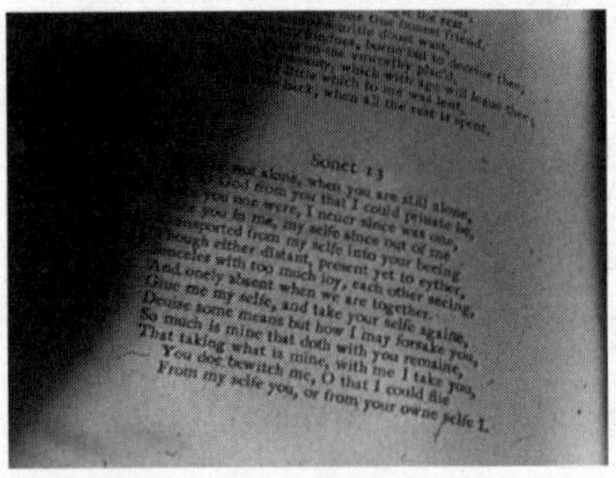

Michael Drayton sonnet in David Gatten's *The Enjoyment of Reading, Lost and Found* (2001). Courtesy David Gatten.

entire project. All of the films are explorations of different kinds of division, and I'm especially interested in the kinds of *division* that create *relationships* that make it hard to take things apart. Drawing the dividing line through the land separated North Carolina from Virginia, but also created a social, economic, political relationship between the two colonies. For me, that line resonates with the idea of Evelyn Byrd and Charles Mordaunt being separated by an ocean in a way that seems to have strengthened their bond. The Drayton sonnet is about the complexity of separation and the fact that to separate from a lover is not simply to divide from another, but from a part of oneself. For me the ideas in that sonnet are at the emotional center of the entire *Secret History* project.

MacDonald: When I saw *The Great Art of Knowing,* I realized that I was (finally!) getting to understand your larger project.

Gatten: That was true for me too! I had been making each of these films separately. I knew they were part of a series, but when I started making *The Great Art of Knowing,* I began to see new connections between the films and how I could actually knit those connections together. When I first started working with the material that becomes the center of *The Great Art of Knowing,* I didn't think I was making a Byrd film. I had seen the exhibition of Leonardo's drawings at the Metropolitan Museum in New York in February 2003 and was *really* taken with his handwriting, partly because it's mirror writing. Also, I noticed that whenever he was exploring something, he would write *and* he would draw in the margins; and the line between writing and drawing is very hazy in a lot of what he did—or at least it was for me, because I couldn't read the handwriting. I decided I wanted to work with this text in the same way I worked with the Bible texts in *Moxon's Mechanick Exercises:* I wanted to lift the text from the pages; and I wanted to explore the lines of text and of the drawings as shapes that evoke language without revealing specific meanings: I wanted to think about the idea that, in order to *understand* something, you have to have both language *and* image.

I was particularly interested in the *Codex on the Flight of Birds,* where Leonardo was trying to understand how flight was possible and how to make a flying machine. I thought I was going to be making a Leonardo film, but then it dawned on me that I was working with *birds* again. In his time, there were many puns on William Byrd's name (his nickname was "the Black Swan"), and he was much involved with birds: he built a garden to attract hummingbirds, he was a birdwatcher, and he wrote about birds. Also, Evelyn drew pictures of birds. So my experiments became a Byrd film, as well as a bird film.

2511 *Kircheri Ars magna sciendi*
KIRCHER, ATHANASIUS . . . Ars magna sciendi in XII libros digesta, qua nova & universali methodo per artificiosum combinationum contextumde omni re proposita plurismis & prope infinitis rationibus disputari, omniumque summaria quaedam cognitio comparari potest. Amsterdam: apud Joannem Janssonium a Waesberge, & vidaum Elize Weyerstraet, 1669.

Athanasius Kircher listing in catalogue of William Byrd II's library in David Gatten's *The Great Art of Knowing* (2004). Courtesy David Gatten.

I already knew that I was interested in the Athanasius Kircher texts that Byrd had in his library: *The Great Art of Knowing, The Great Art of Light and Shadow, The Ecstatic Heavenly Journey.* I started reading about Kircher, and somehow I connected the text of *The Great Art of Knowing,* which is sometimes referred to as the first book of symbolic logic, to Leonardo's attempts to understand flight. How is it that we can understand something? Everyone who I was reading at that moment was an empiricist of some sort, believing that through our *senses* we can accumulate knowledge. I started collecting different people who were looking at birds and trying to understand flight, and, of course, in time that brought me to Marey. Leonardo and Marey became my parentheses around five hundred years of people looking at and trying to understand the flight of birds.

In Kircher's *The Great Art of Knowing,* one page lists twenty-seven different "principles or subjects," which Kircher breaks down into three categories. In my film, those three columns first appear in Latin and then are translated into English. Kircher set out to create a system by means of which you could know all there is to know about the world. I used Kircher's twenty-seven categories as my structuring device for this film, and also as the overarching structure for the entire film cycle. Each of the films has three sections plus an introduction; and in the end, there will be nine films with three major sections each: those are *my* twenty-seven terms to try and organize "all there is to know" about the Byrd family, the formation of America during this period, et cetera.

All of the films in the cycle come from looking at specific books that were in the Byrd library, but each film also makes use of a text that was not in his library. In *Moxon's Mechanick Exercises,* it's the Gutenberg Bible; in *The Enjoyment of Reading,* the 1925 pamphlet of the same name was certainly not in Byrd's library; in *The Great Art of Knowing*, I'm using Leonardo's *Codex on the Flight of Birds* in the center section—again, not something from Byrd's library—in conjunction with the Kircher text, which *was* in Byrd's library.

MacDonald: Kircher is a fascinating figure and one of the first Europeans, if not *the* first, to understand the potential of projected light for entertainment and education—just one of his accomplishments.

Gatten: Yes, he was amazing. I came to know about Kircher through Kenny Eisenstein. In 1999 or 2000, when he was studying with Tom Gunning at the University of Chicago, Kenny sent me a photocopy of a chapter from a book that Gunning was teaching [*The Great Art of Light and Shadow: Archeology of the Cinema*, published in a translation by Laurent Mannoni in 2000 by the University of Exeter Press]; this chapter was on secret writing, and it included a description of Athanasius Kircher's amazing system for sending written messages across great distances.

MacDonald: What's the system?

Gatten: If you have a giant mirror on top of a mountain and you write, backward, on the surface of the mirror with charcoal, and if you put the mirror at a certain angle at a certain time of day; and if, a mile away, your friend on the other mountain has a certain size lens at a certain angle at a certain time of day, the shadow of your words will reflect from the one mountain to the other and be focused by your friend's lens onto a flat surface.

I loved this idea, and I re-created it in my studio, using the sun coming in the window to project words up onto the wall. Actually, I had started exploring that before I realized that Byrd had the Kircher book in which that description appears.

MacDonald: There are a number of particular images in *The Great Art of Knowing* that I can't identify. One of them is a bottle or a jar that we see more than once. There's also a piece of optical equipment. And there is something that looks like a mirror with water drops.

Gatten: The jar is a little porcelain inkwell. The optical device is a small microscope; the auction of Byrd's library included both books and philosophical instruments: compasses and small microscopes and magnifying glasses. That's actually my grandfather's college microscope. And the third object is sand and oil encased between two thin sheets of glass, with a wood frame; you can turn it so that the sand moves from top to bottom and then settles into new patterns, then you turn it again and the sand settles again. It was sitting in my window with the light coming through it and I started filming, not knowing what I was going to do with what I shot, but when I saw the results, I saw a connection with the Byrd materials.

MacDonald: A couple of times you put it near Evelyn's texts.

Gatten: For me it's the "underwater sequence." That's the floor at the bottom of the ocean; it's meant to evoke Mordaunt's drowning.

MacDonald: One of the opening texts in *The Great Art of Knowing* is an entry from Byrd's secret diary. What an interesting character! What do you think he means by "I danced my dance"?

Gatten: He does calisthenics every morning. He calls it dancing; *The Dancing Master* was a manual for calisthenics. In diary entries during his later life, he shortens that phrase to "I danced."

MacDonald: At the end of the film we see what I assume is the last entry in his diary: it concludes, "I am ready"; I assume he means ready to die. The irony is that he had such a regulated life that his last day is virtually the same as any other day.

Gatten: Yes! For years at a time, the entries will be almost identical; the only difference will be how many lines of Latin he read and whether or not he said his prayers.

MacDonald: In your "Codex on the Flight of Birds," there's something I think I'm not getting. I understand that you're working between writing and drawing and that you're doing a wide range of experiments with how to abstract off of the da Vinci material, but it's a long section and after a certain point, I'm not sure I'm getting anything more.

Gatten: Maybe you're working too hard. Again, I took the number twenty-seven, divided into three parts, and I used that as a structure within that section. As you say, I'm looking at this line between drawing and text, and trying to move through a certain number of combinations to see what the process will yield. I do something nine times, then I do something else nine times, and then something else nine times. That structure helped *me* work through that material, but it's not something that I expect the audience to apprehend; it's not like watching the Taka Iimura film *1 to 60 Seconds* [1973] and at a certain point realizing, "Oh, this will be over when he has executed this number of variations."

MacDonald: How exactly were you working with that da Vinci material?

Gatten: It's all my Scotch-tape transfer process where I put Scotch tape onto the page and boil the paper away so that the glue from the tape soaks up the ink and is then contact printed onto high-contrast stock, which creates a negative; then I edited that negative in A, B, C, D rolls and also optically printed some of the material to slow it down and change the rhythm.

Working that way is very much like a kid using silly putty to lift images from the comics and then being able to stretch the faces—basically it was a return to childhood. In 1996, I did a series of folders using this process:

every Sunday morning, I would put splicing tape on different parts of the Sunday *Chicago Tribune,* lift the text or drawing off, and make these folders. I liked the process, but I didn't have any film idea for it yet.

Eventually, I did have an idea of how to use the process in a film, and then I explored how to get the strongest image. I found I needed hot water to soften the paper. Figuring out the process happened over time, but basically it was fairly simple.

MacDonald: In "Causes and Effects," the third part of *The Great Art of Knowing,* you intercut between moments of reflected light and close-ups of books (often emphasizing the pages as strata), and poetically arranged lines that arrive on screen on three levels, stay on screen for a certain amount of time, then fade out. Some of the sources of those lines are obvious—for example, we get a revision of a couple of lines from Evelyn Byrd's diary—but I don't recognize where all these lines are coming from. What are we reading there?

Gatten: That section starts off with a title page from *A Catalogue of Writers Both Ancient and Modern from Whom This Narrative Is Drawn,* and then I'm looking back at specific lines from William Byrd, from Evelyn Byrd, and from the English translation of the text from Leonardo's *Codex on the Flight of Birds.*

I don't know if you remember, but years ago, when you and I were walking through Treman Gorge in Ithaca, you said, "You should definitely look at Marta Braun's book on Marey" [Marta Braun, *Picturing Time: The Work of Etienne-Jules Marey (1830–1904)* (Chicago: University of Chicago Press, 1992)], and I did. I didn't use any Marey *images* in *Secret History of the Dividing Line,* but that third section has seven or eight lines of Marey text, including the line about how it's better not to speculate about those things we do not know and come up with false explanations.

The other dominant text in that section is Wittgenstein's *Tractatus.* "The world is all that is the case," the first line of that section, is the first line of the *Tractatus.* And a number of the last lines are from the end section of the *Tractatus.*

MacDonald: A lot of people have tried to do poetic timing in film, mostly not very successfully. This is an unusual but effective way of doing it.

Gatten: As a viewer, you can read things in at least two different orders at any given moment, and I wanted that. Again, I'm working with twenty-seven; there are eighty-one lines in that section; twenty-seven texts on each of the three levels of the frame.

When *The Great Art of Knowing* was shown in Italy last fall, they subtitled the whole thing! It was quite an experience to watch all this computer-generated text flash up on a screen *below* the screen; it changed the rhythm of the film completely, not to mention the color and the light quality, but it was fascinating.

The other thing about that third section is that the texts that appear in three lines are interrupted not only by the images but also by nine texts that appear as blocks, rather than as individual lines. These longer quotes are from some of the same sources: the Evelyn Byrd diary, William Byrd's diary, Evelyn Byrd's letters, Marey . . .

MacDonald: Near the end, we get this one particular kind of reflection, quite gorgeous; it suggests birds in various stages of flight caught within a single image. Do you mean to evoke Marey's chronophotographs?

Gatten: Those are words shadowed on a mirror bounced off the wall through a lens, modulated by the shadows of leaves blowing in the wind, also being put through that apparatus—so it's *words* that suggest birds in flight. I spent three hours every afternoon for ten or twelve weeks sitting in the studio waiting for the light to arrive and looking through the camera. I probably only filmed every third day, but I spent hours waiting for the wind to be right, for the shadows of leaves to be the right size.

This film starts at sunrise. Early on, there are nine shots of dawn light coming through old windows in the house. At the end, I use afternoon light.

MacDonald: There's a poignant moment in the passage of text from *The History of Virginia* that describes Byrd's garden. The author explains that Byrd grows Indian honeysuckle in his garden, which is alive with hummingbirds so tame that they brush the writer's face. It's always interesting to realize how plentiful and unafraid wildlife was during the early centuries of the European development of North America.

Gatten: One of the three garden images that you see in that section actually *is* Byrd's garden. The two close-ups of the flowers are from the very first roll of 16mm film that I ever shot, in Weena's parents' garden in Wake Forest.

MacDonald: Byrd's garden still exists?

Gatten: Oh, yes. The house on the James River is still there; it's not open to the public as many of the old houses are, although the grounds, including the garden, are open several days of the week. About half a mile away, if you want to go exploring, you can find Evelyn's grave. I've been there twice, and I'll go back.

MacDonald: A question about the exhibition of the films in the *Secret History* project. *Moxon's Mechanick Exercises* and *The Enjoyment of Reading* are meant to be shown at eighteen frames per second, and *Secret History of the Dividing Line* and *The Great Art of Knowing* at twenty-four frames per second. Given the difficulty of showing at silent speed these days, why did you choose it for the first two films you finished?

Gatten: With *Moxon's Mechanick Exercises* I chose eighteen frames per second because I wanted the subtle flicker that the slower speed creates, and I wanted that text to move slowly. When I made *The Enjoyment of Reading,* I decided the project was going to stay at eighteen, but I gradually realized that this decision was creating a serious problem for most anyone wanting to show the films; it's hard enough to find 16mm projectors these days, much less projectors that can show at eighteen frames per second. So I've changed to twenty-four.

MacDonald: I know that you travel and often perform with these films. As you're making them, to what extent do you assume that you're going to be present when they're shown?

Gatten: Never. I don't even assume that any particular film will be shown with another film. For most of their lives so far, single films have traveled to festivals without me. During the last several years I've been lucky enough to be able to present the films in person, but still, probably two-thirds of the time, the films are out there by themselves.

MacDonald: Can you talk a bit more about the remaining films in the cycle?

Gatten: Another big film that I decided *had* to be done involved the division of labor on Byrd's plantation: slavery. Byrd owned thirteen other people, and that's partly why he could *buy* all these books and spend so much time reading them. I knew I wanted to do a film on that, but for a long time didn't know how, because there were no books about slavery in his library. But then I found *Halfpennys Principles of Architecture,* about how to most efficiently design your plantation—so division of *space* as it effects and conditions and produces the division of labor became my way into dealing with slavery and race. There's a good image there, the architectural plans of the great house and its subordinate dependencies. That'll be the seventh film: *Halfpenny's Principles of Architecture.*

The ninth and final film, *The Ecstatic Heavenly Journey,* will be the ghost story.

MacDonald: What's the next film you plan to complete?

Gatten: The next one will be the fifth film, which will use Robert Boyle's *Occasional Reflections upon Several Subjects* from the Byrd library as a guiding text. The Boyle book is going to be colliding with *The Book of White Magic,* published in the 1920s, basically for unhappy women to try and figure out their lives: there are ninety-five different questions; you choose a question and then close your eyes and point to a table of symbols and then use a grid to tell you what page to turn to, and the book will answer your question. The questions are wonderful and very poetic.

MacDonald: Sounds like the *I Ching*.

Gatten: Very much. So *Gadbury's Doctrine of Nativities, containing the whole Art of Directions and annual Revolutions: whereby, any man (even of an ordinary capacity) may be enabled to discover the most remarkable and occult Incidents of His Life* will be the next film.

Confessions of a Feminist Porn Watcher (Then and Now)

Finally, here's a proper subject for the legions of feminist men: let them undertake the analysis that can tell us why men like porn (not, piously, why this or that exceptional man does not), why stroke books work, how oedipal formations feed the drive, and how any of it can be changed.

B. Ruby Rich[1]

Pepe Le Pew was everything I wanted to be romantically. Not only was he quite sure of himself but it never occurred to him that anything was wrong with him. I always felt that there must be great areas of me that were repugnant to girls, and Pepe was quite the opposite of that.

Chuck Jones[2]

For a long time I've been ambivalent about pornography. Off and on since early adolescence, I've visited porn shops and theaters, grateful—albeit a little sheepishly—for their existence; and like many men, I would guess, I've often felt protective of pornography, at least the more standard, heterosexual varieties.[3] I know nothing at all about the child porn trade, which, judging from news articles, is flourishing: I've never seen a child in an arcade film or videotape or in a film in a porn movie house. And though I've heard that many porn films involve women being tortured, I don't remember ever coming in contact with such material, except in Bonnie Klein's *Not a*

1. B. Ruby Rich, *Chick Flicks: Theories and Memories of the Feminist Film Movement* (Durham, NC: Duke University Press, 1998), 273; Rich's essay, "Anti-Porn: Soft Issue, Hard World," originally appeared in the *Village Voice,* July 20, 1982.

2. Chuck Jones's comment is from "Chuck Jones Interviewed" by Joe Adamson, in Danny and Gerald Peary, eds., *The American Animated Cartoon* (New York: Dutton, 1980), 130.

3. During the past quarter century, the nature of my access to pornography has changed, and the two sections of this essay reflect this change. When I wrote "Confessions of a Feminist Porn Watcher" in 1983, I accessed pornographic films in public theaters and in the arcades attached to sales outlets for pornographic materials; later, I owned several 8mm porn films and an 8mm film projector; and in recent years, I have relied on two DVDs, one of which is the focus of the addendum.

Love Story (1981), a polemical documentary on the nature and impact of porn films. On the other hand, I've long felt and, in a small way, have been supportive of the struggle for equality and self-determination for women; as a result, the consistent concern of feminist women about the exploitation and brutalization of the female in pornography has gnawed at my conscience. The frequent contempt of intelligent people for those who "need" pornographic materials has always functioned to keep me quiet about my real feelings, but a screening of *Not a Love Story* and a series of recent responses to it—most notably the B. Ruby Rich review quoted above—have emboldened me to assess my attitudes.

Not a Love Story's fundamental assumption is familiar: pornography is a reflection of a male-dominated culture in which women's bodies are exploited for the purpose of providing pleasure to males by dramatizing sexual fantasies that themselves imply a reconfirmation of male dominance. And while it is tempting to accept this seemingly self-evident assumption, at a deeper level, I find it unconvincing. The pornographic films and videotapes I've seen at theaters and in arcades *are* full of narratives in which women not only do what men want and allow men to do what they want but effusively claim to love this particular sexual balance of power. Yet, given that males dominate in the culture, why would they pay to see sexual fantasies of male domination? Wouldn't one expect fantasy material to reveal the opposite of the status quo? Further, if going to porn films or arcades were emblematic of male power, one might expect that the experience would be characterized by an easy confidence reflective of macho security.

For me, however—and, I'm guessing, for many men who have visited porn arcades or film houses—these periodic visits are always minor traumas. While there is an erotic excitement involved in the decision to go to a porn arcade, this is mixed with fear and embarrassment. From the instant my car is carrying me toward pornography, I feel painfully visible, as if everyone who sees me knows precisely where I'm going. The walk from the car to the door—and later, from the door to the car—is especially difficult: will someone drive by and see me? This fear of being seen has, in my case at least (as far as I can tell), less to do with guilt than with a fear of being misunderstood. Even though the frequency of my experiences with pornography has nothing at all to do with the success of my sex life—I'm at least as likely to visit a porn arcade when I'm sexually active as when I'm lonely and horny—I always feel the power of the social stigma against accessing pornography. Unless the people who see me have been in my situation, I'm sure they'll deduce that my visit to the arcade reflects my inadequacy or some inadequacy in the person I'm living with, that either I "can't get any" or I'm not satisfied with what I can get. As a result, I try to look at ease during the walk to the door: any evident discomfiture on my part, I warn myself, will only fuel whatever laughter my presence has provoked.

Once I'm inside an arcade or a theater, this anxiety about being seen continues, though with a different slant: will I run smack into someone I know? Of course, anyone I would run into would be unlikely to misunderstand the meaning of my presence. But such a meeting would interfere with what seems to me the most fundamental dimension of going to a porn arcade or movie house: the desire for privacy and anonymity. Meeting someone I know would, I assume (this has never happened to me), force us to join together in the phony macho pose of pretending that our interest in the pornographic materials around us is largely a matter of detached humor, that we've come for a few laughs.

The concern for privacy determines the nature of the interaction of the men (I've seen women at porn theaters, but never in porn arcades) involved with porn. Of course, theaters are constructed so as to impede the interactions of members of the audience (I always feel a pressure not to look at people on my way out), but the structure of arcades makes some interaction between strangers almost inevitable. In retrospect, the nature and apparent meaning of this interaction always seems rather poignant. Because of our shared embarrassment about being in this place together and, perhaps, because of our awareness that our presence is a sign of an erotic impatience our casual stances belie—for whatever reason, the men I've seen in porn arcades seem to allow themselves a detached gentleness with each other. For my part—and, judging from my limited observation, I'd guess my experience is pretty standard—I move in an unthreatening way; I am careful not to make eye contact with anyone. When eye contact is unavoidable, I put my mind on erase. When I walk out of a porn arcade, I take with me no functional memory at all of the particular faces I saw there, though each visit has confirmed my feeling that in general, the faces are those of quiet middle-class men pretty much like me.

I've always assumed that, essentially, those of us who coexist with one another for a few minutes in porn theaters or arcades share the embarrassing awareness that we're there for the same thing: to look for a while at forbidden sexual imagery that excites us and, finally, to masturbate. In my experience, the masturbation itself seems less important as an experience than as a way of releasing the excitement created by the imagery. Even though most men seem to look rigorously frontward in porn theaters and even though porn arcade booths are designed so as to provide enough security for masturbation, the idea of being seen masturbating has always seemed so frightening to me (and, I assume, to others: I've never seen or heard anyone masturbate in an arcade) that I've never felt free to get deeply involved in the act the way I can when I have real privacy. At a porn arcade I usually keep myself from masturbating for ten or twenty minutes, until I'm ready to leave; the act itself rarely takes more than fifteen or thirty seconds, and as soon as it's over, I'm on my way to my car. I move quickly because, often, despite my confidence that the other men I see have much the same experience I do, I leave terrified that someone will enter the booth I've just left, see the semen on the floor—impossible in the dimly lit booths—and yell after me. I've never masturbated in a theater (though on rare occasions I've seen others do so), but only later, outside the theater, in the privacy of a car or a men's room.

Since the reason for braving the kinesic complexity of the porn environment is exposure to the pornographic materials themselves, it's important to consider what these materials really are. Over the years I've developed what I hope is a generally accurate sense of the motifs that dominate standard porn fare directed at heterosexual men, and I've thought a good deal about why these particular motifs seem so pervasive. I'm speaking of "motifs" here rather than "films" because the films seem centered (both in terms of the time allocated to specific imagery and in terms of the viewing gaze) on specific configurations, "acts." Even though there's always a skeletal narrative, this is so obviously a function of the need to create a context for the motifs that one doesn't need to pay particular attention to it—except insofar as it raises the adrenaline by slightly withholding the awaited imagery.[4] The empty nature of the porn narratives is confirmed by the booths, which, in my experience, all present Super-8mm films in loops, usually two or three films to a loop. Since each quarter, or whatever the fee is, buys only thirty seconds or so of film (then the film stops until another quarter is deposited), one doesn't automatically see a film from start to finish. The motif structure is also reconfirmed by the announcement on booth doors of the particular acts that are featured in particular booths.[5]

4. In this sense, the porn narratives seem rather similar to those of Georges Méliès's films, where narrative is primarily an excuse for cine-magic tricks.

5. Once I've decided to go to a porn theater, I go immediately, without checking to see when the features begin or end (if the theater runs shows continuously); as often as not, I arrive in the middle of a film. When a theater runs only one or two shows a day, I usually postpone a decision about going until just long enough before the beginning of the show so that the decision can be followed by immediate action and minimal waiting for the film to begin. I've nearly always left before a feature is over; after one film has led up to and past its most stimulating motifs, I've waited only long enough to calm down and not leave the theater with a visible erection. I've never sat all the way through a double feature of porn films.

For me, the obvious amateurishness of the production values and the acting has generally added to the titillating mood, since what the characters do to and with one another is all the more outrageous *because* it's so patently done for the camera. In fact, some acts appear so uncomfortable and pleasureless for the actors that the camera's presence seems the only possible explanation. Our consciousness of the films as films is maintained by the camera angles, the length of shots, and the lighting, all of which are usually (or at least this is how I remember them) overtly functional, providing a clear view of the sex acts. In most of these films, "aesthetics" are rigorously avoided in service of clarity.

The motifs themselves generally involve a relatively limited number of sexual interactions. Sexual intercourse in a variety of poses is nearly inevitable, of course, but it's rarely the clincher in a film. Judging from my limited experience, blow jobs (especially ending in ejaculation into the woman's mouth or on her face) and anal intercourse seem the present-day favorites. Sometimes they involve more than a pair of partners (two men have intercourse—one vaginally, one anally—with one woman; two women provide a blow job to one man; a woman gives a blow job to one man while another has intercourse with her) and/or a mixture of ethnic backgrounds. While the women involved seem to mirror conventional notions of attractiveness, the men are frequently quite average-looking: nearly any man will do, apparently, so long as he has a large erection.

No doubt the psychology of wanting to view sexual performances on a movie screen is complex, but over the years I've been aware of two general functions of the experience: one of these involves its "educational" value, the other its value as psychic release. When I was younger, my interest was in seeing just what the female body looked like and how it moved. Sexuality, as I experienced it as an adolescent, was something that usually occurred in the dark, in enclosed spaces, and under the pressure of time. Often I was more engrossed in the issue of "how far I was going to be able to go" than with really seeing and understanding what I was doing. In those days (the fifties), there were no porn films or arcades, but newsstands were beginning to stock *Playboy, Nugget,* and a variety of other girlie magazines, and my hunger to see women's bodies—and to be able to examine them without the embarrassment of being observed by the women—resulted in periodic thefts of these magazines. For me, these thefts were serious extralegal transgressions; I was terrified of being caught, arrested, and made an example of.

These early magazines seemed a godsend to me, and they provided the stimulation for countless hours of masturbation. But they were also carefully censored: the focus was on breasts, though there were frequent side views of demurely posed buttocks; all vestiges of pubic hair were, for some strange reason, erased from the photographs (I didn't realize this until I was sixteen and had the shock of my life during a heavy petting session!). One can certainly imagine a culture, like that of the Polynesians, in which the bodies of members of the opposite sex would not be visual mysteries, where we could be at ease with seeing one another. But though that is not the case in the United States, men continue to grow up under considerable pressure to know "how to handle" women sexually: we're supposed to know what's where and how it works. Looking at girlie magazines may seem (and be) a callous manipulation of female bodies, but its function was never callous for me. I was powerfully drawn to girls, but my complete ignorance of them frightened me; the magazines were like a nightlight: they allowed me the fantasy (I always knew it was an illusion) that I'd "know what to do" the next time I got to see and touch a flesh-and-blood girl.

The functioning of pornographic imagery as a means of allowing men to examine the bodies of the opposite sex seems an important aspect of porn films and videotapes, which are full of extreme close-ups of cocks thrusting into cunts. The ludicrous lack of romance in such imagery is often mentioned in condemnations of pornography, but its function seems more scientific than romantic, more like Muybridge's motion studies than a Hollywood love story. And it seems to me that the value of this visual option continues to be defensible, at least in a limited sense, given this society's pervasive marketing of rigidly defined standards of attractiveness. For one thing, direct sexual experience with a conventionally attractive woman is, or seems, out of the question for many men, and yet it's come to be one of the definers of a life worth living. Pornography provides a compromise by making visual knowledge of such an experience a possibility. Second, many men feel supportive enough of women to take them seriously when they complain about the invasion of privacy implicit in the unprovoked leers and comments they continue to endure on the street. I'll go to considerable lengths to avoid intruding in this way, but I have to fight the urge to stare all the time. Some of the popularity of pornography even among men who consider themselves feminists may be a function of its capacity to provide a form of unintrusive leering.

I've become conscious of a second aspect of this first function of pornographic materials, the "educational" function, during the past few years. Feminists have made us aware of the politics of staring at women, but the culture at large—particularly the culture as evident in the commercial sphere—tells us constantly that looking at women is what men (and women) are supposed to do. Looking at other men continues to be another matter entirely. Of course, spectator sports, and other forms of physical performance, allow for almost unlimited examination of how bodies function, but knowledge of the naked male body continues to be a tricky matter for heterosexual men. In conventional American life, men are probably naked together more often than women: in shower rooms, most obviously. And yet, as is true in porn arcades, the kinesics of the interaction between men in such places are very precisely controlled. Men certainly don't feel free to look at other men; our lives are full of stories about how one guy catches another looking at him and punches him. Never mind that I've never witnessed such an incident: a taboo is at stake, and potential embarrassment, if not danger, seems to hover on the edge of it. This situation is complicated further by the fact that even if men felt free to look carefully at one another in shower rooms, or wherever, a crucial element of the male body—how it functions during sexual activity—would remain a mystery. Of course, I know what my own erection looks like, but so much stress is placed on the nature of erections that it's difficult not to wonder what the erections of other men look like (and how mine looks in comparison).

One of the things that distinguishes the pornographic materials available in porn movies and arcades from what is available on local newsstands—and thus, implicitly, one of the things that accounts for the size of the hardcore porn market—is the pervasive presence of erections. In fact, to a considerable extent, theater and arcade porn films are about erections. The standard antiporn response to this is to see the porn film phallus as a combined battering ram / totem that encapsulates the male drive for power. And given the characterizations of the vain, strutting men on the other ends of these frequently awesome shafts, such an interpretation seems almost inevitable. And yet, for me the pervasiveness of erect penises in porn has mostly to do with simple curiosity. The darkness of porn houses and the privacy of arcade booths allow one to see erections close-up. The presence of women has its own power, but in this particular context, one of the primary functions of the female presence is to serve as a sign—to others and to oneself—that looking at erections, even finding them sexy, does not mean that the viewer defines himself as a homosexual.

A second function of the pornographic experience involves the implications for men of a number of cultural attitudes that feminists have often seen as subtly detrimental to women. Most people now recognize that the constant attention to the "beauty" of the female body, which has been so pervasive in the arts and in commerce during recent centuries, may involve more than a respect and love for women—that it may be a tactic for keeping them more involved with how they look (and to a considerable extent, with pleasing men) than with what they do, or can learn to do. Further, the emphasis on a pristine ideal of beauty, as feminists have often pointed out, has frequently alienated women from their own bodies: real odors, secretions, processes have frequently been seen as a contradiction of the Beauty of Womanhood. On the other hand, the same cultural history that has defined women as Beautiful has had, and to some extent continues to have, as its inevitable corollary the Ugliness of men; women have been defined as beautiful precisely in contrast to men. Now, even if these definitions are seen as primarily beneficial to men, in the sense that not having to be concerned with appearances allows them more energy and time for attaining their goals and maintaining their access to power, I sense that the definition also creates significant problems for men, especially in the areas of love and sex, where physical attractiveness seems of the essence. It's true that in recent years, we've seen a growing acceptance of the idea that men, too, can be beautiful. And yet, just as the pressure to see women as "the weaker sex" continues to be felt in a culture where millions of women dramatize the intrinsic bankruptcy of that notion, many men—I'd guess most men—continue to feel insecure about the attractiveness of their own bodies.

Perhaps the most obvious aspect of male sexual functioning that has been conditioned by negative assumptions about male attractiveness is ejaculation. Even among people who are comfortable with the idea that men can be beautiful, semen is often (if not usually) seen as disgusting. Is it an accident that many of the substances that our culture considers particularly revolting—raw eggs, snot—share with semen a general texture and look? Accidental or not, I've heard and read such comparisons all my life. I remember the shock and fear that followed my first orgasm. Without knowing it, I had been masturbating in the attic of my aunt's house, where I had discovered a pile of girlie magazines. The unexpected orgasm was astonishing and thrilling, but at the end of it, I discovered, to my shock, that my shirt and the magazine were covered with a substance I hadn't known existed. I cleaned myself up (even at that early point I was clear that for my relatives—especially my mother and my aunt—the mysterious substance would be a form of dirtiness), and I spent the remainder of the day walking around with my arms and hands in odd configurations in front of my shirt in the hope of avoiding detection. From that time on, I was alert to the fact that every indulgence of my desire for sex would produce disgusting evidence, the discovery of which, I was sure, could be humiliating.

Now, I'm well aware that to accept a mucus-like substance that comes out of one's own body is a different matter than accepting such a substance from another's body. I not only understand but can also empathize with the revulsion of many women to semen. Nevertheless, I suspect it creates the same problems for many men as the widespread squeamishness about menstruation has caused women. There are instances of course—in the midst of passion—when semen is temporarily accepted, even enjoyed by women, but these moments tend to be memorable exceptions. For the most part, even between people who love each other, the presence of semen is at best a necessary evil. Many women are concerned about the danger of "bleeding through" during menstruation, presumably because they feel, or fear that men feel, that menstrual secretions make them sexually undesirable; dozens of products have been marketed to protect against such an occurrence. I feel a similar concern about semen and must face a very special irony: the fact that it surfaces precisely at the moment of my most complete sexual abandon.

To me, pornography has always seemed understandable as a way for men to periodically deal with the cultural context that works against their full acceptance of themselves as sexual beings. The fantasies men pay to experience in porn arcade booths and movie houses may appear to be predicated on the brutalization of women. But from a male point of view, the desire is not to see women harmed but to momentarily identify with men who—despite their personal unattractiveness (by conventional cultural definitions), despite the unwieldy size of their erections, and despite their aggressiveness with their semen—are adored by the women they encounter sexually. Only in pornography will the fantasy woman demonstrate happy acceptance when a man ejaculates on her face. As embarrassingly abhorrent as it always strikes me, the hostility toward women that usually seems to hover around the edges of conventional film pornography (in the frequently arrogant, presumptive manner the male characters exhibit, for example) and that is a primary subject matter in some films, seems to be a more aggressive way of dealing with the same issues. In these instances, the fantasy is in punishing resistant women for their revulsion. Of course, the punishments—usually one form or another of rape—often end with the fantasy woman's discovery of an insatiable hunger for whatever has been done to her. This frequent turnabout appears to be nothing more than a reconfirmation of the stupid, brutal myth that women ask to be raped or enjoy being raped, but—as sadly ironic as this seems—it could also be seen as evidence that, in the final analysis, men don't mean harm to women, or don't wish to mean harm to women: their fantasy is the acceptance of their own biological nature by women.[6] I've always assumed that porn and rape *are* part of the same general problem, though I've always felt it more likely that porn offers an outlet for some of the anger engendered by men's feelings of sensual/aesthetic inferiority than that it serves as a fuel for further anger. But I'm only speaking from my own experience. I've rarely spoken frankly about such matters with other men who use porn.

To try to understand the reasons for the huge business of making and marketing pornographic movies is not necessarily to justify the practice. One can only hope for increasingly definitive studies of how porn functions and what its effects are.[7] But, however one describes the complex historical fac-

6. The inclusion of anal sex in porn films seems to confuse this, at least if one assumes that anal sex is annoying and painful for most, or many, women. Yet a decision not to press for fulfillment of such a desire because its fulfillment will cause pain doesn't necessarily eliminate the desire. I would guess that for many men, the anal sex in porn films functions as a way of giving harmless vent to a desire they've decided not to pressure the real women in their lives about (harmless, that is, unless one assumes the women in the films feel they are being harmed, something I have no information about).

7. One recent attempt to assess porn's effects is Dolf Zillmann and Jennings Bryant's "Pornography and Sexual Callousness, and the Trivialization of Rape," *Journal of Communication* 32, no. 4 (December 1982), 10–21. Unfortunately, this study's central finding—"our investigation focused on sexual callousness toward women, demonstrating that massive exposure to standard pornographic materials devoid of coercion and aggression seemed to promote . . . callousness (in particular, the trivialization of rape)"—is based on testing procedures and supported by assumptions that raise nagging questions. The study's conclusions are based on a test of the impact of pornography on students exposed in groups, in a college setting, to "massive," "intermediate," and "no" amounts of conventional, nonviolent pornographic film. But in real life, porn films are seen in a very particular environment, at least in most instances I know of: in a public/private context outside the circle of one's friends and family, in places one is embarrassed about going into, and often in tiny, toilet stall–like enclosures. Wouldn't the meaning and impact of porn films be different given so different a context? Was there some reason for limiting those tested to students and in particular to undergraduates "at a large eastern university"? Were these people previous users of pornography? What was their motivation for participating in such an experiment?

Bryant and Zillman face some of the possible implications of their experimental procedures for their results, but they assume that, at most, students might have guessed the researchers were attempting to legitimize pornography and therefore would have distorted answers in the direction of a general social attitude that, the researchers contend, is strongly supportive of pornography and implicitly legitimizes it by giving it legal status. My sense of the general attitude toward porn is the opposite of theirs. Certainly, the legality of pornography doesn't prove that society approves of it: picking one's nose is legal, but hardly acceptable in society's eyes. My guess is that most people (including many or most of those who use porn and/or are supportive of its being available publicly to people of legal age) agree that porn is creepy and disgusting. And most people nowadays are well aware of the frequent conjecture that exposure to porn is an incentive to rape; even if we're dubious about the assumption of cause/effect in this instance, the contention creates concern. If the students tested were relatively new to porn, their massive exposure must have come as something of a shock, and if they were jolted—particularly by seeing such imagery in an institutional, unprivate context—might not some students have answered the rape questions posed later as a means of acceding to the widely held assumption that people who see porn films will be motivated by the films to rape women?

tors that have brought us to our present situation, the fact remains that in our culture men and women frequently feel alienated from their own bodies and from one another. Pornography is a function of this alienation, and I can't imagine it disappearing until we have come to see ourselves and each other differently. We don't choose the bodies we are born with; natural selection, or God—or whatever—takes care of that for us. And though we can't change the fact of our difference (and regardless of whether we choose to accept and enjoy this difference by being passionate about our own or the opposite sex, or both), surely we can learn to be mutually supportive about our bodies. My guess is that porn is a symptom not so much of a sexual need but of a need for self-acceptance and respect. If we can come to terms with that need, as it relates to both sexes, my guess is that porn will disappear.

ADDENDUM, 2008

Now that most pornography is shot and distributed directly on video, without first opening in a theater or receiving the notoriety of a work collectively witnessed by a large group, the text's temporal context is even less apparent. The tape slips onto a shelf, is rented or not, and its possible sociological or historical impact recedes into the background. This apparent timelessness, though, is only the illusion of a group of texts that the parent culture would prefer to disown: part of the challenge of reading them is to put them back into time, to note the historical demarcations in the seeming monolith, the way they are as much about change as about repetition.

Linda Williams, *Hard Core*[8]

I too had received identity by my body,
That I was, I knew was of my body, and what I should be, I knew I should
  be of my body.

Walt Whitman, "Crossing Brooklyn Ferry"[9]

Twenty-five years have passed since "Confessions" was published, and as Linda Williams suggests in the epigraph, much has changed, though much remains the same. Certainly, one thing that has remained the same is my dread about writing openly and personally about pornography. My original decision to write about my experiences with porn was made the week

8. Linda Williams, *Hard Core: Power, Pleasure, and the "Frenzy of the Visible"* (Berkeley: University of California Press, 1999), 268–9.

9. The final lines of part 5 of Whitman's "Crossing Brooklyn Ferry" (originally called "Sun-Down Poem"), in *Selected Poems, 1855–1892: A New Edition,* ed. Gary Schmidgall (New York: St. Martin's Press, 1999), 137. I am grateful to P. Adams Sitney's chapter on Marie Menken in *Eyes Upside Down* (New York: Oxford University Press, 2008) for this reference.

before my wife had surgery to remove what turned out to be fibroids in her uterus, and I was terrified that she might not live. I decided to write the piece on the day of the surgery and during the recovery, to fill those hours when I could not be with Pat in the hospital; I hoped that writing an embarrassing essay about ideas I felt committed to might help distract me for a few hours. Fortunately, I am not writing in such circumstances now, but there is still considerable embarrassment about being seen as "exposing myself" in public (I'm a *grandfather,* of two young girls!).

On the other hand, recent decades have produced considerable research and writing about pornography, which, of course, is liberating: obviously, what I suggest about pornography here is at most a tiny, barely visible part of an ongoing discourse. In any case, to republish "Confessions of a Feminist Porn Watcher" *without* an addendum has seemed problematic, both to my editors at University of California Press and to me. To publish the original essay without further comment would be a way of arguing for honest discussion about pornography while avoiding honesty *now.* I am going to assume that my writing frankly about my own experiences, once again, however briefly, may provide a way into the activities and thinking of a considerable number of men (I am sure my experiences must be reasonably typical), and a way of providing a sense of some of the ways in which boys and men of different ages have used pornography during the past quarter century.

Not long ago, one of my sons told me, "Every man has a stash." My stash has always been small. During the past few years, I have relied on two DVDs that I bought from Adult World here in Utica, New York: one produced by Anabolic Digital (number 8 in the *Explicit* series), the other produced by Hustler Video (number 6 in the *Barely Legal* series). I have always hidden whatever porn is in the house: from my children when they lived at home, from my wife of thirty-plus years (it would embarrass me if she were to see the covers of these DVDs), and to some degree, I suppose, from myself (the DVDs seem to give the lie to what I think of as my feminism). I have never wanted to study porn very seriously, since studying it would mean seeing a lot of it; I'm not sure I would trust my motives, and there are too many other forms of cinema that matter more to me.

Although the way in which I access porn has changed in twenty-five years, the particular nature of what I am drawn to has been relatively consistent. I have never been drawn to the more exotic forms of porn—fetish material, S&M, violence, child porn. What I am drawn to seems relatively conventional, at least judging from my infrequent scans of porn store shelves. In the old theater and arcade days, porn was presented as a set of acts within a narrative, but the advent of computers and DVD players seems to have eliminated most vestiges of narrative, both in the material itself and in the way the new technologies allow us to access this material. In other words, the new technologies allow us to be quite clear about which particular motifs within the spectrum of a two-hour DVD are most effective in creating the excitement necessary for masturbation. And knowing the effectiveness of these motifs allows one to conjecture about what exactly it is that instigates that excitement.

It seems to me that there are three general functions of the forms of porn that I am drawn to. Two of these were clear to me when I wrote "Confessions," though as a senior citizen I have a somewhat different perspective on them now; the third is an extension of the second, made particularly clear by my Anabolic DVD. When I was working to remember my earliest engagements with porn during the writing of "Confessions," I remembered the "educational" value of porn for young men growing up during a remarkably repressive and secretive era (the 1950s and early 1960s). This educational value is long gone: one hour of prime-time television or a single movie makes more nudity and dramatized sexuality available to audiences than months of desperate adolescent searching could have uncovered in those days. Nudity, especially of women, and overt sexual innuendo are ubiquitous. Obviously, though, the bodies marketed on TV, in the movies, and in magazines are very particular bodies: buff, slim bodies that often seem less like living organisms than like sculpture, and (on the new weight-reduction reality shows) obese bodies, grotesquely fascinating in the way Divine, Edith Massey, and Jean Hill were in John Waters's early films.

The most evident function of contemporary pornography seems pretty much what it always has been: porn imagery provides safe visual and auditory knowledge of, even a kind of participation in, certain sexual experiences that are, or are perceived as, unavailable. The most pervasive motif in the porn I'm aware of is the "cum shot": specifically, ejaculation into the mouth or onto the face of a young woman. Indeed, this action seems the essence of much pornography. My Anabolic DVD is entitled *A Cum Sucking Whore Named Kacey;* nearly every episode ends with a cum shot, and the DVD concludes with its only special feature: a "cum shot re-cap." To the extent that men can be understood as identifying with the men in porn performances, the implications of the pervasiveness of the cum shot seem obvious. Even if one has the good fortune to be with a woman who is not averse to fellatio, over the course of an extended relationship, the romantic excitement that can make ejaculation into the mouth or onto the face a pleasure tends to diminish, particularly for the partner. If one loves one's partner, demanding that she perform activities that are repellent to her is untenable. Much the same is true of anal intercourse, which has become far more conventional in recent years, at least in porn films, than it was when I wrote "Confessions."

Watching such activities in a porn dramatization provides a convenient substitute for performing them, a way of "knowing" the experiences without fully engaging in them.[10] In other words, on one level porn offers opportunities to indulge that portion of our heterosexual desire that we feel is suppressed by the gender roles modern conventional society expects us to play and/or by our commitment to a beloved within a relationship. Our evolutionary biology may suggest to us that the more partners we impregnate, the better for our species, but our status as socialized beings suggests that we control that relentless evolutionary hunger. Within this context, pornography—used as a catalyst for indulging in masturbation—seems analogous to those safety ramps on highways that allow trucks to exit the highway during a long downhill run if their brakes fail.

In "Confessions" I argued that the lure of pornography is more complex than it may first seem, certainly more complex than it seemed to many women who decried its pervasiveness in the late 1970s and early 1980s. Much conventional porn seems a confirmation of both heterosexuality—women are displayed and used for men's pleasure—and a deep-seated misogyny. At first glance, this does not seem to have changed much over the past quarter century. With a single exception, the men who use "Kacey" in my Anabolic DVD seem remarkably unengaged with her; she provides them with pleasure, but they seem utterly detached psychologically. The exception is the segment of the DVD devoted to the sexual interplay of Kacey and an African American man who does express his pleasure and his gratitude to her for this pleasure, to which Kacey appears to respond in kind. (The fact that this is the only segment of the DVD in which a lone man performs with Kacey suggests the continuing power of racial taboo: I am guessing that the interracial sexuality in this segment was assumed to have the prurient power of Kacey's interaction with two or more men in other sections of the DVD.)

A central contention of "Confessions" was that for many if not most men, a second function of what appears to be heterosexual porn is in fact the opportunity to gaze at the erections and ejaculations of other men. This continues to seem incontrovertible to me, since erections and ejaculations are

10. Of course, I recognize that while these activities are "convenient" for those who use porn materials, they may be at best hard, unpleasant labor for the young women performing. I must hope—recognizing the considerable likelihood that this is a self-serving delusion—that these women are better treated and better paid than may have been the norm for the women performing in porn films twenty-five years ago.

the subjects of nearly all close-ups within porn and provide, literally and figuratively, the climax of most porn episodes. Further, the frequency with which two or more male partners have sex with a single female in porn not only confirms the priority of male sexuality in these films but records men having sex "together." In the "gang-bang" segment of my Anabolic DVD, Kacey is the lone woman among many men—or should I say, many erections and ejaculations—and in several other episodes on the DVD, two men orgasm and ejaculate onto Kacey, one immediately after another. Even the general detachment of nearly all the men on this DVD, their seeming obliviousness to this young woman's considerable attractiveness, confirms that the motivator of their sexual excitement is not their desire for a woman but a fascination with their own erections and ejaculations and those of other men. It is clear in all these multiple-male, one-woman episodes that the men not immediately engaged in intercourse or receiving fellatio are watching other men perform and appear to be stimulated by what they see.

While I would not argue that all men who are excited by seeing male sexuality in a porn DVD are repressed homosexuals, I would suggest that their excitement in watching men in porn does provide a stimulation and release of that portion of their desire that *is* homosexual and that they have, therefore, repressed. My assumption here is that in general, our desire involves a fundamental combination of the desires of both the sexes that produce us: that just as we are combinations of male and female DNA, our libido combines male and female forms of desire. Because of our individual biological natures and the particular circumstances within which we grow up, one or another aspect of this complex desire may come to be primary for us—and we may come to define ourselves as "heterosexual" or "homosexual"—but those nonprimary aspects of desire do not disappear, and are often revealed by, and indulged in, pornography.

Assuming that my Anabolic DVD is typical of at least one range of recent pornography (the DVD was produced in 2002), there's a suggestive change in porn filmmaking strategy. It is a change that confirms some of the implications of the central fascination with erections and ejaculations in "heterosexual porn," and it provides porn's third function. Kacey continually breaks the fourth wall and looks at the camera as she is performing. Kacey's consistent visual connection with the viewer confirms our connection, our complicity, with her.

In *Orlando* (1992), Sally Potter's remarkable adaptation of the Virginia Woolf novel, the "male gaze" is confronted by having the protagonist look at and speak directly to the audience from within the narrative; this is Potter's method of creating what she calls a "connectedness" between Orlando

Orlando (Tilda Swinton), with Shelmerdine (Billy Zane), meeting the viewer's gaze in Sally Potter's *Orlando* (1992). Courtesy Sally Potter.

and the moviegoer. Even when Orlando suddenly transforms from male to female partway through the film, our ongoing exchange of looks with the character has caused us to feel intimate enough with the particular personality that lies beneath her sex that we accept this change as just another strange thing that has happened to a person we know; Orlando has become like a friend with whom we share knowing glances during social occasions.[11]

Especially since we rarely see the faces of the men (or anything in their faces besides their concentration), the gaze we seem to exchange with Kacey becomes a kind of personal connection, almost the only such connection in the DVD, since (again, with the exception of the segment with the African American man) Kacey doesn't make eye contact with any of her partners (except very briefly during a few transitional moments, when the performers are reorienting themselves, apparently at the request of the director).[12] This

11. See my interview with Potter in *A Critical Cinema 3* (Berkeley: University of California Press, 1998), 418–19.

12. Scott Stark's remarkable film *NOEMA* (1998) is a montage of moments from porn videos during which performers are reorienting themselves for the next segment of the performance. During these moments, they seem to become vulnerable—the opposite of their apparent assurance during the performances themselves. Stark creates a haunting, surreal ballet from these moments.

is confirmed by the fact that during many of the close-ups in which Kacey looks at "me," her male partner or partners are only partly visible; sometimes only their erections are on-screen. Kacey doesn't *speak* "to us," as Orlando does, but she continually vocalizes her pleasure openly and passionately, whereas the men voice only a few relatively detached sounds during ejaculation.

As I watch and hear Kacey have sex with one man after another, or with two men at once, the illusion of personal connection created by her gaze at "me," and by her vocally sharing her reaction to the sex, tends to create a powerful, erotic identification not with the men but with Kacey. At this level of the experience, when I am watching this DVD, I am identifying *as a woman* during a series of sexual engagements with men. Of course, here again, the woman's presence may be functioning simply as a sign that the man's enjoyment of the spectacle of male sexuality is not evidence of homosexual desire. But I think more is involved. This dimension of the DVD recalls both Hesiod's explanation of Tiresias's blindness and Linda Williams's *Hard Core.*

As the reader may remember, Tiresias, who had been both man and woman, was asked by Zeus and Hera to decide whether women or men had more pleasure during sex. When Tiresias answered that women had far more pleasure, an angry Hera blinded him, and in response, Zeus provided Tiresias with his legendary abilities as a seer. Linda Williams uses this classic myth to suggest "that hard-core pornography is a speculation about pleasure that begins, as does Tiresias, from a phallic perspective, journeys to the unseen world of the sexual other, and returns to tell the story. An ideal of bisexuality drives the quest for the knowledge of the pleasure of the other: that one sex can journey to the unknown other and return, satiated with knowledge and pleasure, to the security of the 'self.'"[13] My Anabolic DVD provides an evocation of Tiresias's experience and an example of Williams's analysis: it offers an opportunity for an aroused male to "become," for a moment, a woman enjoying the sexual experiences of male fantasy. However we understand the complex implications of Kacey's gaze at the camera, it is clear that here, in private, by using pornography, a man can become a "seer," at least of what some particular sexual fantasies might look and sound like, might feel like, were he able to become a woman (or were he willing to become a gay man) and participate in them.

One final thought. For many if not most men, what we see and hear in pornography is not, of course, what we want most deeply and *know* that we

13. Williams, *Hard Core,* 279.

want most deeply: abiding intimacy with a partner, within which sexuality is an ongoing, evolving pleasure. And we want to experience the excitement and pleasure of sex with our partner, as part of this intimacy, not simply as a series of detached "acts" within a performance. The porn I've discussed here, and the porn I've been aware of all these years, has nothing to do with this quest for intimacy—quite the opposite. Which raises the question: Why would one continue to use pornography if one had found real intimacy?

I believe that even when we achieve intimacy with a loving partner, most of us refuse to abandon another, earlier intimacy: that pleasure in our own bodies and in our own fantasies that begins in early childhood and continues throughout our lives. Stan Brakhage's *Vein* (1965), which intercuts between his infant son fondling himself and time-lapse imagery of stars moving through the night sky, suggests that this early pleasure, perhaps the first pleasure we can control, has cosmic implications. The rediscovery of our bodies at the onset of puberty reenergizes and sexualizes this early pleasure, which—even in the midst of other intimacies—remains basic to our sense of self, a sense of our physical self as *our own*. In Jean Genet's still remarkable film *Un chant d'amour* (1950), imprisoned men are depicted as pleasuring themselves with abandon. Despite—and to some degree because of—their confinement, these men continue to find erotic pleasure in their own bodies and in their own fantasies. A man may dream of an intimate, fulfilling relationship with a woman or with another man (and may even be lucky enough to find one), but his relationship with his own body remains one thing that the societal prison he lives in cannot entirely control. He takes pleasure in himself, therefore he is.

Interview with George Kuchar (on the Weather Diaries)

Since the late 1950s, George Kuchar has been a remarkably prolific moving-image maker. At first, he collaborated with his twin brother, Mike, on a series of 8mm melodramas that simultaneously imitated and critiqued the Hollywood films the brothers haunted local New York City theaters to see. In films like *Lust for Ecstasy* (1963) and *A Town Called Tempest* (1963), they revealed considerable awareness of the rhetoric (and absurdities) of Hollywood films. By the mid-sixties, the Kuchars had become part of the New York Underground scene, and a major influence on what would come to be called "trash film" (John Waters: "Really, George and Mike Kuchar influenced me more than anybody" [interview with Waters in Scott MacDonald, *A Critical Cinema* (Berkeley: University of California Press, 1988), 227]; see pp. 34–43 in this volume for a discussion of trash film).

After 1964, George worked independently of his brother, producing dozens of 16mm melodramas. It is difficult to think of a more amusingly insightful and visually arresting critique of the independent filmmaking process than *Hold Me While I'm Naked* (1965) or of a more funkily elegant journey into the bizarre than *A Reason to Live* (1976). By the 1980s, Kuchar had settled into a rhythm of regularly producing 16mm melodramas with his students at the San Francisco Art Institute, where he has taught film production since 1971, and at least one 16mm melodrama of his own. From time to time, however, Kuchar has also revealed a somewhat different sensibility, one more directly diaristic and autobiographical (the melodramas are often deflected autobiographies). *Encyclopedia of the Blessed* (1968), for example, is a lovely diary of his travels with artists Red Grooms and Mimi Gross.

By the mid-1980s, the economic accessibility and improving technological options of video had attracted Kuchar. He quickly became committed to the new medium—and impatient with those "purists" who were holding out against video in the name of film. If he had been a prolific 8mm and 16mm filmmaker (of major American independents, probably only Stan

Brakhage has been more prolific), his output in video has been astonishing. In fact, the Video Data Bank has produced a separate catalogue just for Kuchar's videos.

While Kuchar's videotapes reveal his ongoing commitment to melodrama, the economic advantages of video seem to have freed his autobiographical impulses. Kuchar has made "Video Albums" (which for a time focused on his dear friend, filmmaker Curt McDowell, who died of AIDS in 1987) and "Video Postcards," travel diaries of trips to American tourist sites with friends. But his most memorable videos are probably the series of what he calls "Weather Diaries," which began in 1986, nearly all of them set in El Reno, Oklahoma, a small town thirty miles west of Oklahoma City in the heart of "Tornado Alley," during May—tornado season. Kuchar has been fascinated with weather in general, and tornadoes in particular, since his youth. During the years when he filmed in El Reno, he was not exactly a "storm *chaser*," since he does not drive; he seems to have visited El Reno in the hope that storms would chase him!

The Weather Diaries are, in a sense, Kuchar's meditation on himself. *Weather Diary 1* (1986), the prototype of the series, is a modern-day *Walden* in which Kuchar confronts nature not, like Thoreau, in the woods, but "in the sticks." In *Weather Diary 1*, the funkiness of Kuchar's cheap motel and his involvement with simple realities, including his own bodily processes, combine with the sublimity of his shots of landscape and skyscape, and with his sensitivity to the tiny beauties of nature in and around the motel, to create a sometimes lovely, sometimes shocking, sometimes funny, often poignant (eighty-one-minute) evocation of a man alone with himself. Subsequent Weather Diaries have varied in mood and effectiveness; but at their best—in *Weather Diary 1*, *Weather Diary 2* (1987), *Sunbelt Serenade (Weather Diary 9)*, and *Season of Sorrow (Weather Diary 12)*, for example)—they are as evocative and provocative as anything Kuchar has done.

The Weather Diaries are also remarkable as depictions of El Reno, and not surprisingly, when Kathy High and Ruth Bradley were planning their programs for "Landscape and Place," the forty-second Robert Flaherty Seminar (held at Wells College in Aurora, New York, from August 3 to 8, 1996), a selection of Weather Diaries seemed virtually inevitable (other programs were curated by Loretta Todd). I was asked to introduce Kuchar and *Weather Diary 1*, which I had recommended to Bradley and High. That this presentation would detonate that seminar's most volatile discussion came as a surprise to me, despite the fact that, a few months earlier, this very tape had created the most volatile discussion of my teaching year. I should have known better!

Kuchar's presentation of *Weather Diary 1* came soon after the screening of three more overtly political pieces, programmed by Loretta Todd: *Kanehsatake: 270 Years of Resistance* (1993) by Alanis Obomsawin, and *Bastion Point* (1974) and *Patu* (1983) by Merata Mita, all three of which witness volatile social confrontations between indigenous peoples (of Canada and New Zealand, respectively) and those who continue to consolidate colonial control. After two hours of hatred between Canadian ethnic groups and two-plus hours of protests in New Zealand, often met with violence, Kuchar's slow-paced video, with its quiet, candid documentation of his personal experiences in small-town America, seemed outrageous to some seminarians, just another self-indulgence by a "middle-aged white guy"—at best, Art for Art's Sake.

When Kuchar sensed the barely repressed anger of some spectators after the screening, he "outed" the hostility by attacking what he saw as the unspoken assumptions that lay behind this hostility. Apparently referring to Obomsawin's and Mita's films, Kuchar complained,

> To see movies used as a huge megaphone to put your cause across—I thought it was atrocious, a horrible thing. Flaherty would turn over in his grave. I've come here and sat through movies that to me are the most vile things I've ever seen in my life. I thought it was disgusting. *I* came here for free—they paid my way. I don't understand how the rest of you put up with it.
>
> So I'm from New York, and I'm considered a "white male"—I've already been *labeled.* But *these* people come from other countries and throw this garbage on you and you take it, and treat the people who do it like gods and goddesses. It's horrible to me.
>
> I hope I'm not talking too much! But to see that beautiful Flaherty film [*Louisiana Story* (1948) had been screened at the seminar] that's survived all these decades and to hear it trashed by people who only think in terms of their sex and their nation and all these land fights—I go to bed having nightmares! There's no beauty in these films, no love of the image, no real care—just get the people being beat on the head and their bloody faces! It's disgusting.

It was a moment full of paradox. For those of us who admired the courage of Obomsawin and Mita in witnessing frustrating and frightening events, Kuchar's attack seemed excessive. At the same time, Kuchar had put his finger on something crucial, not so much about these particular films (though Claude Lanzmann, Peter Watkins, Alain Resnais, and Su Friedrich have shown that there is no necessary contradiction between witnessing social and political horror and a love of the image, that indeed, these two concerns can be synergic), but about the presentation and reception of many political films at the seminar. For most seminarians, the anger, pain, and violence witnessed in the Obomsawin and Mita films could be quickly put aside—after all, another film was scheduled, and the tight seminar routine would continue. But for Kuchar, witnessing the events in these films and then walking over to enjoy a snack or dinner was obscene. It was giving him nightmares.

Another paradox of the Art-for-Art's-Sake-by-Privileged-White-Males response to *Weather Diary 1* on the part of some seminarians was that of all the films screened at that Flaherty Seminar, those by Obomsawin and Mita (and Flaherty himself) probably had the most substantial budgets and the most consistent institutional support (Obomsawin is a fixture at the National Film Board of Canada). Further, despite being made by women with indigenous roots, these films looked pretty much like non–indigenously produced films that have witnessed social confrontation: George Stoney's *You Are on Indian Land* (1969, also produced by the National Film Board of Canada), for example. While Obomsawin and Mita have struggled to achieve something like consistent access to conventional budgets and professional equipment, Kuchar has struggled to prove that challenging, intimate videos can be produced with virtually no budget at all, and that struggling for access in the usual way is playing the media industry's antidemocratic game. That his video shook the Flaherty at least as powerfully as Obomsawin's or Mita's films seems to prove his point.

In the end, I was suspicious about the reaction to *Weather Diary 1* at the forty-second Flaherty. The objections to the video claimed to be motivated by high-minded political concerns, but when I showed the tape to a class at Utica College a few months before the Flaherty Seminar, it was a close-up of a turd in a toilet that shook many students, and I suspect that that turd, along with several other personal revelations (at one point Kuchar masturbates), was a primary instigator of the anger of some Flaherty seminarians.

Looking back, I also suspect that Kuchar arrived at the Flaherty Seminar with some prejudice toward it; for years, the Flaherty had been discussed in avant-garde circles as hostile to forms of independent filmmaking other than social realist documentary, and Kuchar, armed with his camera, came ready to document this hostility if he found it. Kuchar did make a video about his Flaherty experience (*Vermin of the Vortex*, 1996, in which aliens abduct Kuchar and take him to the seminar), and he wrote at length about it in "The Big Stink," available in his and Mike Kuchar's *Reflections from a Cinematic Cesspool* (Berkeley: Zanja Press, 1997), 108–23.

Kuchar and alien in *Vermin of the Vortex* (1996). Courtesy George Kuchar.

The following conversation with Kuchar about the Weather Diaries was begun by phone, in June 1996, and was continued, after the Flaherty event, by phone and by letter.

MacDonald: Peter Hutton mentioned to me that your first job was working for a TV weather show.

Kuchar: That's right. In the sixties I worked for a company that serviced NBC. I was assigned to do weather maps for this local weatherman, Dr. Frank Field. Remember him?

MacDonald: I do!

Kuchar: I would put a sort of scientific realism into my rendering of the weather. If it was a warm front, a little nimbus cloud. Frank Field was surprised; he said, "How did you know the clouds looked like this?" I told him, "Weather is my hobby."

MacDonald: How early was weather your hobby?

Kuchar: Well, in New York, weather was nature to me. I used to look out at the weather sometimes, and there'd be an electrical storm, or I'd go into the city and there'd be a big blizzard. To me, weather was the intrusion of nature into the city; and it was able to shut the city down at times. Except for living near Van Cortlandt Park, weather was my only close-up experience with nature.

And then I started reading about weather. The best books were by Eric

Sloane, a painter who painted beautiful pictures of clouds. The books he did for the Museum of Natural History really turned me on because they were an artist's view of weather, rather than a military kind of view, with mathematics and equations. At that time, the Weather Bureau was kind of regimented—at least when I was there. There were a lot of military people, and when they were changing shifts, they didn't even speak to each other! Things like that could kill your interest in the weather.

MacDonald: In your early 8mm film *A Town Called Tempest* you seemed aware of exactly how to do a movie tornado. You and Mike used toys and obviously homemade sets, but the tornado sequence is very effective.

Kuchar: Every time I go out, I look at the clouds. I study weather.

MacDonald: Was your first trip to El Reno in 1977, when you made *Wild Night in El Reno* [1977]?

Kuchar: No, that picture was made about four years after my first trip. I had been reading about all those Great Plains electrical storms and tornadoes, and I knew all kinds of stories of people who witnessed the storms. I decided I'd better go and see for myself what the storms are like. The first time I went, I only stayed two or three days. I went back to Oklahoma City the following year and found the YMCA, the one that got damaged by the bombing in 1995. I got a very good room: one wall was all windows, and there was a good roof area you could go up onto. The first time I stayed there, there were no storms for two weeks, but the last week was big. I've gone back ever since.

Oklahoma City was especially dead on weekends, so I decided maybe I ought to get out of the city and go west, into the farmland. So I took a bus and got off at El Reno, thirty miles away, because it seemed far enough from the city to give me a sense of the countryside, but close enough so that I could get back when I needed to take an airplane home. I thought El Reno was a nice place, so I started going there every year.

Later, I learned that the town has a history. It was one of the places where the people who were in the Oklahoma land rush left from. All the potential settlers gathered there to make the dash into Indian territory. It's strange to think that such a dump was the scene of this spectacle.

The only other interesting thing about El Reno is that they have a big prison facility there; it's where they incarcerated that guy who blew up the Federal Building in Oklahoma City [Timothy McVeigh and Terry Nichols were the primary conspirators in the bombing of the Alfred P. Murrah Federal Building]. Jon Jost was also locked up there when he was an antiwar demonstrator.

MacDonald: There has always been an autobiographical, sometimes even a diaristic, quality to your films, but when you started to make the Weather Diaries, the autobiographical dimension became the foreground.

Kuchar: Well, I was stuck, I guess. I knew I wanted to make a video while I was in El Reno, and I wanted to include weather elements in it, but when I was there, nothing was happening a lot of the time. So I started making pictures of what *was* around: what I was eating, my daily activities, what was in my room. Also, I wanted to have some activity, so I wouldn't get too lethargic and just watch television all the time. I began putting myself into the videos. Then, since I was editing the early Weather Diaries in-camera, staying in El Reno got to be fun. Making the videos kept me absorbed.

MacDonald: Was there also a second editing stage, once you got back to San Francisco?

Kuchar: In those early Weather Diaries, most of the editing was done there in the motel room. When I made *Weather Diary 1,* I was in El Reno about three and a half weeks. My camera lets you go back to earlier footage, say a week later, and insert new stuff without making glitches. You're able to edit cleanly. When I left El Reno, *Weather Diary 1* was all finished.

MacDonald: So it looks like you're on vacation, but you're actually in production.

Kuchar: Yes. It's exciting, because you never know what's coming next, and so the picture is constantly changing, week by week.

Weather Diary 2 was doctored up after I got back home because I was starting to fall apart toward the end of my stay that year. I finished editing that one at home, though whole sections were edited in-camera.

MacDonald: Weather Diary 3 takes place in El Reno, and then you do a second Weather Diary in Milwaukee. Did you plan to do two Weather Diaries that year?

Kuchar: No. I felt that since there were no storms in El Reno that year, I'd go to Milwaukee and maybe there'd be storms there. But it didn't work out; in Milwaukee there was hardly any weather at all, so the video turned out to be about people who were stuck in Milwaukee.

MacDonald: Weather Diary 6 was like a return to the style of *Wild Night in El Reno.* There's no sync sound.

Kuchar: Yeah, just pictures and stuff. I have a second version of that one. I edited *Weather Diary 6* in-camera with a camera that added dropout to the image—white dots here and there. For a few weeks after finishing it, I was happy. Then the dropout began to annoy me. All I could *see* was dropout. So I thought, hey, how about I just put a whole ton of white dots on the thing and have scratches on it too. So the second version, which you probably haven't seen, looks like a film that was found in a garbage can. That's the version I'm happy with now. It's also got a different sound track.

Every time I do a Weather Diary, I try to go in a new direction because I don't want to repeat myself. I'm always looking for new material.

MacDonald: There are always differences from one Weather Diary to the next, but there are also elements that keep repeating. One obvious example is that there are "turd shots" in *Weather Diaries 1, 2,* and *3;* and then, having created the expectation (at least in those viewers who see the Weather Diaries as a series), you surprise the viewer in funny ways. We *hear* you shitting in *Weather Diary 4;* and in *Weather Diary 5,* we see you sit down on the toilet and we get ready for a turd shot, but it *doesn't* happen. Then, in *Weather Diary 6* there's *animated* shit.

Last year, I did a video history course at Utica College, and when I showed *Weather Diary 1,* some students were really shocked by the turd shot; one or two never recovered, and one student stopped speaking to me! For them it was like The Turd from Beneath the Sea.

Kuchar: Oh, I'm so sorry. It *was* a big one! [laughter]

MacDonald: When I'm traveling, and I assume this is true for you too, bowel movements take on considerable psychic size, so it makes sense to me that when you're alone in your room for weeks at a time, you grow conscious of your bowel movements.

Kuchar: I'd always felt deprived of that aspect of life in other pictures. It seemed ridiculous to me that movie people don't take a shit, so I decided to put that into my pictures.

For me, it's fun. It's my version of splatter.

MacDonald: The openness of your videos, their personal intimacy, frightens some people. Their media training has caused them to recoil from such candidness.

Kuchar: Yes. Everyday life has become more horrifying than heads being blown off.

MacDonald: As you go through the early Weather Diaries, you're more and more open about your sexual desire. In *Weather Diary 1* sexuality is a subject, but it's not gendered. But your desire for guys becomes increasingly clear later in the series.

Kuchar: Well, I was just interested in exploring different subjects. I said to myself, "Well, you haven't done *this.*" Know what I mean?

MacDonald: Do you think of yourself as gay?

Kuchar: Strange things are always surprising me. I've never been able to put my finger on what I am. I say to myself, "Maybe I'm this," but then I see some other thing and think, "I wonder what *that's* about; I should try *that.*"

In the Weather pictures, I'm always looking for new angles, and I just thought it was time for that to come into the series.

MacDonald: Have you shown the Weather Diaries to the El Reno people?

Kuchar: No.

MacDonald: Do you think you'd never be allowed back into town?

Kuchar: [laughter] You know how it is. It's Middle America: the people are a bit on the overweight side; mostly they like going shopping. They have no interest in *my* videos.

I sent a tape to a woman one time, and she never responded, so I thought maybe she thought it was disgusting or something. Finally, on a later visit, I asked, "Did you get the tape I sent you, and did you like it?" And she said, "Oh, that tape. Yes, very nice." But they mostly like watching country music shows and stuff like that.

Once, some people in this little gallery in Tulsa found out about the Weather Diaries and contacted me: "We'd love to have you come and do a show." So I said fine, and showed them a whole evening of the Weather Diaries, two separate shows. People of all ages came—men in suits, elderly ladies—and they loved it. They were very proud that I would come to Oklahoma every year. They gave me five hundred dollars, and were very nice to me, then drove me back to El Reno.

MacDonald: We see some of that experience in *Sunbelt Serenade.*

Kuchar: Yeah, that's right.

MacDonald: Do the El Reno people think of you as an artist or as a tourist?

Kuchar: The people at the motel? They know I make pictures; they know I'm interested in weather and storms. They take me as a strange family member who visits every year. But they welcome it. They're grateful that I come, and they take my money. I don't pay that much; the motel is cheap—sixty dollars a week!

The same year as that Tulsa show, a television crew from England was doing a piece on twisters and storm chasers, and somehow they had seen one of the Weather Diaries in England. The producer had called me up in San Francisco and said, "Can we come and see you in El Reno?" I said, "Sure." So he came to my room with a British lady producer and a crew with an Australian cinematographer. They asked me about the storms, why I was there, and it all wound up in their documentary. I think it turned out to be mainly a documentary about frustration because that year nobody had come upon any storms. So they focused on the people who chased the storms when there *were* some. I think the piece was called *Storm Chasers.* They sent me a copy.

Anyway, they played it on Channel 4 in England and I got a rave review! A woman wrote, "A star was born last night," and focused her review on me because, she said, everyone else had seemed kind of frightening.

Later it was broadcast here, on the Discovery Channel, but I got chopped out—except for one close-up that couldn't be removed. They must have thought I was too strange for the American audience. The American version was narrated by Bill Curtis; it's in video stores.

MacDonald: Could you talk about the experience of showing Weather Diaries at the Flaherty?

Kuchar: As I've mentioned before, I was never made so aware of the perceived differences between people (skin color, sex, class distinction—all surface features). It was not a celebration of the differences but, rather, a way to isolate people from one another, a way to view other people as an enemy. The films and videos I saw seemed to be programmed to create a feeding frenzy of hatred. From the remarks I heard in and out of the theater, the enemy was identified as the "white male oppressor."

During the discussion after *Weather Diary 1*, I refused to answer a question posed to me by a handsome, Middle Eastern–looking man, because instead of simply asking how I felt when I was in a particular location that I had videotaped, he put too many adjectives into his question: "How do you *as a white male* . . . " There was no *me* in the question anymore. To answer his question would have meant that I accepted the role he was implying with those adjectives: the role of the white oppressor.

I didn't want to tell him that I couldn't possibly answer his question as it was phrased, because it was all very embarrassing to me. I didn't want to correct him in public, and I didn't want to fight with him. So I mumbled off into inaudibility. But this became the turning point that got me ready to blow. He was trying to push me into a place I refused to go—he and the statuesque programmer from Canada [Loretta Todd]. She had come down from the north like a cold wind out of the Canadian wilds to chill the hearts of all attending—a very striking, articulate woman who is so possessed by the spirits of her ancestors that they animate her big-boned beauty into steamroller action. She was hell-bent on smashing the Flaherty Seminar into a heap of scalps and constructing a totem pole to the annihilation of Art for Art's Sake. People stayed away from her in droves, and she stayed away from them. She was an excellent programmer and an impressive speaker, bringing a weight and importance to the proceedings, and she arranged for some wonderful guests to present their work.

One of these guests brought a movie that is very important to what I'm trying to say. This guest (a lovely woman [Alanis Obomsawin]) made a movie about an Indian boy who had hung himself because no one gave him love [*Richard Cardinal: Cry from a Diary of a Metis* (1986)]. He was an orphan and never in a home long enough to be nurtured into maturity. It made me realize that what we bring into our homes and lives, we should love. When it's a plant, you give it water and sunlight. If it's a cat or dog, you know that you must care for the creature for as long as it lives. You must do that for people too, even though they're terribly complicated. Luckily, people get older and move out, so they're not dependent on you all their lives! Anyway, it was a wonderful picture, and very moving. So was the filmmaker.

The Flaherty film the seminar screened, *Louisiana Story*, was also very inspiring. It not only oozed oil, but harmony!

Unfortunately, what I detected throughout the screenings was a mood of escalating political unrest, a pervading PC toxicity, and a trigger-happy tendency to take aim at our shadows. Our shadow selves had to be murdered to protect the Clean. The magic mirror on the wall, the movie screen, was where everyone seemed to want to be because *there* we could be represented on its surface the way we were told people should be represented. There was no more need to look out a real window to see what real folks were all about.

In that rectangular reality lurked the enemy, too. The enemy clubbed and smashed heads. Nobody seemed to turn off their camera and help the poor smitten victims. I mean, what can we, the audience, do when we see these films? Walk into the movie and help out? No. All we can do is watch it. It's not real life—that came and went a while ago. Everybody gets worked up and mad, but nobody, evidently, has a solution for all these turf wars and injustices.

During the discussion of *Weather Diary 1*, someone else expressed shock that I would dare to use a phrase in my video, a phrase even more awful, apparently, than the "n" word: "Dairy Queen Fatso." It was all getting too ridiculous and sadder by the minute. Who was training these young people to think like this? And why did the elders sit silently?

Anyway, at the Flaherty, I saw films and videos that were doing a lot of good in the world, and I expressed that to the makers individually. But there was something wrong. Agendas were hinted at, but not expressed openly. Everything looked okay on the surface, but you could sense that there was something else lurking underneath.

I decided to hell with it. When I found myself confronted with this hidden something that we all knew was there and that we all recognized, I blew up and attacked not only the seminar itself but the films being screened, because I wanted us all to see the face that was haunting that event. Then I sat back, and we all watched the demon come out in all its mean-spiritedness, hatred, and horror. Truly a gruesome experience! But I guess it had to be done.

Did you notice what it was like the following day when I had to get up again to answer questions about *Sunbelt Serenade* and *Season of Sorrow?* It was another world. I think we had all seen each other more clearly; it was like a weather front had come through, clearing the air.

I didn't want to personally attack individuals during the Flaherty because I don't want to squash people. There's too much killing of the human spirit in our schools today as it is. I liked a lot of these people because they were very idealistic, sweet and beautiful souls who were somehow being corrupted by a twisted education that was making them all talk alike. I'd heard it all a thousand times before—stock responses full of stock phrases and a lot of silliness. And, as a facet of human nature, mean and rotten. But we've got to see all the facets of this nature of ours, and so I hope it was a learning experience for all.

I'm just as rotten as everyone else, but at least I have the courage to show that on the screen and not try to clean it up for the TV public. But I hope there's beauty there, too.

Film History and "Film History"

It is, perhaps, inevitable that we construct mythic versions of our lives, and each evolving component of our lives that we consider important. That is, out of the myriad sensations and thoughts we experience, we focus on a few that, at any given moment in our lives, seem to have been the most important—"important" meaning pivotal in helping us to become the people we believe we are. The aspect of my life that I tend to mythify most frequently is a function of my self-definition as a film history professor and a scholar specializing in independent cinema: I often return to particular film experiences in explaining to my students how I came to commit so much of my time, energy, and passion to such an "offbeat" dimension of modern media. In recent years, I have tended to fasten on four particular filmgoing experiences as being the most important for me, and I have been able to enunciate, at least to myself, what lesson I learned from each. I hope the reader can bear with my unmitigated self-indulgence as I describe these four experiences; I do not describe them because I think these particular experiences, or my "mythic story," are of unusual interest, but because of several common denominators in these experiences that will allow me to develop an argument that *is* important to make.

I grew up as a filmgoer and attended movies with my parents and friends from early on. I have no idea which films I saw first, or which ones I was enthusiastic about as a child—my parents died when I was in my twenties, and my formal interest in cinema did not develop until they were gone—though I am sure some of these must have been the Disney animated features of the 1940s. On weekends when I would stay with my grandmother in Nazareth, Pennsylvania, I would spend Saturday afternoons at the Broad Theater, where I remember seeing *Gone with the Wind* and several John Ford films. While all these experiences had an impact on me (I still have a great admiration of Ford and have made my pilgrimage to Monument Valley), the most important film experience of my youth, and the first of the four pivotal experiences in my cinema myth, was going to see *King Kong* at the State Theater in Easton, Pennsylvania, in the early 1950s. I remember this experience for a variety of reasons, including the fact that it may have been the first time I took a bus downtown to see a film by myself.

At the time, I knew *nothing* about *King Kong*, except that someone—it must have been my parents—had suggested that this was a film I *ought* to see and that it was a film that I was now "old enough" to see on my own. I may have known something about a giant ape, though even this is questionable; television was not a primary venue for Hollywood films as yet, and since *King Kong* had been out of distribution for nearly two decades, there was very little information about the film available, at least to a young boy like me. So I arrived at the theater virtually a tabula rasa and bought my ticket. Did I see a poster of the giant ape as I was walking into the theater?—because, by the time I was choosing my seat, I was choosing on a strategic basis. The State Theater was designed with two aisles separating the large center section from the two smaller side sections. I remember making a conscious choice not to sit in the middle, where "the best seats" were, but to sit in an aisle seat in the right-hand side section, not quite halfway down the aisle: I wanted to be able to make a quick, unembarrassed escape if the film turned out to be too much for me to handle. As I remember, the theater was reasonably full.

I did not find the beginning of *King Kong* very alluring; nothing seemed to be happening, and I was worried that perhaps this was just another of those melodramas that adults seemed to enjoy. Indeed, my primary interest for nearly the first hour of the film was Faye Wray, who was as erotic a presence on-screen as I had ever experienced (remember, this was in the heyday of the Production Code, and *King Kong* had been made during that magical moment in the early 1930s, soon after the coming of sound, when moral restrictions on American commercial films had been loosened, and before the Catholic Legion of Decency forced Hollywood to "clean up" the industry). In any case, Carl Denham and his collaborators arrived at Skull Island just as I was running out of patience, and their sneaking up on the Skull Island natives doing a Kong ritual quickly reenergized me.

The following fifteen minutes of *King Kong*, culminating in the shackling of Ann on the sacrificial altar, were the most exciting moments of my young filmgoing life; during the moments of silence after the chief directed the natives to signal Kong by ringing the immense gong on top of the wall, I was simultaneously terrified and thrilled. I was, literally, on the edge of my seat, ready to run up the aisle and out of the theater. In fact, I was having a powerful urge to yell to the audience, "Get out while there's still time!" And then, there, right in front of me, to my utter astonishment, tearing through the trees, was Kong himself, freeing Ann and running into the

Publicity still for *King Kong* (1933) by Merian C. Cooper and Ernest P. Schoedsack.

woods with her (just what I wanted to do!), and then doing battle with assorted dinosaurs: I was in heaven. *This*, I remember thinking to myself, *is a movie!*

When Kong had fallen to his death, and I staggered out of the theater, I felt like a new person: I had faced my fears and had stood firm, and the payoff was clear: I had had the best time of my life in a movie theater and as good a two hours of pleasure as I was ever to have. I had realized, obviously without being able to articulate it, that art, cinematic art in this case, was one of life's primary pleasures. It was not something one did instead of living; it was part of living itself. But the experience offered more than pleasure, it offered *empowerment*. That cinema could confront dimensions of my complacent self, and make me stronger, was my first lesson.

The second lesson did not come for another several years, and it took nearly seven years to learn. The process began at a small theater in Greencastle, Indiana, in, I believe, the fall of 1963. I was a senior English major at DePauw University—at the time enamored of the British Romantic poets and the British novel—for whom movies were a preferred weekend entertainment. I had heard about an "interesting" new Italian film from someone (it must have been a professor; at the time none of the students I knew took cinema seriously as an intellectual pursuit; indeed, when one of our favorite professors suggested that "it might be interesting to have a course in film history," we thought he was joking and laughed pretentiously at the idea). The film's numerical title certainly suggested it would be unusual. I walked alone to the theater to see *8½* (1963) and sat near the back in the reasonably crowded theater, curious to see what the fuss was about.

The fuss, it turned out, was pretty much about nothing—or so it seemed to me. Not long into the film, I began to be amazed that so many people in the audience could be so utterly phony! Here was a remarkably chaotic, virtually indecipherable black-and-white film that offered no apparent pleasure, and a good number of people in the audience seemed compelled to pretend they were enjoying the experience, at least judging from their laughter. After awhile I began to make comments out loud: "Yeah, *this* makes a lot of sense!" and "Laugh it up, phonies!" and possibly, "Sure, it's from Italy; it *must* be good!" I don't remember anyone telling me to shut up, so it may be that I just *wanted* to say these things out loud, or that I said them so softly that only *I* could hear them clearly. In any case, I don't know if I stayed through *8½*. I do have a vague memory of amusing my frat brothers with stories about the phonies pretending to understand this totally stupid movie.

Six years or so later, I went to see *8½* again. I was now a Ph.D. student in English at the University of Florida, supporting my schooling by teaching undergraduate courses in the Humanities Department, and *8½* had been made an assignment for the humanities students. There seemed to be considerable respect for the film among my colleagues, and I figured I should give the film a second chance. Of course, the moment it began, I understood what I had not understood at that earlier screening: that Fellini begins the film in a dream, *before* he reveals "reality," and further that *8½* gives no special signal when it moves from "reality" to daydream or night dream and back. I had grown up with Hollywood's clear signals between what was real and what was imagined and had not understood what now seemed so embarrassingly obvious. But the lesson—that like a work of literature, a film might take time to understand, and might require a developing sophistication—was an important one. I was soon, like so many of my generation, passionate about "foreign film" and its challenges to Hollywood convention.

My third lesson occurred at the end of my graduate studies, once I had decided to try and find a job teaching both American literature and film history, during that moment at the end of the 1960s when student demand for film courses was so strong that courses began to be offered by people with virtually no expertise in the field. I decided to attend a two-week summer film institute at Kent School in Kent, Connecticut. The guests during the seminar included the screenwriter Robert Anderson, the actress Teresa Wright, the critic Molly Haskell, and, most important, at least for me, Andrew Sarris from the *Village Voice.* One evening early in the institute, Sarris presented a 35mm print of Buster Keaton's *The General* (1926). At this time Keaton was, for all practical purposes, a memory. We knew what he looked like, that he was called "the Great Stone Face," but the Keaton films had been out of distribution for decades, and most American viewers had seen only those clips that were included in silent-film compilations made for television—clips that removed action from its original timing and context.

Sarris, who had been instrumental in bringing Keaton back to American audiences, introduced him as a consummate American auteur and then ran the film. We were astonished. As everyone knows now, *The General* is visually spectacular, full of subtle awareness, thoroughly poignant, and it was as funny a film as I had ever seen. I laughed with an abandon I had not experienced since childhood. I had come to understand that all great films were "foreign films," only to realize that Americans *had* made great films—often, of course, in the face of considerable resistance from the money people in Hollywood. My discovery of Keaton led me to a years-long exploration of Hollywood auteurs, guided by Sarris's *American Cinema* (New York: Dutton, 1968); and to the *Village Voice,* where I began reading Sarris's column religiously, as well as Haskell's, and another critic that I previously had not heard of: Jonas Mekas.

My fourth and final pivotal moment came in two installments, the first at a Saturday film symposium on April 29, 1972, hosted by the State University of New York at Binghamton (since 1992, Binghamton University); the second, sometime later, at a three-week institute hosted at Hampshire College by the University Film Study Association under the leadership of Peter Feinstein.

The announcement of the symposium at Binghamton had not made clear what kind of film was to be the focus of the event, but, as a young film professor with virtually no training, I was hungry for any education I could find. The symposium was an afternoon screening of several films, followed by a discussion. My memory tells me four films were shown: *Soft Rain* (1968) by Ken Jacobs, *Serene Velocity* (1971) by Ernie Gehr, *Barn Rushes* (1971) by Larry Gottheim, and *The Act of Seeing with One's Own Eyes* (1971) by Stan Brakhage (Jacobs and Gottheim were faculty members at Binghamton and led the discussion after the screening). Of course, memories are fragile. Recently, Richard Herskowitz, a graduate of the SUNY-Binghamton cinema department who was present at this event, sent me the program notes, which list three films I no longer remember seeing that Saturday (assuming all the films that were announced were screened). Apparently, *two* Jacobs films—*Nissan Ariana Window* (1969) and *Adjacent Perspectives* (1971; this is a stand-alone excerpt from a longer film, *The Russian Revolution* [1969; now called *Globe*])—were shown. *Soft Rain* is not mentioned in the program notes, though Jacobs thinks it might also have been presented. And Ricky Leacock's direct cinema classic, *Happy Mother's Day* (1964), was also included (I do remember Leacock being present).

Whatever the precise nature of the program, I do not remember ever being more furious at a film event. The Gehr film was tremendously frustrating and exhausting (those who have not seen *Serene Velocity* should know that for the film, a hallway at SUNY-Binghamton was filmed with a zoom lens in four-frame bits so that during half an hour we move from midway along the zoom lens first one way, then the other; as the film evolves, the switching between images of the far and near ends of the hallway can seem increasingly dramatic and disconcerting); the Gottheim film (a series of eight approximately three-minute, roll-long, tracking shots past an upstate New York barn in different lights), was, simultaneously, painfully slow and—I had to admit—appealing, even within this moment of general puzzlement and fury; and then came Brakhage's painfully vivid exploration of the process of autopsy, filmed in the Pittsburgh morgue: thirty minutes of silent horror. When the lights came on, and the post-screening discussion began, I expected the audience to stand and roar its disapproval, and was shocked to discover that people seemed to be discussing what we had seen as if the screening had actually been worthwhile. I remember nothing that was said, only the kind of intellectual terror you feel when a field you thought you understood is transformed into a mystery, and your familiar "intelligence" into a brand-new stupidity.

On my way home that evening, I regaled my companions with acerbic wit and righteous indignation in response to what seemed to me an outrage, but within weeks of the screening—weeks during which I thought continuously about the films—I decided that I admired all of them and, much to my own amazement, wanted to *show* them, first to my film history students, and then to local audiences. My sense of what it meant to teach film, and how one might demonstrate the full range of aesthetic possibilities inherent in cinema, was already changing. And Gottheim's film, along with the other Gottheim films I saw during the following months, was beginning to transform my commitment as a scholar. My writing had been focused on American literature; it was not long before it occurred to me that whatever scholarly abilities I had might be of particular use to what seemed the underserved field of avant-garde film.

The second half of this fourth pivotal moment occurred a year or so later, at the summer film institute at Hampshire College, which I had registered for because it seemed likely to offer a confirmation and an extension of the Binghamton experience. Many things happened at this institute: I have fond memories of a course on ethnographic cinema taught by John Marshall (it began with Kubelka's flicker film *Arnulf Rainer* [1960]) and a course in underground film, focusing on West Coast experimental film (and especially the work of Jordan Belson), taught by Sheldon Renan. But my pivotal experiences were two evening film presentations by filmmakers introduced by Peter Feinstein—the first, a screening of the first three parts of Hollis Frampton's *Hapax Legomena: (nostalgia)* (1971), *Poetic Justice* (1972), and *Critical Mass* (1972); the second, a screening of *Reminiscences of a Journey to Lithuania* (1972) by Jonas Mekas.

In both cases the responses to the screenings were as powerful for me as the films. At the Frampton screening, Feinstein introduced Frampton, who introduced the films—though I do not remember Frampton's comments. What I do remember is that while the audience seemed to enjoy *(nostalgia)*, and about one quarter of *Poetic Justice* (those unfamiliar with this film may want to know that it presents a screenplay, one page at a time, at a rate of approximately six seconds per page; each of four tableaux is made up of sixty pages; viewers "shoot the film" as they read/watch). Once the beginning of the second tableaux had made clear that Frampton's film was not going to alter its minimalist strategy, most of the audience rebelled. The screening room was a conventional academic lecture hall with no rugs, with nothing to muffle sound, and those leaving seemed to take pleasure in stomping as loudly as they could on their way up the stairs and slamming the doors on their way out. A considerable din lasted for around twenty minutes—after which only about a quarter of the original audience remained in the room. Of course, once *Poetic Justice* was over, *Critical Mass* rewarded those who had stayed. I was so thrilled by the three films that I was up half the night, writing notes and trying to come to terms with Frampton's remarkably active engagement of my intellect.

The Mekas screening was a reprise of the Frampton screening, though, of course, *Reminiscences of a Journey to Lithuania* is a very different kind of film from *Hapax Legomena*. *Reminiscences* is focused on Mekas's first trip back to his native Lithuania, and to his mother, after leaving home thirty years earlier to escape the Nazis and then, after the war, finding Lithuania closed to the West. The long central section of *Reminiscences* is filmed with

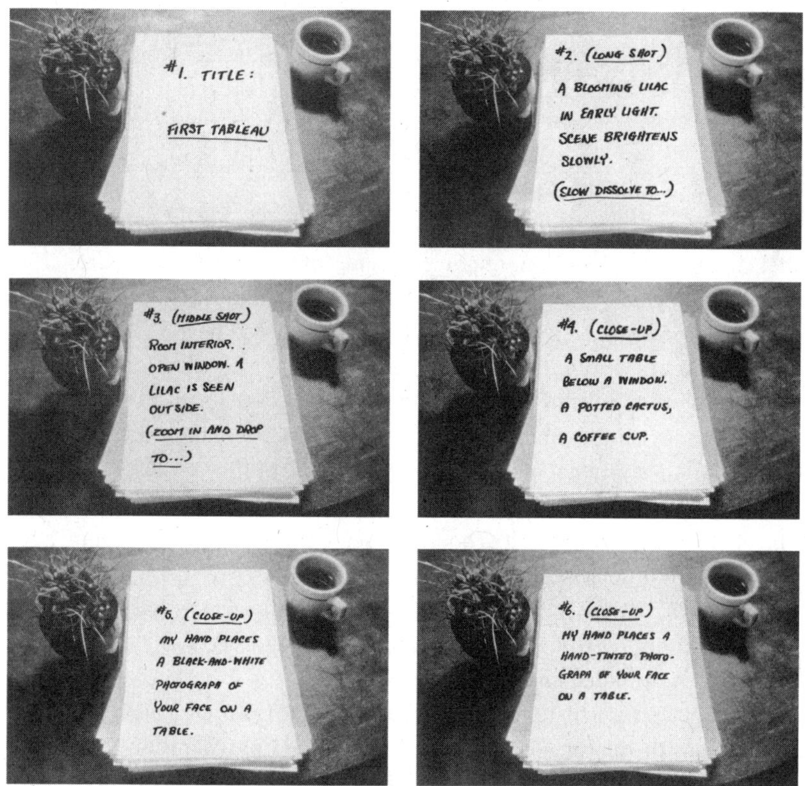

The first six pages of Hollis Frampton's screenplay in *Poetic Justice* (1972).

a highly gestural handheld and single-framing camera, so that Mekas's imagery offers only glimpses of the family, farm, and village he left behind, glimpses that express his own nervousness and excitement and the evanescence of his memories and of this moment. The section documenting his return to Lithuania ("100 Glimpses of Lithuania") is framed by an early section reviewing his life in New York City as a slowly adjusting displaced person, and by a final section focusing on a gathering of friends (Mekas, Annette Michelson, Ken and Flo Jacobs, Peter Kubelka, and Hermann Nitsch) in Vienna, where we realize that Mekas's original family, regardless of how much he loves and remembers them, has, for all practical purposes, been replaced by this new artistic family.

Reminiscences of a Journey to Lithuania is a lovely and moving film—and as a result, I was shocked to hear the fury of some in the audience when the lights came on: "YOU RUINED THE FILM, YOU ASSHOLE!" "YOU HAD A

GREAT SUBJECT BUT MADE IT IMPOSSIBLE FOR US TO SEE!" "HAVE YOU NO SENSE OF CINEMA AT ALL?!" Mekas handled the attacks gracefully; he seemed used to it. For me, this experience confirmed the lesson I had learned from the Frampton screening: I realized that it was possible for me to respond deeply and positively to films that the majority of my colleagues in the audience might absolutely loathe.

Fundamentally, each of the experiences I have described revealed to me that cinema could be far more powerful and interesting, far more transformative, than I had previously recognized. Second, all these experiences were arranged and organized by people who had imagined new possibilities for film exhibition, whether these involved reviving earlier classics, importing films from other parts of the world, or presenting new forms of cinema that functioned as critiques of the "normal" film experiences I had grown up with. Further, all these pivotal moments were the result of *theatrical film-viewing experiences.* In some instances these experiences did lead to my reading about film history and to my using books to search out films I would not have known about otherwise. But what was pivotal was experiencing the films in a theater with other spectators. To put this another way, what was crucial was not simply *learning about* film history, but rather *being part of film history* as it unfolded and expanded.

For, in fact, film history *is* precisely *the history of what is shown and seen,* just as the history of literature is the history of what is published and read. A comparison might be of use. Emily Dickinson is generally recognized as one of the two most accomplished American poets of the nineteenth century and one of the dozen or so greatest American writers. She is studied throughout the American educational system; her poetry is easily available in virtually every bookstore in the English-speaking world and online; and most educated people would be able to identify a poem as Dickinson's were it read to them. In other words, the "Divine Emily" is an important part of American and world literary history.

And yet Dickinson's existence as a canonized poet is not, as most of those who have had more than fleeting contact with her career are well aware, a result of Dickinson's own efforts. A few of her more than seventeen hundred poems were published in her lifetime (ten, according to most scholars), but Dickinson was an intensely private person and writer, and it seems fair to say that no one during her lifetime had any idea of the extent of her oeuvre or of its remarkable quality. Indeed, so far as we know, even though Dickinson knew she was dying, she made no formal arrangements for her life's work, beyond entrusting the poems to the family maid, Margaret Maher. The reason, the *only* reason, Emily Dickinson is part of literary history is that, after Dickinson's death in 1885, her younger sister, Lavinia, discovered the poetry while she was going through her older sister's drawers, decided the poetry was important enough to outlive its author, and set to work to have at least some of the poems published. She was successful, and as a result of Lavinia's efforts and the support of Mabel Loomis Todd and Thomas Wentworth Higginson, Dickinson remains an important part of our cultural surround.

This dimension of Emily Dickinson's career can be understood as a cautionary tale for those who care about film history. At least within the academy, the term "film history" has come to mean something quite different from what film history actually is. "Film history" seems generally understood as the written chronicle of the films that have been produced since the invention of the *cinématographe.* In fact, however, the written chronicle of film history, no matter how detailed and accurate it may be, is *not* film history itself. Film history is not a written chronicle; it is not even the history of the films that have been made. Film history is the set of theatrical (and nontheatrical) experiences that the written chronicle of "film history" pretends to survey. If a film is made and not seen, it cannot be part of film history, any more than Emily Dickinson's poems would have been a part of literary history had they been destroyed. Further, if a film has been made and seen, but is no longer available to audiences, it ceases to be part of film history, even if it continues to be part of "film history."

To think of a "film historian" only as someone who writes about the evolution of cinema is a perversion of terminology, a perversion that has had problematic implications for film history itself, because this definition has been accompanied by a tendency on the part of "film historians" throughout academe to make themselves responsible only to writing about film. Those individuals who have made a commitment to film history itself, with all the difficulties and challenges that exhibiting cinema on an ongoing basis involves, are something of a rarity, especially in academic circles. In fact, academe, like a corrupt union, has created systems that implicitly reward "film historians" for avoiding the labor of actually doing film history: serious efforts at cinema exhibition in academe are rarely encouraged or rewarded, at least compared with the often less challenging process of writing "film history." And since so much of what is produced by film artists is, as a result, not seen by audiences, film history itself is increasingly jeopardized.

It is true that students study film history in classrooms, so that at least for the duration of the course in which they are enrolled, they are an audience seeing films. But, by definition, these are private screenings, screenings that are increasingly constricted both by technical compromises (many in academe use pirated videos or DVDs of films meant to be shown in 16mm) and by the inevitable impoverishment of film history that occurs as a result of the lack of any serious, public film exhibition program outside of the classroom that might confirm and expand on what occurs in the classroom. Academics in film studies in a good many institutions of higher learning seem to have decided that the job of creating a living film history, a film history that expands beyond commercial entertainments and beyond the private screenings within classrooms, is not theirs; and they have enforced this decision by focusing almost exclusively on "film history" to measure expertise and academic accomplishment.

Interview with Karen Cooper

Those who care about the full range of cinematic accomplishment, especially those of us who chronicle film history and guide our students toward a fuller understanding of it, often take film exhibition for granted. Our focus is on films and filmmakers, and on the popular and scholarly discourses about them. As a result, it is easy to underestimate our reliance on those women and men who devote themselves to the exhibition of accomplished films that would never find their way into the nationwide network of multiplexes. The sad fact is that there may be fewer accomplished, creative exhibitors than there are accomplished filmmakers or film scholars. This undervaluing of exhibition (and much the same could be said of distribution and preservation) within both the popular press and academe has problematic implications for all cineastes. If those whose labors make it possible for the rest of us to see the films we need to see are not recognized or honored, how will the next generation come to understand that this kind of contribution is worth the labors and sacrifices involved? It would be one of the supreme ironies of modern cultural history if, after a generation of the production of scholars, critics, and theorists of film by institutions of higher learning, film history itself—meaning the gathering of audiences to share the experience of a broad range of motion pictures—were less alive than it was before the arrival of film studies into the academy.

In this country, alternative exhibition has a long history, from the Little Theater movement in the 1920s to the workers' screenings of the 1930s; to the rise of a film society movement, spurred by Frank Stauffacher at San Francisco's Art in Cinema and Amos Vogel at New York's Cinema 16 during the 1940s and 1950s; to the arrival of cinematheques, film archives, and the midnight movie phenomenon during the 1960s and 1970s; and, most recently, to the proliferation of film festivals and of microcinemas during the 1990s and early 2000s. These diverse adventures in film exhibition not only have assisted audiences in keeping up with accomplished film artists working outside the commercial industry but also have provided a practical reason for independent film artists to make films. As Jordan Belson has said, "If that outlet [Stauffacher's Art in Cinema] had not been there, there wouldn't have been any incentive to make films. Might as well paint" (Belson in Scott MacDonald, *Art in Cinema: Documents toward a History of the Film Society* [Philadelphia: Temple University Press, 2006], 174).

Innovations in independent exhibition require committed individuals who can find the time, resources, and energy to do their work, despite the likelihood that their efforts will be largely overlooked except by the filmmakers whose work they show and the audiences that come to see the films. And innovative exhibition venues that become established cultural institutions that can be counted on by audiences and filmmakers alike require individuals of unusual persistence, resilience, courage, and economic common sense. The epitome of such an institution is New York's Film Forum, which was established by Peter Feinstein on the Upper West Side of Manhattan in 1970 as an alternative screening space for independent films, with fifty folding chairs, one 16mm projector, and a $19,000 annual budget. Karen Cooper became Film Forum's director in 1972. She moved the venue downtown to Vandam Street at the southern end of the West Village in 1975. In 1980, Cooper led the construction of a twin cinema on nearby Watts Street; then, in 1989, when the Watts Street cinema was demolished by developers, she oversaw the construction of another new venue on West Houston Street, where Film Forum remains.

During the past thirty-plus years, Cooper has worked doggedly to make Film Forum a crucial addition to moviegoing opportunities in one of the world's great film cities and an important opportunity for independent filmmakers to meet a public and to receive critical response. Today, Film Forum is a three-screen cinema, open 365 days a year, with 250,000 annual admissions, 472 seats, more than sixty employees, a membership of 4,500, and an operating budget of $4.1 million. Film Forum's three screens present premieres of independent films from around the world, programmed by Cooper and Mike Maggiore, and repertory retrospectives covering the history of commercial cinema, programmed by Bruce Goldstein. It has become difficult to imagine the New York City film scene without Film Forum.

Cooper's longevity as Film Forum director is itself remarkable, as is the fact that she shows no signs of wavering in her commitment to independent cinema and independent exhibition. I have interviewed Cooper twice: first, for *Afterimage* (vol. 11, no. 4 [September 1983]); and again, during January 2008. During the intervening quarter century, Cooper's energy and commitment seem not to have diminished an iota. She was and remains one of the heroes of American film exhibition, not only because of her service to so many independent filmmakers and audiences but because she has dem-

Karen Cooper in 1982. Photograph by Gerry Goldstein; courtesy Film Forum.

onstrated, as effectively as anyone in this country ever has, that independent cinema can be economically viable, even in a culture dominated by Hollywood. One can only hope that her work will become a model for a new generation of women and men who care enough about the public experience of cinema to see that it lives and grows.

SPRING 1982

MacDonald: A lot of us fantasize about running a serious movie theater, but you actually do it. How did you get to do it? What's your background?

Cooper: I'm thirty-four years old, and I was born and raised in New York. I wasn't a movie maven as a child. I was more interested in dance and theater. In high school I studied modern dance with some of Martha Graham's most interesting followers—people like Sophie Maslow and Jane Dudley. When I was eighteen years old, I spent the summer running an Off-Broadway box office for the Fugs—my first stint in "show biz." I also did press and public relations during two other summers, for WNYC Radio and the Berkshire Theatre Festival in Stockbridge, Massachusetts. At Smith College and at the University of London, I studied English literature. I think I fancied myself becoming a writer.

In looking for work, I sent résumés to a variety of periodicals that dealt with dance, literature, and film concerns; I wanted to write from a critical standpoint. After about a year I had a response from *Filmmaker's Newsletter,* now defunct, which had originally grown out of an underground moviemaking tradition. One of my tasks as a sort of all-round slave was to write about what was happening in independent film in New York. I had no background whatsoever. I was introduced to the world of Ed Emshwiller and Maya Deren and Stan Vanderbeek and Stan Brakhage—names that are famous to anyone who knows the slightest thing about this kind of filmmaking, but were new to me. Being a rather obsessive-compulsive personality, I went to see just about everything that was on a screen, whether it was at Millennium or Anthology, the Whitney or Film Forum.

Film Forum was not my brainchild. It was founded in 1970 by Peter Feinstein. I became attracted to Film Forum because Peter showed a great variety of work, and you didn't have the feeling that you had to be initiated to go there; it wasn't a cult audience. He was bringing this work to the general public, albeit a very small one: audiences sometimes ranged downward from a half dozen! I got to know Peter, and one day he said, "I'm getting married and I'm leaving for Cambridge, Massachusetts. Would you like the Film Forum?" No one had ever offered me my own business before, so I jumped at the chance. I said, "What makes this official?" And he said, "Well, whoever has the rubber stamp has the power." To this day I have the rubber stamp in my drawer.

MacDonald: Your schedules are notable for their variety. Was Feinstein's the same kind of variety?

Cooper: I considerably broadened Film Forum's programming. My first year's schedule included Peter Robinson's feature-length documentary *Asylum* [1972], on R. D. Laing; Stan Vanderbeek and Ricky Leacock retrospectives; *The Sunshine Sisters* [1972] by George Kuchar; the Academy Award–winning animation *Frank Film* [1973, by Frank Mouris]; Steve Dwoskin's avant-garde *Dynamo* [1972]; the Spanish documentary *Vampir* [*Cuadecuc Vampir,* 1972] by Pere Portabella, starring Christopher Lee; and experimental, animated, and documentary shorts by Ira Wohl, Kathleen Laughlin, Vincent Grenier, Eli Noyes, Stan Lawder, and Lillian Schwartz.

Today's programming is every bit as eclectic. In the next few months, we are presenting Johan van der Keuken's surreal, environmental treatise *The Flat Jungle* [1978]; a new German-made documentary on Sterling Hayden, *Pharos of Chaos* [1983] (as a double bill with three of Hayden's best features); Chris Marker's philosophical-poetic essay *Sans Soleil* [1983], shot in Japan and West Africa; *Born in Flames* [1983], a feminist fantasy by Lizzie Borden, set ten years *after* a socialist revolution in the U.S.; a documentary program: *Rockaby* [1981, by Chris Hegedus and D. A. Pennebaker], on the making of the Samuel Beckett play, and *Joe Chaikin Going On* [1983, directed by Stephen Gomer], a portrait of the actor-director; two anthropological documentaries shot in Papua New Guinea, which deal with the sometimes hilarious results when white colonialist culture is subverted by primitive peoples; Peter Lilienthal's first made-in-America feature, *Dear Mr. Wonderful*, starring Joe Pesci [1982]; and *The Horse* [1982, directed by Ali Özgentürk], a gentle narrative from Turkey reminiscent of *The Bicycle Thief* [1949, directed by Vittorio De Sica].

Getting back to the early days . . . I went to Cannes that spring [1972]. At the time, Cannes was still responding to the events of May 1968, which had inspired the creation of the Directors' Fortnight—a kind of alternative festival to the main competition. The Directors' Fortnight brought in a tremendous variety of new and exciting directors, many of whose films were more experimental than the work one associates with Cannes. I brought a number of those films to the Film Forum the following season, including Werner Schroeter's *The Death of Maria Malibran* [1972] and, later, *Willow Springs* [1973]. I began to develop ties with local cultural embassies such as Goethe House—people who are very sympathetic to having their national work shown in New York City. They would bring films to New York via diplomatic pouch, making it financially feasible for me to show them. By the way, it really is a pouch, a big leather pouch.

MacDonald: Was Film Forum grant supported?

Cooper: It ran on a shoestring. We still run on a shoestring. The operating budget was about $20,000 when I took over. Now it's above half a million. Then, the equipment consisted of one 16mm Bell & Howell projector. The seats were fifty folding chairs. The theater itself was a small pleasant loft space on the Upper West Side that doubled as a day-care center.

MacDonald: When did you expand?

Cooper: We moved to the Vandam Theater, a two-hundred-seat Off-Off-Broadway theater next door to SoHo, in 1975. That was made possible through a three-year Ford Foundation grant. The reasoning with which I approached Ford was that there was a tremendous amount of high-quality film that was not studio-produced—from avant-garde to documentary to animation to political film to sociological and anthropological studies—which was not being seen through commercial circuits or even on PBS, and the audience was proven. I could show figures for the years of growth we'd experienced on Eighty-eighth Street, and given a larger, more comfortable theater and a better location, we'd be able to be more self-sufficient. In fact, we did grow while on Vandam Street, but we were still only in a position to present 16mm, and

The Film Forum theater on Vandam Street, New York City, with wall decorations by Robert Breer. Courtesy Film Forum.

that was a space designed for legitimate theater, not film—film requires a big screen, which means a high ceiling and a rake for the seating.

MacDonald: Did you set up specific criteria for what you would show? How does what gets on your schedule get there?

Cooper: I don't have a pat answer. It's a matter of taste and subjectivity and instinct for what's happening at the moment. That's not to say that I only show films that have a built-in popularity. I don't, and our box office testifies to it. Some films are wildly popular; others crawl along. But some of those that are least popular are the more exciting work and will be appreciated in years to come. I simply see as much as I possibly can. I write letters. I make phone calls. There's a very extensive grapevine in this country and abroad of people who make films and want them screened. I go to film festivals; I go to Berlin every year; if I can afford to, I go to Cannes; I go to the West Coast.

MacDonald: When you were programming at the beginning, were you setting out to create an ideal independent screening program, or were you trying to find those areas that, say, Millennium and the Collective for Living Cinema didn't service?

Cooper: I didn't—I still don't—want to step on the toes of my colleagues, who do very fine work in presenting for the most part more avant-garde and more experimental work than I personally gravitate to. And, like the artist who makes the painting or film he or she wants to make, I very much want to show films I want to show, films that I have a strong intellectual and gut feeling for, and, for the most part, those films don't overlap with the pantheon of work that Anthology Film Archives deals with or with the specifically avant-garde filmmakers that Millennium champions. I would say the biggest overlap would be with the folks at the Collective, because they're eclectic. Also, I made a conscious decision early on that I wanted to maintain the original format that Film Forum had pioneered—to present work that is an alternative to the commercial cinema but to present it in a format that comes as close as possible to the standard movie house format. Films are presented on a repeating basis; program notes are made available; critics are contacted. The key to all this is that we premiere films: 99 percent of the presentations at Film Forum 1 are premieres. This means we get extensive press coverage for our programs.

Should I describe the theater? In 1981, we moved to a space that was totally renovated with the help of a $400,000 low-interest loan from the Ford Foundation. Turning an empty garage into a twin theater cost more than half a million dollars. We raised over $100,000 from other private and public sources and from individual contributions. Now there's a key financial deal here that made the Ford money possible. Since we were building a twin cinema, it made good sense financially to bring in a profit-making exhibitor to license one of the two screens. Dan Talbot, who for two decades has been New York's most important art-house exhibitor at his two cinemas, the Lincoln Plaza and the Cinema Studio, and a marvelous distributor (New Yorker Films), looked at the space when it was still a messy garage and said, "That's where the projectors go. That's where the screen should be." He could visualize it, and he was enough of a gambling man to take a chance. We agreed to a contractual agreement that would provide Dan with a theater and allow us to be able to count on a certain number of dollars coming in every month. Ford could then count on receiving regular repayments for their loan. So it was really a three-part deal. The theaters were designed by Stephen Tilly and Alan Buchsbaum, and today we look like a real movie house, with marquee. For months I thought, "Oh God! A marquee. How vulgar!" But I've grown to love it. Dan chooses films at Film Forum 2 and does his own publicity. He's presented some superb retrospectives: R. W. Fassbinder, Werner Herzog, Luis Buñuel. His somewhat less esoteric programming brings in a wider audience than might otherwise find their way to independent films. Theoretically, the independent films earn more money as a result of the complementary relationship the two screens maintain.

I don't want to sound too sanguine about our financial position, because in fact we rely quite extensively on public moneys: the New York State Council on the Arts and the National Endowment for the Arts play a vital part in keeping us afloat. I don't know if people are aware that it costs thousands of dollars for a movie house to stay open every week. We have a full-time staff of sixteen people. The projectionists are unionized and make a considerable sum. The equipment itself needs constant maintenance. Film Forum 1, which I program, guarantees the filmmaker $500 a week against 30 percent of gross ticket income. In a case like *Atomic Café* [1982, by Jayne Loader and Kevin Rafferty], a film can make considerable money; in two weeks it made $29,500. The filmmakers did not take any financial risks, didn't put up a penny for that exposure—though of course they made a film that took five years and several hundred thousand dollars—but they did receive over $8,800 at the end of two weeks. Even more important, they received marvelous press coverage and had a tremendously enthusiastic audience. The film moved to a commercial cinema, the Waverly, and ran about two months. It has also opened in about a dozen other cinemas nationwide.

MacDonald: Is it inconceivable that such a theater could function without public money?

Cooper: Without any funding—I think it is. At the point when you say, "We're going to run on the box office," you have a psychic click: you start looking at films and asking yourself not just "Do I like it? Is it important? Is it exciting? Is it innovative?" but "Just how many people want to see this? How much money is it going to make or lose?" I do ask myself those questions, but I also show work I know will lose money but which I think is worth the loss because it deserves to be seen by however many, or few, people show up. I can take that risk because I have public and private funds as part of my budget. They provide a financial cushion that is essential in keeping you honest.

MacDonald: I've heard Bruce Conner say that public support of film series at places like colleges and museums has tended to create a situation where programmers ignore any concern with building an audience and, as a result, destroy what audience might otherwise be there.

Cooper: That's ridiculous! It's an outrage that a country as affluent as ours could consider spending more money on military bands than on the National Endowment for the Arts. I am a strong supporter of both public and private moneys for the arts; film gets a very miserly share of arts funding. I doubt very much that programmers in college settings are just sitting around thinking, "Well, the grant money's coming anyhow. Who cares if only ten people show up?" Running a movie theater or any other kind of screening house is often tedious work; it's seeing that the film has arrived and that the projector is running and that your staff is on time. Mies van der Rohe said, "God is in the details." He was right. Much of the time it's not creative and it's not even fun. I don't think anyone does it unless they feel there's a chance for the sense of fulfillment that comes from seeing an audience arrive to see the films.

By the way, two people whose work certainly preceded Film Forum's, who really were pioneers in bringing unusual films to an American market, are Amos and Marcia Vogel, who ran Cinema 16. For considerably more than a decade, they presented independent films from all over the world to New York audiences that ranged upwards of five hundred. This came long before the late-sixties mushrooming of film exhibition in New York City and the rest of the country. And they did it before there was any public funding for exhibition. They did it on the basis of the box office and subscribers.

MacDonald: How does your board of directors function?

Cooper: Traditionally, a board of directors helps you raise money, and my board of directors has been very useful in that regard. They make recommendations, provide contacts, make a needed phone call—that sort of thing. My chairperson, Nancy Boggs, is always in touch with what's happening with new artists and new films. She's an important source of information. Another board member, Ray Silver, was the producer of *Hester Street* [1975, directed by Joan Micklin Silver] and has directed a number of films of his own, including *On the Yard* [1978]. He'll travel to foreign film festivals and make suggestions. There are also businesspeople on the board who work with me in creating budgets and developing marketing strategies.

MacDonald: Do you make all the decisions about programming yourself?

Cooper: Yes.

MacDonald: I got interested in avant-garde filmmaking about the same time you began programming. For me this was largely out of sheer pleasure. I'm amazed that avant-garde film is still looked at as something only academics can enjoy.

Cooper: That attitude probably comes from the growth of film schools and graduate programs that have students studying *Serene Velocity* [1970] and *Wavelength* [1967] and writing theses on them. All of that's fine, but it does put the work in an academic ghetto. On the other hand, on many occasions, I see avant-garde films that excite or provoke me, but which nevertheless I wouldn't show at the Film Forum because they wouldn't work well in what is essentially a conventional format. Film Forum is different from the screening situations throughout the country where you come together with filmmakers and artists and others who are cognoscenti, where there is a lecture or discussion with the filmmaker afterward, and where there's a rather high level of interchange. Ideally, I'm sure, those artists would like their films seen by a larger public. I've been in the business of exhibition—and it is a business—long enough to know that it's naïve to expect this to happen.

MacDonald: How did Benning's *Him and Me* [1982] do? That's probably the most avant-garde film you've shown during the last couple years.

Cooper: It did very well, but we're right next to SoHo; there are many artists and filmmakers who are excited about seeing a new James Benning film. He has a strong New York following. But it's tough to make an experimental film that speaks to a reasonable number of people, that does not require an audience already versed in its vocabulary. Bruce Conner is a formal filmmaker, but his use of pop music and his wonderful sense of humor and of the macabre make his films more accessible than most avant-garde films.

Another aspect of all this is marketing. The early independents, the avant-garde in particular, pooh-poohed conventional forms of marketing, and they've maintained a holier-than-thou attitude toward the marketplace. As a result, they tend to stay in a ghettoized area. It's significant that you can hardly think of an independent filmmaker who makes a living on his or her own films. Even the most successful filmmakers teach for a living or do some commercial work on the side to bring in the rent. An exhibitor can only bring work to a larger audience by marketing it in a professional, sophisticated manner. That's something I've felt very strongly about from Day One. Publicity means program notes, stills, biographical data on the artist, press screenings in advance of the opening; all the elements that go into opening *Jaws* and *Superman* can be co-opted to sell independent films.

And there has to be a good relationship between exhibitor and critics. They're going to ask, "Is this film for me?" If it isn't, you have to tell them the truth and not waste their time. That way you don't lose them for the next film, which might be just up their alley. We do press mailings of approximately 350 pieces every two weeks. We have a general mailing list of 14,500 names, and we take weekly ads in the *Village Voice* and the *New York Times.* All of this has to be done in a very conscientious, ongoing fashion. I'm very fortunate that Janet Perlberg, who's been my assistant the last year and a half, has a wonderful feel for publicity. She does a terrific job.

I think there's a rather sad state of affairs vis-à-vis independent films in this country. If you ask the person on the street what they know about modern dance, they might not know Yvonne Rainer, but they'll certainly recognize Martha Graham or Paul Taylor. They may have a conventional sense of it, but they will have *some* sense of it. If you ask them what they think of independent films, and they've never been to any, they'll probably say, "Pornography?" There are a lot of reasons for this, but the attitudes of the exhibitors and the filmmakers are partly to blame. We have to come off our high horses and get the word out. We can't just speak to ourselves.

There are other reasons as well, of course, which we're not responsible for, and I think one of the important ones is that the independent film experience is constantly confused with "going to the movies." And in some cases that's fine. While it's true that James Benning's work runs through the same projector as *Airplane II*, you have to differentiate in the public's mind that one's a work of an artist speaking in personal terms and the other's mass entertainment. Both have a certain entertainment value, but a viewer needs to bring to the Benning film a desire to be challenged intellectually.

There's also the hype to which people are subject. There's no way we're going to compete with the tremendous prepublicity which comes with a multimillion-dollar Hollywood film. It's a question of integrity. I don't make exaggerated claims for independent films. The audience's expectations have been molded by the commercial industry. It's our job to create a different set of expectations.

MacDonald: Do you think of this theater as a SoHo neighborhood theater or as a New York theater?

Cooper: Both. I have no independent survey that tells me where my audience is coming from. My guess is that for more difficult works, we're probably drawing on the local Village/SoHo/downtown audience. Films that have a broader appeal—we premiered Robert Altman's *Health* [1980], which is a studio-made film that the studio refused to release—draw from all over the city, and New Jersey, Long Island, and Connecticut.

MacDonald: From the beginning, you made a commitment to a broad range of documentary and to animation.

Cooper: I feel both those forms are very important and get short shrift elsewhere. I'm not interested in documentaries that tell you both sides of the issue. I want to see one person's very strong opinion, a film which backs up a point of view no matter how controversial. I also turn down lots of documentaries in which the filmmaker's heart is in the right place, but the form is so conventional as to be uninteresting or predictable. Also, as a political person, I think each of us has a responsibility to be aware of the kind of world we live in and what a mess it is. I am concerned with social justice and with trying to make the world a better place. While I don't think film per se is going to do that, it can certainly awaken us to the issues.

MacDonald: You premiered, at least in New York, *The Battle of Chile*

[1976, directed by Patricio Guzman]. Did you have a hand in getting that film into the country?

Cooper: The Battle of Chile was already distributed by what was then called Tri-Continental and is now Unifilm. That was a wildly successful screening—I think in part due to the fact that Pauline Kael wrote about the film at length and brought all kinds of people to see it who probably didn't know Film Forum existed. There are other films that I see abroad which are then brought in specifically at my request. Of course, when the film is here, every effort is made to bring in American distributors to have a look, in the hope that it will be able to stay here and get wider exposure.

MacDonald: Do you have much difficulty getting foreign films you want?

Cooper: There are all kinds of bureaucratic hassles along the way. Many films have accumulated inch-thick files of correspondence. The problems don't come from a lack of cooperation from either the filmmaker or the distributor abroad; it's simply that letters go unanswered or never arrive. A film we presented in July 1982, *The Swiss in the Spanish Civil War* [1982], was one of the all-time hard films to get. I saw it at the Museum of Modern Art during Swiss Film Week in 1974. I love the film. It's a wonderful subject: the relationship of the Spanish Civil War to the events of World War II. The filmmaker, Richard Dindo, located people who left Switzerland to fight on the side of the Republican army, and who maintained their radical persuasion throughout their lives. The film is not so much about their participation in a war some thirty-five years ago, but about their radicalism today, compromises they've made or have refused to make in the course of their lives since the Civil War. The one print in existence with English subtitles somehow ended up in a Mexican cinematheque, and for years there was no way to budge it. Two years ago I ran into the filmmaker at the Berlin Film Festival. Another year and a half passed. Then one day I got a call from a Swiss colleague who told me, "The film is on its way from Kennedy Airport."

MacDonald: Is there a lot of good film that we don't see because nobody is willing to pay for subtitling?

Cooper: Yes, but you can't say, "Who are those bastards who are not willing to plunk down $20,000 to have the film subtitled?" That's what you're talking about: $5,000 to $20,000. Subtitling is done with no guarantee that a film will have strong nontheatrical markets. Whether they expect to make money opening the film theatrically in a few major cities is less important than the fact that they have a work which they feel they can sell over the years to universities, museums, and schools. But a film like *The Swiss in the Spanish Civil War* seems to be about a narrow subject. Nontheatrical distributors in New York City looked at it and turned it down. They have to keep their businesses alive and be realistic about what they can market. They're not supported by the New York State Council on the Arts. To answer your question, yes, there are many films which don't get distributed, and even more get exhibited on a limited basis but don't find distributors in this country and simply go back to Switzerland or wherever to sit on some cinematheque shelf.

You asked about animation. That's an area of independent filmmaking which is mostly ignored. It's not on public television, and you no longer see an animated short before the feature. People miss that. But the kind of independent animation which is being done in this country and abroad is really quite different from the cartoons we grew up on as kids, and it deserves to be seen in a dignified setting, as work of value in and of itself—not just as the teaser before the feature. I think living with an animator, George Griffin, has sensitized me to the extraordinary quality and variety of work being produced.

MacDonald: Do you read much criticism?

Cooper: I read all the film magazines, and I scrounge through *Variety* every week. I consider that groundwork. Seeing the film and having my own response to it is the key to whether we'll show it here.

MacDonald: Are there particular critics whose views or tastes you feel particularly comfortable with?

Cooper: It's hard to say because there are so few critics who regularly review noncommercial releases. When it comes to feature films, more often than not, I agree with Vincent Canby at the *New York Times.* I have a lot of respect for his taste and integrity. He'll write as much or as little as he feels a film deserves, and he has no qualms about panning work *or* raving about it. I like the fact that he never gives an independent film the sympathy vote, damning it with faint praise. The *Times*'s coverage of Film Forum's programs since 1971 has been a critical element in our success. Roger Greenspun, who was at the *Times* in the early seventies, was interested in difficult and obscure films, and it was his enthusiasm, I believe, which made the first reviews possible.

I also value Jim Hoberman's judgment at the *Village Voice.* He's sympathetic to avant-garde, political, and animated films often ignored or misunderstood by less engaged critics.

MacDonald: What's the least pleasant part of this job for you?

Cooper: Housekeeping. I've never been much of a housekeeper in my own home. Now I've got a theater and a few thousand people coming in every week. I feel strongly that it has to be kept clean, look good. The whole experience of seeing the film should be pleasant from the moment you enter the theater until the moment you leave. I'm a bit of a maniac when it comes to upkeep. And yet it's a crashing bore.

MacDonald: Do you have plans or thoughts about expanding, about a chain of Film Forums?

Cooper: Oh God! The last thing I want is a great big anonymous organization. We're open 365 days a year; Film Forum 1 screens films Monday through Friday three times a day, and Saturday and Sunday four or five times a day. Not even the post office runs on Christmas! What I'm getting at is that if there was more happening, I wouldn't be able to give it the kind of attention I do now. I welcome other people using Film Forum as a model. As far as I know, though there are literally hundreds of screening situations for independent films, we are the only *autonomous movie house* open every day of the year dedicated to independent film.

WINTER 2008

MacDonald: Let me start with a question I didn't ask when I interviewed you twenty-five years ago. At what point after you took over Film Forum did you think you could actually make a living as Film Forum director? When the Vogels started Cinema 16, they decided this was how they would make their living, and I think their making that commitment helped them be successful. Most people who do alternative film exhibition support themselves in some other way. Of course, in asking this, I'm assuming that this *is* how you make your living . . .

Cooper: Oh, definitely! It's not only how I make my living; it's *my life.* I *always* assumed that directing Film Forum would yield me a living.

MacDonald: Even early on?

Cooper: From Day One. Perhaps it's naïveté. Even in 1972, a hundred dollars a week, which is what I got for running Film Forum, was not very much money. I think for a year or so I received food stamps. Our standards were different then. In 1972, I lived in a cheap, tiny studio apartment with no children or mortgage; and the consumer culture was not as ravenous as it is today. For our generation, coming off the sixties, money was the least of our worries: we wanted to do something worth doing. In 1972, I had a second job, working for Nadine Covert at the Educational Film Library Association. I helped her put on their annual festival.

But to answer your question: it never occurred to me that Film Forum couldn't or shouldn't support me. I think the bigger issue was whether it could support *itself;* could the kind of films I was committed to presenting reach

The current Film Forum marquee on West Houston Street. Courtesy Film Forum.

enough people to give Film Forum a future? I always thought the *films* had a future, but whether the public was ever going to recognize them in a significant enough way to support Film Forum was the bigger issue. From the beginning, Film Forum supported two people, in fact: me and a projectionist-assistant.

I am, by nature, a hopeful person. A lot of the ways in which Film Forum has changed and expanded happened in large part because I *believed* they were doable. Unless you start with that attitude, that these things *are* possible, then they're *not* possible. There's nothing mystical or spiritual about any of this; I have a very pragmatic, can-do personality.

MacDonald: In our earlier interview we both felt that, on some level, you were carrying on what the Vogels did at Cinema 16. Recently, when I looked through the Film Forum schedules for the past twenty years, I realized again that your programming is very close to Cinema 16's. Art in Cinema, Frank Stauffacher's breakthrough San Francisco film society, was primarily focused on art, while Amos Vogel was primarily focused on creating better citizens.

Cooper: It's interesting that you bring up Amos and Marcia because

George [the animator George Griffin; he and Cooper have been together since 1972] and I went to visit them this past weekend; they are both quite elderly and ailing to some extent, but they have great spirit. Amos was always a very political person, and his political awareness informed Cinema 16; as is clear from the title of his book *Film as a Subversive Art* (1974) [New York: Random House, 1974; a facsimile edition, published in 1974, is available from D.A.P. Press], Amos was interested in subverting the culture as well as the political system. Frankly, I don't think I'm as bohemian in my gut reality as Amos, but politically, we are on the same page.

One difference between my programming and his is that in the 1940s and 1950s, many independent filmmakers made short films; they didn't think in terms of a more conventional, feature-length format. Perhaps because the world has become a tougher place or maybe because filmmakers today are more savvy about marketing, a person who might have made a fifteen-minute documentary in 1949 will try to make an eighty-minute film that has a possibly of getting into theaters.

MacDonald: Up until the early 1980s, you used to do a lot of programs of short films. Is the change a function of the fact that audiences just didn't come to those shows? There are still a lot of people making interesting short films.

Cooper: There *are* a lot of people making short films, *but* a greater percentage of independent filmmakers are making longer films. I mean, look at Matthew Barney: he makes very bizarre and interesting movies—interesting to me: we've shown the entire Cremaster cycle—some of which are extraordinarily long. If Barney had been working in the early 1950s, he would have made eight-minute shorts. Artists and filmmakers think in different terms today.

And you're right, audiences are resistant to seeing programs of short films. That's a shame. Short stories aren't any less important than novels, but it's the novels that sell.

MacDonald: When you think back over the last twenty-five years, what other changes do you see in your programming?

Cooper: Actually, I see more consistency than change. Look at the films coming up this spring: each is a dramatic film with a strong political trajectory. *Ezra* [2007, directed by Newton I. Aduka] is about that extraordinarily tragic phenomenon of child soldiers in Africa. *Chop Shop* [2007, directed by Ramin Bahrani] is about a twelve-year-old Latino boy and his older sister who make a living by selling stolen goods to "chop shops" in Willet's Point, Queens. Essentially, both are about exploited children. *Blind Mountain* [2007, directed by Li Yang] is a Chinese movie about young women sold into marriage, but marriage as slavery. And *Alexandra* [2007] is a wonderful Alexander Sokurov film about an elderly woman visiting her nephew who is a soldier; we can see the futility of these young men's lives devoted to war. These are four films that I would have been proud to show twenty or thirty years ago.

The biggest changes in recent years have been brought about by technology. The fact is that I could preview these films because DVDs travel around the world so easily. I have always been concerned with bringing foreign films to New Yorkers and with using film as a way of speaking across cultural boundaries. But that was much harder to do when I was starting out. You had to go to film festivals to take in a broad range of international movies. I still go to festivals—Berlin and sometimes Toronto and IDFA [International Documentary Festival, Amsterdam]—but it's less necessary now, plus DVD is such a wonderfully sharp, convenient medium.

MacDonald: Do you still do all of the programming of the premieres, what used to be called Film Forum 1?

Cooper: No, I don't. For the last ten years or so, I've been working closely with Mike Maggiore, who is also the head of publicity for the premieres. He's become co-programmer. As we speak, Mike is at Sundance, scouting new work. We're a good team. I'm more oriented to the documentary than Mike, but Mike has the better eye for oblique and difficult narrative filmmaking. We complement each other.

MacDonald: Are you looking at films all year-round?

Cooper: We look at work constantly. We show films 365 days a year, and we look at films 365 days a year. Mike and I read extensively about works in progress. We're very proactive about getting our hands on work that sounds interesting.

MacDonald: Do you personally see everything that Film Forum shows before it's screened?

Cooper: Absolutely. If we're showing it, I've seen it. I'd say I see 80 percent of the screeners that come in. I don't see the others because Mike has said they're definitely not for us. If we're in any doubt, we both look at the film.

MacDonald: About how much time do you spend each week looking at film?

Cooper: Six to ten hours, usually at night and on weekends. People sometimes think "Gee, you just look at movies all day, what a great job!" Running a movie theater, day to day, takes a lot of time and energy; we need to *find* the time to look at the work we need to see.

MacDonald: Your brochure says you have fifty-nine employees . . .

Cooper: It's sixty now, of whom about twenty-five are full-time. There are four of us here in programming and publicity for the premieres. There are four people in Bruce Goldstein's office (Bruce and three others who do the repertory programming). So, eight people in programming and publicity. Then we have a couple of additional people in development; and a technological team of three guys (Richard Hutchins, Craig Balen, and Jeffrey Cranor). Dominick Balletta is the general manager: he likes to say he keeps the planes flying. There are concessions people, box-office people, ushers, a janitorial staff; and we have a fellow who comes in and fixes broken things every Saturday morning at 5:00 A.M. (when you're open every day, you have to use all twenty-four hours to keep things running). If a projector is doing something it shouldn't, it has to be fixed immediately because it has to work the next day at one o'clock in the afternoon. We have twenty-four-seven contracts with HVAC (heating, venting, and air-conditioning) companies; and Roger Getzoff services our booth.

God knows what's going to happen to the city when Roger Getzoff retires, because he keeps all the better theaters running. He's the über-projectionist.

MacDonald: You're pretty close to the 9/11 site; how did 9/11 affect Film Forum?

Cooper: We're about a mile north of the World Trade Center, and we were closed for three days, which was nominal, but like just about every other cultural institution in the city, our audiences were really soft for a year. After 9/11, people stayed home. They were nervous, for good reason, and they didn't travel into another neighborhood, especially downtown.

We also took a hit, a different kind of hit, in the 1980s, when VHS arrived and rental stores popped up all over the city. And now, Netflix is doing a superb job of getting DVDs out to people, and very often picks up on films right after we've shown them, so to some extent we're competing with Netflix—but, of course, so is the Metropolitan Museum of Art and everybody else.

People have the option to stay home and see movies or go out. They also have the option to stay home and cook their own dinner or go out. Restaurants continue to thrive because there is something ineffable about the experience of a meal with friends. The same is true of experiencing a good movie in a crowded theater.

MacDonald: How closely do you work with other exhibitors in the city who program some of the kinds of films that interest you?

Cooper: There's no formal relationship between Film Forum and other exhibitors, nor do the other exhibitors have formal ties to one another; but of course, everyone knows everyone—it's a small world.

We're opening Pere Portabella's *The Silence before Bach* [2007] at the end of January, which I was happy to find through the Museum of Modern

Art's retrospective of Portabella just a few months ago, so other people's programming certainly has some effect on me. *I'm Not There* [2007, directed by Todd Haynes] played at the New York Film Festival; we're running it now. For the most part, however, because we do premieres, we show everything first.

A lot of this has to do with the way the *New York Times* works: the *Times* is no longer running full reviews of either the New York Film Festival or New Directors / New Filmmakers (a MoMA, Film Society of Lincoln Center program), which is a plus for us, because we can get the full review at the time we play the film theatrically. That kind of publicity is our lifeblood. And that's another thing that hasn't changed since our earlier interview or, really, since Day One. Free publicity, meaning good critical coverage, is key to independent films getting an audience.

MacDonald: When you say "premiere," you mean the first theatrical run in New York City?

Cooper: Yes.

MacDonald: When you think back over the last quarter century, are there particular moments that you're especially proud of?

Cooper: Chris Marker, and Werner Herzog's documentaries, and the early films of Fassbinder. Patricio Guzman's *The Battle of Chile,* Werner Schroeter, Syberberg, Chabrol, Fred Wiseman's documentaries, *The War Room* [1993, directed by Chris Hegedus and D.A. Pennebaker], and *Paris Is Burning* [1990, directed by Jennie Livingston]. I'm proud that we're showing a lot of the new Romanian cinema now. Recognizing important directors who are appreciated in their own countries or regions, but not in the U.S., and getting them to American audiences is important. It breaks down barriers.

MacDonald: I remember when you showed *Daughters of the Dust* [1992, directed by Julie Dash].

Cooper: That was a coup. It would have been sold out here for endless weeks, but we had other films playing on the screen we use for open-ended runs, so it moved on to a commercial theater, where it played for months. *Daughters* was a breakthrough in that it reached an audience of black middle-class women for whom films were not made, and are still not made. At best, Hollywood makes a few silly comedies about black women, but a sophisticated look at African American culture has yet to be produced by the industry.

MacDonald: Are there things that you've done as a programmer that you now regret?

Cooper: My god, I'd be a fool if I could look back over thirty-five years of programming and not say, "What a mistake *that* was!" My biggest mistake was a certain narcissism that I had in the early years. This goes back to the short-film programs we were talking about earlier. In the seventies, I would try to find ways of making connections between certain shorts; I'd see two or three films that I thought really worked together. I'd come up with a theme and then would run around looking for other films to fill out the show. But ultimately the program wouldn't live up to my Big Idea. For instance, I did a show I called "Single-Frame Dance." Every film involved working with single frames, either using animation or the optical printer, or some other method. The problem was, in order to make my Big Idea work, I had to include films that were less impressive than those that had attracted me to begin with. I used this approach a number of times with different concepts until finally reality set in. I learned that *my* ideas are much less important than the *films'* ideas.

Programming is like pulling a rabbit out of a hat. For instance, right now, we're playing *Doc* [2007], a film by Immy Humes about her father, Harold L. Humes, who was a literary figure in the late fifties and early sixties, cofounder of the *Paris Review.* He was friends with people like George Plimpton and Norman Mailer and Paul Auster; in fact, Auster is coming to the theater tonight to introduce the film with the filmmaker. I realized that the film had a very limited audience, an audience that was interested in that moment in cultural history and might be interested in the story of this remarkable and strange man, his personal tragedy, and the family tragedy it perpetrated, so we decided to run the film, but only for a week. *Doc* earned nearly $11,000 in that week—a sizable amount, and Humes's reprinted books, *Men Die* and *The Underground City,* sold out.

Most of our premieres run for two weeks, and then if they do really well, like *I'm Not There,* they'll play on an ongoing basis for months. But there's no formula, no rule.

MacDonald: I've shown Benning's recent films and Peter Hutton's a lot during the last few years . . .

Cooper: Oh, Hutton is a wonderful filmmaker!

MacDonald: And my experience is that audiences now love their slow, meditative work—I'm talking about comparatively general audiences. I'd urge you to look at *casting a glance* [2007], Benning's newest, about Smithson's *Spiral Jetty,* and Hutton's short Iceland film, *Skagafjörður* [2004]—they'd make a wonderful double bill that your audience (I consider myself part of your audience) would love.

Cooper: I think what you say about audiences enjoying meditative work is true. We showed *Into Great Silence* [2005, directed by Philip Gröning], two and a half hours of a lot of silence, and it did very well. We played it for a couple of months. Meditative. Beautifully shot.

I should say more about our repertory programming. Bruce Goldstein, who's been director of repertory programming since 1987, is a critical part of everything that happens here. In fact, Bruce's programming brings in the major part of our admissions dollars.

MacDonald: How much do you two collaborate?

Cooper: I'd say we work 90 percent separately; occasionally, there's a way in which we two can and should relate. For instance, in February, Bruce is reopening *Don't Look Back* [1967], the Pennebaker documentary on Dylan, tying into the fact that we've been running *I'm Not There* since the end of November. Tie-ins do occur, but for the most part we operate autonomously.

MacDonald: Are you in touch with other nonprofit, autonomous theaters? I'm thinking of the Coolidge Corners Theater in Boston.

Cooper: I'm not. I know Upstate Films in Rhinebeck, New York, which often shows the same films we're showing, but they also tend to show a lot of art films that in New York play at Lincoln Plaza, Angelica, and Sunshine. BAM has a great screen for independents, but it closes down for a couple of months of the year, and right now they're playing films like *Juno* and *There Will Be Blood*—films that play in commercial venues throughout the city. There's not the same full-time commitment to independents that we have.

MacDonald: Have you had censorship problems?

Cooper: Amazingly, no. I've never had a problem with any of my public funders: the New York State Council on the Arts, the NEA, the New York City Department of Cultural Affairs—they've all been terrific. Our annual budget is $4.1 million, and maybe $200,000 comes from those three funders: not a large percentage, but certainly important.

MacDonald: One of the things that makes Film Forum unusual is the way you've been able to build financial support. The number of people thanked in your brochures, the number of organizations thanked, has expanded immensely. How much of your time is spent developing new financial possibilities?

Cooper: More and more. And I wish that were not the case. For a good many years, no more than 15 or 20 percent of my time was spent on financial issues; today, it's easily half. The building we're sitting in was just purchased for Film Forum through the generosity of two major donors. The reason we approached them about buying this building is that, as all good New Yorkers know, there's nothing like real estate for an investment that appreciates. We now own a valuable asset that gives us the ability to expand our office space, so we can hire more staff. We've never had the space to accommodate interns; now we will. We also have two rental apartments that will generate perhaps a hundred thousand dollars of income annually. We *always* need to find new ways of raising money.

MacDonald: Is the reason you need to raise all this money the fact that New York is getting increasingly expensive?

Cooper: To survive, a business, even a nonprofit cultural business, has to reach a certain level where there's enough happening—where there's a dynamic relationship between the organization and the public and between the organization and the press—to be able to sustain itself through good times and bad. The cost of everything *is* higher, yes, but it's also that the world we live in goes faster and is always changing. Lots of young people come to Film Forum, but I don't think it's a generation that's as savvy about movies as their parents' generation was; bringing those people in takes a lot more effort. I understand that Paris, which has always been the world's greatest city for moviegoing, has lost a number of theaters because landlords can get a lot more money by selling condos than by selling tickets to movies. This struggle by independent film exhibitors to stay alive is a worldwide phenomenon.

MacDonald: The nature of your board has changed over the years. What do you look for in board members? I notice that Vivian Ostrovsky is on the board, and David Grubin.

Cooper: Vivian is herself a programmer, for the Jerusalem Cinematheque, and an experimental filmmaker. We just played a film of hers called *Ice Sea* (for which my husband did the graphics). A film that she made on her cell phone will be at the Museum of Modern Art on February 20.

The board is twenty-six people, and it's a mix, actually always has been: lawyers, arts people, businesspeople . . .

MacDonald: Do you approach them, or do they approach you?

Cooper: It goes both ways. Usually, I approach them because a current board member recommends a friend or colleague they feel has something to offer. There are boards and boards, of course. Our board doesn't hear about leaky roofs or the Con Ed guy. Ours is about fund-raising and about seeing around corners, thinking about where we're going to be in ten years, and what we need to do to make the future possible. I want people who have vision and who approach things from different vantage points. David Grubin, as you know, is a documentary filmmaker; Vivian Ostrovsky, an experimental filmmaker; Vivian Bower is an artist; Shelley Wanger is an editor; Gray Colman is an attorney; Richard Lorber is a film distributor who has a background in art history. Richard has been a remarkable chair for the past three years, and before him Ned Lord was the chair: Ned is in banking at UBS and brought a very different point of view, a corporate point of view.

I think the mix is important, and a degree of collegiality and a feeling for what it is that Film Forum does and why we do it . . .

MacDonald: Does the board have any input into the programming?

Cooper: None at all. Which is the way it should be.

MacDonald: Do they try?

Cooper: You bet! [laughter]

MacDonald: So where *are* you going? What's around the corner for Film Forum?

Karen Cooper in 2007. Photo by Robin Holland; courtesy Film Forum.

Cooper: Well, we've just come around one corner, by creating an endowment fund at the beginning of 2000, with a Ford Foundation grant of $1,250,000; the principal on that fund is now over $3,000,000. And we've turned several corners with technology, building the databases and learning to use e-mail effectively: we e-mail thirty-nine-thousand-plus people every week about the programming, about in-person events, and live musical accompaniment. Learning to take advantage of the new technologies is very critical to our future. We just installed HD in the booth, which was rewired; and we put in $150,000 worth of new theater seats. People complained for years that the seats were uncomfortable, and they were right.

MacDonald: Any plans for another theater?

Cooper: We have plans, but they're not entirely ours. Columbia University is expanding their campus. This is a multibillion-dollar expansion, and I've been told it will not be completed in our lifetime. Columbia approached me three years ago about making a new Film Forum part of their expansion, and we've been in discussions with Gregory Mosier, the director of their arts initiative. We're about to present him a more formal proposal with some numbers, for a four-screen cinema that would show both premieres and repertory programming. But this is years into the future. I've learned that institutions as large as Columbia move slowly; it's a marathon, not a sprint.

MacDonald: Do you ever think of retirement, or do you plan to do this until you drop?

Cooper: Drop.

Sources for Films

I have done my best to locate a source for every film mentioned in *Adventures of Perception*. If a film is not listed, I have not been able to locate a source (an exception: most of the early films described in "The Attractions of Nature in Early Cinema" are not listed but are available at the Library of Congress American Memory website).

Organizations that are the source for several films are identified in the list of distributors. The list of films is alphabetized by title; the filmmaker's last name follows (in parentheses), then the relevant sources. The listings are for film prints (usually 16mm), except when DVD or VHS is specifically indicated, or when Amazon is listed as a source.

Distributors

CC	Canyon Cinema, 145 Ninth Street, Suite 260, San Francisco, CA 94103; www.canyoncinema.com; phone/fax: 415-626-2255
CFDC	Canadian Film-makers Distribution Centre, 299 Queen Street West, Suite 204A, Toronto, Ontario, M5V 1Z9 Canada; www.cfmdc.org/home.php
DER	Documentary Educational Resources, 101 Morse Street, Watertown, MA 02472; www.der.org; 800-569-6621
EAI	Electronic Arts Intermix, 535 West 22nd Street, 5th floor, New York, NY 10011; www.eai.org; 212-337-0680
FC	Film-makers' Cooperative, c/o The Clocktower Gallery, 108 Leonard Street, 13th floor, New York, NY 10013; film6000@aol.com; 212-267-5665
FDK	Freunde der Deutschen Kinemathek, Potsdamer Strasse 2, 10785 Berlin, Germany; fdk@fdk-berlin.de; 49-30-26-95-51-00
FR	First Run Features, 135 Waverly Place, New York, NY 10014
LC	Light Cone, 41bis, Quai de la Loire, 75019 Paris, France; www.lightcone.org; 33 1 46 59 01 53
LUX	18 Shacklewell Lane, 3rd floor, London E8 2EZ, UK; www.lux.org.uk; 44 20 7503 3980
Milestone	Milestone Films, P.O. Box 128, Harrington Park, NJ 07640-0128; www.milestonefilms.com; 800-603-1104

MoMA	Museum of Modern Art, Department of Film, 11 West 53rd Street, New York, NY, 10019; www.moma.org/research/studycenters/index.html#circfilm
NFB	National Film Board of Canada, Postal Box 6100, Centre-ville Station, Montreal (Quebec), H3C 3H5; www.nfb.ca
Sixpack	Sixpack Film, Neubaugasse 45/13, P.O. Box 197, A-1071 Vienna, Austria; office@sixpackfilm.com; 43.1.526.09.90.0
VDB	Video Data Bank, School of the Art Institute of Chicago, 112 South Michigan Avenue, Chicago, IL 60603; www.vdb.org; 312-345-3550
Zeitgeist	247 Centre Street, New York, NY 10013; www.zeitgeistfilms.com; 212-274-1989

Films

Acera or the Witches' Dance (*Acéra ou la bal des sorcières;* Painlevé): lesdocs.com (DVD)

The Act of Seeing with One's Own Eyes (Brakhage): CC

Alexandra (Sokurov): Amazon

All My Life (Baillie): CC, CFDC, FC, LC, MoMA

Alone: Life Wastes Andy Hardy (Arnold): CC, Sixpack

Alpsee (Müller): CC, FDK, LC, SF

American Dreams (lost and found) (Benning): CC, CFDC

Anemic Cinema (Duchamp): MoMA, www.unseen-cinema.com (DVD)

Apotheosis (Ono): MoMA

Arnulf Rainer (Kubelka): CC, SF

At Sea (Hutton): CC

Atomic Café (Loader/Rafferty): Amazon

The Awful Backlash: CC, FC

Baadasssss (Mario Van Peebles): Amazon

Ballet mécanique (Léger/Murphy/Ray): www.unseen-cinema.com, www.re-voir.com (DVD)

Barn Rushes (Gottheim): CC, FC

Bastion Point (Mita): 2 West End Road, Herne Bay, Auckland, New Zealand

The Battle of Chile (Guzman): icarusfilms.com

Beach Events (Hancox): CFDC

Beaver Valley (Disney/Algar): DisneyDVD.com

Behind the Scenes (Gehr): CC, FC

Bells of Atlantis (Hugo): MoMA

Berlin: Symphony of a Big City (Ruttmann): Amazon

Black and Tan (Murphy): on *The Best of Jazz and Blues* DVD, Amazon

Black and White Film (Huot): CC
Black Narcissus (Powell): www.criterion.com (DVD)
The Blood of a Poet (*Le sang d'un poète;* Cocteau): www.criterion.com (DVD)
Blood of Jesus (Williams): Amazon
The Blood of the Beasts (*Le sang des bêtes;* Franju): on *Eyes without a Face* DVD, www.criterion.com
Blues (Gottheim): FC
Body and Soul (Rossen): Amazon
Budapest Portrait (Memories of a City) (Hutton): CC
Bush Mama (Gerima): www.facets.org
casting a glance (Benning): jbenning@calarts.edu
Castro Street (Baillie): CC, CFDC, LC
Chang: A Drama of the Wilderness (Cooper/Schoedsack): Milestone
Un chant d'amour ("A Love Song"; Genet): Amazon
Un chien andalou ("An Andalusian Dog"; Buñuel/Dali): Amazon
Chop Shop (Bahrani): www.noruzfilms.com
Chronicles of a Lying Spirit (by Kelly Gabron) (Smith): CC
Confessions of a Black Mother Succuba (Nelson): CC
Corn (Gottheim): FC
Critical Mass, part 2 of *Hapax Legomena* (Frampton): FC
Cue Rolls (Fisher): morganhfisher@yahoo.com
Culloden (Watkins): www.newyorkerfilms.com
Curried 7302 (Conrad): conrad@buffalo.edu
Damned If You Don't (Friedrich): CC, CFDC, LC, www.outcast-films.com (DVD)
Darwin's Nightmare (Sauper): Amazon
Daughters of the Dust (Dash): Amazon
De Profundis (Brose): CC
Deep Blue (Byatt/Fothergill): Amazon
Deseret (Benning): CC, CFDC
Disappearing Music for Face (Shiomi): on Fluxfilm Program, FC
Do the Right Thing (Lee): Amazon (DVD)
Documentary Footage (Fisher): morganhfisher@yahoo.com
Dog Star Man (Brakhage): CC
Doorway (Gottheim): CC, FC
Down the Hudson (American Mutoscope and Biograph): www.unseen-cinema.com (DVD)
Down to the Bone (Granik): www.moviesunlimited.com
Dripping Water (Snow/Wieland): CFDC, FC
Eaux d'artifice (Anger): CC, www.fantoma.com (DVD)

Edvard Munch (Watkins): www.newyorkerfilms.com
11 × 14 (Benning): CC, CFDC, FC
El Valley Centro (Benning): CC, CFDC
The Emperor Jones (Murphy): www.criterion.com (DVD)
Empire (Warhol): MoMA
Empty House (Kim): www.ginakim.com
The Enjoyment of Reading, Lost and Found (Gatten): www.davidgattenfilm.com
Entr'acte (Clair): www.re-voir.com (DVD)
Erogeny (Broughton): CC
Ethnic Notions (Riggs): www.californianewsreel.com
L'étoile de mer ("Starfish"; Ray): MoMA; on *Avant-Garde* 1 DVD, www.kino.com
Eureka (Gehr): CC
Evil.8. A Bigger Picture (Unseen) (Cokes): EAI
The Evil Faerie (Landow): on Fluxfilm Program, FC
The Exterminating Angel (Buñuel): EmGee, 818-881-8110; www.facets.org (VHS)
Eyeblink (Ono): on Fluxfilm Program, FC
Fade to Black (Cokes): EAI, VDB
Fällan ("The Trap"; Watkins): peter.watkins@orange.fr, peter_r_watkins@hotmail.com
Film about a Woman Who . . . (Rainer): CFDC, Zeitgeist
Film No. 5 (Smile) (Ono): MoMA
Fireworks (Anger): CC, www.fantoma.com (DVD)
Five Long Takes (Dedicated to Yasujiro Ozu) (Kiarostami): www.mk2.com
Flaming Creatures (Smith): FC, CFDC
The Flicker (Conrad): CC, FC
Florence (Hutton): CC
Fly Away Home (Ballard): Amazon
Fog Line (Gottheim): CC, FC
Forest of Bliss (Gardner): DER
Four Corners (Benning): CC, CFDC
4 Little Girls (Lee): Amazon
Four Shadows (Gottheim): CC, FC
The General (Keaton): www.image-entertainment.com (DVD, with Alloy Orchestra)
Genesis (Nuridsany/Pérennou): www.thinkfilmcompany.com (DVD)
Gently Down the Stream (Friedrich): CC, CFDC, LC, www.outcast-films.com (DVD)

Geography of the Body (Maas): CC; FC; on *Avant-Garde 2* DVD, www.kino.com
Gina Kim's Video Diary (Kim): www.ginakim.com (DVD)
Gloria! (Frampton): CFDC, FC
Goshogaoka (Lockhart): Blum and Poe, 2042 Broadway, Santa Monica, CA 90404; www.gladstonegallery.com
Grass: A Nation's Battle for Life (Cooper/Schoedsack): Milestone
The Great Art of Knowing (Gatten): www.davidgattenfilm.com
Hallelujah (Vidor): Amazon
Hapax Legomena (Frampton): FC
Hardwood Process (Gatten): CC
Harmonica (Gottheim): CC, FC
The Head of a Pin (Friedrich): www.outcast-films.com (DVD)
The Hellstrom Chronicle (Green/Spiegel): Amazon
Hide and Seek (Friedrich): CC, CFDC, www.outcast-films.com
High Kukus (Broughton): CC
Highway Landscape: CC, FC, MoMA
Him and Me (Benning): CC, CFDC
Hitler! (Holden): CFDC
Hold Me While I'm Naked (Kuchar): CC
H_2O (Steiner): MoMA, www.unseen-cinema.com (DVD)
Ice (Murphy): CC, FC, MoMA
Images of Asian Music (Hutton): CC
In Marin County (Hutton): CC
In Titan's Goblet (Hutton): CC
Inauguration of the Pleasure Dome (Anger): CC, www.fantoma.com (DVD)
Into Great Silence (Gröning): Amazon
Invisible Light (Kim): www.ginakim.com
James Benning—Circling the Image (Wulf): www.germanunited.com; reinhard.wulf@wdr.de
The Journey (Watkins): CC, www.facets.org (VHS)
Journeys from Berlin/1971 (Rainer): Zeitgeist
July '71 in San Francisco, Living at Beach Street, Working at Canyon Cinema, Swimming in the Valley of the Moon (Hutton): CC
Kanehsatake: 270 Years of Resistance (Obomsawin): NFB
Killer of Sheep (Burnett): Milestone (DVD)
King Kong (Cooper/Schoedsack): Amazon
The Kiss (Ortiz): LC, LUX, www.vtape.org, www.videoart.virtualmuseum.ca, www.imaionline.de
Landfall (Hancox): CFDC

Landscape (for Manon) (Hutton): CC
Landscape Suicide (Benning): CFDC, FC
Lemon (Frampton): FC
Line Describing a Cone (McCall): CC
The Living Desert (Disney/Algar): DisneyDVD.com
Lodz Symphony (Hutton): CC
Looking at the Sea (Hutton): CC
Los (Benning): jbenning@calarts.edu
Lost Lost Lost (Mekas): FC
Lot in Sodom (Watson/Webber): on *Avant-Garde 1* DVD, www.kino.com
Louisiana Story (Flaherty): Home Vision Entertainment (DVD)
The Love Life of the Octopus (*Les amours de la pieuvre;* Painlevé): lesdocs.com (DVD)
Lumière and Company (Moon): Amazon
Making "Do the Right Thing" with Spike Lee (Bourne): on *Do the Right Thing* DVD, Amazon
Man of Aran (Flaherty): Amazon
The Man Who Could Not See Far Enough (Rose): CC, CFDC, LC
The Man with a Movie Camera (Vertov): Amazon
Manhatta (Sheeler/Strand): www.unseen-cinema.com (DVD)
March of the Penguins (Jacquet): Amazon
Mario Banana (No. 1) (Warhol): MoMA, www.filmpreservation.org (DVD)
Meshes of the Afternoon (Deren): FC, MoMA, www.mysticfire.com (DVD)
Metamorphosis (Gerson): FC
Methuselah (Painlevé): lesdocs.com (DVD)
Microcosmos: Le peuple de l'herbe ("The People of the Grass"; Nuridsany/Pérennou): Amazon
Moana (Flaherty): Amazon
Money (Hills): CC
Mother's Day (Broughton): CC
A Movie (Conner): Michelle Silva, filmscratch@yahoo.com
Movie Stills (Murphy): CC, FC
Moxon's Mechanick Exercises, or the Doctrine of Handy-works Applied to the Art of Printing (Gatten): www.davidgattenfilm.com
Multiple Maniacs (Waters): www.facets.org
My Father's Dead (Ortiz): LC, LUX, www.vtape.org, www.videoart.virtualmuseum.ca, www.imaionline.de
Namib Desert, Africa's Hostile Dunes (National Geographic): National Geographic
Nanook of the North (Flaherty): Amazon

Nature's Half Acre (Disney/Algar): DisneyDVD.com
nebel (Müller): Mueller.film@t-online.de
Necrology (Lowder): CC, CFDC, FC, www.filmpreservation.org (DVD)
Never Forever (Kim): www.ginakim.com
New York Near Sleep for Saskia (Hutton): CC
Night Mail (Grierson/Wright): MoMA
9-1-75 (Benning): FC
NŌ (Lockhart): Blum and Poe, 2042 Broadway, Santa Monica, CA 90404; www.gladstonegallery.com
Nobody's Business (Berliner): CC, FC, Milestone, MoMA
NOEMA (Stark): CC
North on Evers (Benning): CC, CFDC
(nostalgia), part 1 of *Hapax Legomena* (Frampton): FC, LC
Not a Love Story (Klein): NFB
Nude Descending the Stairs (Huot): FC
¡O No Coronado! (Baldwin): CC
Oh Dem Watermelons (Nelson): CC, FC, MoMA
One Way Boogie Woogie (Benning): CFDC, FC, FRF
One Year (1970) (Huot): FC
Orlando (Potter): Amazon
Palindrome (Frampton): FC
Paris Is Burning (Livingston): Amazon
passage à l'acte (Arnold): CC, FDK, LC
Patent Pending (Berliner): ajberliner@aol.com
Patu (Mita): 2 West End Road, Herne Bay, Auckland, New Zealand
Peliculas (Clancy): pclancy@kcai.edu
Pens@o Globo (Müller): CC, CFDC
Phi Phenomenon (Fisher): morganhfisher@yahoo.com
pièce touchée (Arnold): CC, LC
Pink Flamingos (Waters): www.facets.org (DVD)
Plastic Haircut (Nelson): CC
Poetic Justice, part 2 of *Hapax Legomena* (Frampton): FC, LC
Portrait of a Young Man (Rodakiewicz): www.unseen-cinema.com (DVD)
Print Generation (Murphy): CC
Privilege (Rainer): CFDC, Zeitgeist
Privilege (Watkins): www.newyorkerfilms.com
Production Stills (Fisher): morganhfisher@yahoo.com
Projection Instructions (Fisher): morganhfisher@yahoo.com
Punishment Park (Watkins): www.newyorkerfilms.com (DVD)

Regarding Penelope's Wake (Smith): LUX
Richard Cardinal: Cry from a Diary of a Metis (Obomsawin): NFB
Riddles of the Sphinx (Mulvey/Wollen): MoMA
Roast Kalvar (Conrad): conrad@buffalo.edu
Rolls: 1971 (Huot): CC
Say Nothing (Noren): ANoren@msn.com, www.archive-search.com
Screen Tests (Warhol): MoMA
Screening Room (Fisher): morganhfisher@yahoo.com
The Seahorse (*L'hippocampe;* Painlevé): lesdocs.com (DVD)
Seal Island (Disney/Algar): DisneyDVD.com
Season of Sorrow (Weather Diary 12) (Kuchar): VDB
Secondary Currents (Rose): CC, LC, www.peterrosepicture.com (DVD)
Secret History of the Dividing Line (Gatten): www.davidgattenfilm.com
Serene Velocity (Gehr): CC
Shoah (Lanzmann): www.newyorkerfilms.com (DVD)
Short of Breath (Rosenblatt): CC
Shrimp Stories (*Histoires des crevettes;* Painlevé): lesdocs.com (DVD)
The Silent World (*Le monde du silence;* Cousteau): Amazon
Simba (the Johnsons): www.safarimuseum.com/museum_shop_cart.htm
Sink or Swim (Friedrich): CC, CFDC, www.outcast-films.com (DVD)
Skagafjörður (Hutton): CC
Sky Blue Water Light Sign (Murphy): CC, FC, MoMA
Sleep (Warhol): MoMA
Snow (Huot): CC
So Is This (Snow): CC, CFDC
Sogobi (Benning): jbenning@calarts.edu
Sonic Outlaws (Baldwin): CC
Sonoran Desert, a Violent Eden (National Geographic): National Geographic
Spectres of the Spectrum (Baldwin): CC
Standard Gauge (Fisher): morganhfisher@yahoo.com
Still Life (Baillie): CC, FC
Stream Line (Welsby): CC, LC
Study of a River (Hutton): CC
Sunbelt Serenade (Weather Diary 9) (Kuchar): VDB
Sweet Sweetback's Baadasssss Song (Van Peebles): Sony Pictures Classics (DVD)
Symbiopsychotaxiplasm: Take One (Greaves): 230 West 55th Street, New York, NY 10019 (35mm); www.criterion.com (DVD)
Symbiopsychotaxiplasm: Take 2½ (Greaves): 230 West 55th Street, New York, NY 10019; www.criterion.com (DVD)

Tarnation (Caouette): Amazon
Teatro Amazonas (Lockhart): Blum and Poe, 2042 Broadway, Santa Monica, CA 90404; www.gladstonegallery.com
Ten Minutes to Live (Micheaux): Amazon
Ten Skies (Benning): jbenning@calarts.edu
13 Lakes (Benning): jbenning@calarts.edu
This Is It (Broughton): CC
Thought (Gottheim): FC
Three Songs of Lenin (Vertov): Amazon
The Ties That Bind (Friedrich): CC, LC, www.outcast-films.com (DVD)
Time and Tide (Hutton): CC
Time Indefinite (McElwee): FR
Tongues Untied (Riggs): Amazon
The Tourist (Moss): rmoss@fas.harvard.edu
Trailing African Wild Animals (the Johnsons): www.safarimuseum.com/museum_shop_cart.htm
Trains of Winnipeg—14 Film Poems (Holden): www.cliveholden.com
Tribulation 99 (Baldwin): CC
27 Years Later (Benning): jbenning@calarts.edu
Two Rivers (Hutton): hutton@bard.edu
Unsere Afrikareise ("Our Trip to Africa"; Kubelka): CC, FC
Untitled (Gehr): CC, FC
Used Innocence (Benning): CC, CFDC
Utopia (Benning): CC
The Vampire (*Le vampire;* Painlevé): lesdocs.com (DVD); on *Avant-Garde 1* DVD, www.kino.com
The Vanishing Prairie (Disney/Algar): DisneyDVD.com
Vein (on *Three Films: Bluewhite, Blood's Tone, Vein;* Brakhage): CC
Vermin of the Vortex (Kuchar): VDB
Victory at Sea (Adams): Amazon
Vormittagspuk ("Ghosts before Breakfast"; Richter): www.re-voir.com (DVD)
The War Game (Watkins): www.newyorker.com (DVD)
The War Room (Hegedus/Pennebaker): Amazon
Water and Power (O'Neill): CC
The Water Circle (Broughton): CC
The Watermelon Man (Van Peebles): Amazon
Waterworx (A Clear Day and No Memories) (Hancox): CFDC
Wavelength: CC, CFDC, FC, MoMA
The Weather Diaries (Kuchar): VDB
What the Water Said, nos. 1–3 (Gatten): CC

When the Levees Broke (Lee): Amazon
Wild Night in El Reno (Kuchar): CC
The Wilkinson Household Fire Alarm: morganhfisher@yahoo.com
Winged Migration (Perrin): Amazon
Workers Leaving the Lumière Factory (Lumière Brothers): MoMA; on *The Lumière Brothers First Films* (Tavernier), Amazon
XCXHXEXRXRXIXEXSX ("Cherries"; Jacobs): en.wikipedia.org/wiki/Ken_Jacobs, www.starspangledtodeath.com
You Are on Indian Land (Stoney): NFB
Zorns Lemma (Frampton): FC, LC

Index

Page numbers in italics refer to figures.

Text: 10/13 Aldus
Display: Franklin Gothic
Compositor: Integrated Composition Systems
Indexer: Andrew Joron
Printer and binder: Maple-Vail Book Manufacturing Group